The Enculturated Gene

The Accumulated Gene

The Enculturated Gene

Sickle Cell Health Politics and Biological Difference in West Africa

Duana Fullwiley

PRINCETON UNIVERSITY PRESS

Princeton and Oxford

Copyright © 2011 by Princeton University Press

Published by Princeton University Press, 41 William Street,
Princeton, New Jersey 08540

In the United Kingdom: Princeton University Press, 6 Oxford Street,
Woodstock, Oxfordshire OX20 1TW

press.princeton.edu

Library of Congress Cataloging-in-Publication Data

Fullwiley, Duana.
  The enculturated gene : sickle cell health politics and biological difference in West Africa /
Duana Fullwiley.
     p.   cm.
  Includes bibliographical references and index.
  ISBN 978-0-691-12316-5 (hardcover : alk. paper) — ISBN 978-0-691-12317-2 (pbk. : alk.
paper)   1. Sickle cell anemia—Social aspects—Senegal.   2. Sickle cell anemia—Genetic
aspects.   3. Sickle cell anemia—Patients—Services for—Senegal.   4. Genetic disorders—Social
aspects—Senegal.   5. Kinship—Health aspects—Senegal.   I. Title.
  RA645.S53F85 2012
  362.196′15271009663—dc23   2011017413

British Library Cataloging-in-Publication Data is available

This book has been composed in Minion and Myriad
Printed on acid-free paper. ∞
Printed in the United States of America
10 9 8 7 6 5 4 3 2 1

For Bachir, and his mother...

For Zemula, and her son

CONTENTS

ILLUSTRATIONS

Figures

Tables

What do postcolonialism, North-South economic disparities, and African peoples' struggles to obtain health have to do with the writing of genetic science? Can patients who live the irregularities and unevenness of priorities that define "global health" actually shape their biological destinies for the *better* when afflicted with a gene anomaly? This book is a medical anthropologist's attempt to document how people enact what it means to have sickle cell anemia, a familiar enough condition, in a place less well known, Dakar, Senegal. In it I argue that patients with sickle cell express the symptoms of this blood disease through their bodies and biology, yet they do so by articulating pain, health, and normalcy in light of idioms of kinship, colonial histories of race, postcolonial population genetics, material medical lack, and failed health infrastructures that mark nearly every aspect of their lives. Ultimately I claim that sickle cell, like any disorder, has no singular disease ontology that could possibly be stripped from the historical and political structures in which people affected live. Social actors—patients and families, as well as scientists, doctors, and healers—have brought about specific experiences of this disorder in their everyday struggles with the economics of health care, in their efforts to reorder their global standing, in their hopes to establish scientific authority, and in the survival tactics they forge through therapeutic social supports with others. Together they conjure sickle cell well-being in the face of systematic health triaging in the global South.

Like the human genome itself, the human social history of sickle cell in Senegal, West Africa has many common identifiable bases elsewhere, which can be compared to similar legacies and cultural understandings of the disease beyond Dakar's shores. It also has many points of difference. In what follows I focus on how people embody sickle cell variation and differential lived expressions of sickling blood through historical, personal, scientific, and political processes that yield forms of life where biology and cultural strategies for living well are perpetually interlocked.

■ The Early Social Biography of Sickle Hemoglobin

In 1945 the renowned American chemist Linus Pauling, who would later receive a Nobel Prize for his research on the chemical bond, learned of sickle
cell for the first time from a colleague. He later recounted that upon hearing
that patients' red blood cells sickled in the venous circulatory system (when
deoxygenated), he almost immediately imagined that a hemoglobin abnor-
mality was at issue (Pauling 1970, 1011). For the next short period Pauling
set several younger scientists training under him at Caltech to work on the
idea that sickle hemoglobin might have a different chemical bond type that
could account for the shape of the deformed (deoxygenated) cells in patients
with the disease, which did not pan out (Gormley 2007, 73). Eventually, they
decided on a line of research that could simply measure the electrical charges
of different proteins in order to determine that they were indeed seeing a
different hemoglobin molecule in people with the disease. Their observation
that "sickle hemoglobin . . . has 2–4 more net positive charges than normal
hemoglobin" was detailed in the now classic paper, "Sickle Cell Anemia: A
Molecular Disease" (Pauling et al. 1949, 546). Even though they had yet to
determine exactly how this variant hemoglobin protein caused sickling, their
study made sickle cell the first molecular elucidation of a genetic condition
recorded in the annals of science.[1]

Yet both before and after the disease's technical role in birthing molecular
medicine, sickle cell anemia was much more than a simple gene disorder.
One might go so far as to call it a cultural icon in the social history of medicine. From the time of Pauling, the blip in the gene sequence that resulted
in an altered form of hemoglobin taught researchers how single Mendelian
alleles resulted in disease (one from each parent would find its way into the
offspring) as well as the genetic basis for this protein change that could result
in disorder (viscous sickle blood jammed veins creating painful blockages).
Yet, sickle cell science could never be neutral or devoid of judgments about
human similarity and difference. Years before Pauling's "molecular disease"
appeared in *Science Magazine*, in 1910 a Chicago doctor named James Herrick
was the first to discover the illness and its characteristic "sickled blood cells"
in a black patient of Caribbean origin. Subsequently, the crescent-shaped cells
routinely revealed themselves in the blood of black Americans. In this way,
sickle hemoglobin became an all-too-reliable weather vane for the climate
of race thinking in the United States, as many physicians had long obsessed
over black versus white biological differences. In a few telling cases, sickle cell
was tasked with diagnosing black ancestry in "the white race,"[2] and in others it was later deployed as a rallying cry for anti-miscegenation proponents
who assumed that the disease originated in "Negroes."[3] Due to the particular
nature of American racism, where the widespread belief that "one drop" of
African blood determined one's biology as black, as well as the social and
political anxieties about white-race contamination that powered such ideas of

hypodescent, scientists who held that sickle cell was a marker for degenerate black blood did not usually distinguish between the types of African peoples who were brought to American shores with it in their bodies.[4]

Across the Atlantic, however, French colonial conceptions of this same hereditary disorder in West Africa were simultaneously similar and yet strikingly divergent. For colonial scientists, it was precisely by looking at different types of African peoples that they made conjectures about race as a scientific concept. Through what they called studies of *"raciologie,"* colonial researchers worked from older notions of cultural and physical differences *between* Africans to theorize about relative degrees of sickle cell in different groups— which were used to imagine the biological bounds of African ethnicities. This idea of *relative affectedness*, in different configurations, would remain central to later scientific narratives of Senegalese sickle cell particularity. It is at these points of conceptual departure where we begin to trace the health politics of sickle cell biological difference in Senegal today.

For French colonial medical researchers in the early 1950s, sickle cell (both trait and disease) constituted a *pathologie exotique*, a tropical affliction that interested eclectic men of science, such as Léon Pales (who held joint military, medical and museum posts in Paris and Dakar) not because it deteriorated people's health per se, but because it was a potential metric to size and order ethnic differences on the ground. With Pales leading several studies, the French followed British surveys conducted in East Africa in the late 1940s in their assumption that one would find different rates of sickle hemoglobin in the blood of ethnic groups defined and classed by language, cultural forms, and, in some cases, homelands. In 1953 French medical administrators were surprised to find that the "more Caucasoid," lighter Peul "race" was revealed to be, in their words, "profoundly black," due to Peul study subjects' sickle cell trait levels, which were higher than the "blacker" ethnic groups of the Wolof and the Lébou (Pales and Serré 1953, 66). Yet it was less the finding of essentially "black" Peul ancestry that threw them for a turn. The real issue was what this finding *meant* for the goal of biologizing local ethnic group boundaries in order to square them with the then divisions of large "West African Races" (these were supposed to obtain as catchall terms like "Peul," "Sudanese," "Guinean," and even "Mediterranean" [Pales and Linhard 1952; Pales et al. 1954].) In other words, Pales and colleagues' scientific objective was to draw blood in order to test the finer points of ethnicity for a serological match with race. The Peul were both a race and an ethnicity for the French, however, and the local ethnic group within the territory of West Africa did not validate colonial researchers' assumptions about the deep ancestry of what they took to be the larger Peul racial group.

Despite the apparent similarities in race logics that were helped by sickle hemoglobin on both sides of the Atlantic, in the then French West African capital of Dakar, Senegal, the scientific emphasis was less on this trait as a biological index of "Negro" blood and its perceived social threat to whites vis-à-vis "admixed" progeny. Rather, key colonial physician-anthropologists, such as Pales, stressed how ostensibly different and *multiple* groups of black Africans *varyingly* exhibited this so-called African pathology across the geopolitical terrain of French West Africa (*l'Afrique Occidentale Française* [the AOF]). The pattern of that variation, it was assumed, would congeal ethnicity and race into a metonymic configuration where mental telescoping would allow researchers to scan the geography of race for ethnicity within it.

In 1950s Dakar, the colonial activity of sickle cell testing fit into prior logics of cataloguing intra-African heterogeneity (Amselle 2003, 84–88). Colonial-era physical anthropologists went so far as to portray populations as spatial, topographical areas defined by relative disease incidence through the visual tools of cartography. The area of Senegal was literally mapped as a geopolitical ethnic tableau of what the French administrators in question called *biologie comparative* for a range of traits, both morphological and serological. For our purposes here, they found that several groups under study during this period seemed to differ in their incidence of sickle hemoglobin as measured by sickling tests—at least initially. Although this historical context is dealt with more fully in a later chapter of this book, I want to stress here that the raw scientific emphasis on the differential penetrance of sickle cell anemia, again, the relative affectedness of the disease in different groups of Africans broadly, set the stage for future scientific thinking about sickle cell anemia as a phenomenon that could distinguish populations of black peoples, one from the other, across different African geographies.

As we will see further on, today French geneticists and Senegalese sickle cell specialists continue to borrow from imagined ideas of African geopolitical identities, albeit now drawn along contemporary nation-state boundary lines, to explain sickle cell biological difference in West Africa. In many ways scientific categorizations of sickle cell have continued to be conversant with both French and West African political rationalities that now draw from more unitary ideas of "Senegalese specificity" into the present. With the 1978 arrival of the very first technologies that permitted scientists to isolate segments of DNA linked to the sickle cell gene, French geneticists rewrote colonial conceptions of multiple, segmented ethnic population blocs, each with their own unique sickle cell occurrence profile, within the territory of Senegal. In the process they updated the colonial-era serological studies that emphasized intra-territorial diversity with more modern, contemporary emphases on collective genetic *Senegalese-ness* for the singular, national population more generally.

Today postcolonial economic asymmetries and "priorities" set by global health agendas that have *overlooked* sickle cell anemia have actually helped bring into being a highly localized version of sickle cell on Senegalese soil. In part because sickle cell anemia was deemed an exotic pathology, rather than as a disease per se, during the period of "*raciologie*" studies in colonial Senegal, specialty medical clinics and general medical education on its effects lagged. Only in the late 2000s have advocates, comprised of affected families and the physicians who treat them, flagged these needs as potential state priorities. They have also pushed their leaders to acknowledge that sickling affects 10 percent of the country's population.[5] Because of the historical official invisibility of the disease in Dakar, coupled with the state's retrenchment of medical social securities after structural adjustment, beginning in 1979, Senegalese patients and doctors have had to struggle to manage sickle cell care, and to find ways to get by with its chronic reality. Of consequence is that Senegalese sickle cell specificity in the present coheres through a dynamic where both sicklers[6] and medical specialists focus on patients' survival tactics, or the ways that people affected "make-do" (*góor góorlu*), as they say in Wolof, in this resource-poor setting. As we will see in the pages ahead, patients and scientific professionals symbiotically feed each other's conceptions of sickle cell gravity or, more often in this case, functional sickle cell *mildness*.

Today physicians in Senegal offer people limited medical treatments, consisting mostly of folic acid, partially due to economic constraints. For their part, many patients adapt to the idea that their disease can be managed with such low-level interventions in the biomedical realm. Yet they draw from other domains of care to complete their health. These include maintaining disease networks of kin-based supports through which one can "share" and distribute both pain and hope; manipulating bodily thresholds for even low-level medications that over time become too costly; and following specific regimens of pharmacopoeia offered to them by specialty healers. In these everyday efforts many sicklers end up vindicating their doctors' ideas that limited medical treatments in this setting, *luckily*, may work after all. I argue that it misses the point to try to freeze the frames of this moving tautology in order to discern which aspects of this dynamic necessarily animate the others. Patients' survival tactics, such as their reliance on widespread botanicals, or, their participation in patient advocacy groups formed through biosocial blood ties that both mimic and renew idioms of kinship solidarity, create a perception that many instances of sickle cell are "managed," cared for, and less clinically urgent. The resultant image of the patient governing his or her symptoms, notably the hallmark "sickle cell pain crisis," gets taken up by biomedical practitioners and outside observers as a picture of health competence, where the active and hopeful agent of his or her own well-being just might be less crisis-stricken by this disorder. Add to this picture of low-tech health the general poverty of Dakar's health infrastructure and we begin to understand Senegalese doctors' investment in mild sickle cell's "success." All of the above combine with Senegalese research-physicians' postcolonial anxieties about obtaining purview over a special population—potential model organisms even—as leverage in North-South research relations with French geneticists who are interested in Senegalese patients' DNA. From these elements, an illness reality of sickle cell "mildness" begins to emerge.

In the not too distant past, a French-led research team established a feature of Senegalese DNA that is important to understanding how ideas of sickle cell "relative affectedness" play out in the here and now. Using restriction enzyme cutting technology (RFLP's) to find markers inherited with the sickle cell gene, the Paris-led research group discovered a series of genetic identifiers linked to the sickle cell gene in different populations in French-speaking West Africa in the early 1980s (Labie et al. 1985; Pagnier et al.1984). In essence, these markers, called "haplotypes," are population genetic signatures. In simple terms they are the underlying patterns in people's genetic sequences—the famous A's, T's, C's, and G's—in and around a specific area of interest, in this case the sickle cell mutation. Given the "optimistic" picture of sickle cell health in Dakar, the geneticists in question ascribed what they took to be a favorable Senegalese phenotype of life to what they saw as a population-based Senegalese genotype in the lab. Taken together, these various events, scientific actions, and human aspirations for well-being in the face of biomedical scarcity reiterated a social reality where patients, families, doctors, and healers, within the clinic and without, focused on patients' health and hope—even as many lived with recurring bouts of pain and despair. What is clear is that sickle cell anemia on Senegalese ground today has been lauded on multiple registers as an instance of relative African vitality, rather than solely as a prevailing pathology. Yet, as this book unfolds, it will become apparent that this disease conception—what I call a *lived construct* of mild Senegalese sickle cell anemia—should not be uncritically understood as a simple celebration of Afro-optimism. Postcolonial optics of Senegalese particularity, genetic technologies used to explain phenotypic differences, colonial legacies of racial science that obscured an emphasis on sickle cell as an actual disease, as well as the educational and medical lag that followed sickle hemoglobin's racialized conceptions, have forced people to improvise survival strategies in the face of spotty sickle cell care in the present. Today economic precarity and what patient activists refer to as continued "state incomprehension" and "neglect" of their disorder add to the social and historical genealogies that spawn the recuperative disease ontology of "mild sickle cell anemia" in Senegalese bodies.

■ From DNA Passports to Genetic Health Identities

In 1984 when the aforementioned team of mostly French researchers, led by a geneticist named Dominque Labie, worked with field staff in Dakar, Senegal, Cotonou, Benin, and parts of the Central African Republic (CAR) to localize haplotypes in the DNA of African patients, they were responding to a larger enigma within medicine that characterizes most, if not all, genetic diseases. That is that many conditions are highly variable and often affect individuals in dramatically diverse ways. For example with sickle cell, only some people with the most common disease genotype (HbSS)[7] have recurring infections, serial and frequent sickle cell pain crises, and, in worse case scenarios, suffer from organ failure and attendant systemic sequelæ that can lead to death. Labie and her colleagues were after an answer to explain the medical observation that Senegalese people seem to manifest "milder" sickle cell symptoms when compared to other African groups.[8] Their gloss on relative population sickle cell health relied on the technical protagonist mentioned above that lives throughout this book, even when it recedes from the main narrative, that of the Senegalese sickle cell haplotype.

Whether they realize it or not, many readers have already encountered the once arcane scientific objects of genetic haplotypes. Population geneticists now routinely analyze them in myriad chromosomal regions to assign population genetic differences to disease study cohorts and to theorize about people's "Old World" ancestral origins. In a somewhat different domain, as concerns male and female lineage markers on the Y chromosome and in mitochondrial DNA, haplotypes have also allowed many Americans to embark on genetic genealogical identity quests beginning in the early 2000s.

In the United States, one need not look very far to see how haplotype markers, as biological tools of social and personal meaning, have become thoroughly intertwined with psychological needs and political conceptions of identity linked to African geography. They are sociotechnological products—never just about biology—that permit people to pack into truncated DNA code what might also be longer experiential life and historical processes of belonging that far exceed genetics alone.[9]

For instance, on April 26, 2008, an African-American television star named Isaiah Washington announced his plan to travel to the small West African country of Sierra Leone to obtain the world's first DNA passport.[10] He often spoke publicly about this new invention that would make him a citizen of the recently war-torn nation based on mutations in his mitochondrial DNA that sequentially resemble those that geneticists have found in the "Mende" people of that country. According to Mr. Washington, Sierra Leone's president Ernest Bai Koroma agreed to give him "and any African-American full citizenship if they can prove that their 'origins' through DNA are Sierra Leonean" (Washington 2008). This extraordinary genetic exceptionalism with regard to Mr. Washington's new possibility for national belonging proves possible when individuals, who are descended from African populations who were dispersed around the globe through the violence of the trans-Atlantic slave trade, are said to genetically "match" contemporary Africans based on specific DNA haplotype patterns that are inherited together.[11]

The idea to link heritage, to create national belonging, and to reconnect black peoples in the "New World" with an African homeland is not entirely new, however. What might come as a surprise to many readers is that the very first iteration of DNA matching capable of tracing a minute portion of one's genome to locales in Africa was already possible for many Americans more than twenty years prior to Mr. Washington's planned homecoming. That is, Labie and her colleagues deemed possible such a limited DNA ancestry quest through sickle cell haplotypes in Americans with the disease, nearly three decades ago. I should say at the outset that African-Americans did not use HbS haplotypes (sickle cell DNA markers) to pursue cultural connections through citizenship in any event.[12] Yet, at the time, Labie's team imagined that their discovery of the initial three African sickle cell haplotypes revealed two potentially important—yet wholly separate, in their minds—directions for future research on the disease. The first, which presaged the now flourishing industry that led Isaiah Washington to seek literal genetic citizenship through his DNA passport,[13] they called "anthropological" identity.[14] The other was what we might call a *clinical identity*. As concerns the latter, these scientists and their colleagues in medical specialties that treat sickle cell's many complications made other links and associations between genetics, health, and culture (albeit less explicitly) on the behalf of Africans more broadly.[15] That is, they used the sickle cell haplotypes to theorize about Senegalese people's *passport* to better health. Specifically, the Labie team wondered if certain of the genetic changes that characterized the Senegalese haplotype could constitute the defining factor that endowed West Africans tested in Dakar with the ability to offset the most debilitating sickle cell complications.

At the risk of stating the glaringly obvious, not all people's engagements with genetic haplotypes do the same cultural work. What is important is how these bits of DNA sequence have been marshaled in the recent American context to fill in larger social voids and historical detachments, yet, as the chapters to follow show, in the French and Senegalese postcolonial setting of contemporary Dakar, sickle cell haplotypes have been used for over a quarter of a century to fill in specific voids in medical knowledge. In particular, African sickle cell haplotypes have been utilized to theorize a pathway of genetic causation that yields different biological outcomes with regard to how people manifest sickle cell disease in the clinic and beyond.

In response to many clinicians' reports about the disparate illness courses of any two sicklers compared, Labie's team relied on the haplotypes (or molecular differences) to speculate why certain sicklers (on a population level now) live healthier lives than others. Prior to the African population genetic studies of HbS, these researchers had noted that some people with sickle cell continue to produce healthy *fetal* hemoglobin, the kind all humans are born with but usually lose after the first few months of life. Given this, the team then went on to hypothesize how their discovery of multiple origins for the sickle cell gene might be the broad "associative" link that would allow the larger scientific community to make sense of sickle cell biological differences seen in patients who lived in different African countries.

As the forgoing suggests, Labie and her colleagues' initial division of the use-value of their findings overlooked a crucial question concerning how people's aspirations for health in the face of material limits, economic constraints, and historical legacies of colonial studies of pathology might influence local framings of disease symptoms. More to the point, their focus on genetics left little conceptual space to contemplate how the domain that is most broadly referred to as "culture" is intimately tied to the historical processes of human interaction that yield observations of biological difference.[16] Instead, Labie and colleagues' hope was merely to elucidate the effect of DNA markers in causing sickle cell biological distinction in the three regions under study. A much-cited idea from their 1984 paper reads as follows:

> [A]n interesting possibility arises with respect to the clinical expression of sickle cell anemia. . . . *The switch from HbF* (Fetal hemoglobin) *to HbA* (the usual form of Adult hemoglobin) *is retarded in sickle cell anemia patients, and genetic diversity among individuals could exist with respect to this feature.* The genetic basis of [such] phenotypic features may be linked to specific haplotypes. . . . Variability in the course of sickle cell anemia may in part relate to the multiple independent origins of the HbS gene. (1773; emphasis mine)

This use of ancestral sickle cell backgrounds to theorize about a broadly lived healthy phenotype, which could account for African variability in illness, rapidly gained traction within biomedicine. In 1985, just one year after their first article appeared in the journal *Proceedings of the National Academy of Sciences* (PNAS), key players on this research team published papers linking the Senegalese genetic haplotype to an increase in fetal hemoglobin (Labie et al. 1985; Nagel et al. 1985). The marketability of this idea—the association between Senegalese sickle cell and better health—has, in its own way, spawned a genetic exceptionalism that now favors the Senegalese by pegging their sickle cell health to a biogenetic cause. Through their specific genetic markers, the Senegalese people are said to exhibit an especially mild form of sickle cell anemia whereby they do not become as sick as others who have the disease in Africa and its diaspora.

■ The ways that the 1984 team of scientists imagined clinical identities differed mechanistically from people's claims to ethnic heritage that congeal in African ancestry tracing quests today, and that were imagined for sicklers more than twenty-five years ago. Nonetheless, scientists who are still influenced by the HbS haplotype findings deploy similar frameworks of geographic ethno-racialization to make sense of sickle cell biological difference in West Africa in the present. In this book I argue that with the HbS haplotype discourse, key French and Senegalese geneticists, hematologists, and pediatricians have made sickle cell genetic sequence variations correspond to a level of observed health in African bodies—bodies that are imagined to be nominally, and nationally, distinct. Following from this, I argue that the very epistemological categories of "Senegalese HbS," and the ontological lived disease that corresponds to it, obtain their descriptive powers through social dynamics of identity and difference rather than through any "natural" means entirely free of such political machinations.

Ideas of difference that cohere through people's imaginaries about belonging are often marked by place and nation. What this book describes on this front for people with sickle cell in Senegal has often been imposed from the outside but blended with social dynamics of survival within. The postcolonial relationship between France and Senegal continues to inform local medical science as well as economically inflect the illness it aims to treat, in emergent ways. Beyond Senegal's shores, population specific differences between geographically located groups are gaining much more salience as researchers renew reports on various forms of biological diversity and distinction in Africans and African-descended peoples broadly. New studies regarding sickle cell often focus on variations in people's levels of fetal hemoglobin as well as the frequency at which they suffer sickle cell pain crises. I argue here, however, that these *effects* in the body should also be considered beyond mere population genetic framings. This is not to deny that biogenetic differences exist. To the contrary, we cannot but recognize that more of them are being discovered by the day, as genetic technologies push on.[17] Instead, I ask, how is it that genetic explanations are allowed to absorb more complex social, medical, and economic processes in instances when observed health outcomes are correlated with genetic patterns, often despite any clear detailed proof establishing causation? What might happen to the seductive allure of genetic "association studies" (where DNA is correlated with a given outcome) if an analysis of sickle cell biological difference in West Africa took seriously the concerted efforts and cultural practices that sickle cell patients themselves have put into surviving in the face of economic scarcity, limited treatment options, and intersubjective structures of care networks that allow them to aspire for health?

Based on ethnographic research I conducted in Senegalese public university hospitals, traditional healing sites, French clinics and laboratories, Dakar market places, and patients' homes over the course of more than a decade, I found that people's ability to make-do with scant biomedical palliatives functionally filled a resource gap in which the state has proved incapable of adequately providing basic health care for most of its citizens. People's ability to improvise self-care with therapeutic autochthonous plants (one of which has been hypothesized to also increase fetal hemoglobin), sometimes coupled with their investment in the numinous powers of their Islamic faith, or at least their faith in the therapeutic value of their social supports forged with caring others, were key factors that shaped their embodiments of this disease. When these actions combined to mitigate symptoms, the result could be reframed as Senegalese sicklers' "positive health outcomes" when seen from a biomedical perspective. Therefore disease embodiment and favorable sickle cell health have been mutually brought into relief as people have found ways to minimize the gravity of their situations.

For many, the motivation to strive for health and the possibility of one's own well-being, even if, as they say, "God has written" [*binde*] this genetic illness into them, is powered by their beliefs that they must find a way to marry and bear their own children. These acts of personhood, and of renewing one's lineage, were of primacy to both men and women. To fulfill them, people felt that they needed to achieve a certain degree of normalcy, where they could manage their pain, so that they might be eligible for marriage in the first place. Men and women experienced different pressures regarding this issue, with men fretting about financial gain and employment, and therefore being healthy enough to work, while women worried about being fit enough for domestic life, to rear children and, most importantly, to be able to bear them at all. Thus, it was not just their own futures that hung in the balance between the pain crises characteristic of their disease and the prospect of variable but viable health. They were impelled by a larger social awareness, a need to achieve an outward sense of normalcy that would allow them to bring life, through progeny, into being in the present for themselves, and beyond themselves. These pressures, however stressful, were also aspirations that made people not only claim to "live well" with sickle cell anemia but to live well despite it. This latter triumphant attitude was both an enunciation of the health they hoped to muster and a denunciation of the long state silence, public health invisibility, and general scarcity of medical resources that many patients faced when they were not feeling quite so well, and when they were more generally seriously afflicted with the deep malaise of another aspect of the future: economic uncertainty and "crisis."

The confluence of issues I raise here must be seen within the macro context of health care in this part of West Africa where the allocation of resources to various disease interests is largely determined by outside donors. From this vantage, it is clear that geneticists, hematologists, and pediatricians in Senegal have continued to characterize their patients as having "better than expected" sickle cell outcomes due to conditions beyond the clinic. These claims are based not only on genetic comparisons with other countries, which, again, show degrees of biogenetic differences among subjects. Rather, Senegalese medical professionals have taken such stances only after sifting the data on biological difference through the sieve of a local health politics of scarcity. By this I mean that they became accustomed to comparing sickle cell with other global-local health priorities that command donors' attention and thus dictate which diseases merit public visibility, "awareness," and subsidies for care. The most paramount in this contest for attention has been HIV/AIDS. Thus sickle cell in Senegal is part of a health economy where donor interests financially circumscribe any given disease's value, and where sickle cell itself had no value in the way of funding, programs, or education until the late 2000s. In this way "mild" sickle cell anemia is, in part, a lived construct of economic triaging and uneven investment throughout Africa, where, as James Ferguson has argued, the "global," in this case global health, does not "flow," but rather "hops" to connect privileged points "while excluding with (equal efficiency) the spaces" and, I would add, health issues, that have not been "connected" to Western aid interests and funding lines (Ferguson 2006, 47). All throughout Africa we are witnessing a simultaneous dearth and excess of funds for health problems and their scientific solutions. In this blotchy matrix some diseases benefit greatly and others remain ignored.

In the historical space where sickle cell has been largely ignored as a health problem, dating back to its colonial use as a marker for African racial distinction in the 1950s, readers may wonder how it was that a conception of sickle cell "mildness," rather than "severity," emerged. It is not difficult to imagine that either conception, if not both, were historically plausible. I argue that in the 1980s health economy in Dakar, the construct of mildness was born both of geneticists' ideas about Senegalese biological capacities to weather the worst symptoms of the disease and of patients' informal economies of securing health through improvisational yet effective methods and networks of care. With that in mind, I do not want to say that "severe" cases of sickle cell in Senegal have never existed. Indeed they have. My strategy in the major part of this book, however, has been to follow instances of how the disease has been varyingly lived as mild, or how stoic subjective expressions of illness—as well as physicians' belief that they are "blessed" with treating a disease "type" that may not require the importation of frontline therapies from the North— both permit and are permitted by the generative, and economically inflected, discourse of Senegalese sickle cell specificity.

In the final chapter of the book I show how, since 2008, sickle cell in Senegal has begun to be partially reconfigured as a severe disorder. This shift came as international patient advocates in France began to network with local patient groups in Dakar to emphasize the importance of campaigning for international recognition so that funding and care subsidies to poor African states might follow. Subsidized medications and hospitalizations, when needed, have been their goals. The state currently covers antiretroviral treatments for people living with HIV/AIDS, subsidizes malaria prophylaxis for the very poor, and also covers aspects of maternal health, such as cesareans and deliveries, with the help of aid from bilateral donors, Nongovernmental Organizations (NGOs) and from the World Health Organization (WHO). After years of political struggle, in 2009 sickle cell patients in France and West Africa succeeded in convincing the global health multilateral institutions, the WHO and the United Nations, to create a resolution declaring sickle cell a global "public health priority." Still today, however, the notion that suggested funding would find its way through these global agencies to local countries, and specific sites, remains a mere hope.

■ My purpose in writing this book has been to bring crucial concerns of cultural and medical anthropology to renditions of genetic science. In detail this means showing how both patients' and medical professionals' economic, health, and political struggles actively shape lived expressions of sickle cell biological difference in Dakar. Historically, this West African locale has deep colonial roots that have promulgated the idea that Senegalese people, for the French, were special. They were the only "subjects" of the AOF who were offered a path to French citizenship.[18] Despite the early studies on *raciologie* that divided then Senegalese subjects by their sickle cell biology, one could argue that the French Republic's political bate of citizenship for urban Senegalese was an effort to supercede the messy differences of life on the ground in favor of a universalized—yet still always African—subjectivity. Keeping in mind both the history of *raciologie* that focused on Senegalese population differences for sickle cell and the political history of special citizenship status for Senegalese natives in the cities of Saint Louis, Gorée, Rufisque, and Dakar, we see a continued pattern of the cultural functionality that scientific (and then ethnological) declarations of relative benefit for certain Senegalese have engendered. The specificity of the Senegalese people as a fact on the ground has been shaped by these older histories that contribute to how Senegalese biomedical practitioners and patients square newer technologies of health care governance, and its omissions, in embodiments of Senegalese sickle cell mildness.

Together histories, politics, and bodies, as biocultural products, must be brought into the increasingly pervasive technical story of haplotypes and population health for sickle cell, as the "first" genetic disease, but also for countless other conditions that now figure in the annals of science. My goal here is to make human history and social practices bear on and, more importantly, to bear out our understanding of genetic data points. In an age when many facets of human life are gaining new senses as biologically destined through the precision of genetics, I chronicle the lives of Senegalese sicklers and document how the state of health care in the global South, international health priorities, colonialism, kinship, and histories of race all mark aspects of how Senegalese sickle cell has come to be associated with a modified clinical picture and favorable biological life course. Biology is not destiny. Nor, as Sociologist Nikolas Rose would have it, is it simply "opportunity."[19] For many in the global South, postcolonial legacies, economic constraints, and struggles to define health options—despite the odds—clearly shape the kinds of chances, prospects, or breaks from genetic destiny people are able to make in the first place.

This is the first book to ethnographically treat a genetic disease in Africa. Not surprisingly the social scientific study of genetics has usually focused on richer locales, where technologies of diagnosis, as well as lay and medical education about them, are more pervasive. Yet, intellectually, anthropologists of science and medicine know that both genetic research and genetic disease surely exist in resource-poor settings and in Africa in particular. Why, then, we must ask ourselves, have not anthropologists ethnographically engaged issues of genetics as sites of science and medicine on the continent? To date, most genetic research in Africa has been conducted in a fragmented way, with Northern scientists working on projects in spurts, or within research units based in their home countries with little to no continued or sustainable tie to local specialists. Although medical anthropologists might encounter genetic conditions in their work on other afflictions, it may be that we as a discipline have overlooked genetic disorders because they are often not officially recognized as public health problems or priorities for African states or for the aid, donor, and humanitarian forces that have increasingly begun to administer health care governance in this part of the world.[20] As with most studies on scientific trajectories of illness, my ethnographic engagement with sickle cell in Senegal provides an aperture onto the societal forces that condition disease embodiment, but that also highlight the possibilities for how power shapes people's subjectivities across the North-South divide. Sickle cell is one window through which we might better understand Senegal's place in the world, its history of special status in the French colonial era, its population's ability to cope with the difficulties of structural adjustment, and, in the postcolonial present, its economic dependency on multilateral institutions, as well as the ways this dependency affects which diseases it is able to prioritize, and which it is forced to neglect.

There are specific lessons to be learned from studying a genetic affliction in the global South. I found that unlike most genetic determinisms that scholars conducting fieldwork in North America and Europe have described, the genetic prognosis of a sanguine form of mild sickle cell in Senegal has neither hardened nor highlighted the absoluteness of disease.[21] In fact it has done the opposite. When the Senegalese government entered into economic structural adjustment in 1979, it was forced to drastically cut health-sector spending. In this context of scarcity, the discovery of sickle cell DNA haplotypes, and the attendant observation that the Senegal type was associated with a better health outcome on the ground, was not only welcomed news, it allowed the condition to remain officially invisible so as never to materialize as a health priority. This went on for nearly three decades until patients began to organize. When prompted by the successes of other diseases to obtain government aid, they finally protested sickle cell's invisibility in the early 2000s. Yet on a broader register, the fact that healthy sickle cell life was reduced to a gene effect at all, nonetheless, has narrowed many specialists' accounts of Senegalese health to a loosely configured but assumed causal pathway explained by the Senegalese haplotype. In other words, at the same time that sickle cell life was optimistically left to its own devices during the onset of Senegal's neoliberal market reforms, scientists' attribution of an advantageous form of Senegalese sickle cell to isolated DNA closed off other explanations of this population's measured biomedical success. In particular, sickle cell specialists' biogenetic rendering of patients' health overlooked how economic scarcity forced people to actually create unofficial economies of health care where their bodies would become sites to manipulate thresholds of pain and to condition decreased needs for painkillers and other low-tech but still costly treatments, on the one hand, and to dissolve the bounds of subjectivity and of pain beyond themselves to be shared, managed, and lived intersubjectively, on the other.

What I hope to demonstrate in this book is the necessity of following emergent sickle cell health in its many biological, political, and cultural directions. Medical anthropologists must explore an inclusive mix of life and be as broad as possible in our analyses of genetic renditions of biological difference, as well as how such differences come to live within the scientific literature through specific grammars, such as association studies. When we recognize that there is always a middle ground between two associated elements, and that this is part of a specific social and historical milieu, we begin to discover whole fields of life and experience. Doing so allows us to see, in this case, how African states, postcolonial health care governance, cultural practices, and disease politics populate the family trees of the exceptional data points that— as DNA markers—are too often saddled with the task of explaining human biological difference alone.

ACKNOWLEDGMENTS

Two observations will become apparent as readers make their way through this book. The first is that any human's success, or failure, largely has to do with his or her structures of support and care. The second is that any contribution to expanding our vision about how the world works is always born of a time and place—a context rich in people and ideas that nurture how we imagine new framings for what is possible. Turning these two lenses on myself, there are many people, structures, and sources of support without whom, and without which, this book would not have materialized.

It was Troy Duster who first introduced me to the world of genetic science. After I got my BA in 1994, he hired me to work on his then DOE-funded project "Pathways to Genetic Screening," which was financed as part of the Ethical, Legal, and Social Implications (ELSI) arm of the Human Genome Project. With Troy's team at the Institute for the Study of Social Change in Berkeley, I learned the feasibility and importance of doing fieldwork in specialty clinics and hospitals, as well as in Bay Area communities where people affected by sickle cell, cystic fibrosis, and the thalassemias were largely classed as "Black," "White," and "Asian" respectively. Troy's calm wisdom and undying conviction that societal human differences (such as race) and biology should not be reductively conflated inspired me to pursue work on sickle cell within medical anthropology more globally.

From my graduate school days at the University of California at Berkeley, in the mid-1990s and early 2000s, Paul Rabinow provided unwavering intellectual engagement and support. He always lent a receptive ear, and then compelled me to see the underside of my assumptions. Although he has had his issues with ethnography, Paul, more than anyone, challenged me to learn from, and to live close to, the fast-moving technical field of molecular genetics. If Paul prevailed upon me the need to expand the ethnographic present to incorporate the anthropology of science in real ways, it was Philippe Bourgois and Nancy Scheper-Hughes who never failed to engage me on realities of race, poverty, North-South research relations, and the importance of showing that most global human differences (in quality of life, health, and other "phenotypes" of well-being) could not be reduced to genetic effects. Others who challenged me to think about the relationships between territory, geography, ethnic belonging, and power in Africa and beyond were Mariane Ferme and Donald Moore.

In Paris several people were crucial in setting me up with resources, office space, and intellectual community. Michel Callon, Bruno Latour, and Vololona Rabeharisoa hosted me at the École des Mines, Centre de Sociologie de l'Innovation (CSI), during three different research stays between 1997 and 2002. Their seminars and invitations to think with them about joint concerns regarding science and embodiment, for Michel and Volo, and everything under the sun, for Bruno, gave me a community of scholars and a comforting retreat at the CSI. This was a priceless gift, especially during the first years of fieldwork when I was still trying to define my project.

In Senegal several researchers helped in times of need. Charles Becker opened his reading room to me, where there is a trove of historical and anthropological resources. Rene Collignon, Arame Fall, Khadime Mbacke, Cheikh Niang and Ibrahima Sow offered helpful insights about the history of medicine, social structure, linguistics, spirituality, and everyday life in Senegal. I could not have done this project without several dedicated and philosophically inclined Wolof teachers both in the United States and Dakar. My sincere gratitude goes to Fallou Gueye in New York, as well as to Rudy Gomis and "Zator" in Senegal. I especially want to thank to Paap Alasaane Sow in Oakland, my long-standing teacher over the years. In addition to Paap Sow, several other close friends in California and Dakar were crucial to expanding my thinking, including Victor Diatta, Idi Sow, and Khadim Thiam. Pape Douda Ndoye also taught me an incredible amount about family ties, loyalty, and selflessness, as well as economic and general life sacrifice. Without him, my knowledge about familial care would have been unknowingly limited.

During my postdoctoral years at New York University, Rayna Rapp signed on as my official National Science Foundation "sponsor," a formal title that completely misses the possibility that a mentor could turn out to also be the humane, nurturing, and mindful friend that is Rayna. I will always learn from her close attention to the details of scientific intervention on the body and mind, as well as her astute renditions of social corollaries for these same phenomena. Emily Martin was also a joyful source of inspiration. From the most casual conversation to formal seminar settings, Emily could always crystallize the absurd and poetic aspects of life and their interconnections with power in the field and at home. Others who showed me support in the Department of Anthropology at NYU during those days include Todd Disotell, Faye Ginsburg, and Fred Myers.

At the Institute of Advanced Study in Princeton, in 2004–5, I met a wonderfully giving and creative bunch of academics who provided endless insights (and laughs), both before and after lunch. Several people made me think harder about affect, economy, and how the relational nature of science and society plays out in various humanities and social science fields. I especially want to thank Caroline Arni, Patricia Clough, Paulla Ebron, Bruce Grant, Sarah Igo, and Helen Tilley.

In a different interdisciplinary setting, the Robert Wood Johnson Health and Society Scholars Program at Harvard provided me with funding to continue fieldwork on sickle cell and to think with specialists in population health about tools and theoretical framings meant to capture health disparities. At the Harvard School of Public Health the faculty most crucial to my success in this program were Lisa Berkman and Nancy Krieger. Both of their sharp minds and attention to the social and theoretical underpinnings of quantitative data have imprinted my thinking in fundamental ways. Allan Brandt and Charles Rosenberg were also invaluable sources of support during these years, providing me with an office in the History of Science Department and encouraging me not to strip my work of its complexity.

A species of gratitude unto itself is reserved for several close friends and colleagues who helped me to rethink critical elements of the book, in whole or in part. Clara Han, Alondra Nelson, Kristen Petersen, Elizabeth Roberts, and Terence Keel all gave wonderfully engaging reads and extensive comments at vital stages. Their creative minds, judicious eyes, and general care forced me to clarify thoughts and to detail dynamics in ways that, again, set me on the eternal path of striving to be a clear writer without sacrificing technical detail. I especially want to thank Terence for always being such a spirited interlocutor, and for broadening my own reflections about our kindred concerns. Margaret Lock deserves special recognition for reading the whole manuscript and for spending a few weeks in the summer of 2010, before the final submission, in a highly productive back-and-forth on several points about which we both care deeply. Her generosity remains unparalleled, and her brilliance leaves me humbled.

The Committee for African Studies and the Humanities Center at Harvard hosted seminars wherein I presented parts of the book in progress. At these events my colleagues in anthropology and African studies, especially Emmanuel Akyeampong, Byron Good, Biodun Jeyifo, Bhrigupati Singh, and Mark Auslander, offered essential feedback. Randy Matory also gave me excellent critical commentary at several junctures. More broadly, I must thank Arthur Kleinman for his friendship and counsel throughout my years at Harvard.

With regard to my students, I had the good fortune to hire three who turned out to be outstanding research assistants. Two anthropology undergraduates, Allison Brandt and Jeff Leopando, continuously astonished me with their smarts and cutting insights. Jason Silverstein, a thinker whose lively mind should not be confined to disciplines, had a helpful hand in too many aspects of the book to enumerate here.

Additionally, I want to thank Mary Murrell for bringing me to Princeton University Press. I must also convey my deepest gratitude to Fred Appel, my editor, who always engaged me with cheerful and professional patience. Others who worked to usher the manuscript into the world were Kathleen Cioffi, Denise Baggett, and Grey Osterud.

The research for this book, at various stages, was supported by the Ford Foundation, the National Science Foundation, the Robert Wood Johnson Foundation, the Social Science Research Council, the USIA Fulbright program to Senegal, and the Wenner-Gren Foundation for Anthropological Research. Parts of two chapters have appeared previously as journal articles. Sections of chapter 2 are excerpted from "Revaluating Genetic Causation: Biology, Economy, and Kinship in Dakar, Senegal," *American Ethnologist* 37 (4): 638–61, which appeared in 2010. Chapter 6 is an expanded and reworked version of "Biosocial Suffering: Order and Illness in Urban West Africa, *BioSocieties* 1 (4): 421–38, which was published in 2007. I thank the American Anthropological Association and Palgrave Macmillan for allowing me to reprint them here.

Lastly, my ultimate gratitude is reserved for the many people who appear in the pages to follow, especially Ibrahima Diagne, Magueye Ndiaye, and Touty Niang. Their willingness to share their lives with me, and sometimes the intimate spaces of their dreams, places me eternally in their debt.

CHAPTER ONE

Introduction: The Powers of Association

In the summer of 2000, as the rainy season started, I made my way to the poor Dakar suburb of Thiaroye to meet a family with multiple cases of sickle cell anemia. There were no paved sidewalks and my shoes sank in the mud when I jumped off the rusty minibus in a line of other hurried passengers. Stray sewer water bubbled from an opening in the street, creating small puddles of grey that were now being abluted by the downpour. Mr. Seck, the man I had come to see, had his niece keep watch for me, "the American from the hospital."[1] She surveyed me like sport as I divided my attention between the faulty gutters and locating the house. When we entered the compound, Seck welcomed me with a hard handshake. The whole family joined around, everyone extending an arm, to introduce themselves with the familiarity and cheer an American usually reserves for a loved one.

Doctors in town had recently diagnosed two of Seck's children, ages eight and twelve, with HbSC sickle cell anemia, a less serious, heterozygous form of the more common homozygous HbSS disease. Both forms of the illness produce the hallmark symptom of this hemoglobin disorder: the vascular pain of arterial vessels clogged with sticky, damaged red blood cells, commonly called "the sickle cell crisis."[2] The children were prescribed folic acid for fifteen days a month and *Doliprane*, the local name of acetaminophen, for pain when needed. In this part of West Africa, a vitamin and a mild painkiller constitute the standard biomedical therapies for this major red blood cell dyscrasia.

Mr. Seck wondered what else could be done. How, he asked, did people in America and France treat this strange disease, which often left his family visibly healthy but periodically made them acutely ill? I then explained what I witnessed in hospitals in those countries, clinical staples of blood transfusions and a specific chemotherapy called *hydroxyurea*. The latter—approved for general use by the FDA only in the mid-1990s—works by stimulating red cell growth of fetal hemoglobin, the kind we are born with, but lose shortly into infancy. Seck, his wife, and every other parent of sickle cell children I met in Senegal knew that as newborns their children were seemingly healthy. "That child was beautiful," one mother recalled, "and then one day her hands and feet swelled up." That *one day* was sometime during the waning of the infant's fetal hemoglobin production, when the "adult," sickle hemoglobin instituted its takeover for life. In Seck's case, his family's pediatrician reminded me that the children rarely experienced "sickle cell crises." The doctor had only begun following them after their recent diagnoses, when Seck's oldest affected child was nearing puberty. The discovery that an illness ran through his bloodline was new news to Seck. Today he was desperately seeking bits and pieces of additional information on the disease—and struggling to make sense of it—since the lab had detected the same hemoglobin configuration in him as well.

After our extended greeting, Seck and his wife each began to ask what I could tell them about the disease. They wanted answers, and hoped that I had come with some explanation about how this malady seemed to suddenly befall only some of the children. Fearful of disappointing, I nonetheless tried to describe the uncertainty of genetic risk. Each birth is the luck of the draw, I offered, "you'll either pass it on, or you will not." I immediately regretted my frankness, but then remembered that their doctor spoke in broader—and sometimes confusing—terms of percentages, probabilities, and finally, "lotteries" when the message of risk didn't appear to stick. A concession was visible on Mr. Seck's face as he receded deep in thought. After a moment or two he began thinking aloud as his body regained the unmistakable confidence of our first handshake and—in between thoughts—he allowed me to join in with my queries about their situation. When we approached the therapeutic mechanics of fetal hemoglobin, he squinted at the seriousness of the treatment I referenced, and then at the complexity of such a regression of one's adult blood back to its fetal kind. He doubted that the Whites of the North (*les blancs*) always had everything right. Moving to a broader experiential register, he began to theorize more generally about comparative difference:

> Here people say that when [then] World Bank president James Wolfensohn came to Dakar he expected his helicopter to land in a graveyard. The vital statistics, the WHO numbers, are bad, you see. When he got here he was confused. We were tall, well dressed, healthy. Senegal may be underdeveloped, but we live well. . . . I guess if we had no centenarians, then we might entertain the thought that we too need an overly sanitized [medicalized], American type of life.

As Seck continued, he was quick to make the analogy between his family's "broken blood cells" that clogged their "piping" and the defective sewer ducts responsible for the fetid mess in the street. The "powers that be, the public works and health ministries," he complained half-heartedly, "don't see a point in investing in either." He then added: "Senegalese live with them, all the same, and we live well" (*On vit avec, quand meme, et on vit bien*). He reminded me of the many vibrant old people in Senegal. Some of the oldest old actually seemed ageless, he mused, since they were born long before the end of colonization. Few Senegalese obtained birth certificates in the early part of the twentieth century. It was therefore a mystery just how long they had witnessed the world as we knew it, with all of its changes and technology, for the "good and the bad."

Seck, like many in the Dakar region living with sickle cell, presented a picture that coupled outwardly contradictory elements. While lamenting the neglect and political invisibility of his family's illness, which implies its seriousness, he simultaneously seemed able to dismiss its gravity, preferring to speak of his family's survival, the viability of the disease, and its "*mildness.*" I encountered this tendency again and again. Mr. Seck, whose children mostly lived crisis-free, furthermore refused to see himself as sick even though their diagnosis had prompted his own. As a military man, he explained, he had endured rigorous training in the heat of the Sahel region for a decade, but the strain and exhaustion had never once provoked the incapacitating symptoms so often associated with the disease.

Another person I followed, whom I will call Aby Kane, brought similar issues to my attention with dramatically different emphases. Although Mrs. Kane had the most serious compound form of sickle cell disease, HbSS, she too refused to see herself as sick—but she had a particular interest in doing so. At the age of twenty-eight, after almost two years of marriage, Aby wanted nothing more out of life, even life itself, than to have a child. Her doctor repeatedly told her to forget the idea. Not only would she put herself at risk for serious delivery complications, the doctor warned, but she would also risk passing on her illness. During one visit to the adult sickle cell clinic, housed in the partially state-funded University of Dakar teaching hospital at Fann, Aby grew furious as her usual entreaty met a wall. Her doctor defensively smiled at her persistence. Turning to me to build a case against the patient at my side, the physician, who had allowed me to observe her clinical encounters for over a year, grew irritated. She gracelessly told Aby to focus on her *own* life and health, and to have her thyroid checked because her "pulse was rattling in her neck." Calling the doctor "negligent and uninterested," Aby quickly asked me if there was someone else in Dakar whom she could consult for a second opinion. She had twice succeeded in becoming pregnant, but neither pregnancy had ended in a live birth.

Although repeat blood transfusion therapy is rarely and hesitantly administered for sickle cell in Senegal, specialists in Dakar know that they must attempt to provide polytransfusion for women with the disease who, despite its medical contraindication, do become pregnant. Both Aby and her husband recounted how in 1999 she was admitted to a public hospital for complications during her second trimester, and no one registered the fact that because she had sickle cell that she might have needed a transfusion. Instead, the sleepy physician on the night shift simply told her husband to tell an intern that she needed a certain prescription. In recounting their story, neither remembered the pharmaceutical detail of the script. They only recalled losing their child after Aby was given too large a dose of an analgesic whose name was now better forgotten. In this young couple's view, general neglect—and specific ignorance of sickle cell disease—in one of Dakar's major hospitals went hand in hand. On her next pregnancy, Aby visited another doctor, received a bad blood transfusion, for which she was not properly matched, and according to her doctor at Fann, she went into septic shock in a matter of hours. She died after being transferred to a hospital that was judged better equipped to revive her. This was in early 2001. In our conversations when she was alive, Aby insisted that her ills were caused not by her disease, since she was rarely sick, but by "a system," perhaps itself in "crisis," where physicians can be both dismissive and uninformed when it comes to matters of sickle cell anemia life—and, in Aby's case, premature death.

■ **Biology and Economy**

Mr. Seck's and Mrs. Kane's stories, specifically their attitudes about sickle cell and its biomedical and political stewards, perform the discursive double duty of protesting public neglect and political apathy with regard to the disease, while promoting a self-based conception of vitality for those who have the capacity to "live well" with it. In their separate accounts, both of them immediately offered me telling bits of their lives to drive home this message of determined survival by refashioning potentially limiting diagnoses into examples of exposing the limits of these diagnoses. Their frustration that Senegal's health ministry, and larger government, has long ignored sickle cell as a public health problem, was articulated alongside their own strength and will to live "normally." This configuration of *crisis* and subsequent contrary *affirmation* of an intuited, lived (but not yet officially sanctioned) description of the nature of things should be familiar enough to social scientists of science. It is the basic prerequisite to scientific (and "political") revolutions, where, as historian of science Thomas Kuhn once noted, a deep "sense of malfunction" leads to "crises" in our approach to assumed knowledge of disciplinary fields (1962/1993, 92). Put differently, when faced with crises without clear solutions, people's belief in the bounded nature of science and truth can begin to wane. Sometimes this belief refuses to materialize at all, or it sediments in ways that geneticists in places like America and France might not expect. What can we make of a situation in which both bodily and economic crisis are consistent aspects of the human experience that the sick hope to normalize? How do people establish health norms, revaluate scientific knowledge, and offer new contours for emergent medical truths that might be better off left unbound?

In Senegal, as in much of sub-Saharan Africa, tropes of crisis that are articulated through economic lack are rarely bereft of human connections that affect how people deal with acute despair, how they get by, and, in some cases, how they understand norms for well-being alongside new definitions of bodily threats (Ashforth 2005, 91; Ferguson 2006, 82; Wendland 2010, 179–80). Thus it was not surprising that people in Dakar easily elided aspects of their lives marked by financial constraints with those of bodily dysfunction. Mr. Seck makes this clear when he articulates the limits of state intervention regarding sickle cell disease, as well as the government's inaction faced with pervasive structural disrepair and poverty that are both visible and invisible, within his body and without. It was hardly a stretch for Seck, and others in the pages to follow, to link the effects of economic crisis and red blood cell obstruction not only in the same sentence but also in the same terms: those of aspirations for normalcy and of the government's inability to meet their everyday needs. Yet broader overlays of economic fate and sickle cell health emerged long before those I heard people recount in the early 2000s. Entanglements of biology and economy characterized sickle cell disease during Senegal's recent postcolonial history, particularly when Northern genetic researchers began to query characteristics of global Southern populations during the period when much of sub-Saharan Africa was on the brink of economic crisis in the early 1980s. In Senegal, recurring severe droughts over multiple years hit the agricultural-based economy just as the world oil shocks of 1973 and 1979 drove up prices and made massive borrowing inevitable (Boye 1993). In 1979 the government embarked on a series of loans from the World Bank and the International Monetary fund that would run into the billions in the coming decades.

During this time, in a lab far removed from Africa's impending economic woes, two University of California, San Francisco-based geneticists, Yuet Wai Kan and Andrée Dozy, pioneered a specific use of a technology called Restriction Fragment Length Polymorphisms (RFLPs) that would prove to be key for the field of population genetics. They showed that specific enzymes could cut genetic strands at specific cleavage points that were "in linkage" (consistently passed on) with the sickle gene (Kan and Dozy 1978). Since the restriction enzymes sectioned the DNA of the majority of African American patients in their sample at one place, and a significant minority at another, the researchers proposed that these "restriction sites" indicated that the genetic loci in question revealed different evolutionary histories of the sickle cell gene (Kan and Dozy 1978, 1980). In their publications on the issue, Kan and Dozy made an overture to others in the field of medical and population genetics to pursue such studies more globally.

Two decades later, French geneticist Dr. Dominique Labie would remember their call as she told me how she and her Paris-based team took up Kan and Dozy's challenge and immediately began to secure funding, logistics, and collaborations for what would become the 1984 *beta globin haplotype* studies in three former French African locales, one of which was Senegal.[3] The Labie team would go on to perform a detailed assessment of Senegalese versus other sickle cell haplotype markers discussed in this book's preface.

Even though Kan and Dozy's discovery was based on the understanding that these markers were likely "without function" (Williamson 1995, 149), researchers like Labie hypothesized that the favorable clinical picture of sickle cell in Senegal could be due to the genetic sequence variant found in people with the disease in Dakar since, they theorized, it likely increased the production of fetal hemoglobin (Labie et al. 1985). It did not take long for hardworking sickle cell specialists in Senegal to add this *conceptual* linkage of favorable Senegalese sickle cell to their cultural and clinical repertoire of healing and of intersubjective relationships of care. Whether or not they had a clear understanding of these DNA markers as such, many specialists in France and the United States (albeit to a lesser extent) also began to imagine that some stretch of DNA in the vicinity of the sickle cell allele was responsible for a biological change in Senegalese bodies. From this point on, Senegalese research physicians drew upon these conceptual linkages in different forms and, in the process, opened up "Senegalese" DNA to a whole social and economic world (of both function and meaning) within government health care sectors in Dakar.

By the time Labie and her colleagues equipped themselves and set up contacts in Africa to help them realize the planned "field studies" inspired by Kan and Dozy's key paper, Senegal's government was in the midst of restructuring its social spending to meet the terms of its first structural adjustment loans (Anseeuw 2001, 250; van de Walle 2001, 1). It was the first nation in the region to undergo structural adjustment and, in the process, to start the economic liberalization trend that would later characterize one aspect of continued indebtedness and economic crisis that still plagues the region today. At the time the small African nation had an international debt of US$1.47 billion, which represented 49 percent of its GDP (van de Walle 2001, 2). At the very beginning of reform, the state instituted austerity programmatic cuts in civil service, education, agriculture, and health care. By the end of the 1980s, government expenditure on health as a percentage of total government expenditure dropped to almost half of what it was in the previous decade. It fell from a mere six 6 percent to slightly above a much more meager 3 percent (Ogbu and Gallagher 1992, 616).

What seems strange in hindsight is that just the year before its first loan and cuts in health care necessitated by reform, the country had committed to implementing the "Health for all by the year 2000" goals defined by the 1978 *Alma Ata Declaration* (Foley 2010, 59). In public health circles globally, Alma Ata stands out in the history of international declarations of planetary goals for human welfare, since it ambitiously defined health as "a state of complete physical, mental, and social well-being, and not merely the absence of disease or infirmity." It also pronounced health to be "a fundamental human right," which, it boldly charged governments with the responsibility of ensuring through national primary health care. In its quest for equality and empowerment of communities, it furthermore tasked what we might call health care constituencies with fully "participating" in securing care with their own means, to the best of their abilities. The political economic philosophy of neo-liberalism was rapidly gaining ground during these years, however. Thus, in reality, the rhetorical work of such discourses of inclusion would of course mask the real ways that people in the global South would have to fend for themselves while overcoming economic and health barriers after structural adjustment. Concepts of "participatory health" would shift the focus from one where many had to navigate multiple layers of exclusion to one that championed their efforts to obtain inclusion at all costs.

The case of Senegalese sickle cell emerged in this global health and liberalizing economic context. Despite Senegal's said commitment to primary care for all in 1978, in reality, this was a time when government health expenditure was one of the lowest in the country's history. Given these two events—population genetic studies in Senegalese bodies, on the one hand, and economic retrenchment of the Senegalese state, on the other—people with sickle cell in this part of West Africa have hitherto been drawn into a curious species of participatory health that no country representative at Alma Ata likely imagined. It was through these emergent normative tropes of inclusion that Senegalese sicklers would be left to their own biological devices to "participate" in securing their own health through their "mild" disease. Economic despair, in one realm, coupled with the exactitude of genetics for well-being, in another, overlaid each other in historical time. Their coincidental correspondence shaped the long-term unfolding of what it would mean to have this genetic condition in Senegal thereafter.

■ **Experience as Experiment**

When I arrived in Senegal for the first time in 1998, many health personnel and medical practitioners in state-run teaching hospitals at the University of Dakar, where I conducted fieldwork, habitually critiqued their government's "neglect" of sickle cell, the absence of funding for both research and care, and the general inexcusable invisibility of the disease. No matter the palpable demoralization brought on by their exclusion from the state's articulation of health problems, they often answered their own needs through recourse to the vague, technical "saving-grace" that individuals in their clinics possessed: "*Senegalese* sickle cell anemia."

Several of the principal hematologists and pediatricians who allowed me to observe the dynamics of their clinical consultations referenced the Senegalese haplotype, even as some qualified patients' health in other terms. In most cases, the idea of a beneficial haplotype had morphed into a general optimism about local sicklers' well-being through hybrid concepts that drew more explicitly from politics and culture than solely from genetics. Several of my informants who were physicians offered explanations of their population's biological success that—even when these departed from or critiqued the genetic narrative—seemed to be derived in part from the scientific discovery about Senegalese sickle cell health that was put in motion by Labie's team. As one hematologist told me in 2000, the now famous haplotype not only "saved" patients, it also "saved busy practitioners the trouble of having to do so." This statement drives home the extent to which mild sickle cell anemia in Senegal is the *involution of inclusion*: it is the contribution of participatory health that is allowed to function via the attributes assigned to a people's genetic biology in the absence of state health care benefits.

I refer to the haplotype as an involution of inclusion since the function of health inclusion that it permits is powered by its own inverse—by this population's extant exclusion on multiple levels. Neither the Senegalese state nor the global North-South donor economy that increasingly sustains it has problematized sickle cell as a worthy issue of concern. Before the late 2000s, sickle cell had not been conceptualized as a site of intervention or care at the most basic level of government investment.[4] Thus, despite its debut within the high-tech performance of modern genetics at the dawn of population gene mapping, and despite the publicity it would receive internationally as part of a crucial imagined aspect of Senegalese advantageous biology, the phenomenon of the disease itself within the country was strangely ignored. Still, its discursive effects helped to shape people's intersubjective modes of self-care and self-governance where both the sick and their biomedical stewards came to experiment with make-shift, low-level therapeutic practices that would come to constitute a lived experience with the disease shaped through economic scarcity. As the haplotype discourse gained currency in medical circles over the years, patients in Dakar lived and survived by experimenting, in practice, with their own bodies, trying to determine what worked, in the form of plant therapies, prayer, diet, and eventually through therapeutic solidarity care networks and their sickle cell advocacy group. Doctors also experimented with minimal treatments, an approach that was economically driven but undoubtedly helped along by a belief in their patient population's predisposition to health. The Senegalese sickle cell experience, in this sense, signifies the passage of life as *experientia* to life as *experimentum* (Licoppe cited in Callon et al. 2001, 112), or experiment, where trials for health became part of the everyday.

Other Views on Experimental Life

Recently scholars of science and medicine in Africa have argued that the irregular ways that people have been left to care for themselves, with either absent states or poorly functioning ones, have made many places on the continent coveted sites for scientific experimentation by actors in the global North. This situation, they argue, is one where Western nations perform a mix of medical humanitarianism and new forms of therapeutic domination that invoke colonial scrambles for Africa, which, they maintain, are now executed through biomedical intervention (Nguyen 2010, 185; Rottenburg 2009, 425–27). Africa, in these accounts, is not so much marginal to the global order as it is central to it: it is highly valued precisely because of its forms of dispossession (cf Tilley 2011, 314).[5] Old formulations of *Afrique inutile*, the land that was judged useless and barely exploitable for gain by colonial powers, have, in some realms, been turned on their head. Now it is precisely the poverty and need on the ground that have remade whole populations as useful (*utile*) for pharmaceutical, field laboratory trials that would prove difficult in more privileged locales (Peterson forthcoming). The allure of global sites of dispossession for research recalls what Adriana Petryna has termed "experimentality" (2009, 30). Experimental, crisis-driven interventions in Africa are rarely adequately scrutinized since, as Petryna has argued, Northern scientists maintain that their treatments "could only be of benefit in such desperate contexts" (2009, 40). Clearly, global science, medicine, health, and governance are not freely gained in this part of the world.

The administration of health governance by ethically compromised, enterprising, unaccountable non-state actors may be heightened in Africa due to the epidemic health disaster of HIV/AIDS. In the wake of crumbling social securities, political instability, the NGO-ization of state authority, and the industry-driven nature of therapeutic solutions, physician-anthropologist Vinh-Kim Nguyen has diagnosed the West's mission to treat HIV/AIDS, given these North-South entanglements, as "government-by-exception" (Nguyen 2010, 13; 186–87). He writes: "AIDS has been defined as an exceptional occurrence worthy of an exceptional response" (2010, 6), while that response from the global North has resulted in a calculus of triaging lives and skimping on the administration of effective therapy (104–05). Anthropologist Richard Rottenburg hopes to expand Nguyen's provocative thesis to a much broader register as he refers to experimentality and government by humanitarian exception as "an empirically massive trend" (2009, 423). Both anthropologists are careful to critique the construction of the exploitative necessities wrought by HIV as well as the compromised health subjectivities that these engender. On this point, Nguyen asks, "what forms of politics might emerge in a world where the only way to survive is to have a fatal illness?" (Nguyen 2001, 6; cf. Rottenburg 2009, 433). If the power of government-by-exception lies in the humanitarian "sovereign's power"—in Nguyen's terms, to triage lives (which renders invisible the many people who do not get HIV-related attention)—what about those whose health problems never make it into official counts and accounts? Who or what wields the power to exclude the health problems left in the shadows? Picking up at this crucial point where these authors leave off, I argue that there is a second-order erasure of other ailing populations that are excluded from view when the scope of "crisis" becomes narrowly singular as we see with the sharp focus on HIV. In much of Africa, disease invisibility has required that affected people deploy experimental technologies of care and form therapeutic networks of advocacy and governmentality in the wake of the state's failure to intervene on their behalf. At issue is the fact that what Nguyen terms the "global health juggernaut" powered by the urgency of AIDS for Africa as a whole—inclusively—itself excludes. To date, scholars have paid little attention to how this layered dynamic of displaced issues actually works, and how people who remain at the margins (given that some "exceptions" have taken center stage) make-do.[6] How, we must ask, do people with life-threatening conditions and potentially fatal illnesses that will not save them (through aid) survive? What other economies and biosocial "saving graces" might mark their hopes for better life?

Without dismissing the importance of HIV/AIDS prevention, research, and medical subsidies, research physicians with whom I worked in Senegal wondered how to get neglected ailments like sickle cell on the table. Even in sub-Saharan Africa, which contains the largest burden of HIV/AIDS globally with 5.6 million cases as of 2009, there are still nations where HIV has not mushroomed into the epidemic crisis that is most visible in the southern tip of the continent (UNAIDS 2010, 28). Empirically speaking, HIV has not overtaken many national populations and may not warrant the same label of "crisis." To cite the 2010 *Global Report* "The HIV prevalence in West and Central Africa remains comparatively low, with the adult HIV prevalence estimated at 2% or under in 12 countries in 2009. [These include] Benin, Burkina Faso, Democratic Republic of the Congo, Gambia, Ghana, Guinea, Liberia, Mali, Mauritania, Niger, Senegal, and Sierra Leone" (UNAIDS 2010, 20). In Senegal, where the adult seroprevalence rate has historically been one of the lowest on the continent, and is currently said to be between 0.07 and 1 percent (UNAIDS 2009), HIV/AIDS government programs are nonetheless massive, taking up 30 percent of the state's allocated budget for health, with childhood vaccination campaigns and malaria prevention trailing behind (OMS 2009, WA540 HS1, 11). Following from this, we might conceive of the health blindspots that officially blot out the all too visible problems that fill Senegalese clinics as after-effects of what feminist philosophers Shannon Sullivan and Nancy Tuana have called "epistemologies of ignorance" (2007). When ignorance is the underside of knowledge, then tracing its contours, they argue, has "the potential to reveal the role of power in the construction of what is known and provide a lens for the political values at work in our knowledge practices" (2007, 2). Issues of ignorance, in the public health context of contemporary Africa, therefore characterize illnesses that are not so much pushed out of view as simply not officially problematized in the first place. Cases like that of sickle cell anemia in recent Senegalese history illustrate the very real underlying dynamics of exclusion within Africa, and of Africa, that are, of course, in no way novel. They were embedded in the colonial subjugation of African peoples on various levels, including the scientific use of race and biological difference for mapping territory as we saw in the preface, at the exclusion of medical care for sickle cell anemia. Today aspects of these legacies merge with the bleak economic realities that shape most people's lives in this postcolonial context where Africa's global standing continues to infuse its populations' biologies, as well as the constructions and functions that these biologies are made to serve.

■ Medical Neglect and Sickle Cell Life Itself

Almost daily I witnessed people go back and forth between frustration and hope in managing their disease, and more specifically in garnering the necessary resources to live relatively normal lives. In toggling their emotions they seemed fully aware that doctoring their disappointment in the state threatened to create a moral cover-up—a veiling of the unfair, unattended breach in the social contract that troubled them in the first place. Many felt stuck in a cycle of aspiring to be well, while they could not always afford check ups, buy their continued stream of prescriptions, or openly pursue hopes to marry and have children. When their mood was light, they would chalk state neglect of the disease up to fashion—a powerful signifier in Senegalese life—by nonchalantly stating that sickle cell was "not in vogue," that "today HIV/AIDS dominates the runways" (*leegi, SIDA moo xew*). Even with the results of their self-care in view, they still hoped that public perceptions of the disease would improve.

There were both political and personal issues at stake in the public health system's permanent triage of sickle cell. Not only would people have to fend for themselves to obtain health care, but it would be left to them to correct other people's misconceptions about their fates. Many people in the public domain held ideas that sicklers could not be productive (or reproductive) members of society. I heard numerous stories from people with the disease about how teachers, friends, neighbors, and would-be in-laws wrote them off as "born ill, to die ill," as "dead before adulthood," as "doomed to never marry," and as "destined never to have children." Although many people with the disease took umbrage with the death pronouncements, it was the prognosis of not being able to bear children that seemed to upset them the most. People like Aby Kane saw their role in life (at least partially) as having children in order to be complete. Whether blatant or more muted, people's anxieties on these issues conveyed the human importance of existing for one's self, in the here and now, and for one's "lineage" in the future and simultaneous past. Socially and biologically, people embodied the past and their future family lines, which they existentially collapsed into their own bodies and beings. Thus, for them, it was their future projected self, extended lineage, bodily and life potential, which onlookers and prognosticators of their fates devalued in their judgments that people with the disease were somehow "less" (*wañeeku*). Through relationships, within families, between certain doctors, healers and patients, and among patients themselves, people strived to socially and economically invest in making the body with sickle cell live well while simultaneously restoring a sense of value to sickle cell existence.

In this process of affirmation patients and their fellow compatriots in medical genetic fields found various ways to subjectively transform the exigencies of life on the ground in contemporary Africa, including economic scarcity and an absence of biomedical resources, into therapeutic media for survival. In this context my use of the term "life itself" refers to people's existential ability to create value in a setting marked by gross medical dearth, to "manage" and "make-do" with everyday aspects of life's difficulties.[7] Yet, life itself furthermore extends to all that constitutes the biological body proper that is central to specialty fields of medicine concerned with making it live better. In amazement about their patients' well-being, despite their lack of biomedical resources, some doctors believed that Senegalese people's mild disease might impart lessons to improve medicine, rather than the other way around.

Michel Foucault (1970, 127–28) argued that a Western European fascination with life itself, or the organism, happened only when biology as a domain of knowledge emerged as a both a subject (a discipline) and an object of study (the living being). This was a historical advance past natural history as the primary field concerned with nature, but also a conceptual shift away from it. Borrowing from Foucault on this point, many anthropologists and sociologists of science describe how life itself continues to change as our concepts of, and relations to, scientific knowledge shift. Social scientists' forays into research on specific cultural forms that shape molecular genetics, pharmacology, neuroscience, fertility, and brain death (to name a few areas that have yielded new tools for conceptualizing our bodies, biologies, and, ultimately, selves) make clear that prior human practices mark and mold seemingly new articulations of what is biologically possible and permissible (Franklin 2006; Fullwiley 2008; Inhorn 2003; Lakoff 2006; Lock 2002; Montoya 2011; Petryna 2002; Rabinow 1999; Roberts 2007; Strathern 1992). These thinkers help us understand what is genuinely novel in the "epistemological mutations" (Rose 2007, 42) that rearticulate how we conceive of our own biology and the biology of others as these foil and fold into self-concepts across global North-South divides.

The fundamental point I want to make in this book is that the two aspects of "life itself" that I emphasize here—people's existential acts of "making-do," coupled with specialists' investments in mild sickle cell as useful for medicine and for their impoverished health system—work together. These aspects of life itself integrate genes, poverty, hope, religious faith, and constraints in care, as well as autochthonous plants, scientific aspirations, and human survival strategies that cannot be parsed as separate. In other words, I argue against the "domaining practices" that, at the broadest level, hold "culture" and "biology" as mutually insular (Vora 2008, 378). Instead, I focus on the material conditions that people negotiate daily to make sickle cell about health, rather than a limiting disease, that have resulted in a socio-scientific reality of mild Senegalese sickle cell anemia in Dakar.

There are many constituent parts to this "biosociality," where nature is modeled, made, and remade through human anxieties and "practice," while "culture becomes natural" in the process (Rabinow 1996, 99). Examples of this dissolution of the nature/culture split abound in patients' self-imposed injunctions for sickle cell normalcy, and the rendering of their genetic fates as mild. These include a will to bear children despite contraindication because "it is the one thing that makes an African woman a woman!" as Aby told me shortly before her death. For Aby, a normal life is pregnant with acts that sometimes blur the bodily risks run by living one's cultural values. With regard to treatments, many strive for a different degree of normalcy by culling the ecological and economic gifts of pharmacopoeia, or "black people's medicines" (*garab u nit ku ñuul*), one of which, when used for sickle cell, has become an acceptable stand-in for pharmaceuticals in this resource-poor setting. In Dakar the hope is that a palliative exists cheaply in the larger environment, not only in the red dirt of the Senegalese hinterlands but also within urban terrains of healing. People's faith in plant therapies draws upon a conception of local nature that is articulated not only as a space that provides an accessible, affordable palliative but one that is also filled with biosocial relationships of care. For instance, the principal medicinal plant used for sickle cell often enters into people's health regimens through the recommendations of caring others who bundle it with friendship, love, and support when they try to intervene to avert further sickle cell crises.

In reality, such biosocial forms of care far exceed the sharing of plants. They surface much more broadly in people's efforts to *partition* pain through therapeutic economies of exchange where they distribute and "share sickle cell blood" itself (*bokk derët*). The explicit invocation of sharing disease pain and sickling blood are powerful biosocial connectors that are driven by local idioms of literal forged kinships. People enact family ties beyond the limits of birth kin to mark and name intersubjective supports, like their patient advocacy group, that affectively draw sicklers together through the disease and allow them to collectively manage their crises, both biological and economic. These and other instances of the ways that people live the exigencies and, in cases like Aby's, the precariousness of everyday life contribute to a specific illness picture where sickle cell is made "mild" enough to allow patients to strive for normalcy.

The larger point to be made here, of course, is that there is no singular disease called sickle cell anemia in the world today. At most there are near universal terms of disease entities that are nonetheless made and enacted differently in different places through people's diverse historical engagements with pathology, concepts of human distinction, global standing, economic well-being, and social structures as basic as kin ties that allow one to get by.[8] And "getting by" is how many people describe their illness. For their part, actors in the medical corps both encourage—in their own pronouncements of mild sickle cell—and reiterate people's general tendency to emphasize their health rather than its impossibility. In this way, sickle cell in present-day Senegal is pushed to succeed as "mild."

More generally, the issue is how economic scarcity itself distributes variants of extant "making-do," such as the lack of biomedical interventions, on the one hand, and the biomedical rewriting of those absences as tolerable, on the other. Senegalese patients are left, or are *let*, to live, yet they do so in a way that reiterates their larger cultural attributes of gumption, faith, and hope that they strive for in other domains, such as work and economic survival.

Foucault made one of his most instructive observations when he wrote that "modern man is an animal whose politics places his existence as a living being in question" (Foucault 1980, 143; cf Franklin 2000; Rabinow 1999). What exactly are these politics that infuse not only "modern" stakes in life but also the biologies of people "outside the Western world" (Foucault 1980, 143)? In *Global Shadows*, James Ferguson argues that the social body is actually a planetary mass whose lifeblood is economic *interdependence*. Parts of that body are atrophying, through neglect and heavy tax, and through over use and expectations of failure. This limb link is true of many places in the global South where human life is shot through with gross planetary economic disparities, and marked by clear global rank that many Africans aspire to change. Thus, rather than focusing on "cultural difference" per se, I follow Ferguson in arguing that we must grasp the ways that inequality works to radically differentiate our experiences of primary "modern goods" (Ferguson 2006, 32; 186). Specifically, the "good" of life itself cannot be conceived of without attention to experiences of health as well as conceptions of healthy biology. We must be attentive to the ways that techno-scientific renditions of well-being come to influence framings of health, in this case, how a concept like the Senegalese haplotype has been charged with explaining mild sickle cell anemia in a context of economic disorder.

I want to enlarge a Foucauldian emphasis on how we come to understand ourselves biopolitically in the world today to include how modern economic differences, societal effects of poverty, and what Ferguson calls Africa's *place-in-the-world* actually *inhere* in scientific understandings of biogenetic distinction for sickle cell in Senegal. In other words, the fact that Senegalese sicklers "make-do" and often render their disease mild marks not only their subjective attempts to normalize the limits of their disease, as discussed earlier, but it also shows how they metabolize the difficulties of their troubled health care system where, first, the state in economic crisis and, then later, global donor priorities have long ignored their plight. As the lives of people with sickle cell in Senegal demonstrate, biopolitical survival tactics of living well, or simply living at all, are in no way reducible to nationalized notions of genetic causality and haplotype differences—the primary concepts that have maintained an explanatory monopoly on Senegalese "mild sickle cell" for over twenty-five years. Nonetheless, as I laid out in the preface, the specific sickle cell haplotype in a population called "the Senegalese" has been allowed to subsume many of these larger processes of cultural reckoning.

■ Localized DNA and the Haplotype Explanation for "Mild" Disease

The scientists responsible for the discovery of the African sickle cell haplotypes named them after the national locales in which they were found. The only exception was the Central African type, which was called "Bantu" by Europeans and CAR (for "Central African Republic") by more politically correct American specialists who continued to follow the logic of the map. Informed by DNA analyses from the chromosomes of twenty-nine homozygous sickle cell patients in Dakar, fourteen from the Central African Republic, ten from Benin, and ten from Algeria (who possessed the pattern of markers identical to those of the Beninois), the research team found that 82 percent of those in Dakar possessed a set of genetic polymorphic sites common to that group. The twenty Beninois chromosomes were perfectly matched among themselves, and the Central African Republic type was 84 percent homogenous as well (Pagnier et al. 1984, 1772). One additional African haplotype was found later in the Eton ethnic group of Cameroon (and was called "Cameroon"). Again, these "upstream" or "downstream" changes (meaning DNA lettering switches toward the end or beginning of the coding sequence in reference to the sickle cell mutation) were noted to be differentially inherited *with* the sickle allele depending on if one was nationally, and ethnically, "Senegalese," "Bantu," "Beninois," "Cameroonian," or "Arab-Indian."

Despite the background on which it lies, the gene for sickle hemoglobin itself, as a protein product, seems to be encoded in Senegalese bodies in the same way as it is in people of any other geographical locale. In addition, the string of particular nucleotide changes (the haplotype) in the beta globin gene cluster has not been solidly proven to cause *functional* changes in biology, differentially, in these marked populations as "whole groups" (by which their high haplotype frequencies, above 80 percent, define them). Put otherwise, in the disciplinary parlance, "most polymorphic endonuclease restriction sites used to assign a haplotype have no known role in the differential transcription and temporal regulation of [this gene]" (NHLBI 2002, 174). In one study conducted in Dakar by local specialists, 11.6 percent of adult Senegalese patients had relatively mild disease manifestations and a fetal hemoglobin level above 15 percent of their total hemoglobin (See Diop et al. 1999, 173, table V). Although the Senegal haplotype (like the "Arab-Indian" haplotype) is "strongly associated" with a high expression of persistent gamma globin (a constituent element of fetal hemoglobin) into adulthood, the causal link between the two remains an open area of research. To date, there have been many theories about what genetic factors could be modulating the amount of

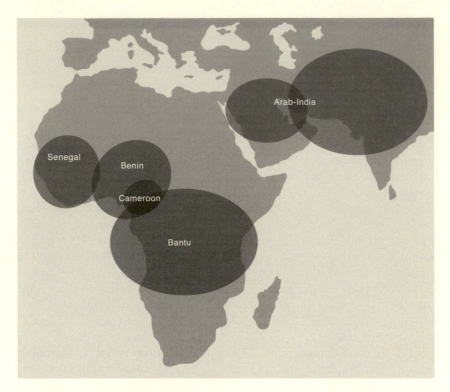

Figure 1.1 Sickle cell haplotype map based on where each mutation was theorized to have emerged. The beta hemoglobin gene that contains the sickle mutation evolved independently in different regions of the world. Although the mutation is the same, the chromosomal background, or sequence on the chromosome that most people from these named populations share, is older than the specific mutation that codes for sickle cell. Courtesy of Elsevier Publishers.

fetal hemoglobin that adults with sickle cell produce at varying levels. Environmental, dietary, and social contributors have yet to be taken seriously in these studies.

Most recently (still within the framework of genetics), in 2008 scientists from the United States, Italy, and Brazil compared patient cohorts and healthy individuals in order to map areas of the genome that might be responsible for persistently high levels of fetal hemoglobin in those with sickle cell and beta thalassemia (also a hemoglobin disorder). Through genome-wide association (GWA) studies, this international group found several novel sequences on chromosome two that appear to be at work in HbF expression (Higgs and Wood 2008; Lettre et al. 2008; Sankaran et al. 2008; Uda et al. 2008). One single nucleotide polymorphic change (SNP) in particular accounted for 14 percent of the variance in fetal hemoglobin levels in an American cohort and for 9 percent in Brazilian patients (Lettre et al. 2008, 11870). These more re-

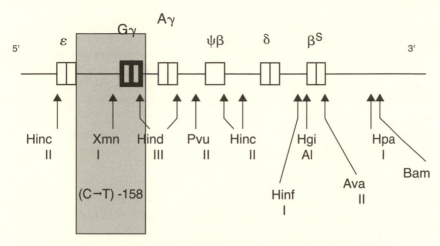

Figure 1.2 The sickle cell haplotype arrangement. The genetic sequence of the beta-globin chain cluster of genes essential to hemoglobin is on chromosome eleven. This image conveys the restriction enzyme cutting sites that indicate sequence variation. The xmnI site signifies the C → T change that defines the Senegalese haplotype. The beta chain contains different forms of hemoglobin that are "turned on" or expressed in the order in which they appear in development. The order of expression begins in the early embryonic stages with epsilon-globin. Shortly after—in the fetal stages to the first few months of life—gamma-globin is produced, which is necessary for fetal hemoglobin synthesis. Finally, there are two adult forms, delta-globin (in very small amounts, usually less than 3 percent) and the major adult form, or beta-hemoglobin. It is this last stage where the genetic change in sicklers codes for sickle hemoglobin, HbS, in lieu of the usual "Adult" beta form, or "HbA." Courtesy of Elsevier Publishers.

cent findings, which include several newly recognized SNPs, as well as a validation of the one that partially characterizes the Senegalese haplotype (−158 C → T), are now thought to account for roughly 20 percent of all phenotypic fetal hemoglobin variation (Lettre et al. 2008).

These discoveries are not insignificant. Yet, in conceding that health outcomes may be linked to some aspect of genetic variation exhibited between people classed within ethnic and national lines, we must also ask what is lost when we focus on small, highlighted gene differences that are in no way generalizable to the majority of sicklers in these nationally named cohorts? Additionally, like many studies that cite multiple genetic markers in aggregate to account for a fraction of a given trait phenomenon, research of this type leaves many unanswered questions, most notably, what accounts for the other ~80 percent of human fetal hemoglobin variation? Important as they may be for explaining life in terms of genes, I nonetheless want to get us beyond these modes of query.

There are two reasons for this. The first is that moving past an emphasis on filling quantitative gaps in genetic knowledge allows us to begin to ask how human biological differences get parsed in the first place. In other words, it allows us to instead think through social "likelihoods of recognition" that allow some *ways of differing* to make cultural sense, while others are not conceived of as salient at all (see Epstein 2007, 142–43). Jean and John Comaroff make a similar point in diagnosing the role of "physical facts" on social constructions of the African body in the Western imperial imagination. Taking from Marshall Sahlins's frame of universal perceptual logics, they write: "categories are themselves just one of a series of available imaginative 'implements.' Whether they will be selected and how they will be used in any context is clearly a function of culture rather than nature" (1992, 71). My point here is that we cannot hold this two-sided relation as separate, beyond the heuristically helpful moment of doing so (Strathern 2005, 87–88). Instead, we must probe the materiality of the natures with which we are dealing for their relational role in how constructions function. What kinds of natures make up the structural fibers of cultural selections that appeal to us, and that answer our anxieties about peoples and their placement in the world? How does the mode of inquiry, specific question posed, or assumed, allow particular material and bodily differences to be marshaled up, or to perform at all?

This brings me to the second reason that I want to move discussions of biological difference beyond a mere quantitative focus. Although sickle cell haplotype mutations may have true biological effects of some magnitude, they form only "partial connections" to a larger life picture where people rely on botanical material objects, which are often prescribed or recommended to them by someone in their larger social worlds of care (Haraway 2003). Donna Haraway calls such topologies of inseparable relational categories— in this case, of people, plants and the scientifically ascribed effects of their interconnection—"naturecultures" (2003, 8). In "getting by" certain Senegalese sicklers embark on a specific therapy regimen that includes the roots of an autochthonous tree called *Fagara xanthoxyloïdes*, or *dengidëk* in Wolof.[9] In France, researchers currently studying fagara believe that it holds some medical promise chemically, as they pursue science on its ability to induce fetal hemoglobin (Dupont et al. 2005). If fagara induction of HbF production were found to be true, this plant could be the source of biological effects in patients that are attributed to the Senegalese haplotype in the first place. Yet, like any element of this relational topology, neither fagara nor fetal hemoglobin acts alone.

Two sisters in Dakar told me about how fagara "made [their] bodies produce fetal hemoglobin" in a context where the person who referred them to the "traditional healer" they now consult worked within the domain of "modern medicine." As historian Steven Feierman has shown in Eastern Africa, the therapeutic effects of medicine are not just about the efficacy of the material at hand. Rather, they often depend on the relationship between patient and healer, and are especially effective when kinships form between them during the healing process (2000, 330–31). In the above case, the healer, who supplied the sisters with fagara, eventually became "friend" and then "family." These distinct yet related appellations emerged when each woman differentially emphasized her life woes and future projects in terms of desired "normalcy." Even after the older sister in this story took fagara long enough to regain a sense of health, "free from sickle cell crises," she was still plagued by serious anxieties of gendered social expectations. She then emphasized that sickle cell "really becomes an issue, when it comes to marriage and having children." At some point both sisters playfully began to refer to their healer as their "husband," since, as the older one said, "no one has married us," in part, because of sickle cell, "so he has." Here, care, protection, and kinship wishes combine to diffuse suffering. This happens in a relational topography of convivial biosociality and through the informal microeconomies of commerce in botanicals of which this healer's larger family, many sons and nephews, also take part.

Keeping these issues in play, we must furthermore go beyond the specific points above to consider why is it that some sicklers experience rare or nonexistent pain crises, and have virtually no fetal hemoglobin to offset the ill effects of their sickle version of this protein. In over one hundred interviews that I helped to conduct in Oakland, California in the mid-1990s, a lifetime with sickle cell would hardly go unnoticed (Duster and Beeson 1996). The American cases were filled with narratives of serial episodes of indescribable pain. Moreover, the treatments of routine blood transfusions and their iatrogenic effects of iron overload—requiring attendant abdominal injections of iron chelation therapy—compounded and often equaled the pain and fatigue of the disease itself (also see Rouse 2009). Given this, how is it that sicklers in a relatively poor country like Senegal are seen to "live better" than their doctors would expect, creating a scenario where physician-researchers in Dakar judge Senegalese sickle cell to be milder than that lived in America and France? I argue that these answers lie in the role of affect, in people's ability to forge biosocial bonds and partial connections to others via their pain, blood, and life, in order to manage economic and health problems more generally.

Shuttling between realms as seemingly distant and disparate as economy and biology, the sickle cell stories I relate in the ethnographic chapters to follow detail how aspects of economic struggle and biological norms cohere in life processes that are less conspicuous and far less contained than population medical genetics' discourses of haplotypes. At stake is our willingness and, in some sense, disciplinary ability, to see that cultural practices and genetic effects are attached before birth. Put otherwise, a certain *pedigree of process* has gone missing from the genealogy of knowledge when it comes to the experience of sickle cell anemia and its "difference" in contemporary West Africa.

The case of sickle cell in Dakar illustrates the power and place of genetic explanations for human well-being. Even if genetic framings often mask the historical and cultural experiences that may lead to a given health outcome, those framings remain present in the ways that medical specialists translate local needs for biological success more broadly. By situating the genetic conception of the Senegalese sickle cell haplotype in a contemporary global order of economic disparity, I aim to contribute to a guarantee that affective underpinnings of health outcomes, constellations of poverty, and material inequality are not blotted out for good in our thinking about biological causation. If a putatively "simple," "single gene disorder" becomes infinitesimally layered when analyzed as a lived cultural construct, then almost all other human ailments—which are increasingly framed as at least partially due to "complex" genetic interactions—must also be seen for more than their genes.[10]

■ Enculturation

As Senegalese biomedical practitioners have long struggled to be taken seriously by their French colleagues, and to be recognized as equals within science proper, several of the doctors who run sickle cell clinics in Dakar dutifully reference the particularity of the Senegalese HbS haplotype, both directly and indirectly. Yet, in the same breath, they can also do double takes and subject this biogenetic explanatory version of difference to other social realities that might account for the unique lived experiences of their patients. In various conversations with physician-researchers over the years, it became clear to me that their own lives and interactions with sicklers provided them with alternative views on what might be going on with their affected population. They recounted people's attitudes about pain, familial ties, religious beliefs, stoicism, and propensity to take traditional medicines, which could all be put to work to derail a sense of crisis. People affected by sickle cell furthermore habitually redrew barriers of constraining economic limitations, while they searched for possible alternatives to get beyond them. Through interconnections between global understandings of Senegalese genetic particularity and a more general recognition of how people manage sickle cell locally, materially, and in the mind, a lived reality of a mild form of this disease has taken hold. It is in this mix of life and lived experiences that the Senegalese population variant of sickle cell has been made to correspond to a social context where people find ways to live better than expected. In this process the gene itself has become *enculturated*.

Enculturation, as the vital adaptation techniques that social groups fashion for themselves, involves making sense of and living with specific referent objects. The referent in this case is the sickle hemoglobin genetic sequence, which becomes enculturated as both patients and biomedical practitioners engage its supposed dictate of fate and subsequent constraints on (or chances for) living a normal life. Even if we settle on defining health outcomes globally in terms of genetic variants in different populations, we must explore the possibility that *somatization* as a theoretical frame so vital to the anthropology of medicine for psychiatry (Kleinman 1977) might also be at work in the differential cultural expressions of "somatic" genes. Medical anthropologists have chopped the logic inherent in psychology's use of "psychosomatic illness," which often targets individual pathos, or the idea that strange bodily symptoms signify all that has gone awry in "one's head." Nancy Scheper-Hughes and Margaret Lock catapulted forward the theoretical importance of somatization in their now classic essay *The Mindful Body* by staking instead that symptoms are socially significant signs of all that has gone awry in the body politic rather than in the patient's corpus per se (1987). Following from this, if we are to begin to sort out differential global phenomena of bodily expressions of illness, as these are related to Africa's place-in-the-world, then we need to actually include the body that is increasingly biologized through its genetic traits. In other words, we need to consider a somatization framework (where body, mind, and society inhere) for disorders that are assumed to be irrefutably "physical," such as sickle cell anemia. So far, the trend in medical anthropology has been a rather large focus on mental health and its "softer" illness categories as the preferred sites to note how psychosomatic conditions are embodiments of social tensions. In attempting to broaden our view, my concept of the enculturated gene animates a second process that I call *sociosomatic genetics.*

When the sickle cell gene in Senegal mediates social relations that range from postcolonial engagements about science equity to public health funding set by North-South donor priorities, when patients conjure healing strategies that range from silencing pain to an emphasis on normalcy at all costs, when the bounty of biomedicine merely consists of folic acid, painkillers, simple surveillance, and the doctor's touch, and when Senegalese traditional plants are believed to curb sickle cell crises, and perhaps incite the biological production of fetal hemoglobin, people absorb these points of social fact, in body, society, and mind, and express an illness result in the process. This is sociosomatic genetics, and it is made possible when people enculturate sickle cell's effects through soma and psyche in a societal context, in this case, of material scarcity. In this dissolution of the nature/culture split, the actors who people this book rework and rewrite sickle cell knowledge to reflect how they manage to get by with a gene anomaly that has little state attention, locally, or acute medical genius, globally, that might have offered them a cure by now.

It bears dwelling on the theoretical and practical importance of the actors here as *living beings,* and as ethnographic subjects who, as a population, have also been the objects of much scientific inquiry. Nikolas Rose resuscitates medical philosopher Georges Canguilhem's idea of vital humanism on this very point when he writes that knowledge incurred from "resisting death" is both the "key to an understanding of vitality and pathology, and the definition of life itself" (Rose 2007, 43). In Senegal, as Mr. Seck points out, experts working for multilateral financial institutions might think that the country is so impoverished that they expect to find a landscape of graves. Instead, "life itself" often floats on medically uncertain explanations of patients' lived success in "naturally" resisting death when compared to other sicklers globally.

Chronicling the ways that Senegalese sicklers succeed at life, despite grim economic indicators, allows us to make sense of how and why geneticists and other disease specialists in Dakar approach care and research in localized ways that often depart from methods and protocols they have learned on training stints in France. At issue is how they deal with the tangible lack of official knowledge, that unacceptable negative reality that haunts this population as an absence of state attention, once they return home.

■ Sickle Cell Health Politics in Dakar and Beyond

For sicklers to say that there was no Senegalese state intervention for their disease was indeed an empirical truth that deeply troubled many of my interlocutors in Dakar long before my first field trip in 1998. Through a series of events to be elaborated on below, government officials, even Senegalese President Abdoulaye Wade and First Lady Madame Viviane Wade, only began to publicly speak on the disease as of 2006, when they hosted the country's first international conference on sickle cell in November of that year. Dakar's sickle cell specialists, some of whom have been invaluable informants for this book, then found themselves in a position that they could not have imagined only a few years earlier: that is, it was they who actually wrote these politicians' speeches on sickle cell for this national event, enumerating the many health care interventions necessary in this nominally "new" era where the disease entered into the state's consciousness. Sicklers, their families, and researchers who work on the disease felt a palpable optimism that funding, research, and especially care would benefit, as the 2006 week-long conference activities ended with an elaborate televised closing ceremony and gala event. This was a remarkable time of historical change—or so it seemed then. To date, little actual promised funding has materialized beyond the state's financing of the highly publicized 2006 conference. Yet, in anticipation of a revolutionary change, or a paradigm shift in sickle cell visibility, patients and practitioners began to speak out about their limited options. Their predicament was framed as "unjust," a cause of "struggle," a political health "crisis" in need of redress. The disease in crisis, however, did not always reflect how sicklers and those in their care networks saw their own bodily plights. For most patients and families, the body might be "sickly" (*xibon*), diminished (*wañeeku*), or, simply, crisis-free (*tane*), for the time being, but "the system" was *perpetually plagued*.[11]

As one principal sickle cell specialist told me in September of 2009, concerning the lagging National Program, "the problem is that we have no state— we have a country, but we have no state." In his frank diagnosis that he merely has "a country" the specialist was referring to the Senegalese people who have worked to give sicklers a voice, most notably members of the local patient advocacy group *l'Association sénégalaise de lutte contra la drépanocytose* (ASD), whose president is a "healthy" HbSS sickler now in his mid-thirties. These patients and affected family members work tirelessly alongside key biomedical practitioners. Starting in 2008, they also began working with various organizations of women, teachers, and youth volunteers to educate larger publics on the disease.

Several local physician-researchers and disease specialists serve as scientific advisors for the ASD. These professionals have made their case for a state-funded national program part of their university research agenda for the disease. Yet after investing the energy to compile data for the basis of educational initiatives to decentralize care beyond Dakar, they have repeatedly found that ministry funds earmarked for the disease were erratic, or, more commonly, simply unavailable. The "treasury is tapped," they were told in 2009, as both flooding and chronic electricity shortages continued to plague the country for the third consecutive year. "The population was at first understanding," one specialist assured me, but when journalists and NGOs began to reveal the level of wasteful spending and clear corruption that has characterized the Wade regime's rule, their patience fizzled.[12] The same specialist complained, "sickle cell had been budgeted in as of 2006, and those funds went to the planning of the international congress. As of 2007, the government said that we had a right to approximately 70 million *cfa* francs [~US$157 thousand], but in reality there were very little funds."

Despite the lack of follow-up on financing awareness initiatives, several government ministers and the Senegalese First Lady have invited specialists and the ASD to piggyback on large public events where they could reach important thought leaders. One such event was at the twentieth anniversary of the microfinance entity, *Crédit mutuel du Sénégal*, where the borrowing agency's president linked his new focus on credit lines for the country's hard-working female entrepreneurs to the Senegalese First Lady's new involvement in sickle cell education. He then handed the microphone to Madame Wade herself who highlighted the importance of women in disseminating such intimate warnings of genetic disease transmission through family lines, and also through society. Mrs. Wade then brought the ASD to its largest live audience yet when she ceded the stage to Touty Niang, the group's vice president, who is also the mother of a deceased child who had sickle cell. Shortly thereafter, the ASD again benefited from Wade's invitation to a similar event on March 8, 2008, on *International Women's Day*, where she and the ASD leadership addressed *Le comité national des enseignantes pour la promotion de la scolarisation des filles (CNEPSCOFI)* [National Committee of Female Teachers for the Promotion of Girls' Education]. Here again Wade and Niang asked Senegal's female leaders to take the message of sickle cell not only to their classrooms but to their extensive social networks of women's groups and to society at large through their extended families.[13]

During this time Madame Wade gave the ASD state sponsorship, not through the funding they sought, but through the social and political connection to her state image and power. The ASD would continue nonetheless to focus on monetary support and subsidies for patients, since Madame Wade's presence and endorsement was heartening but still fell short of actually changing their daily lives. Many of the most active ASD members are unemployed, and they complain that even the low-tech interventions of folic acid and quarterly medical check-ups are too costly to sustain over a lifetime without draining family resources. Hospitalizations throw many families into debt. Their real goal is state-subsidized health care.

Like those in the ASD, Senegalese country sickle cell specialists, who also attended these events, lamented a frustrating inertia that plagued them on the real issues they wanted solved. These include formal plans of action with regard to the education of doctors and subsidizing needed tests, but, first, equipping health centers with the basic testing technologies in question. A particular problem today is the low number of sites that perform electrophoresis analysis. Electrophoresis is the tool that allows one to differentiate sickle cell disease from the single allelic "dose" of sickle cell trait. The current technology of Emmel testing used by most health centers only detects sickle hemoglobin, which partially accounts for why many people with the trait are told, and believe, that they have a disease.

Local Dakar specialists organized two meetings, in 2008 and 2009, to write a countrywide "strategic plan," complete with a budget and justification, which has yet to receive government approval. As of March 2010, it still languishes in the office of "non-communicable" diseases at the Health Ministry. During these planning sessions, specialists used their own personal finances to write a comprehensive care manual for non-specialists that details the disease and how to intervene on its many complications. Once published, disseminated, and, specialists hope, followed up with training sessions, this single document could immediately begin to address the problem of care being centralized in Dakar. In a March 2010 interview with Mr. Abdou Fall, the minister of health who held office at the time of the 2006 international sickle cell congress, he explained to me that part of the problem is one of political leaders "passing on the baton—or not." Senegal has had four health ministers since late 2005, when sickle cell was allotted a theoretical budgetary line. Each new minister changes aspects of the previous cabinet, while the plans of predecessors often get tabled or reordered in terms of priority. This happened several times with regard to sickle cell. Meanwhile specialists like Dr. Ibrahima Diagne and concerned advocates like Mrs. Niang must decide whether to continually solicit and educate new politicians, or succumb to their own frustrations about the lack of subsidized care, the desperate need for broad medical training, and the continual scarcity of resources that prevent proper testing, diagnosis, education, and awareness throughout the country.

I witnessed different physician-researchers—and members of the ASD —hold their tongues for fear of sabotaging this new nominal state interest, which was nonetheless valued because it was so hard-won. To this end, in their bleaker moments, several of my informants wondered among themselves whether the recent state attention to the disease on the part of the First Lady was actually a step back, rather than forward. Since "there is little action tied to her discourse," one physician-informant lamented, it could be that Madame Wade's presence "simply motivates government ministers to verbally commit their interest for no other reason than to curry her favor."[14] In more optimistic moments, this same informant nonetheless pointed to the social sphere to indicate that real strides were being made: sickle cell visibility could not have happened without everyday people, the sick, and their families, who had no power, until they came together.

This political mobility that simultaneously focused on debility and the prospect of normalcy with the proper supports took shape between patients and families in France and Senegal, as well as in other places in the French-speaking world. To capture it as a movement, they created the Francophone Network for the Fight against Sickle Cell Disease (*Réseau francophone de lutte contre la drépanocytose*), or RFLD. The Francophone network emerged as a rare assembly of patient groups and key sickle cell specialists in France and Africa who, in a hybrid structure—part "patient advocacy association" and part "research scientists"—continue to work to make sickle cell disease an international health priority today. Their initial hope in the early 2000s was that the organization would become a source of much-needed funding to begin "consciousness raising" (*sensibilisation*) in Francophone Africa. The political steps to achieving visibility included working to have sickle cell recognized as a "public health problem" by the UN and the WHO. In the WHO program that first adopted it, however, sickle cell was subsumed under the larger umbrella of "non-communicable diseases" (WHO 2006a). Neither its genetic nature, nor what the implications of that nature would be for models of prevention, were specifically attended to in that categorization.

In an effort to strengthen its international appeal, the RFLD changed its name to the International Organization for the Fight against Sickle Cell, or OILD, in 2005. It nonetheless remains a Francophone entity. Because the patient and professional components of this hybrid network were each "frustrated by the Anglophone dominance of sickle cell knowledge, and its largely American bias," as its president, Madame Edwidge Ebakisse-Badassou, told me in 2002, the OILD possesses a clear politic of promoting *French* speakers' awareness of sickle cell. This ethos was furthermore evinced by the RFLD's early sponsorship and collaborative ties with the *Agence de la francophonie* itself, whose current secretary general is Abdou Diouf, former Senegalese head of state who succeeded Leopold Sédar Senghor within the self-same political party, *le Parti Socialiste* in Senegal. In addition, through a series of efforts on the part of the OILD, Vivian Wade was educated on the disease for the first time in Paris in 2003. The very persuasive (even cunning) Ebakisse-Badassou convinced Mme Wade, along with three other African First Ladies, to serve as political sponsors—*les marraines* (godmothers in French)—for the nascent network. This is how sickle cell disease became one of the many health talking-points of Senegal's *Première Dame*. In a matter of months the condition became a noticeable, even if mostly nominal, preoccupation of Mme Wade's semi-governmental organization called *Association éducation santé*. As one advisor for the health minister told me in September of 2006 when I asked about the sudden emergence of the National Program, "Well, it happened overnight. When it interested Madame Wade, it interested us!"

To date there has been one key intervention for which sicklers can thank Mme Wade. Beyond the ministries, Wade's influence surpassed the merely nominal when she asked the industry-development-charity-foundation arm of the telecommunications company, the *Fondation Sonatel*, to donate funds for a vaccination campaign specifically for sicklers, in 2008 and 2009. In a deal struck with *Sanofi-Pasteur*, a large pharmaceutical company who offered the vaccines at a reduced rate, over a thousand people with the disease were vaccinated against pneumococcus, meningitis, salmonella, measles, mumps, and rubella. Specialists on the ground could not enumerate the preventive costs of this intervention, but felt it to be huge. Yet, as of 2010, there has been no actual allocation of *state* resources to help poor and more severely affected sicklers to obtain medical care, such as hip-replacement surgery needed by some patients but, at the equivalent of three thousand U.S. dollars per procedure, lies far beyond the reach of most. This is the case, even though in 2008 the Senegalese prime minister promised specific funds for interventions of this type.[15] Mme Wade, for her part, is adamant about following the lead of the OILD and shifting attention away from the Senegalese state, for which she demands the population's understanding because of its low global standing and sheer powerlessness to assume the costs of the disease in her view. A European, French native whose *métisse* children have dual citizenship, Viviane Wade has lived between France and Senegal for most of her and her husband's adult lives. She knows Senegal well and, now, as a state insider, her passionate appeal is not to France but to the UN to advance sickle cell care.[16] By following the OILD's lead she is also placing one of Africa's health problems into a global dynamic that draws on some notion of interdependence, rather than the more common French-Senegalese postcolonial dynamic of stark asymmetry that still orders much social and economic life on the ground.[17]

■ Life before Biological Endpoints

Medicine, as it meets with the life sciences, is often where trial and error, experimentation (Fr. *expérience*), is responsible for new directions in therapy, as well as in thought. On this point there are at least two instructive lines of inquiry that have partially taken place on Senegalese ground that power this book. Both have focused on units of life that have been "associated" with improving sickle cell manifestations through observational studies. These studies, though many in number, have never fully shed their airs of experimental observations. That is, they have not quite resulted in the production of solid or indubitable scientific facts but they have nonetheless been deposited within cultural nexuses of meaning that have allowed them to grow into truths. The first life unit concerns the Senegalese haplotype.[18] The second involves local belief in the healing powers of the fagara plant. The medical role of this botanical therapy has been sporadically studied and theorized to ameliorate sickle cell and other conditions of "fatigue" in West Africa. People's belief in fagara's efficacy makes one wonder whether medical observations of good sickle cell health outcomes in this population that are attributed to genetic data endpoints, in this case "Senegalese" genetic sequences, are possibly literally rooted in what is now Senegalese soil.[19] I say possibly because the science on fagara is just as complete, or incomplete, just as speculative, or compelling, as the genetic science that posits haplotype variation as the causal mechanism at work in Senegalese sickle cell mildness. For some, fagara is seen as the key to managing this disease; for others it is derided as damaging to and distracting from real medical pursuits. This was especially true once its efficacy was injected with a large dose of skepticism after it was linked to a controversy of medical charlatanism in France and Benin in the years 1999 and 2000.

In Dakar, biomedical research physicians have repeatedly expressed interests in conducting an *in vivo* fagara trial, but they have never mustered the will and the "resources" to pursue this idea beyond a proof of concept, due to the Benin scandal and the criticism they feared from their Northern colleagues in Paris. Their professional pressures (being overextended in their day jobs) combined with scientific uncertainties (plants are not their areas of expertise), while present politics (wanting to be taken seriously in global sickle cell circles) merged with anxieties of being belittled (by their French colleagues) and a desire for legitimacy in the future. They nonetheless went back and forth on praising the promise of this plant. The fact that they were of two minds about fagara mirrors their descriptions of "mild" sickle cell as simply due to "the haplotype," at times, and/or, as due to less well-defined processes—patients' "attitudes," perhaps mixed with the benefits of plant therapies and their religious faith, at others.

People with the disease did deploy multiple representational strategies that both blended and held separate ideas derived from Islamic theo-logics and sickle cell science techno-logics. Many thought that God willed their "special" existence, or, in the words of one, "had chosen" him for "attention and affliction as a Muslim marked by a handicap who might stand out from the millions of other believers in the world." In such cases the disease was presented as an indicator that an all-knowing God had decided to "test" the individual, to put him on a path of struggle, whereby repayments of spiritual boons and rewards would be forthcoming in the afterlife. For others, faith allowed them to question the limits of science and entertain the idea that a miracle might befall them through the powerful prayers of an imam, or,

through the blessings bestowed on a traditional healer's plants. I heard educated self-assessed healthy sicklers even outright deny that this genetic condition written into their blood and bloodline would necessarily affect their
progeny, if God so willed it. This latter denial was hard to disentangle from
a point blank acceptance of their condition and an ability to minimize its
gravity when the sick and their close kin face searing economic constraints,
which, for many, are what effectively cripple their chances for biological and
social normalcy more broadly.

These subjective embodiments of religious, economic, and social options—
and limits—are furthermore reiterated through language itself, or what
Martin Heidegger called "the house of being" (1993 [1947], 236). In verbally
qualifying their illness experiences, many Senegalese reduce their disease, or
(s)lighten it quantifiably, by articulating and enacting beliefs about their "quality of life." People's linguistic reordering of everyday concepts, often through
amusing wordplays, allowed them to execute diverse representational truth
strategies that affected their illness attitudes as well as scientific knowledge
in the specialty clinics where they receive care. Such locutions as grawul (the
Wolof version of the French phrase c'est pas grave—"not an issue"), mangi
góor góorlu sénégalaisement (I'm getting by "Senegalese-ly"),[20] or alternately,
Yallah baax na (God is great) proved to be vehicular palliatives in many areas
of life for people confronting hardship. Here localized maxims furnish a large
stock of remedial expressions: du daara (it's nothing); mangi ci kawaam (I'm
on top of life's difficulties); and, too often when ill, tane naa (I'm better). In
short, bringing gravity into proximity with the ordinary and what "ought to
be" provided subjective therapeutic verbal injunctions to meet medically and
economically untreatable ends.

When people live their illness experiences through ideas to minimize suffering and articulate miracles of health, the illness picture itself solicits a response from existing models of sickle cell disease and, in Senegal, prompts
them in new directions. Medical philosopher Georges Canguilhem might
have called this mix of affairs an instructive example of "vital normativity"
(1991, 136). Yet what can anthropologists learn about the social-biological
nexus of disease embodiment from an ontological reality where quantitative population genetic markers and patients' spiritually inflected attitudes of
health mutually rely on each other?

Lurking somewhere in the many unknowns that characterize the Senegalese haplotype, certain medical practitioners in Dakar have come to believe
that a "Senegalese attitude" (l'attitude sénégalaise) of optimism, helped by
an earthly spiritual relativism when faced with the most dismal prospects,
deserves immediate attention. As "Senegalese ourselves," they exclaimed,
they believed that many of their patients possessed the mentality that things
"grave" could be partially doctored with the turn of a phrase. For one specialist, this "attitude" might provide an alternative explanation to the HbS haplotype sénégalais in improving life on the ground.

Perhaps conveniently, neither the haplotype nor the attitude has been thoroughly defined. The lack of definitive truth surrounding these concepts allows them to circulate in various arenas, medical and non-medical, where they maintain functional ambiguities that are nonetheless productive. Yet what to do with the frustration that I anticipate here in advance, for some readers, that this book will not resolve or attempt to present "the truth" or "scientific answers" to what is *really* going on concerning the efficacy of the fagara plant in the test tube, the causal underpinnings of fetal hemoglobin as linked to the HbS haplotype, or even the Senegalese "attitude" by engaging with psychology or psychiatry? Should we leave it to medically ordered double-blind trials to get at these questions? Is the lack of effort to do trials of truth a reflection on inadequate funding, or interest? I argue that although these may be the right questions in some instances they will not provide adequate answers about how Senegalese mild sickle cell has come into existence. Nor will they get to how and why fagara "works," or to how attitudes of optimism and faith are embodied, given other energies and powers at work in many realms in West Africa that imbue gaps in scientific knowledge with hope and possibility rather than doubt. Many people I met in Dakar viewed "holes" in science, or unknowns about reality, not necessarily as voids but as spaces where possibilities could happen. They are spaces where constellations of social truths are made, and also function forcefully as positives for chance, rather than solely as negatives, or nescience.[21] In this way the genetic determinism of the Senegalese haplotype is also an endless source of biological as well as cultural indeterminism.

■ **Causation and Culture**

The lived experience of mild sickle cell disease provides an exceedingly important case of study for medical anthropology as well as the anthropology of science on a global scale today. Since the 1984 sickle cell haplotype research, the "observation" that Senegalese sicklers enjoy a "s/light" case of this hemoglobinopathy has been assumed to be due to mutations near the sickle cell gene in Senegalese people. Today, this kind of observation-gene correlation, known as "an association study" in molecular genetics parlance, constitutes the bulk of "gene" findings in the field of genomics. Increasingly, the ubiquity of such associations has been facilitated by the shared databases that researchers have created from research facilitated by the Human Genome Project and the Haplotype Map Initiative. Beyond these global projects, more recent forays into personal genomes (full genomic sequences of people's coding regions) are beginning to reveal that some DNA mutations that had long been associated with disease have at least been partially wrongly labeled. That is, certain loci have been designated as disease culprits in clinical studies that consisted of sick individuals, not of the random human population at large.

On this point, geneticists are beginning to see that healthy individuals who—the case of several South Africans whose genomes were sequenced in 2010—are quite old have never suffered from these same diseases even though they carry these same mutations (Shuster et al. 2010, 946). In other words, we still have a ways to go before we can confidently interpret what it means to possess many DNA sequence variations. It is quite possible that genetic studies on disease and the interpretations of "associated" alleles that follow suit have been clinically defined, in part, by the phenotypes and health outcomes of people who present themselves at hospitals and who are therefore enlisted in genetic research in the first place.

Still, today the international genetics community continues to locate large numbers of DNA sequence variants and deposit them into shared databases like Genbank whereby scientists worldwide then correlate them with disease and myriad other phenotypic endpoints. By endpoints, I am referring to the reductionistic explanations that emerge when observed lived experiences (such as a mysteriously well-tolerated form of sickle cell in Senegalese bodies) are presented in terms of genetic variants, such as the C to T genetic code switch that constitutes the Senegalese haplotype. Sarah Franklin has succinctly noted that the logic implicit in such scientific shorthand is characteristic of many studies within biology whereby the process of observing, classifying, and studying an outward result of a phenomenon or object is "conflated" with the entity itself (2001, 306). Similarly, Margaret Lock points to the category fallacy inherent in such conflations when what she calls a "folk-reconstruction of biological history" is made to do political work in creating self-contained forms of putative genetic identification (1997, 286).

For most disorders, the association studies permitted by the large-scale gene mapping projects of our time are recent and speculative, while more in-depth work is relegated to the near future. The difference with sickle cell is that its genetic nature was discovered more than half a century ago, while the mutations around the gene were found in the late 1970s the early 1980s. As of 2010, the discovery of the disease is a century old. Thus, in this case, we are presented with a slight historical advantage and opportunity to unpack such associations, or at least to ethnographically map the space located in the thinly described "pathway" between what health researchers term "causation" and "outcome." Culturally, scientifically, and historically, the space of the said "pathway" is too often left unexplored. It is my view that we need to analyze disorders with framings larger than those offered by association study structures of explanation. An emphasis on causal sequences unnecessarily narrows our thinking to 1:1 relationships, linear directions, and streamlined effects. An anthropological approach to disease manifestations analyzes the rhetorical work performed by causation discourses while highlighting the power dynamics and health effects that they permit, and preclude.

■ **Difference and Diagnosis**

In cultural anthropology, genetic disease difference localized to a people might be understood within the discipline's long historical obsession with societal "contrast" in order to situate the aleatory nature of seemingly biological norms (Mead 1973 [1928], 27). Today, points of comparison do more than denaturalize difference. They get to what Clifford Geertz, in his exasperation with the "culture concept" (and the various successive movements to articulate societal human difference while avoiding it), named "commonalities of diagnosis" (2000, 257).

The colonial past and recent economic history of aid and "cooperation" make the United States[22] and France obvious points of societal comparison when it comes to Senegalese sickle cell. In order to explore cultural variants of biological norms, and examine the lack of genetic universals on a local level, I follow a thread similar to that of Margaret Lock in her pursuit of societal contrasts in biomedical descriptions, to query the flipside of Geertz's locution. That is, I examine the *un*-commonalities of diagnosis. Scrutinizing divergent diagnoses pushes anthropological inquiries into science and medicine onto new ground. This terrain layers on what Lock has termed "local biologies" (1993b, 38–39; Lock and Nguyen 2010, 90–92). An engagement with this concept proves useful in my own inquiry into how scientific and medical renditions of the sickle cell experience in Senegal, as well as human experience itself, come to be seen through optics of biological specificity and distinction. Discourses of the Senegalese population's physiological uniqueness, on various registers, anchor analytics of science as concepts of genetic difference take shape within and across geographical and national bounds. Through such processes, people who are the objects of sickle cell scientific study in Dakar (when compared to other Africans on the continent and abroad) accumulate and instrumentalize descriptions of "difference" and "mildness" in their own narratives of health and disease that sometimes parallel, but often diverge from, the genetic explanation of the Senegalese haplotype. Many people in Dakar saw Senegalese bodily traits and population characteristics as "distinct," and qualified them through idioms of location, language, race, ethnicity, historical moment, culturally specific practices, and, sometimes, genetic variation. In my ethnographic work, I explored how and in what arrangements these framings and the realities that brought them into being became important qualifiers for actors in Senegal to explain local illness expressions. I also traced how historical, social, and economic practices around health, including how colonial scientists suspended sickle cell from medicine proper, have had a hand in current public health policies of non-intervention. These legacy effects carry over to the material management of sickle cell care, including people's reflexes to heal themselves with plants and kin-based support networks that condition bodily expressions of this illness in the here and now.

In detailing the course of how diagnoses become "*un*-commonalities," as they take on particular meanings and are varyingly lived in different societal contexts, I find the theoretical framing of what scholars in the field of science and technology studies (STS) have called "co-production" useful to the extent that it is one attempt to capture the mutual collapse of variegated life processes into precise scientific facts. Defined as how the "natural sustains and is sustained by the social order" (Jasanoff 2004, 275), "co-production" of course goes beyond the two binaries of nature and society that the prefix implies.[23] Any fieldworker can attest to the untidy spin-offs that are not equally "sustained" by the orders of either nature or society in systems of "production." More to the point, there are clear instances when categories, bodies, populations and problems have *long* preceded the scientific naming that, in fact, *rearticulates* (rather than produces) their meanings and usefulness for technological projects and promise (also see Wailoo 2003, 236). Part of the problem lies with our available language.

As a discipline that describes *processes*, anthropology resists catchall terms—most self-consciously, "culture" itself. In cultural anthropology, current acceptable terminologies tellingly refer to method: thick description, participant observation, ethnography, fieldwork. It is through recounting and delineating process that ethnography expands and creates new possibilities of understanding (Marcus 1998, 14). In the relatively new subfield of the anthropology of science, description proves increasingly important as genetic explanations of humanity and human difference packaged as DNA "coded data" are being produced at such orders of magnitude that leaders in genomics today pride themselves on having "dare[ed] to break ranks with the prevailing view that biological research must always be conducted as a hypothesis-driven enterprise" (Collins, Morgan, and Patrinos 2003, 286). For the leaders of genomics at the U.S. National Institutes of Health (Francis Collins), the U.S. Department of Energy (Aristide Patrinos), and the UK Wellcome Trust (Michael Morgan), data-driven (empirical) research has been repackaged as a "science-driven process." To borrow their language, this approach translates into an "association-study" driven process—and one that grows exponentially by the year.

It is my view that anthropologists of science and biomedicine might well renew a commitment to ethnography precisely because it is an induction into sites where social forms are increasingly rendered into coded sequences, as are bodily states in all of their complexity. As concerns medical anthropology, many significant aspects of what we study as bodily affect (that are linked to political and economic effects) may be missed in renditions of human and ecological experience reduced to genes—even if this "cultural tendency" itself within laboratory life constitutes new aspects of the human experience of interest to many anthropologists (Abu El-Hadj 2007; Fullwiley 2007; Helmreich 2009, 52–53; Montoya 2007). How contemporary bodily states are situated within old and new cultural practices speaks volumes about not only which scientific objects, in this case genetic mutations, might be signaled as important, but also why and how such signaling makes sense at all.

In *Encounters with Aging*, Margaret Lock tackled an iteration of this very problem in her examination of how the socio-physiological experiences of menopause in Japan and North America emerged differentially in the field of endocrinology. When examined across the divide of these two locales, menopause was both qualitatively and quantitatively different: survey researchers sought to describe symptoms that women reported—ranging from depression to shoulder stiffness to "hot flashes"—as well as to gain an understanding of common temporal markers of female midlife. As an idea in two contrasting societies, "menopause" was both a response to the ways that female bodies aged and a series of statistically-based correspondences *of* aging *to* concepts in endocrinology. In North America the concept signaled "deficiencies" and "decline," notably of estrogen and reproductive capacity, and thus emerged a "disease of aging," synonymous with the end of menstruation. This looked strange against a Japanese concept of *kōnenki*, or "the turn of life," where the cessation of menses was often minimized—or, more commonly, altogether ignored (Lock 1993b, 41). When women did report similar symptoms of hot flashes, key Japanese gynecologists thought patients could be taught to "overcome" these with "discipline" of the autonomic nervous system through meditative practices (1993b, 30). Although such narratives of discipline run throughout her work, Lock focuses on a much more complex set of entanglements. Of particular importance is that Japanese women tended not to fixate on physical changes of their own bodies, nor could they, as they increasingly bore the individual burden of the post-war "graying" of Japan. Here, social, familial, and economic pressures pushed them deeper into "servitude" as the seemingly natural caretakers of their (husbands') elderly parents amid declining social supports given new welfare state reforms (1993b, 130; chap. 5). Additionally, and more provocatively, Lock contends that Japanese women also experience an impermanent, but nonetheless temporarily stable, population-based biological difference when compared to their European and North American counterparts (Lock 1993b, 38–39, 373). She remains resolute that Japanese women's biological expressions and symptoms of middle-aging, compared to North Americans, cannot be adequately described by cultural constructions of illness alone and that the universal body of biomedicine is a fiction (Lock 2007, 217–21; Lock and Nguyen 2010, 90).

Even if our tools and language remain weak in their ability to articulate how it happens, anthropologists of medicine—with Lock central to the field—have long been committed to showing how "biological" bodies are thoroughly shaped by cultural, political, and economic forces, while these same forces empower those in medicine to describe the normative course of the body's biology and pathophysiology. Lock's compound construction, "local biologies," may be interpreted by some as potentially forfeiting the complexity of social-cultural-biological processes, both local *and* global, to an age-old reductionist vision of biological determinism that she clearly intends to out-vie. Her initial framing tried at once to address the problem that anthropology has had in describing complex processes of how social life gets into the body and how biological expressions contribute to the cultural norms we live by in patterned ways. Most recently she and co-author Vinh-Kim Nguyen reviewed the various sites (disciplinary, global, scientific) that both shape and draw from population-based, biological outcomes and difference. They implore anthropologists and others to recognize how "local biologies" are essentially "artifacts—snapshots of ceaseless biological differentiation frozen in time" (2010, 90; cf Montagu 1972 [1951], 47–48). Here they add the term "biosocial differentiation" to "local biologies" to pinpoint the ways in which the physical differences of bodies that Lock highlighted in *Encounters* cannot be disentangled from history, culture, politics, environment, and medical nosologies throughout time and over space. In this new approach, local biologies are the result of a *longue durée* of evolutionary and social processes (2010, 90), while it is "biosocial differentiation" that makes physical differences congeal in different "kinds" of bodies through cultural and political complexities at certain historical junctures (Lock and Nguyen 2010, 108).

An engagement with a local-biologies framing for thinking about the case of "mild" sickle cell in Senegal is instructive on several counts. The environmental, historical, linguistic, and economic issues that I outlined previously are embodied within people's biological expressions and lived experiences with this disease in Dakar. Second, although there is less of an emphasis on the standardized biomedical body when dealing with a disease that largely affects people of the African diaspora—and differentially so—it must be acknowledged that there are Western-generated norms of "best practices" and protocols that pressure Senegalese doctors to reify or contest both sickle cell disease and the illness effects of sickle cell trait. It must also be acknowledged, however, that marked biology as the site and articulation of human difference has historically been reserved for "non-white," "non-standard," "non-universal bodies" that have often been excluded from the concept of the universal biological body altogether, fiction or not (Epstein 2007; Vaughan 1991). At the level of the genome, inter-individual variation is proving to be massive compared to inter-group genetic differences, regardless of the group. Full genome sequencing is just one burgeoning arena that drives home the point that biosocial "difference" is made meaningful through, *inter alia*, cultural beliefs, trends in science, and ideas of race. Clearly there is no universal body. My point here is that in denouncing it, the stakes differ varyingly for people as one crosses the meridians that separate East from West and, in this case, latitudes that separate North from South.

In my own emphasis on the processes of correspondence between social and scientific forms, as well as descriptions of human difference in the field, I describe the historical effects, social conditions, and present outcomes of what I take to be *localized* biologies. In contrast to Lock's term, my superadded emphasis on localization furthermore takes seriously how scientists themselves construct and put into place reductionistic, and at times and racializing, genetic categories and therefore have a hand in eliding the biological outcomes they observe and the genetic distinction in bodies that may or may not be biologically meaningful. For sicklers in Dakar today, sequence variants on their eleventh chromosomes are pegged to strict territory boundaries drawn around Senegal. This localization happens through constant references to notions of nationalized population biology and historical ideas of cultural difference more broadly.

It is not just potential forms of racialization that are at stake in these moves. More importantly are the blind spots they create for other visions and understandings of biosocial processes. Of primary consequence is a medical unwillingness to see how people in Senegal construct survival strategies to address an under-researched disease, in terms of adequate affordable treatments, and how they condition their bodies to space crises through fagara ingestion and, or, through communal support networks where they recount processes of literally sharing and distributing their pain with the result of mitigating it. Secondly, focusing solely on human genetic difference as the cause of "mild" sickle cell misses the economic global health politics that, on the one hand, overlook everyday diseases throughout the global South and that, on the other, both force and allow people to create biosocial informal economies that rewrite their possibilities for health. Too often the local biologies that individuals fashion into a milder illness expression become conflated with the local biologies of a genetic signature that characterizes this population's sickle hemoglobin sequence: each is frozen within the same frame, which naturalizes sickle cell difference as inherent to this population and nation. Although I want to emphasize this specific dynamic, the history of this present and its racial underwriting are nonetheless also important.

While the *longue durée* of evolutionary time has made people from India to West Africa acquire sickle cell anemia at different points in human evolution (traceable in the patterns of haplotype markers they carry around their sickle cell gene) the acquisition of sickle cell DNA cannot be parsed from the biosocial uptake of hemoglobin S as a marker for African ethnic difference in the shorter *durée*. Here, colonial agents of medicine deployed racial optics to map human differences in blood onto the geography of then French Africa that, in part, created specific legacies for contemporary forms of embodiment, lived experience, diagnostic categories, care, and public health political responses to sickle cell anemia in contemporary Dakar. Although colonial physician-scientists were not aware of haplotypes, they reanimated race as an epiphenomenon of ethnicity and African difference that previously existed in this part of Africa, and that would see new a lease on life when beta globin haplotypes were discovered. An even shorter *durée* of economic crisis that began with structural adjustment also partially constituted the lived construct of "mild" sickle cell alongside people's affective responses to the postcolonial state's neglect of this disease. Meanwhile, also in the shorter *durée*, specialists in Dakar have tried to advance research and care for sickle cell patients, in part by training in Paris, professionalizing globally and, in the process, continuing apace within a scientific nexus of Western geneticists and hematologists who still today emphasize the Senegalese population's "difference." As we will see in chapter 5, Senegalese specialists' interactions with certain French geneticists who are interested in new haplotype studies are fraught with frustration due to the fact that their Northern colleagues often parochialize medical trends outside of the global North, geneticize the uniqueness of African bodily expressions, dismiss local practices of healing with plant therapies, and ultimately treat them unequally when it comes to past and present collaborative research.

Anthropologists have long shown how culture and place prove powerful tropes through which identity, ethnicity, territory (Appadurai 1988, 37; Comaroff and Comaroff 2009, 96–97; Moore 1998, 346; Raffles 1999, 324), and, most recently, human biological differences get mapped (Montoya 2007; Pálsson 2007; Rabinow 1999; Taussig 2009). The case of sickle cell in Senegal is an early example of a trend, now more pronounced, where scientists who hail from many parts of the globe increasingly molecularize human groups as "distinct" whereby they rigidly think of sample populations' genes as naturally linked to their assumed geographical homelands (Fullwiley 2007, 22; Reardon 2005, 2007). Elsewhere (Fullwiley 2008) I have argued that it is because of these groups' imagined stark biological differences that they have been targeted for population genetic studies in the first place.

■ **Why Study the Case of a Genetic Disease in the Southern Hemisphere?**

Medical and scientific technologies, unevenly distributed and applied, clarify the nature of inequality. Physician-anthropologist Paul Farmer has characterized the medical haves and have-nots along global meridians where the world's poor are affected by "geographical chance" (2003, 207), their fates exacerbated by structural violence and the "terrorism of money" at the hands of multilateral institutions (2003, 10). My focus is on actors whose "happenstance" has landed them on the unluckier sides of the global dice but who are faced with an illness that even the resource-rich North is still pondering how best to treat.

The major therapies for sickle cell in the United States and France carry several serious risks. Hydroxyurea, the principal frontline therapy, poses a risk of inducing cancer, and it is still unclear how safe it is for long-term use. In the short term, patients often complain of hair loss, blackening of the fingernails, and other signs of cell death that make them anxious about their care choices. While on this treatment, patients must consent to temporary sterility: men are advised to freeze a portion of their sperm before treatment as a precautionary measure should they ever want to have children, while women are warned not to become pregnant at all. In the case of blood transfusion therapy, besides the risk of intravenous infections for hepatitis, HIV/AIDS, syphilis, as well as other diseases that sometimes succeed in getting through blood security systems in the North, and that surely pose greater risks in parts of Africa, this treatment causes the iatrogenic disease of iron overload. To remove the excess iron from sicklers' bodies, painful and long intravenous iron-chelation treatments come to constitute a secondary disease for patients who suffer through them. For sicklers I interviewed in Paris and Oakland before going to Dakar, these issues were the source of much anxiety for their own health as well as the source of tension between them and their providers when they "had enough." Most health practitioners understood that "non-compliance" in the case of a chronic and life-long disease was not about bad behavior, but about exhaustion. In the case of transfusion therapy, doctors in Dakar are trying to establish a secure system. Yet, with regard to hydroxyurea, it is not totally clear that they would want to import what one characterized as "a serious chemotherapy," even as it is hailed as a success for sickle cell in the North.

The solution that Farmer puts forth to redress the gap in global health care as attending to basic human rights is filled with the hope that biomedicine has succeeded in sustaining life in the face of the most basic causes of "stupid deaths," at relatively low costs (2003, 205). Getting the world's poor access to simple treatments, like vitamins and antibiotics, is indeed the bulk of what has and continues to save lives in places like Senegal. Yet what about more medically complex, clinically ambiguous, and expensive treatments? When we move to other registers, away from the infectious diseases that concern anthro-pologists like Farmer, to relatively high rates of a genetic trait (again, in Sen-egal, an estimated 10 percent of the population has sickle hemoglobin), I argue that a different kind of reflection is needed. It is one that requires carefully examining context, available technology, and people's (doctors included) cul-tural unwillingness to entertain treatments, like hydroxyurea, that cannot be decoupled from their risks. In the case of hydroxyurea, when consent to take the drug is also consent to become infertile, even if "temporarily," with no guarantees for future germ cell normalcy, the barter for such treatment is lost in advance as most people weigh their personal ethical commitment to having children at any and all costs. A different emphasis on the question of medi-cal futility must be posed. Not only are these treatments expensive, they may also not be warranted in a place where other practices may be responsible for increased fetal hemoglobin (the therapeutic point of hydroxyurea), while the very human conditions they require—in this case, a willingness to tinker with one's biological capacity to bestow a lineage—cannot be taken for granted.

Querying medical futility from this vantage, "high-level" treatments, like hydroxyurea, may not only be dangerous but redundant. They are dangerous because the techniques of monitoring this chemotherapy prove too costly to be done correctly for most patients in Dakar. They may be redundant because, as a group of French scientists has now set out to corroborate, fagara may confer the same desired protective effect as hydroxyurea—increased fetal hemoglobin (Dupont et al. 2005). This scientific effort has entered into what Foucault called a "game of truth" (1984, 387). Now the stakes are to legitimate fagara once and for all, while simultaneously filling in the empty space enveloped in associations of Senegalese sicklers with better life chances. Experiments on this specific botanical have been underway in France since May of 2009.

If certain therapeutic practices long known to the global poor produce similar effects as the pharmaceuticals they cannot afford, trajectories of what Didier Fassin has called "the embodiment of inequality," or how historical inequities write themselves into "physical" realities (2003, 54; 2007), may inform local researchers' actions of devising ways around the very need for the newest revolutionary treatments developed in the global North. This is not slipshod leechcraft. It is a serious pragmatics of care where doctors question key aspects of French and American protocols by discerning what keeps their patients well in the technologically barren Senegalese state clinics.[24] Following physician-anthropologist Claire Wendland (2010, 24), I ask what happens to the "moral order" (as economy) of science and medicine when doctors, like their patients, must eke out care practices that are shaped by histories of structural violence, resource scarcity, and unequal footing with their counterparts in other areas of the globe? How do Africa's materially and technologically impoverished clinics force African biomedical practitioners to create resources through other means? In what ways exactly do upwardly mobile Senegalese biomedical doctors balance multiple emergent realities of better than expected health outcomes, which they also witness in the "mild" case of a local form of HIV, that of HIV-2? Senegalese physician-researchers have found ways to sketch local research programs linked to health care that create opportunities for patients to enroll in years-long clinical surveillance that both patients and doctors come to speak about in beneficial kinship terms (see Gilbert 2009).[25] By rooting structures of observational research within care, local specialists begin to upend Western assumptions about the continent as a general and consistent site of disease. They also deploy various articulations of Senegalese specificity to scramble colonial hierarchies that persist through inequalities in the postcolonial world.

For instance, while I witnessed doctors encourage patients to strive for normal futures and demonstrate faith in their physiological success, I also heard key higher-ups in the Senegalese medical corps marshal cultural and biological "difference" to speak about sickle cell distinction and survival in optimistic efforts to bypass medical inequality altogether. In a different sort of revolutionary action than that described by Farmer, the discursive strategies bound up in "mild" sickle cell anemia become technologies in and of themselves in the absence of others. Seen in this way, Mr. Seck's contradiction described in the opening pages of this chapter dissolves, and the protest-

affirmation ensemble inherent in his story takes on deeper significance. Like Seck, certain Senegalese biomedical practitioners incorporated the material limits (*ce qui manque*) into discourses about Senegalese self-sufficiency, social and vital capacities, and, at times, "African adaptability" to otherwise life-threatening disease states. Various doctors I encountered resorted to a national and sometimes "African-centered" reliance on local "biological" resources as a response to political and economic stratification that often leaves their population unable to afford basic medical needs. If the haplotype and the medicinal plants—which may in part account for people's health—are indeed specific to Senegalese ground, then a different kind of "geography of chance," where local specificity is associated with better health comparatively, overlays that described by Farmer.

On yet another register, biomedical practitioners in Dakar are attempting to change the "chance" associated with their geographical positioning. They are fully aware that inequality works through biological and social facts at the heart of the science in which they participate. In an attempt to redress unfair carryovers of colonial power relations, several of my informants in the research sector confronted geneticists in France who proposed collaborations that seemed exploitative of Southern scientists, and that would never be accepted by those in luckier locales. The physician-researchers I observed initially refused offers from Paris to collaborate on a "revolutionary" new haplotype study in 1999. To do so was to broker an image of their own self-sufficiency while demanding that "the French" take them seriously as intellectual, and human, equals. These Senegalese men and women of science wanted to make it clear that they were not simply "indigenous doctors" or unwitting couriers who send their patients' DNA up North for studies but are not acknowledged among co-authors on the resultant publications—an unfortunate practice that took place in the recent past on more than one occasion.

These local dynamics and their global connective points take place within a larger scientific context where geneticists are focused on population comparative biology to better understand human variation in illness expression. With the increased inclusion of different global populations in research there are many opportunities for the involution of inclusion, where exclusions are made possible by historical inequalities and asymmetries. This history of vulnerability makes invitations to "participate" in global science less about choice than about pressures to happily accept the conditions one is offered.

■ **The Chapters**

The ethnography begins with a focus on how sicklers with varied economic situations and philosophical stances succeed in transforming their disease states into "health" statuses through a range of normalization techniques. The president of the *Association sénégalais de drépanoctyose* himself lives by a personal regimen of norms that link his refusal to be sick to a lifetime of managing economic scarcity. In his adult life, the leader of Dakar's grassroots sickle cell movement, Mr. Magueye Ndiaye, continues to consciously raise his thresholds for basic needs—as basic as the need for food itself, which he simply often could not afford. Scarcity for Ndiaye is explained through banal non-events that many people take for granted as necessary for sustenance, as he once told me flatly: "when I could not buy breakfast, I surely would not be buying folic acid supplements." Magueye's want, which he transformed into a source of strict training, has left this thirty-five-year-old HbSS sickler with a profound sense of control over his lived experience and his own ability to create individualized biological norms for life and his survival that better suit his optimistic attitude for the future than those espoused by biomedicine. Maguey's subjective norms became particularly evident when it came to re-production, or transmitting a heritage through children. "Science has lim-its!" he exclaimed, even if at that moment he, in relative health, had resigned himself to spawn his "heritage" through the patient advocacy group he leads rather than passing on either of his SS genes to a child to mix with those of his would-be fiancée, as she too was an SS sickler. I chronicle these issues, as well as the links between informal economies of health care, "mild" sickle cell biology, kinship, and the societal "sharing of blood" in chapter 2.

In chapter 3, others who live with Magueye Ndiaye's same nominal form of sickle cell (HbSS) focus mostly on quelling their symptoms, notably pain crises, through the use of autochthonous medicinal plants like fagara. For one thirty-nine-year-old woman who was trained in biomedicine as a nurse's assistant, fagara ingestion resulted in the visible induction of new biological norms and bodily states of felt health. For her and her more symptomatic sister, their sickle cell pain crises subsided and fetal hemoglobin levels rose "because of this traditional medicine." In this chapter, I also explore the exten-sion of people's life sustaining relationships to healers and palliating plants to examine the therapeutic economic relations that fagara, as a central yet al-ternative therapy, conditions. This botanical treatment also permits relations between structurally integrated, yet nominally separate, healing domains termed "traditional" and "modern," as it reveals tensions and anxieties among and between researchers in the global North and South over whether plant therapies can "cure" a genetic disease.

As I argue throughout, when faced with sickle cell, patients in Dakar have tried to remake the severity of their disease as "mild," viable, and even nor-mal. Their attitudes inform and follow their practices of economically find-ing ways to distribute sickle cell severity across the social sphere so that no one person is left to suffer or manage this disease alone. Chapter 4 examines how Senegalese French-trained research-physicians in Dakar have adopted similar low-tech strategies and health interventions within the biomedical realm. It focuses on how doctors rationalize economically triaged care, while chronicling their methods for doing so in Dakar's principal sickle cell clinics. These are the pediatric care site at Albert Royer Children's Hospital and the *Centre nationale de transfusion sanguine* (CNTS), or the National Blood Transfusion Center, where most adult patients are followed. Although physicians often take cues from the social realities that define their patients' lived experiences with this disease, their own clinical limits and technological constraints also inform the alternative assemblages of care they construct. In addition, specialists' varied philosophies of sickle cell management and their personal approaches to engaging patients as people with the capacity to live relatively normal lives also determines what Annemarie Mol has called the "logic of care" in this setting (2008). In a general sense, specialists in these two clinical sites create consultation services where they can get by with fewer biomedical therapies than their research and training stays in Northern countries initially led them to believe. These doctors are fully aware of more globalized biomedical notions of what one "should do" for sickle cell. Instead, they make local health needs, material realities, relationships, and even spiritual safeguards part of their medical and moral engagements with those in their care.

In examining how genetic knowledge came to congeal in the ways that it does for biomedical practitioners in Dakar, I also explore how Senegal's colonial past informs present possibilities of conceiving of sickle cell difference. In chapter 5, I chronicle how in the 1950s sickle hemoglobin was tested in the blood of various Senegalese ethnic groups to determine the bounded nature of population-based race and ethnic groupings within the AOF. These colonial uses of HbS to scientifically define group belonging were later interrupted by RFLP technology starting in the late 1970s.[26] RFLPs allowed researchers to pinpoint DNA variants around the sickle cell gene and thus provided new ways of measuring and lumping human physiological distinction in terms of unified "national" genetic difference, which were based thereafter on haplotype patterns. With RFLP technology in hand, in 1984, geneticists made African sickle cell differences come to light within contemporary geopolitical frameworks, differently configured from those of the colonial era. New technologies *and* political rationalities account for the shift. Finally, this same chapter chronicles how discourses of ethnic population purity continue to drive Parisian scientists' interests in new sickle cell research for which they hope to enlist Senegalese collaborators in the here and now.

As philosopher Gaston Bachelard once wrote, "all absolute barriers proposed to science are the mark of questions badly posed" (1936/2002, 75). Chapter 6 explores how "culture," in the form of "Senegalese attitudes" that are seen as less than buoyant, has sometimes proved to be a barrier that Senegalese biomedical professionals propose as contrary to science on sickle cell "trait" (heterozygous sickle cell, or HbAS). Yet they also see culture as mutable, or less than absolute, since they are attempting to "correct" people's thinking that sickle cell trait also constitutes an illness state. In the biomedical parlance of the United States and France, they hope to convince people with the trait that they are simply (healthy) "carriers." Sickle cell disease is a classic recessive Mendelian condition. In order to inherit the disease, a person must receive two alleles, one from each parent. When only one sickle mutation is present (and pairs with "normal adult hemoglobin," or HbA), then the person in question has the sickle cell trait (HbAS), not the homozygous condition understood by most in the global North as the illness (HbSS). Yet symptomatic people with only a *single* S allele, or HbAS, in Senegal have refused this "foreign" medical norm and are currently protesting its purported truth that they are merely "asymptomatic carriers." At many points in the field, it became clear that contrary to majority medical opinion in the United States, most Senegalese think of the heterozygous sickle cell trait as a potential disease and thus live with, and treat it, accordingly. Several Dakar specialists have taken this instance of a culturally divergent embodiment of diagnosis to be a "psychosomatic" problem. Yet this mind versus body configuration is proving to be an uneasy one, especially since there has been little definitive research, either locally or globally, to categorically rule out the possibility of bodily symptoms caused by sickle cell trait heterozygosity. Furthermore, Senegal is a country where HbAS was never epistemologically dissociated from sickle cell disease, despite recent attempts to do so.

This state of affairs collapses what many American readers with biomedical knowledge of this issue will take to be two separate genetic statuses. I argue that we must bracket our own under-researched medical understanding of the trait as a simple "carrier state" in order to enter into the life-worlds of people who struggle with it as a disease in much the same way as those with full-blown SS do. This is not to say that either the American or the Senegalese situation is "right" and the other "wrong." The murkiness around the issue benefits from a continuous publication stream of case studies and tentative science on possible symptoms and impaired biology in trait carriers, while the scientists authoring these papers seem wary of pronouncing the trait to be a disease (see Kark 2000 for a review). Sickle cell trait suffering may not be arbitrated by science anytime soon. The Senegalese case makes it painfully clear that many people who claim HbAS as a disease refuse to rethink their suffering as naught and will continue to believe they are sick regardless of whether medicine corroborates their experience.

On the surface, the sickle cell trait story in Senegal provides a striking departure from the primary point of interrogation of this book—that of *mild* sickle cell anemia. If sickle cell disease is mild in Senegal, how it is then that the trait proves more "severe"? I argue that "trait patients" struggle to "order" what for many is a severe sense of life's disorder more generally. That is, they consciously conscript the biological, physical element of their HbS in an effort to create new norms of a delineated disease entity, rather than continuing to live by a medically amorphous one. If only nominally, life becomes more manageable, as the source of their suffering is at least defined. More broadly, people with both sickle cell anemia and sickle cell trait in Senegal find stability and intersubjective belonging in linking their disease status to the lives of others, most notably through their patient advocacy and support association, the ASD. In this sense, a culturally based "clinical identity" mixes their shared blood trait with a larger societal network of care. Finally, in light of chapter 5, chapter 6 shows how sickle cell trait suffering also makes clear how cultural understandings of race shape medical nosologies, while it raises questions about African diasporic *non-universality* with respect to medical interventions, bodily forms, and the *un*-commonalities of diagnoses assumed to be commonly shared.

Most trait carriers I interviewed for this book and beyond (for a separate case-control study on sickle cell trait in Dakar) believe and feel bodily that calling this heterozygous state benign is a gross misrepresentation. If this were true, specialist Dr. Ibrahima Diagne confided, "Senegal would have a major public health problem on its hands," since at least 10 percent of the population would be directly affected. The doctor does admit, however, that those with the trait *may* feel pains and fatigue periodically, but these symptoms "should not come to constitute an illness."

Chapter 7 further explores issues of patients' tenacity to shape science, through advocacy now on an international level, and investigates the ways that making a disease public in Africa often entails locating it within discourses of humanitarian "crisis," emergency, and global health prioritization. In this way, tireless patient advocates of African origin living in France created the sickle cell disease umbrella organization of the OILD, which succeeded in getting sickle cell anemia the attention of the World Health Organization and the United Nations in 2008. The latter established the first "World Sickle Cell Day" on June 19, 2009. The OILD's strategy of making sickle cell visible to these multilateral institutions consisted of linking the disease to other pressing global health problems for development through means that often deployed *uncertainty* as "data." They used the dearth of statistics and the lack of epidemiology on sickle cell in the global South, coupled with assumptions about massive rates of death due to the disease. Through statistical aggregations and associations with communicable infections and other diseases of the blood, sickle cell would become a serious concern that resulted in the 2008 UN Resolution A/63/237 instituting "Sickle-Cell Anaemia as a Public Health Problem." The General Assembly officially inaugurated the possibility of new funds, programs, and partnerships that would encourage member states to establish research and care infrastructures to combat sickle cell in late 2008 and early 2009. The final chapters of this book show how the work of the OILD both empowered and frustrated its own Senegalese sickle cell "UN Member State," the ASD patient advocacy group in Dakar, which had its own ideas about how global monies and its local state attention should be directed in the here and now.

■ **Explicit Politics of Knowledge**

In 2011, as this book goes to press, two elements of Senegalese sickle cell ontology continue to create tensions and solidarities among patients in Dakar. These are sickle cell trait as an illness category and the potential construct of sickle cell disease itself as "severe." The politics of visibility concerning the latter have begun to sideline trait sufferers within the ASD, which is now lobbying the state for health benefits for those with HbSS. Nonetheless, because trait patients feel themselves to be sick and now are (only recently) being told that they are not, they have become some of the most vocal patients in the public sphere. On the one hand, the ASD needs them, especially to guarantee the population numbers required for the state to actually establish (fund) a country program. On the other hand, ASD advocates with full-blown HbSS have begun their urgent demand for state health subsidies largely based on the handicaps and costs of "severe" homozygous patients. Yet, with the prospect of health care coverage in site, trait carriers want to be included in any such policies that severe patients might enjoy. Although there may be power in numbers, the heterozygous trait population is increasingly threatening the new and fragile gains of those with homozygous HbSS disease.

Sickle cell trait illness is one instance where local practitioners are fighting against Senegalese disease specificity rather than courting such an idea. The stance of their science politic, like that of once rallying around the notion of the "mild form" for the disease itself, takes place in a health care context defined by the absence of economic resources, available manpower, and an appropriate social and clinical space to accommodate a potential "epidemic" of sickle cell trait illness—or not.

Finally, with regard to the ways that biomedical specialists have benefited from the localization of "mild" sickle cell anemia, I argue that the disease in Senegal proves to be an instance of what many thinkers from the continent have termed Afro-pessimism (concerning disease, economic scarcity, crisis, and death), which is nevertheless joined to extreme Afro-optimism (about local biodiversity, therapeutic economies, and scientific leverage afforded by advantageous biological contingency). Now I turn to how people's enactments of illness allow each stance to fully enable and abet the other.

CHAPTER TWO

Healthy Sicklers with "Mild" Disease: Local Illness Affects and Population-Level Effects

Reality is not a crucial appearance underlying the rest. It is the framework of relations with which all appearances tally.

—Claude Merleau-Ponty 2006 [1962], 349

As discussed in the last chapter, clinicians and geneticists in Francophone sickle cell circles have adopted an optic of seeing African sicklers in terms of population groups that exhibit differences in disease expression. However, a key slippage occurs when scientists observe biological "outcomes" and assume, as a first response, that these should be attributed to distinct genetic sequences, which those same populations possess at different frequencies. This chapter examines how such scientific methods and assumptions may miss complex congeries of behaviors and relationships that influence people's disease experiences and biological expressions of sickle cell anemia.

By engaging cultural frameworks of relations, notably of kin ties and social safety nets that mitigate sickle cell suffering for many, I hope to enlarge the conceptual terrain of how we view causal factors for varied disease manifestations. Because disease causation is increasingly conceived of in molecular terms, the notion of "population," for the purposes of indexing a genetic effect, seldom includes analyses of the social relations, familial bonds, economic constraints, and survival strategies of the group in question. By analyzing local Senegalese discursive practices that name their sickle cell "mild," I bring *affects*—which extend beyond emotions to patients' shared sentiments and the family ties that inspire health—into this picture. Put simply, people's moral concerns of caring for the other, of going to incredible lengths to make family and loved ones live in health, is the human, intersubjective substrate that undergirds an experience of alleviated sickle cell stress, both bodily and socially, in Dakar today. I want to emphasize that affect structures people's actions of *entraide*, or what Senegalese people loosely term "solidarity."

45

Phenomenologically speaking, a "reality" of sickle cell mildness in Dakar is the biosocial framework of relations with which health appearances tally. This is to say, reality is not a truth to be excavated, if only the social analyst could dig deep enough. Rather, it is made through care practices, political contingency, and social engagements where human actions contribute to and partially determine life possibilities.

As a disease "of the blood" that runs in families and that is also a societal issue, sickle cell in Dakar lends itself to expressions of kinship and social bonds that go beyond metaphor. Here, people enact "living well" with this disorder through pragmatic relations with others who, as we will see further on, "share their sickling blood." This happens within specific forms of biosociality that extend beyond the discrete referent of genetic material proper (Rabinow 1996). The bonds that people in Dakar form through this disease include putting an accent on the shared propensity of their blood to sickle, their commonly experienced pain that sickling brings on, and the widely referenced economic constraints that force people to train their bodies and their households to focus on relative health. In their efforts to manage both sickle cell crises and a larger structural crisis in their country's health infrastructure that limits optimal biomedical care, people forge therapeutic economies where they circulate and share both pain and well-being.

In the absence of official normative medical attention and resources for the disease, patients and biomedical professionals alike have done their part to fight for established programs for sickle cell as an "awareness" issue of importance for the population. In piecemeal ways they have imagined various strategies to attach awareness on the disease to a range of problems that currently benefit from state health care subsidies, such as malaria prevention and maternal-child health programs. Awareness for sickle cell, however, has not yet adhered in any sustained fashion. To complicate matters, many specialists have ended up investing more time and energy to a particular discourse of "mild" sickle cell that has now embedded itself in doctor-patient interactions at the principal sickle cell clinics in Dakar. Even as they see patients suffering, the country specialists who run these clinics tell themselves that things "could be much worse," and push their patients to focus on maintaining health through monitoring, quarterly check-ups, and adherence to a folic acid regimen coupled with mild painkillers when needed. There is little that can be done in the clinic, however (as we will see in later chapters), beyond these minimal interventions, which is why health seeking for sickle cell almost always goes beyond biomedicine. Although the sick take notice of and find comfort in the doctor's touch, comment on the feelings of goodwill they sense from mindful providers, and, in some cases, pronounce a "family tie" with the person overseeing their health or that of their child, it is outside of the clinic where they find significant therapeutic gains. These are in social supports and structures of family-based collective actions where people work to change the experiences of those suffering with sickle cell for the better. Certain aspects of these new relationships, however, may seem to fly in the face of traditional notions of disease prevention for genetic disorders, which advocate avoiding marrying someone with whom one might pass on the condition. Nonetheless, when people flout such rationality, they often find a sense of solace, support, and normalcy within their own circles of mutual care and concern.

Increasingly within their organized patient network, Senegalese sicklers have begun to create groupings and even romantic "couplings," that many know are not "recommended," but that they stress have provided them with a culture of "confidants" and "loved ones who can really understand them." Women who may have feared trying to find a husband willing to marry someone with the disease were also apprehensive about entering into a potential spouse's extended family. They imagined that other people's families, especially potential mothers-in-law, might be unforgiving of the limits posed by their illness. Some medical providers balked at the suggestion that the patients for whom they had worked so hard to ensure survival into adulthood "would, at their turn, have their own sickle cell kids if they married other sicklers!" Nonsuffers could not understand this behavior, especially when it came to "educated" people with the disorder, or those with some university training. Yet, as one woman with a degree in pharmacy proclaimed at a public meeting, "I have a body with a disease, but I have a heart too. All I'm saying is that if my husband shares my disease, his family would already know what sickle cell does, and would understand me. I would be marrying into a situation where they, especially my mother-in-law, would not expect for me to perform the impossible." Another told me, "Our society is not one where adoption comes to mind for most people. So yes, having children is a problem. But I know a couple that just adopted a little girl. We could begin to change ideas about adoption." As of 2010, within the patient advocacy group in question, there are at least a half a dozen couples that claim to extract therapeutic value from their supports of romantic love, as well as from the larger advocacy network. In so doing they normalize their life prospects by entertaining marriage and the possibility of a future family. Through their affective ties they also succeed in enacting their biology as "milder" than it would be without these biosocial links.[1]

Even before people formally joined such advocacy networks they often built relations that yielded informal therapeutic economies where the materiality of kinship was distributed not only through shared biologies (their "shared blood") but also through the care that these biologies conditioned. It was in this context that many sicklers in Dakar referred to deep "feelings" of wanting to intervene in the lives of others, and then acted on these impulses to do so. Their actions overlaid a social matrix where many also found their well-being through more traditional forms of family, where people affectively came to embody the investment in their health that a relative's love and economic sacrifice had underwritten for their survival.

Given how Dakar's public health spending has traditionally passed over their disease, many active patients have recently found themselves in a bind over how far to take their idioms of "shared blood" identity when it comes to constructing an image of themselves as both "children" of the state and "a family" unto themselves. They currently live a strange configuration of "cultural intimacy" (Herzfeld 2005, 50), where their rejection of official norms is tentative, since the idea of preventing the disease that the National Assembly proposed through prenuptial testing in 2010 must also still find its legs (Sané 2010). People with sickle cell are actively trying to figure out how to deal with a mode of state management that threatens to compromise their hopes of simply being with their disease, as well as living with, dating, marrying, and mutually supporting others who are also affected. As will become clear, living with sickle cell in the Senegalese nation-state is defined by a biopolitics where these internal dilemmas and questions about how to go forward define people's aspirations for normalcy through what Paul Rabinow, in his engagement with Niklas Luhmann, calls "provisional foresight" (2008, 60). Here the present (life as one knows it) and the future (probabilities that cannot truly be known) are two sides of a "respectable uncertainty" where people try and try again, incessantly correcting and adjusting to a reality that comes to be other than what was at first expected (Rabinow 2008, 60). In other words, personal action does not follow a moral closure where agreed upon norms are socially and biologically performed. Engagements of care themselves are morally shared activities. The human commitment to others, even as one is still figuring out the moral complexities of his or her interventions, is a defining act of solidarity and practical assistance (also see Kleinman 2006, 78–79). In most cases, such moral actions also undergird morale, as they require people to possess wells of tenacity, perseverance, and adaptability (Mol 2008, 78–79).

Examples of these human(e) moral configurations of affective attachment take varied forms, as the cases in the second half of this chapter demonstrate. Yet before we get there, I show the ease with which people wield the materiality of "shared blood," while reviewing anthropological reflections on kinship and the social life of informal economies in Africa.[2] This background will provide the framework to see how mild sickle cell anemia becomes biosocially structured through political-economic contingency and networks of informal therapeutic economies in Dakar in the absence of state resources.[3]

■ **Biosocial Ethics of Care**

Magueye Ndiaye, the current president of the *Association sénégalaise de drépanocytose*, or the ASD, clutched his thin, albeit "healthy," sickle cell body, and rocked forward to emphasize the point he was about to make. "Why can't I just take his pain? It's frustrating." He was referring to a small boy he had just met at Albert Royer Children's Hospital. The boy's mother had heard Magueye speak publicly about his own disease during a recent event aired on radio. She ran into him at the hospital when he was trying to convince a social worker

to work with a patient. The boy's mother congratulated him on his "achievement," which, she explained, was not convincing the social worker but (at that
time) "living to the age of thirty-one." She asked him to come visit her son,
who might see himself in Magueye, a healthy adult living with his same blood
disease. The boy in question apparently feared that he would never grow up
because he was a "*drépano*" (Fr. sickler). Magueye continued to recount the
story and his emotional dilemma when faced with the child in pain.

> He couldn't handle the crisis. . . . Since I'm rarely sick, I often visit people
> at the hospital. In my mind, I try to take their pain, to share it in some
> way. If only people could know that are not suffering alone. I think
> about this a lot. I wonder—if only there was some way that you could
> actually take someone else's pain for a while. . . . If you could just pull
> it out from them, and take it on, I would. People don't think about this,
> but, why not? . . . Just take his pain and let him rest.

For Magueye, the inability of people to "think" about pulling out the other's
pain, leaving it isolated in a single body, was a fundamental lack of what historian Julie Livingston calls "moral imagination" (2005, 19). Magueye also recounted stories of when his own doctor's reflex of empathy forced him to step
out of his more distant role at times, and to treat Magueye like family. Recalling a time when the doctor saw Magueye seriously distraught, he told me, "it's
like big brother little brother," as the physician reached in his wallet when his
patient could not afford needed medications. In the midst of both living and
describing such an outlook, within the ASD, Magueye developed a discourse
of "sickle cell" familial solidarity through idioms of shared blood. "We have
the same sickle blood running through our veins," he would tell other sicklers, "therefore, we are family." Magueye easily drew on the Wolof inclusive
term for family, "*nu bokk deret*" (lit. "We share blood"), or, alternately, "*sama
bokk la*" (s/he is "shared," my relative). Such biosocial relations of caring, in
different configurations, allowed people to find a certain naturalness of affinity through kin idioms that whittled down clear distinctions between subject
and object, personal "ownership" of suffering and disease, and self as separate
from the other in pain.

Kinship understandings and varied forms of biosocial affinities are a crucial source of both physical and cultural practices of survival in Senegal more
broadly. It is through such relations that sicklers in Dakar are able to reduce
their disease burden, in some cases, and experience their sickle cell status as a
kind of existential normalcy, in others.[4] People whose better health outcomes
I present in the latter part of this chapter are of the same genetic population
described by scientists in chapter 1, who imagined Senegalese HbSS carriers
to live a "mild" disease because of specific patterns in their beta globin genetic
sequence. How, we might ask, can genetic science consider social relations
of care and the intersubjective ethical concerns of people like Magueye who
strive to extract the other's pain through biosocial affinity and solidarity?

Sicklers, their families, and newly created disease advocacy networks of persons "attached" as kin absorb, emotionally redistribute, and in some cases, deflect sicklers' pain and suffering. These networks of support, of both literal and metaphorical kith and kin, provide subtle and direct sources of alleviation and improved health. At issue is that kinship ties, like genetic data points, must be seen through their constitutive parts. They too must be detailed in terms of their pedigrees of process. The outward, nominal understanding of kinship structures in Senegal—as specific kinds of human connection forged and sometimes improvised in light of material scarcity—are filled with elements that are seemingly distinct from European or North American commonplace understandings of social bonds, in this case, building a disease support structure as a political need, or gifting medical care as an economic good. Too often, economic ideas that break down the imagined barriers of one's own body to make someone who is suffering live better do not explicitly surface in terminologies of relatedness.

Kinship and Economy

Anthropologists have long been interested in how biology, economy, necessary goods, and relatedness fuse in particular ways across a range of diverse societal settings. As Marilyn Strathern demonstrated in her seminal article "Kinship and Economy: Constitutive Orders of a Provisional Kind" (1985), the ordering of kin connectedness encompasses economic exchanges as relations themselves, where both relatedness (marriage, for example) and interpersonal ways of relating (exchange of goods) cross over (2005, 67). In this crossover, kinship systems often function through abstractions as, for instance, symbols of connectedness are enacted through the delivery of prized goods, such as cattle, power, wives, or daughters to one party on the part of the other (Comaroff 1980, 38; Hutchinson 1996, chap. 4; Strathern 1985, 205). Strathern, borrowing from John Comaroff, uses the term "constitutive order" to signal the singularity of kinship as a particular institution in which seemingly disparate elements, such as things and persons connected to and also exchanged by families, merge. She then backtracks heuristically to say that these "separations" may never actually have been distinguished in the first place for many people around the globe (Strathern 1985, 201; Comaroff 1980, 38). Here one of Strathern's keenest insights bears repeating: in many cases, "anthropological analysis establishes itself only through distinctions"—such as kinship and economy—"even when it wishes to collapse them" (Strathern 1985, 201). The collapse of particular categories, or, rather, of making instances of their oneness explicit, may seem jolting at first glance. Yet Strathern and others who have revived recent anthropological interest in kinship would focus less on the "two" parts, or terms, of this relation, and more on the *relation itself* (Carsten 2000; Strathern 1985, 201). Building on this, what would it take for anthropologists to add still other "parts," such as biological traits, or bodily expressions of genetic illness, to this relation of oneness? Clearly, kinship is often co-configured with ideas of biology at some level. My hope, following Sarah Franklin, is to "defamiliarize the very nature" of what it is for any phenomenon "to be strictly biological" (2001, 303).

This brief review of kinship essentials allows us to segue to *relations* themselves in Dakar where sicklers' kin and biosocial attachments indeed generate many resources that often yield better health outcomes for them. Sociosomatically, those affected distribute and share the intensity of their genetic disease with others. Through openness and a willingness to take on each other's pains, many have succeeded in mitigating the severity of suffering alone. Here it is the constitutive order of kinship, economy, and biology that allows individuals a leg up in their struggle for personal and family health in a context where they experience daily that the formal economy and the state health system work against them. For many, very little monetary wealth would not preclude, a priori, the possibility of health. In fact these two realities, like kinship and economy, cross over and converge within biosocial frameworks.

My use of the term economy is wide-ranging. At one level, I focus on Senegal's informal medical economy where people "make-do" in order to get necessary medications, tests, or traditional medicines, or else by simply waiting out illness episodes with large quantities of patience and faith. This informal economy of healing takes place against a general societal backdrop of economic scarcity in Senegal, even in Dakar the wealthier capital. Scarcity that constrains people's purchasing power also characterizes the context in which people enact what Janet Carsten calls broad "cultures of relatedness" (2000, 34), which help many sicklers find meaning, vitality, and eventually better health through resources and social bonds formed by *being-together-in-the-world* and finding degrees of normalcy in doing so. Through their affective commitments, siblings, spouses, partners, parents, and friends often contribute portions of their limited financial means to care for those with sickle cell at great expense given that their overall budgets were frequently stretched to the point of incurring debts. This investment in the sick family member, patient, or comrade who shares the political struggle to organize in the form of disease advocacy often reoriented people's own visions of "normal" norms that were rooted in explicit Senegalese customs that emphasize the necessity of marriage and biological reproduction. As some people overtly questioned and then reworked social norms of marriage, they suspended or sublimated others, notably with regard to reproduction. Many continue to debate whether or not potential spouses, with the disease in some cases, and without it in others, would detract from their health. Some worried, despite themselves and their desires, that romantic involvement with someone who also had the disease or trait could condemn them to social isolation and rejection on the part of their birth family members. It was often through these conversations that people became immersed in imagining new norms that would take sickle cell health—rather than pathology—as their foundation. Economic supportive ties do not always co-constitute kinship and lived biology, however. Yet, when they do, we can begin to see how the work that the bond, or chain, of kinship achieves, as a form of relatedness that is not at all confined to birth-family blood links, very much parallels Michel Foucault's idea of "governmentality." It is not accidental that Foucault writes: "Power relations, governmentality, the government of the self and of others, and the relationship of the self to [the] self constitute a chain, a thread." He further elaborates that it is around these notions that "questions politics" and "questions of ethics" connect (2005 [1982], 252). This ethical work rooted in relationships happens at a level below the "state" proper; at the level of people with similar conditions, families, comrades, and loved ones.

■ **The Social Life of Economy in Africa**

When the state is not a key player in cultural and medical processes, as has been the case with sickle cell care in Senegal, its absence easily becomes a consequential target for complaint, protest, and action.[5] An analysis of how sickle cell in Senegalese bodies comes to be understood as mild in the absence of state resources and even public discourse (before 2005) will benefit from a brief foray into the recent anthropology of economic activity between the global North and South regarding Africa. As certain thinkers have made clear, informal wealth and resource creation have become central to official state functioning (Ferguson 2006, 103; Roitman 2004, 19), in the present case, to sickle cell health care functioning. All over Africa people are formulating new sites of authority and health efficacy to build their own "public-political foundations" in lieu of, and in addition to, the said state (Mbembe 2001, 76). Taken as an aggregate, with many individuals hustling to attain the goods to secure survival, Senegalese sicklers ameliorate their prescribed fates, partake in rendering their disease "mild," and often attain adulthood despite a staggering lack of medical technology and standard interventions and resources that constitute sickle cell care in the United States and France.

Anthropologists tracing the roots of similar trends have honed in on the economic circuits, state body politics, and the unevenness of resources in the global system that often selectively neglect the planet's poorest countries (Ferguson 2006). In ethnographic work focused on the ability of people to secure wealth despite their minimal resources, anthropologists James Ferguson, Julia Elyachar, and Janet Roitman offer critiques of the telos of modernization, development, and growth strategies that have left the world's poor to survive by "informal" means. In pointing out the failures of global logics to incorporate impoverished nations into more equitable market relations— through structural adjustment programs, as well as more palatable programs to empower those in poverty through microfinance or decentralization made possible by the upsurge of NGOs—this recent economic anthropology highlights the role of informal actors that sustain state coffers and civil institutions. People's economic survival strategies, which at one time may have been deemed "below" or "outside of the state," are no longer formally *un*official because they serve functions of governance (networks of care) and provide new forms of wealth (networks of value) that the state no longer does. Instead, various instances of what Roitman's informants have embraced as "fiscal disobedience" (not paying tax, while generating their own "tax/price")[6] are proving to be an integral part of economic development and individual livelihood in satisfying certain basic needs and, in some cases, procuring extravagant goods that allow the official structure of the state its power and even varied forms of sustenance (Elyachar 2002, 500; Fassin 1992, 95–97; Ferguson 2006, 101–2; Guyer 2004, 163–64; Roitman 2004, 22).

The fundamental lesson of this recent anthropology is that economy must be understood broadly—perhaps in its original sense implied in the orthographic rendering *oeconomy*, from *oikos* (house) and *nomos* (norms)—with the norms that govern "the private," the interior, the intimate sphere of human activity being crucially important for understanding how the minutiae of the everyday moves public life. This emphasis gets us beyond statistical indexes of unemployment, national income, rate of growth, and price levels. Real people and the circulation of goods important to them, wealth creation through investment in social bonds, the sociability of indebtedness and interdependency, as well as an extensive notion of reproduction as a kind of "futures contract," or at least a social contract with generations to come, are all in play in Senegal. If one looks, close enough, however, even more traditional economic indexes and history reveal the importance of the "home," and the private interior sphere, as a wedge to manage poverty's most debilitating effects.

■ **Poverty in Numbers**

In January 2004 the Senegalese Ministry of Finance, the national Forecasting and Statistics Office, and the World Bank jointly issued a report called "La pauvreté au Sénégal: De la dévaluation de 1994 à 2001–2002" (Poverty in Senegal: From the Currency Devaluation of 1994 to 2001–2002). These experts optimistically pronounced that Senegalese individual household poverty rates declined from 61.4 percent in 1994 to 48.5 percent in 2001–2. When the surveyors disaggregated the domain of "household" and counted individuals, the numbers looked less impressive. In real population terms, 67.9 percent were said to be impoverished at the time of the 1994 currency devaluation compared with 57.1 percent in 2002. These claims and their attendant comparisons were made on the basis of Senegalese Household Surveys I and II (*Enquête sénégalaise auprès des ménages*, or ESAM I and II, carried out in 1994–95 and 2001–2, respectively).

The "Poverty in Senegal" report recognizes the importance of methodology, acknowledging that, "the differences in poverty estimation can be a result of poverty indicator, poverty line, and poverty measure choices" (Ministère de l'Économie et des Finances et al. 2004, 7). Yet it fails to discuss the discrepancies in method between the two instruments that produced these disparate numbers. It also cites another report, based on a survey of the same population sample in 2001, tellingly called "Enquête sur la perception de la pauvreté au Sénégal" (The Perceptions of Poverty in Senegal Study) (Direction de la Prévision et de la Statistique [DPS] et al. 2001). In comparison with the reported results of ESAM II, the "Perceptions" document found that, of all urban households questioned, 73.3 percent reported that their communities were impoverished. Nearly three-quarters of the population saw themselves and those around them as worse off than simply "poor." When surveyors queried heads of households in rural areas, the numbers in "Perceptions" climbed as high as 94 percent (DPS et al. 2001, 5)—nearly the entire rural population. These figures stood in stark contrast to those in the ESAM II report, which indicated that only half of the nation's households lived in poverty.

In the "qualitative," more methodologically transparent "Perceptions" document, the three primary "manifestations of poverty" were ranked in order of importance as follows: "difficulty in feeding one's family," "lack of work," and "not having the means to secure health care for family members." These indicators were also among those most described by Senegalese sicklers and their families I met. The "Poverty in Senegal" report attributes its discrepancies with the "Perceptions" document to reliance on economic science ("objective equations") versus subjective views ("degrees of satisfaction") (Ministère de l'Économie et des Finances et al. 2004, 5). But this judgment misses a crucial social fact underlying the numbers. Within the domain of the "household," an experience of dire poverty may be somewhat alleviated. When individuals were asked to rate the community around them (which implies all that the state has not furnished) as separate from their own private households, and kinship networks, they offered a much bleaker view.

People's subjective experiences of what economists call "objective poverty" must be understood in the context of Senegal's recent economic history. In 1979, Senegal was the first sub-Saharan African nation to enter into an International Monetary Fund-World Bank structural adjustment program (Anseeuw 2010, 250; van de Walle 2001, 1). A country largely dependent on agriculture in the form of peanuts, a monoculture crop that used 80 percent of the state's arable land despite efforts to diversify, Senegal quickly fell short of its promises and the IMF's payment schedule because of both a multi-year drought and a history of state care for its farmers through subsidies and loans when needed (a laudable commitment on the part of the strapped state). In 1979, falling world market prices for peanut oil dealt another blow. Then, the rise of petroleum prices in 1979 aggravated the downward spiral of Senegal's currency. It was against this backdrop that (then) Prime Minister Abdou

Diouf approached the multilateral institutions to initiate "a policy dialogue" (Delgado and Jammeh 1991, 9).

Between 1979 and 1990, through a confusing set of starts and stops, Senegal entered into various borrowing agreements. At the end of 1979, the government signed a "Medium-Term Program for Economic and Financial Adjustment," which provided the framework for its first Structural Adjustment Loan (SAL I). The agreement was based on neoliberal market reform: "liberalization, higher agricultural prices, and stricter economic criteria for investment projects" (Delgado and Jammeh 1991, 9). One of the first projects to be cut in the retrenchment was the costly agricultural aid structure, the *Office national de coopération et d'assistance pour le développement*, or ONCAD, on which many peanut farmers depended. Still, the SAL I was abrogated because the state continued to pay subsidies to its farmers. The multilateral institutions revoked the terms of that agreement in 1983, but the country was given a second chance for reform, which was set out in the "Economic Adjustment Plan in the Medium and Long Term" (or PAML, after its French acronym), a few years later. The PAML covered rules on market reorganization from 1985 to 1992 and led to SAL II in 1986. It then provided the framework for the SAL III in 1987 and SAL IV in 1990 (Delgado and Jammeh 1991). The 1990s saw a continued pattern of extended borrowing, and more banking acronyms entering the picture.

During the implementation of structural adjustment, the Senegalese state was seen as undisciplined, with excessive "expenditures" for public-sector employees and farmers. The IMF then instructed the government to diversify the economy beyond peanuts and to pare down the size of its civil services. Of consequence, these policy imperatives lead to massive employment cuts in agriculture, education, and, by extension, health care, since public university hospitals (*centres hospitalier universitaires*, CHUs) were essential to treating the population at large. In many ways these sectors have never recovered, since they have not successfully grown enough on their own through private, or participatory, means. What we see in Senegal during this period is the inception of a pattern that was later repeated in many African countries that underwent structural adjustment: declines in wages and wage employment in the formal sector not only resulted in job losses for countless individuals but also severely compromised governments' ability to provide health education and welfare services broadly (Turshen 1999, 60–61). In addition, subsidies on gasoline, imported vegetable oils, wheat, utilities, and transportation were "gradually eroded" in order to bring domestic prices more in line with world markets (Somerville 1991, 157). For ordinary Senegalese, buying these basics posed a problem from the very start of neoliberal reform. Then, through what many economists describe as an almost natural measure to make the region's exports more desirable, in 1994 the IMF devalued the *cfa* franc by half.[7] With staid humor and cynicism, people often refer to the devaluation as a *dévalisation*, meaning to rob someone of their possessions. Senegalese saw their purchasing power radically diminished overnight. Shortly thereafter, in 1996, the Senegalese state implemented new reforms in the health sector based on user fees for services as recommended by the WHO-UNICEF sponsored 1987 Bamako Initiative. The specifics of the initiative, founded on an ethos of participatory health care, often overlooked constraints that, in practice, quickly rendered such neoliberal ideals into a greater sense of diminished empowerment for people, rather than increased freedoms and autonomy (Foley 2008).

Finally, in 2000 Senegal was added to the unenviable list of the world's poorest and most indebted countries. This was also the year that the political party that had been in power since decolonization, the Socialist Party (PS), ceded power through free elections to the opposition, the Democratic Socialist Party (PDS), which was led by Abdoulaye Wade. As we will see in later chapters, ministers in Wade's cabinet, and even Wade himself, made several promises to address sickle cell care during his first term. In 2006, when the Wade government initially promised the population public funds for a national sickle cell program, the monies were almost immediately diverted to the agricultural sector because of "more pressing economic needs."[8] A year later, in 2007, when both sicklers and their doctors expected the funds to finally be forthcoming, the monies were redirected to cover presidential election costs—an election that resulted in Wade's second term.[9] Throughout his rule, Wade has increasingly embraced neoliberal economic policies and privatization.[10] Many people who believed in Wade's 2000 campaign platform, which was "change!" (*soppi!*), are now unable to fathom just how much more difficult everyday life for them has become with regard to matters pecuniary. Tropes of crisis circulate broadly, and as concerns the many sicklers and their families I knew, their "crises" were fundamentally about money, but also about sickle blood.

People often contemplated how difficult it was for them to sustain the chronic cost of keeping their children with sickle cell "crisis-free" and alive, yet they also offered expansive conceptions of kin-inspired safety nets that blended economic and social supports, a pattern perpetuated in the establishment of the sickle cell care network, the ASD. Their predicaments made me realize that despite the many recent optimistic reports on Senegal's economic growth, from those published by the World Bank, to profiles generated by the World Health Organization, increased income means little when life—and maintaining it—simply costs more than it did in the past, and when the state shouldered what are now withering social securities. Today the GNI per capita for the country has nearly tripled since 2000, now at US$1,560, in "objective terms," yet more than half of the Senegalese people—56.2 percent—still live on less than two dollars a day (United Nations Development Program [UNDP] 2008). What this overall increased income means, when viewed against a reality where many live on less than two dollars daily, is that the heightened demands that people "participate" in securing their own health have made many switch from relying on currencies of money to investing in improvised currencies of care that might partially absorb their disease pain and life difficulties. Economically, these two terms, pain and life difficulty, share the same idiom in Wolof, *defa metti*.

Now I turn to people's specific stories that illustrate how economic, affective, and material exchanges that inflect social bonds, and vice versa, absorb disease pain. As we will see, people manage the scarce resources they have, while trying to create a stock of care remedies, which draw on varied practices, including manipulations of bodily thresholds, gifting therapeutic goods, and undertaking subjective "training" dictated by household cash flows and constraints in this wider context of prolonged economic uncertainty (Antoine et al. 1995; Duruflé 1994). For many, economy must be thought of more broadly than purchasing power and available health care goods. Home economics—such as a father's calculated investments in a sick daughter's well-being—and the human attachments to therapies circulated in society, such as discounted vaccinations offered by a friend, or fagara purchased by a sympathetic onlooker, also make it clear that the sociability of goods and shared sentiments sustain relationships and establish interdependence through networks of investment and debt-gifting (Elyachar 2002, 510; Roitman 2004, 74). In some cases, these processes yield a biosociality that is just as contingent as the notion of economy itself (Roitman 2004, 2–3).

■ **Home and Health Economics: Training the Family for Healthy Disease**

When I first heard a Senegalese sickle cell geneticist question the relationship between the mild disease and the Senegalese haplotype, it was in reference to a particular patient whom I will call Rokhoya Sylla. "Perhaps she's a statistical aberration," Dr. Diagne, the principal hematological pediatric sickle cell specialist at Albert Royer, confided. Rokhoya had grown up under his care. I met Rokhoya shortly after her nineteenth birthday. She had virtually no fetal hemoglobin, the physiological marker often associated with the Senegalese haplotype, but had been "crisis-free" for over five years. Diagne dubbed her his "healthiest patient." He half joked that, in fact, she was probably "healthier than your average normal-hemoglobin-carrying Senegalese."

It was apparent from the outset that Rokhoya was an excessively shy young woman. She only spoke to me in short sentences, about things like school and her family, and "yes, they were fine." She did complain to me that she had recently been forced to leave high school before earning her diploma. She wanted another chance at an education and was interested to learn any details I might have about possible support from the Rotary Club in Dakar. Why was she forced to leave school? I asked. "Because of my [Hb]SS," she offered. The classroom had proven a dangerous environment. Although the curriculum inspired her, sixty-five students were crowded into a small room where the teacher smoked "long cigarettes" and often closed the windows.

She told me that she "suffocated" because her red blood cells needed oxygen, and that she often fell sick. Rokhoya's parents both held "good jobs." Her father was an accountant and her mother a university administrative assistant. She was the fifth of twelve children, and two of her older siblings were living abroad to attend college. Her parents sent a substantial portion of their combined salaries to their children, one in France and the other in Spain, totaling US$450 a month. "It's an investment in the future, that's why I do it," her father told me. The family owned the four-story house where they lived and Mr. Sylla rented out the bottom two floors for income. His accounting and fiscal management skills were strictly applied to themselves. They barely made ends meet.

When Dr. Diagne first introduced us, Rokhoya was enrolled in a trade school, pursuing a degree called *enseignement technique féminin* (technical education in feminine work, loosely equivalent to home economics). She was expected to master cooking, sewing, crocheting, and "conversation" (*causerie*). Rokhoya crocheted beautiful robes out of thin yarn, without using a pattern, to fit her form and planned to eventually produce garments to fit women of all sizes. The requirement that she master "*causerie*" made me pause, for Rokhoya was not a conversationalist. I initially found her a difficult informant. She seemed utterly uninterested in conversing with me, or anyone, except out of politeness when she was addressed. Even then, she would answer with the fewest possible words—perhaps a private economic exercise that she had perfected. When I first visited her house to interview her and her family, I mostly engaged with Rokhoya's parents and siblings, all of whom wanted me to know the twists and turns of their story. As we all talked, Rokhoya stared silently into the room, offering bits and pieces of information only when I persisted in questioning her. She could not bear to look strangers in the face. If her head was not lowered, her eyes darted elsewhere. I decided to leave her be, to see where the conversation would take the rest of us and whether she would ever feel compelled to join in.

Mr. Sylla wanted to speak in English when he could, impressing his wife and children, who sat on the floor. I tried to steer him back to French or Wolof, which he used interchangeably, so that the children might participate in our conversation rather than being intimidated by their head of household and the foreigner (*tubaab*) here to learn about Rokhoya's disease. Mr. Sylla had an imaginative memory, going beyond lived facts with inventive details. His wife and children corrected him. "No she was hospitalized for a bone infection, not a crisis." Rokhoya only participated at strained interludes, to correct her parents regarding the dosage and frequency of her medications. She "had taken fagara" for a few months in her early teens, but did not think that it had helped. She also nodded reservedly when her parents described their meticulous home-care and their optimism about her health as a consequence of it. Years later, she would tell me, through a flood of tears dammed up only by desperate aspirations for breath, that her father's care saved her life. I first heard this care described in the following exchange:

Mr. S: Where we live—we live in an airy apartment. A crowded, enclosed space [*la promiscuité*] is dangerous for her. We rent out the bottom apartments, the ground floor, so that we can take these top floors. We also have an open roof [with a courtyard, kitchen, and bedrooms] so that she can breathe pure air. She has her own bed, her own room. This way she has her own air.

Mme S: And no one is allowed to light the incense stand in her presence. . . .

Mr. S: Incense—smoke of any sort, really—when there is a smoker here, we intervene right away and say: "we are all, the whole family—is allergic to cigarettes, all of us [*tous*]." Even when there is a smoker out crossing the street in front of the house, the children will come and tell me, "Papa, there is someone smoking in the street." We are allergic to cigarettes, and do not permit anyone to bring cigarettes near Rokhoya. This training [*entraînement*] is key. No one crowds her [*ken du ko xatal*]. She has everything—a practical environment to prevent her crises, to space her crises. We operate this way and pray to God that we start to tend toward actually eradicating her disease. . . . We are optimistic. This is an incurable malady. . . . One of her doctors told us that there is a vital relation between the disease and man.[11] The essential thing for us is to correctly care for her and to promptly give her the assistance she needs. We are guided by these objectives, and we are optimistic.

As if to demonstrate their vigilant guardianship, a few minutes later, a report of a smoker came from the part of the house where Mme Sylla had gone with Rokhoya to retrieve her handiworks to show me. "There is someone smoking here . . . !" Arame Sylla yelled. "Is there a smoker in the building?" Mr. Sylla shouted out down the hall. No one responded. "It's not in the house, it must be outside," he continued in his normal voice. He then resumed our conversation.

It is important to constantly keep an eye on her, and to believe in God, and to strive for the best well-being possible. As they say in French, "*Tout homme en bonne santé est un malade qui s'ignore*" [A man in perfect health is simply an unknowing patient]. It's rare to find a [human] being that suffers from nothing at all. We have inculcated ourselves with this mindset [*esprit*] and we live this mindset in our family. All that she needs is support, our aid. . . . She has certain talents, her handiwork, and the will to work. We've helped her choose a trade—home economics—

which she is now finishing. All she needs is a supportive environment
that will permit her to succeed.

I later learned that none of Rokhoya's closest friends knew about her condition. "They never asked, I never told," she responded, when I inquired about
her discretion.

Six years later, in 2006, I visited her father's house again. Nearly the same
scene unfolded. The children were taller, and this time they sat on chairs and
cushions lining the walls. Mr. Sylla spoke English, his wife Wolof, and the
children eyed me and tried to join in when they could. Rokhoya was still
silent. I spent the afternoon with them and then took Rokhoya with me to an
ASD meeting I needed to attend at the CNTS. In the taxi we talked more than
we ever had. She was then twenty-five, had gotten married, and had borne a
child. She and her new family still lived in her father's house. "This is best,"
she assured me. Her husband was a close neighbor from her childhood. Their
mothers had arranged the marriage, and the couple was happy to reunite after
many years apart. Rokhoya's family had moved away from the neighborhood
where her husband had lived and where she was born and had lived until her
father bought the four-story apartment. "He has always been family to me,
even when I went years without seeing him. He knows my family, and we all
live together without a problem." Our conversation then veered back to the
sickle cell disease association, newly publicized on television in a sustained
way in the preceding weeks, as we passed billboard after billboard displaying a literal sickle cell poster-child, a seemingly healthy newborn infant. The
state was getting ready to host its first international conference on the disease,
and awareness messages lined the highway and were flooding the media. We
were both surprised by the coverage: sickle cell had finally seemed to garner
state attention. We spent four days meeting and talking, and I introduced her
to dozens of sicklers who were part of my larger project and who were also
members of the ASD. Rokhoya had abandoned clinical follow-up once she
became too old for her doctor's pediatric consultations. She had never been
to the CNTS, and did not have friends her age who were also sicklers. This
was all about to change.

As the ASD meeting started and the agenda was read aloud, it seemed clear
that Rokhoya recognized herself and the outlines of her life in the issues enumerated by the group's president, Magueye Ndiaye. She kept looking around,
scanning the room to take in ASD's members who called themselves a family
of "shared blood." Magueye reiterated multiple times throughout the meeting
that this family of blood was bound by sickle hemoglobin as the medium of
their kinship.

The airy CNTS cafeteria, which opens onto a courtyard shaded by mango
trees, where the group usually met, was under construction. After some
commotion about finding a space where they could all fit, they decided to
convene in the waiting hall where patients usually lined up to have blood

drawn during hours of operation. There were two large open doors and a smaller window through which air could move. The meeting lasted for over two hours. About forty-five minutes into it, when an argument ensued over access badges to the international conference, Rokhoya started to cough violently and asked for water. She told me that she was suffocating because there was "no air." I directed her to the water cooler upstairs and pointed out the open doors and windows. She went to drink and to breathe. She then came back for the duration of the meeting without incident. I wondered about the coughing and the claim to be suffocating. Was this an affective plea to return to the safe haven of her father's house? Was she not truly "at home" with the many others in the room who were sharing her air, and who also needed "more oxygen"?

The remainder of the ASD discussion consisted of a back and forth about which members would get a *carte blanche* to the upcoming international conference. I also wondered if these the high emotions linked to the group's politics were what had "suffocated" her. As the meeting ended and we were able to talk, she assured me that she was fine and that she wanted to meet the group's president. I now noticed that her eyes were slightly wet, as she continued to softly cough and to pat them dry. When the small huddle around Magueye started to thin, she approached him to pay her membership fee to join the association. They were both "healthy" sicklers, Magueye joked. He got her to laugh by teasing that he was more "successful" than she was because he was older. Her sympathies with him and the others were clear. She would return again. She also convinced her father to join. Eventually most of Rokhoya's peers in the ASD began to refer to Mr. Sylla as their father as well.

In the week that followed Rokhoya's first encounter with the ASD, she began to tell me about her desires, her plans, and finally her frustrations. Members of the association immediately took her in as they spent eight-hour days together in their information booth at the conference and traveled together to its remote location (the ultra-rich district of *Les Almadies* at the luxury hotel *Le Méridian President*). It was in part because of a profound realization that she was "not alone in this disease" that she began to express her feelings more openly. Her disease had been "mild" but at what cost? The normalization of her illness was rooted within the love of her caring family, yet it was also situated within a context of broader economic precariousness, which she observed all around her. Most recently, she had suffered from survivor's guilt as she witnessed a neighbor with less educated and capable parents die from the same disease because, in her words, "he lacked my health." She also understood that her near-total health was rare, and she simply credited her father's care. Nonetheless, by gauging the worst cases of the disease around her and comparing them with her own, she imagined that her livelihood was due to a very thin buffer, family care, which separated her suffering from that of others. Rokhoya suffered nonetheless; she lived emotionally bewildered at the thoughts of her special status, her family's sacrifice, and the biosocial inequality that somehow cast the die in her favor. We planted ourselves in a quiet corner of the hotel, away from the conference commotion, to talk. We had never done a taped interview before without her family present, but now she was ready to tell me her story. Overlooking the city, she pointed out a mosque nearby. She then playfully attempted to find her neighborhood within the city sprawl before she settled into her chair. Her smile began to fade.

DF: When I first started talking to your father about your disease it was clear that his care played a large role in your health. Can we talk a bit about that, and how you see your father's actions? It's important that I also understand your take on things.

RS: What you're saying is true. Sickle cell demands care, and understanding, and support. When you're tired, you need rest, you need air, and a way to avoid getting stressed or tired about small things. And my parents, they understood me—[she begins to cry], when I was tired, they— [she stops and can no longer talk] . . . they supported me. [Through tears, her language gets confused] everything they did, nothing ever lacked [*sama dara defa mesul manqué*]. They did things for me first, then thought about the others. I came first.

I asked if she wanted to stop the interview. She gulped and shook her head no. She regained her voice and we continued.

DF: When you first realized all of this, how did you feel?

RS: When I was small, before I really understood the disease, I felt guilty. They would take better care of me than the others. I was special. Later we found out that some of the others had sickle cell too [sickle cell trait] . . . [begins to cry again]

DF: What is it that is making you cry? What is it that is touching you to make you cry like this?

RS: I've just lived so much. The disease, you can't understand. . . . And when you asked me about my father—I just can't explain [chokes up].

DF: I'm sorry [*massa waay*].

We stopped the interview. I handed her tissue after tissue until her face was dry of tears. Her eyes were locked on the city, to avoid looking at me, as if seeing me meant exposing more than she could bear. She then balled up the whole disintegrated mass of Kleenex in one hand and clenched tightly. She forced a smile to say she was "fine" (*ça va*). She began to gather herself emotionally again as we sat in silence for a while. Small reminders of the world— birds cutting into the view, a maintenance man below—allowed her to gradually speak again, if only to comment on the scene. She eventually found her way back to a not-so-lost thought and resumed the story of witnessing her neighbor's recent death from sickle cell because his family "didn't have the knowledge, the means, or the interest" required to keep him alive.

In our exchange, Rokhoya's tears appeared to me to be a metonym for the well of emotion she had guarded quite carefully through years of silence. When we stopped the interview, she allowed me to sit with her, as she tapped her hand on the arm of her chair and nodded to me to both wait and to just be with her. Her tears gave speech to that which was beyond language (or at least communication with a non-sickler like myself); as she told me during our interview, "You can't understand." Silence, for Rokhoya, expressed the non-verbal dimension of communication, in this case of illness, that non-sufferers presumably cannot know because it eludes the linguistic tools usually used to convey intimate life experience (Morris 1997, 27). What Rokhoya's stunted silence made clear to me was that although I could never be sure that I could actually understand, I felt an ethical obligation to try, even if that meant leaving exposed that undeniable gap in experience between myself, the anthropologist, and the woman trying to speak through her pain. As she seemed to want to talk and overcome the physical blockage of her gasps, it appeared that our interactions may have enabled her to see what was at stake in her health, why it so conflicted her, and more importantly, to what extent it was a societal issue far exceeding her as an individual (Kleinman 2006, 210–12). In the days we spent together at the Méridian, Rokhoya gradually breached her silence with more ease, especially once she found the sickle cell patient group and was able to listen to her own experiences recounted in the stories of its members. In the group, she found a family of shared blood whose proclivity to, and semi-normalization of, silent suffering mirrored her own—except for the fact that their organization was now giving a voice to the void.

As for how Rokhoya felt about her biological family, the message she wanted to convey may have been interrupted by her emotions but was nonetheless clear. She loved her father and was deeply grateful for the life and health he helped her to achieve. All that he had done, she explained, probably meant that he "loved her more" than his other children. She later told me that she bore the name of Mr. Sylla's mother. Through this assimilation, his mother was able to live on through her. In this custom of nominal incarnation (*turaandoo*), their relationship was doubly knotted: he was centered in a timeline of parental affection where Rokhoya, diseased or not, embodied the bonds of familial past and future beyond any straightforward notion of lineage.

If Rokhoya's disease was made "mild" by the medical care she received, it was only because that attention was complemented by an extraordinary degree of familial investment and "training" (*entraînement*), as her father put it. Given his limited means, with the number of people he had living in the household and whom he was supporting abroad, the fact that Rokhoya had her own room speaks volumes. He not only provided all of the materials she needed to continue her schooling and pursue the trade the family had chosen for her, and that she was quite happy to follow, but he also wanted her to have "her own air to breathe," a notion I never encountered in conversations with anyone else in Dakar. Mr. Sylla believed, like health philosopher Georges Canguilhem, that "in order to discern what is normal or pathological for the body itself, one must look beyond the body" (1991 [1966], 201). In applying this idea, Mr. Sylla believed that "health is a set of securities and assurances, securities in the present, assurances for the future" (1991 [1966], 198). His daughter's chances for the future, and her belief that she was important to its making, may have kept her crisis-free since she was a child.

Rokhoya's father not only implored her to live beyond the confines of her illness but he also made-do to ensure that she had decent care. He always bought her the needed vitamins, painkillers, and vaccines while he had her blood work done at the expensive, and usually reliable, *Pasteur Institute* in Dakar, where he had friends who would sometimes perform analyses and vaccinations at a discount. His rational philosophy of health was enabled by his ability to buy her lifelong prescriptions, and through them (largely folic acid supplements and sometimes traditional medicine), Rokhoya was able to stave off her crises and approach a degree of normalcy. This state of near-health was normalized by the family's adherence to the idea that *everyone* lives in a state of health defined as "life in the silence of the organs" (Canguilhem 1991, 101). For them, the imagined dormant disease in all of us could begin its cry, if it had not yet done so, at any time. Rokhoya was no different from anyone else in the human masses of the eventually sick, except that she already knew her disease and was therefore a bit more enlightened on this matter of eventual risk than most. Other HbSS sicklers constructed ideas of the normal very differently—through an impetus to build family to supplant strained or failing solidarities of birth kinship and national citizenship (state care). This happened through dire economic lack, rather than relative economic prosperity.

■ Training the Body for Minimal Need

> He lost his appetite. . . . He lost his "taste" for food,
> and now he lived on coffee.
> —Scheper-Hughes 1992, 179

Magueye and I sat under a whirling ceiling fan, which did little to break the heat in the enclosed courtyard of the new French bistro across the street from the children's hospital. I had made it my ethical duty to fatten him without his knowing that I harbored such a strange project. Instead, I played on his penchant for hospitality and said that I had no one to eat with, as it was Ramadan, and asked him to keep me company during lunch. Because of his disease, he was not supposed to fast, but he was fasting anyway. I succeeded in talking him out of it, theoretically, with the help of a doctor, and then immediately with the promise of pasta *avec sauce béchamel*. Practically speaking, I knew that Magueye fasted on most days anyway—not out of choice but due to circumstance. He had become rail thin and it bothered me, not solely because my very presence next to him implicated me in the global inequalities I palpably felt after the seven-hour trip between JFK and Léopold Sédar Senghor airports, but also because it was clear that today Magueye was working as hard as anyone in the humid heat of September in Dakar. He was on his self-appointed rounds visiting sicklers throughout the hospital sector while living on fewer calories than nutritionists think humanly possible. He was over six feet tall and could not have weighed more than 130 pounds.

As we sat down, he commented on the skills of the waiters, the rules they were breaking, their inability to carry more than one plate at a time. He was an expert in restaurant management—a strange paradox, given that lack of food was the tool by which he trained his body for scarcity, constantly raising his threshold for alimentary needs. Magueye was good at making his disease seem less like an inconvenience and more and more like a way of life.

The waiter brought us a basket of sourdough rolls to hold us over until our order arrived. Magueye picked one up and smiled.

> You know, I used to eat one of these for lunch every day when I was a kid. But it wasn't just for me. It was for me and my friends—those of us who couldn't go home for lunch, because we didn't have bus fare. And if we did go home it wasn't clear that there would be much to eat. So we shared this little thing [his eyes fixed on the roll he'd begun to twirl in his hand like a toy].

Magueye's account made me wonder about the sharing of food in general in Senegal. Families and guests usually eat from one plate, sometimes (traditionally) with their hands—a social fact that bespeaks the intimacy of eating with others in general. But, more specifically, whenever I offered children something they would share it among themselves, whether they were poor or not. (This seemed a natural tendency so very different from children I encountered back home, my dear nephews being my referents for this comparison). I often gave food to street children (*taalibe*), who would rush to me when they saw me near the busy thoroughfare on my way to the transfusion center. They too, even in their very dire situations, would divide whatever they were given among themselves, even if the biggest boys would take larger shares leaving the little ones with stark lessons about might being right.

Magueye was the youngest of nine children. His father was a military man, a *gendarme*, and his mother, a Peul woman, lived (and continues to live) off her cows. After his father's death, when Magueye was just fourteen, he moved to Dakar from his village of Khombole to live with his older brothers, who were in the city attending school. Why did they not provide for him? I asked.

> I don't know. I think I was too young to question it. That's how it was. My brother gave me 200 *cfa* a day [40 cents]. I had to take two buses

to school, which means a transfer and paying again, so I had to content myself with the little change I had left to get something to eat. My friends and I, we would go in on the roll together. We couldn't go home if we wanted to. There was no way around it.

Magueye presents this situation as normal, and for other poor sicklers in Dakar who recounted "not being able to go home for lunch," the assumption indeed was that they would fend for themselves, or, more likely, wait for evening when they might eat at home.

Later he related this training in surviving scarcity to the fact that he lives well *with*, and not in spite of, his sickle cell disease.

> MN: I have learned to manage my crises largely without all of those pharmaceuticals. It's awful to be dependent on something—it's a hard thing to feel dependent on medications. It's especially difficult for me because I don't even have access to pharmaceuticals. I don't have the means to buy the meds. Sometimes I have a prescription that sits [*qui dort*] for six months. I don't have a cent to buy them with. Given all of this—the lack of means, access, the hospital costs—I say to myself, listen, since I can't access medications, I don't have the necessary means to always be buying myself medications—while I know that I need them incessantly, always!—then why not use another therapy? What I call psychology. It's mental. It permits me to get by.
>
> DF: The access you're referring to, is it principally an economic problem?
>
> MN: For me it's entirely economic. The meds are at the pharmacy. [There's no disruption in the supply these days.] But I can't . . .
>
> DF: Which medications? Folic acid tablets?
>
> MN: Folic acid is what we need at a minimum and, you know, the price is around 2000 *cfa* a month (US$4). I can go a whole month without having 2,000 francs, a whole month without 2,000 francs. Imagine! And, I have other things to take care of, too. I have my breakfast to contend with. I have tons of things that will come first. It's not possible [to spend 2000 francs on medications].

I inquired about how he coped with his dire economic situation.

> DF: How do you live? [silence] . . . on a daily basis? You are unemployed. How do you do it?
>
> MN: I also ask myself how I do it. How?
>
> DF: You don't have a daily allowance, DQ [*dépense quotidienne*][12]?
>
> MN: I don't have a DQ. And I can't ask anyone for anything, but things come, just like that. It's weird.
>
> DF: In the morning, for example . . . recount your day for me.

MN: This morning, for example, I knew that I had my round-trip bus fare taken care of by the health ministry [since he was helping them organize the upcoming sickle cell conference]. And other than that, I had 5 cents [25 *cfa*] in my pocket, or something like that. So, I buy a little baggie of coffee along the side of the road, the 5-cent sachet and I drink it calmly and slowly. It's my breakfast. Sometimes I don't have . . .

DF: Only a 5 cent cup of coffee?

MN: Yeah. Sometimes I don't even have that. I drink a glass of water, and then I'm on my way. And you know, in this way, I have learned— naturally, I have no appetite. It's innate with me. Everyone knows— eating [*le manger*], or not eating, has never held me up. This, in any case, permits me to self-manage better [*de mieux m'auto-gérer*]. I tell myself that there is not a set hour for lunch. Just because it's twelve noon doesn't necessarily mean that it's time to eat. No—that has never been part of my schedule.

DF: I see.

MN: Sometimes from sunup 'til sundown I simply drink water. But I'm well in these conditions. That's it. As soon as it is evident that I cannot have what I *want*, I content myself with what I *have*. If I have a glass of water, I drink it and I'm on my way. If I have a cup of coffee, I drink it and I'm on my way. If I have nothing—I'm on my way.

Magueye's case recalls Veena Das and Ranendra Das's observation with regard to chronic sufferers in urban India that "within both the medical system and within the distribution of power and resources within the household (or economy) there operates a patterned non-recognition of severe disease that helps to absorb serious pathology within the normal" (2006, 194). Similarly, in Senegal, when economic privation characterizes the life worlds of those with chronic disease, people normalize illness as an aspect of the everyday. In part, it is this patterning that renders Magueye's disease "mild." Yet Magueye was not always able to manage his disease with ease. He also told me of times when he was in dire need and local specialists, all of whom knew him well, would let him "borrow" money—which, it was understood, did not necessarily have a repayment date—to stock up on folic acid. The main specialist at the children's hospital, who was also from Khombole, opened his wallet when he once saw Magueye tear up a prescription he could not afford; he also bought Magueye shoes and other necessities when he traveled to France soon afterward. Magueye's personal doctor at the CNTS would periodically "get hit up for bus fare, a few francs here and there," when he was in need. "It is no longer like doctor and patient," Magueye told me, and that is when he said, "It's more like big brother-little brother. He looks after me."

Magueye, like other sicklers I knew, initially diagnosed himself after learning about the signs and symptoms of the disease in a natural science course in middle school. He was fourteen. His teacher recommended that he see a doctor, who made the diagnosis official. When I asked if his parents had detected anything wrong during his childhood, he said that his mother first noticed a strange swelling of his hands and feet when he was only a few weeks old. They were on a long road trip in the Casamance region, where his father had been stationed for the military. "It was hot," Magueye imagined, and "I was dehydrated." His mother said that he did not stop crying for nine hours once the "hand-foot syndrome" set in. His parents were confused about his recurring symptoms and took him to traditional healers for years. Some of the healers cut his small body with razors and inserted herbal mixtures into the thin slits. Others gave him tonics and infusions of various plants. Still others would write Koranic verses, neatly fold them into squares, and enclose them in leather casings, which he was to string around his body for protection. In this medley, which he described as a "barrage of therapies of *hazard*" (Fr. *chance*), he was sure that fagara was included in the mix. He recalled a plant that sent vapors to his nose, "like mint," and that had a particular smell and taste. As an adult he learned that this plant was fagara when a friend in Dakar began buying him small sachets from the market when he was not well. "I could never forget that smell," he told me.

■ Streamlining Survival

> When we think of the world's future, we always mean the
> destination it will reach if it keeps going in the direction we can
> see it going in now; it does not occur to us that its path is not a
> straight line, but a curve, constantly changing direction
> —Wittgenstein 1980, 3

Magueye received his high school diploma, which, in the French system, demands a rigorous test (*concours*), after the second try in 2000. He was twenty-four years old. He enrolled in university, negotiating to do one semester a year, but even that proved too much for him. He soon dropped out and decided to pursue English courses at the American Cultural Center in Dakar the following year, but he fell sick. He decided to change course again and opted to go to cooking school. He had never had an appetite, but the high culture of French culinary practice intrigued him. He finished his training and had job offers soon afterward. He was proud of himself for finishing the course, and for having a trade, but also had to admit to himself that the heat of the kitchen, the stress of the line, and the long hours on his feet were not compatible with his illness. He now caters private parties on occasion, about five times a year in good years, and still hopes to build a client base. His catering "contracts" usually stipulate that he work long hours, often until early in the morning following an event, while they pay no more than US$10 for the night. He always welcomed these opportunities, however stressful the labor.

Magueye spent his days, for the most part, at the adult sickle cell clinic and in the teaching hospital environs, where he would look for sicklers who might be in need of support. He gave them everything he had. As if proposing a plan that I might help him realize, he often talked about imagining ways to change the nature of suffering, to be able to transfer actual physical pain between sicklers who were "overloaded with crisis." Sometimes over coffee, he would imagine a kind of "transfusion" technology that, like a blood transfusion, would instead transfuse suffering by exporting it to another person who could better bear it. Other times he imagined that God would have to "update human capacities," and biological nature, to make this possible. He thoroughly enjoyed these musings and would laugh at himself for wanting things otherwise. In 2004, when he was twenty-eight, he was voted president of the newly formed Senegalese sickle cell disease association. This voluntary work made him feel useful on several levels:

> Every morning I go the National Blood Transfusion Center. I don't actually work there, but it's like a second home. I feel at home there because that's where the sicklers are and at least over there I feel I'm serving a purpose. I counsel them, I orient them, I share pain with them. Sometimes they ask me to come to their homes, or parents will ask that I come and see their kids because they refuse to take their medications. Sometimes they ask me to come and talk to their families about how to live well with sickle cell, how to manage it. Many people ask me, in disbelief, if I'm even an [Hb]SS sickler. Why? Because I have learned to live with it. It doesn't throw me off. I'm at peace with it. And I love these people. I am always thinking of them. I'm always thinking of how to advance things here in Senegal for their benefit, how to help them live with the pain. It's good, because it busies me. When I'm unemployed and I'm just sitting around idle, that is a much more difficult situation to be in. It's better to feel useful, especially for a cause.

Clearly the ASD served a double purpose for Magueye. For many of the people with sickle cell I encountered in Dakar, creating a *heritage*, a family line, was a special kind of investment they deeply believed in, but it stymied them in practice. For Magueye this notion of legacy was strong, but he constantly questioned his desire for it because the woman in his life, whom I will call Safietou, was also an HbSS sickler. Magueye was not yet sure what to do about his dilemma, because, genetically, there was no room for doubt: they could only have SS children. In their case, with the calculations of risk settled, the matter at hand was whether or not to continue their relationship, to live it only in private (a near impossibility given familial pressures to marry), or, perhaps, to think about other forms of heritage.

MN: If people don't want SS sicklers to marry each other, it's because they are thinking of their children, about the family that you will found. But what if we aren't necessarily thinking about that?

DF: So you do not want children?

MN: I'm just saying that, for the moment, we don't have the future figured out—marriage or children. We simply want to be able to support each other, mutually. Each of us knows, on the inside, that we are both sick. But, we understand each other—between us we've established a climate where we don't consider ourselves sick sicklers. We live, we go out to clubs. We go to the beach, like "normals." What is the problem? The essential thing is to be happy.

DF: And if you want children, eventually? Can you stay together and forgo having children? Would that be too weird? We see lots of childless couples in the United States, for instance.

MN: No. In our society, that is not recommended.

DF: Why not, if the child would be sick?

MN: You know, I'm going on what I am. In the Muslim faith it is said that you must marry and have children to augment the race, you know?

DF: The race?

MN: The race—to augment the number of Muslims in future generations. When one is born into a Muslim family, you are Muslim, and you continue reproducing Muslims. That's how it is. We are here to increase the number of Muslims.

DF: The Muslim race, is that it?

MN: No, not the Muslim race, but the black race, you know. There is not, technically speaking, a Muslim race [laughs].

DF: "The black" race? Doesn't Islam first come from Arab culture?

MN: Well, to augment the genealogical tree—well the tree is there, I'm here, but no one has the right to simply stop the tree with themselves. Like if I refuse to have kids . . . the line stops with me, the line becomes extinct, and that is a problem.

Magueye's quip about "race" is more precisely about lineage. Many Senegalese recounted that, to be a good Muslim, one must have children. This was stated less as a pressure, than as an opportunity to please God and to partake in the larger outlines of conduct he proposed to humanity. This is largely why adoption is not seen as a viable option for most couples, although it is not uncommon for people to take in other people's children, usually those of a relative, once they have had their own. Senegalese Christians had similar views. Magueye then continued,

When I talk to my friends about marriage, I get into discussions about the point of marriage. What is it for, at the end of the day? And they say that it—well, they don't exactly say that it is for having children, but they say that it is a way to preserve—if you die one day, to see you through the person you have left behind. Then I say, "instead of creating a person, I can create a thing, through which you will be able to see me." I can forgo marrying, do without having children, and instead fight for a purpose and build so that Senegal has a specialized center for sickle cell where the fight to better sickle cell care will live on. And everyone will say, "Magueye Ndiaye, he was part of this." That, too, is a *heritage*. It's like a son one leaves behind after death, who will continue to serve the world. So don't tell me that it is imperative to have an actual son or daughter. Sometimes I defend myself with this rationale. . . . Sickle cell is my heritage, and I depend on it [*j'y tiens*]!

Magueye nevertheless did want to marry and have children. He constantly discussed it with an older, motherly friend whose HbSS child had died recently. They both got animated, and sometimes argued furiously, when she told him not to get too involved with the woman he loved. The friend, Mrs. Touty Niang, was also part of the governing body of the ASD. As Magueye and I continued our initial conversation about marriage, I attempted to think with him about his future possibilities and heritage, given his relationship. He admitted a future with Safietou might not be possible, given the pressures from his biological and other relations on two completely linked fronts: marrying someone with the disease and not being able to have (healthy) children.

MN: I can tell you that right now everyone is talking to me about marriage these days. Everyone brings it up, I don't understand why.

DF: Do you think that it would be possible for you and Safietou to marry, [Hb]SS and all, and that the two of you could have the association as your heritage, and forgo having children?

MN: If it was just the two of us, we could do it. The problem is that each of us is issued from a family, and everyone knows that we Senegalese have a very, very heavy social context to deal with. I can decide as an individual to make such a decision, she could too, but they will never let us live in peace, as we would like. Maybe it could work if we left the country. In order to live your life in peace, without considering the family—it's not possible, unless you are disowned. If you do something like this, you will be banished. No one in the family will speak to you again.

DF: Because of not having children?

MN: No, because you're living your life the way that you see fit, disregarding their familial expectations. . . . It's difficult. Me, I don't want to commit to a decision like that.

DF: So, what would be the basis of the exclusion? Is it the fact that you've married another SS sickler, or the fact that you've decided, in doing it, that you don't want to have children? . . . What kind of exclusion do you imagine?

MN: I think—I tell myself that the exclusion will essentially be because you've decided not to have children, and that you've decided to marry an SS, while everyone knows that that just isn't done [*que c'est pas normal*]. So, these are decisions that you can make, when you love each other, but there is the family that imposes itself, and the family can then decide to never speak to you again, and you'd live with your wife in solitude. That would be awful. At the very least, we need our families.

DF: So you really do think that your family will reject you?

MN: Yeah, you know there are families . . .

DF: Yours?

MN: Yes, mine. There are certain things that are not pardonable, frankly. I'm sort of spoiled because I'm the youngest and all, but there are issues that they just will not tolerate. Even the Association [ASD] would not forgive me for that.

DF: Your other family . . .

MN: [laughs] Yes, my second family. Even my doctors would say, that Magueye, he did it on purpose, so just leave him to live alone with his malady. In any case, I do know that there is a pretty strong possibility that *I will* marry another sickler. Frankly, it could happen. I'm not *deciding* on this. It's not my wish, but I'm not fleeing the possibility either. I'm not *seeking* it, but also, I'm not against it. . . . Medicine has its limits, you know. Science—has its limits! . . . I am really tempted to do it, you know, maybe to prove that we could have healthy children. Sometimes I even wonder if I really have sickle cell. I've taken the test many times over, but sometimes I really don't believe it.

Senegalese family pressures to reproduce, the physician's lectures against knowingly bearing children who might have the disease, and even the mission statement of the ASD in its "fight against sickle cell" have laid out certain norms of conduct that collided with Magueye's hope to pursue his relationship with Safietou. For a time, he continued it anyway, refusing to "make a decision," as evident in our discussion when he rattled off a few rounds, back and forth, about how he is not actively for or against such unions. At the end of the above conversation about being with an SS sickler, Magueye brandished his own health as a means to question the interdictions and the prognostic capacity of science to determine whether or not his own child would be sick. There is a part of the scientific narrative that he knew to be true. He felt, however, that it had limits, given his level of health and the individualized norms that he had achieved through methods on which science may have little comment. For Magueye, having children at all costs was also an expectation framed within Islamic theo-logics. Augmenting his family line was, moreover, framed as increasing the Muslim population of God's children.

In this conversation, Magueye's idea that he and Safietou should just marry and experiment with having children, to "prove" that they could be healthy, despite the technical impossibility, drives home the extent to which his own norms had come to trump those of science on this question.

Magueye Ndiaye's biological thresholds however, are anything but fixed. After the 2006 international conference, his stress from being the public face of the ASD, his unpaid work at the CNTS, and his side attempts to make money to save for marriage brought on two painful crises, one of which landed him in the hospital in the winter of 2007. Safietou spent most of her days and evenings with him, which made it obvious to Dr. Diagne and other providers in the CHU (who were increasingly defending the ASD and promoting sicklers' rights on the public stage) that the two were romantically involved. Diagne was visibly frustrated and worried that Magueye seemed to be flouting the message of the ASD on prevention. I rarely saw him as flustered as when he told me, "Magueye simply cannot do this! He has to take his responsibilities seriously (*prendre ses responsabilités*)." Diagne was not overly forceful with Magueye on this, however, telling him instead that he was his "own man" and would have to make his own decisions. A few years later, in 2010, Magueye told me that Diagne, whom he called his "spiritual father" in the context of this conversation, made it very clear to him that he could marry Safietou but that he would have to resign as president of the ASD if he chose this path. Diagne had no power to fire him, but Magueye understood that he could suffer a public crisis of legitimacy if, as the ASD's president, he openly married a woman with sickle cell. Magueye also referred to Touty as his "spiritual mother" in his account of how she also asked him to "think of the consequences." The decision to end his relationship with Safietou was a moral dilemma that made Magueye realize that the network he helped create in order to permit those with the disease to share pain, and also hope, was subjectively inseparable from him. He could not imagine life without it and began to realize how much he relied on the very supports he helped bring into being for others. There was no question of sacrificing his work with the ASD to pursue a love that was about his own wants. To do so would have been more "selfish" (*égoïste*), he said, than social. In this way, he made the decision to leave Safietou for the same reason that brought them together in the first place: because they shared so much, starting with the same disease.

During the following years, in 2008 and 2009, Magueye tried to reconcile his feelings and kept himself busy with several projects to better the plight of sicklers in Senegal. In addition to working on a vaccination campaign funded by the telecommunications company's charity organization, *Fondation Sonatel*, he drafted plans for two interrelated projects of his own. The first consisted of a plan to start what he described as a "nonprofit health insurance-micro-credit agency for sicklers" (*une mutuelle d'épargne et de micro crédit qui servira comme mutuelle de santé en plus*). In his conception, people with the disease would be the shareholders, pay a set monthly premium, and be able to borrow larger sums for projects, for hospitalizations, and for pharmaceuticals when necessary. This hybrid of economic and health support would, according to his business plan, "come to the aid of economically vulnerable patients and further develop a cadre of solidarity within the ASD," out of which the *mutuelle* would be run. The problem was of course capital. Magueye hoped to find investors who would front the initial money, and hoped that some of the many projects that most of the ASD's unemployed members had imagined for their economic futures might come to fruition, such as the boutique Rokhoya hoped to open upon finishing her latest set of courses in 2010. Magueye had already succeeded in enlisting a pharmacist who is an HbAS sickler (i.e., who carries the trait) and who felt a personal interest in sickle cell *entraide* to provide medications at a discounted rate for those within the ASD who might join *la mutuelle*. He told me that he prayed daily that such a concept would not dissolve into fantasy. He even began reading up on aid policies to consult the WHO representative in Dakar about the multilateral institution's specific country plan for Senegal, which listed supporting such insurance plans for medical coverage.

Magueye's second project was a quasi-ethnographic study about sickle cell and relationships. He sought my help to formulate research questions on intimacy and sexuality based on major themes that he and others had lived. "There are so many people suffering from fears that they will never find anyone, and there are others who wonder about how the disease affects sexuality, with symptoms like priapism," he told me.[13] "I can't count how many women don't think that they will ever be loved because they have this disease. They feel lesser (*wañeeku*). They need to know that they are not alone in this." Magueye's very position as president of the ASD made him a natural confidant for both men and women, and he wanted to somehow catalogue all that he was hearing into some kind of formal study with "data."

During these years it became clear that the moral dilemma that Magueye faced with Safietou was partially structural; he felt a deep connection, a closeness, a sense of family with sicklers. He often said that he "loved them," adding, "I even love the ones with horrible character flaws, who I'd *love to hate*! It's impossible." Thus, not surprisingly, he later became intimate with another woman, again a healthy HbSS sickler, whom he dated quite seriously in secret, fearing reprisals from her family and from the ASD's biomedical supporters.

In recent years Magueye has noticed that, in several cases, close relations among others in the ASD have gotten serious. In one instance he was asked by two sicklers' families to come to the man's home to "counsel" the couple. Afterwards, he told me, "I realized that they were deep in this, and they were absolutely not going to let each other go. What can I do? I understand them. As their president, and confidant, I am not going to encourage people to get together. No. But if they do, I'm not going to discourage them either." Yet, his own relationship, like the previous one with Safietou, could not go on because of his public role. After a year into this relationship "a university

trained, polite fellow from a good family," according to Touty, asked for Magueye's second girlfriend's hand in marriage. She refused. Her family could
not understand why she "chose to remain alone."

Magueye then took it upon himself to pull himself out of what was becoming a painful pattern and resolved to marry a non-HbSS woman, "as a
safeguard," he said, to keep him from becoming too close to women with
the disease. "We have no future, it's useless," he told me, and himself. Almost as a seeming reflex, Magueye went to his other family, his birth kin,
for a suitable wife. This is not uncommon in Senegal, but what is interesting
about Magueye's choice at this conjuncture in his provisional efforts to eke
out his future is that, for much of his life, his birth family could not provide
for him so he created bonds of sharing and solidarity with others, from the
kids with whom he had shared bread for lunch to the sicklers who offered him
a heritage. Now, when two love relationships with women, who were not of
his same Peul ethnic group and who were not birth-blood kin, threatened to
compromise his family relation to the ASD, he almost naturally went to this
other "bloodline," and decided to marry a cousin from his natal village, with
his mother's help. He recounted the story simply: "I was home for the Tabaski
holiday and I saw her around, and meant to talk with her, but lost track of
her that night. I asked my mother about her, and my mother said, 'That one?
She will be your wife.' " He talked to his cousin indirectly about marriage over
the next few months. While they dated, she let him know that "he wasn't the
only one with an illness." She was not talking about sickle cell, however, as
she had not been tested at the time. Perhaps sensing his anxiety about being
understood, she gave him a laundry list of all of her "ailments," from chronic
allergies, to frequent colds, to snoring, to let him know that she was capable
of comprehending the chronicity of his disease. He said that he laughed at
first but then realized that she was serious. She wanted him to know, perhaps
like Mr. Sylla, that what made anyone normal was that "we all suffer from
something," as she later told me.

Magueye had his cousin tested for sickle cell at the CNTS in the fall of
2009. He worried because, as he said, "everyone knows that consanguineous
marriages pose the same risk as marrying someone in the ASD," his other
family. Even though people from the Peul ethnic group are sometimes seen
to be more at risk for sickle cell because of popular understandings that Peul
rates of first-cousin marriage surpass those of other groups, Magueye's wife-
to-be did not have the disease, or the trait. He came to believe that her genetic
lot was more than luck (*chance*); he began to see marriage to her as both his
biological destiny and opportunity. Soon afterward, Magueye announced his
wedding to his ASD confidants, specifically, to one of his former loves. Out of
what I took to be one of the most selfless forms of care for him, she took the
lead in planning the wedding ceremony within the ASD.

Magueye, a self-pronounced "healthy sickler," created various relations,
enacting kin ties on multiple registers, and ended up marrying a cousin

from his Peul ethnic group who does not have sickle cell but who nonethe-less shares his "other" blood at the level of the family, as she was the favored wife that his mother had likely chosen for him, a choice that he may have secretly resisted for a time. In forgoing his "selfish" love relationships based on shared understanding and suffering with other HbSS sicklers, Magueye was nonetheless able to maintain the biosocial future of the ASD, his heritage with other sicklers who share his diseased blood, in a biosocial nexus that medical anthropologists have called a "kinship of affliction" (Health, Rapp, and Taussig 2004, 204; Rapp 1999, 277), which for Magueye was always and equally a kinship of affection.

In Senegal, as elsewhere, biological kinship remains an impressive force that continues to shape people's options for the future. The thought of his family's reprisals if he should brazenly marry a sickler, that is, enact a clear social and biological reproduction of his own condition, muted Magueye's initial hopefulness with Safietou that he might one day have had a "normal" child with HbSS disease. In fact he knows it is "not normal" to even con-sider it. He and his cousin are now expecting a child, who will not have his disease. In conversations with other sicklers I met in Senegal, the domain of marriage is where the level of health and the new norms sicklers acquire through informal care strategies collide with the limits imposed by the ge-netic rules and societal taboos related to passing on their disorder. Magueye could not "just up and marry whomever he wants." Instead, he created other options for eventually bettering the plight of people with the disease. These ranged from bringing intimacy into public discourse on sicklers' well-being as a human need that they should claim for themselves, to trying to create a formal mechanism that would allow people to economically share and sup-port life projects, as well as acute economic or health crises, through literal and figurative micro-credits of accumulation and exchange of shared senti-ments within *mutuelles* of health.

As we will see in the following chapter, other sicklers also relied on expan-sive forms of economy and kinship to manage health and to negotiate bodily norms and health thresholds. Here, familial and biosocial networks overlap with the informal sector of healing as concerns other forms of life, specifically, of therapeutic plants.

CHAPTER THREE

The Biosocial Politics of Plants and People

The Dakar neighborhood of *Fas*, named after Fez in Morocco, is just minutes from the city center where wide avenues and multistory buildings dominate. Arriving in Fas, however, is a quick reminder of how Dakar's city planning, initially organized for the French colonial administration, peters out when one leaves the urban center and the adjoining area of *le plateau*. The *plateau* was the central hub of French West Africa's colonial and economic administration, and has since retained government buildings, as well as banks, international hotels, and major hospitals. *Ville*, as locals call it, still stands in stark contrast to many parts of working-class neighborhoods (*quartiers populaires*), like Fas, as well as those surrounding it, *Fann-Hock, Gueule Tapée* and the *Medina*, where the immediate terrain resembles more rural parts of the country. In these dispersing sectors of Dakar, sand paths serve as both street and sidewalk. They are flanked with cinderblock structures that seemed to appear overnight, suddenly filling voids in the landscape. Thrusts of busyness often animate open storefronts whose densely packed insides seem to uphold their makeshift supports. Throughout these neighborhoods, canteens and commerce stands offer foodstuffs, beauty products, electronics, and fabrics from locales as far away as Cincinnati and Dubai.

In Fann-Hock, amid a row of houses with only the bottom halves painted, an indiscrete "clinic" is marked by a sprawl of bundled botanicals left to dry in the heat. The healer inside welcomes patients one by one as they queue up in his doorway. His sons and nephews who staff the clinic are dressed in what were once white lab coats. A few of the men hunch over to tend to the medicinal plants strewn out over the sidewalk.

Dakar's jumble of vital expansion and dense accessibility still validates French ethnologist Georges Balandier's observation, more than fifty years prior, that "In its physical aspect as in its human aspect, the city is seeking its form in confusion" (1966, 176). This mix of form, colonial legacy, urbanism, therapeutic botanicals, and constant shuffle of old and new is "confusion" in its literal sense, an intimate intermingling in which the distinction of elements is lost by fusion.[1] In this configuration we see a slightly varied continuation on the theme developed in the previous chapter: across the physical landscape, people enact therapeutic networks that are sustained through their desires for economic and biological normalcy and stability. In this chapter I present an additional element of the therapeutic economies that people forge, namely a specific aspect of Senegal's pharmacopoeia used to treat sickle cell, the medicinal plant *Fagara xanthoxyloïdes*.

In many instances people with sickle cell understand this plant to be a specific, localized medicinal form of life as well as an economic good. Whether they are patients, healers, or doctors, people often solidify the therapeutic powers of fagara through human relations of care, which they frequently described and enacted through linkages of kin. Their intersubjective supports are key to the functioning of the informal economy that allows fagara to circulate and bolster sickle cell health. Rooted in direct interpersonal relations, people's propensity to take fagara also extends beyond themselves. This botanical is local, but it does not stay put. Its back and forth across lines denominated as "traditional" and "modern," its sale, its gifting, its promise in the global South as a therapy to space sickle cell crises, and (later) in France as a powerful alkaloid with wider potential, allow it to override boundaries that demarcate domains that may be seen as conceptually separate, such as a genetics lab and a traditional healing clinic. Fagara is not, however, a widely welcomed, uncontested object in all settings, at all times, as we will see in the later part of this chapter. In both its contestation and its circulation, it is a relational node in a health market that opens onto larger societal trends of healing, scientific authority, and global standing.

It bears stating that the terrain of Dakar itself, its "elements," both human and physical, undermines any attempt to cast the city as a traditional outpost of Africa that is now simply checked with aspects of modernity. Dakar—the place and the people—repeatedly "dazzled" Balandier in its refusal of nostalgia, so much so that he had to remind himself that "there is no point indulging in regrets" (1966, 11, 177–78). Clearly the mix of cultural forms and practices that bond in the relational oneness that I describe here is not entirely new. What is novel in my articulation is that the biosocial life of fagara operates within therapeutic economies structured through kin supports within a larger global-local context of medical scarcity and North-South health priorities for Africa that traditionally have not included sickle cell anemia. Because of this, people invest their hopes in fagara, making it, like the "mild" Senegalese form of the disease, an object that is threaded through with discourses of success. This happens as people make do with this therapy, this exigency of life on the ground. Their aspirations for health are entangled with their hope that fagara will alleviate sickling symptoms, that it will produce a biochemical—even genetic—change. Therefore, for some, fagara may be the aspect of life that actually *makes* sickle cell mild in the first place.

In *Pouvoir et Maladie en Afrique*, Didier Fassin noted the internal accessibility of Senegal's urban terrain for people constructing healing itineraries. Through ethnography conducted with several Senegalese research assistants from various ethnic groups, he also illustrated how healers with different cultural heritages depended on social relationships to establish reputations of success. They did this by drawing from domains that could not ever adequately be pegged as strictly "traditional," since they worked with and within formal political structures and exchanged freely with biomedicine, often even comparing notes with the physician-anthropologist Fassin himself. Within this medically pluralistic terrain, people afflicted with illness set out on pathways to health that were not necessarily premeditated or systematic, but instead took direction from both "structural" and "conjunctural" causes and events that lead them to multiple sites (Fassin 1992, 118). In quite similar relational contexts of healing that I describe here, structural issues that come into play often have to do with a person's life chances, their perceived role in society, their social expectations about marriage and their anxieties about parenting, while the conjunctural may be more acute. Issues such as finishing school with hopes to find work, locating treatments to do so, hearing from a colleague in biomedicine about a renowned healer, ending a stressful relationship, or falling in love with someone who offers care can also place the patient on the course to heal, even if derailment sometimes awaits. For their part, various practitioners offer care strategies that draw from, reiterate, and complement those of other professions who possess genealogies of knowledge that are different from their own. Here, multiple objects of healing (plants, persons, and family) enter into relations of care where, as in the previous chapter, subject and object boundaries also partially dissolve.

As these boundaries fade, it quickly becomes apparent that monocausal explanations for why Senegalese sicklers fair well with this otherwise debilitating disease fall short of the mark. Only by giving attention to people's networks of care and kin, coupled with the healing practices that these relations engender, can we further observe how the experience of mild sickle cell in Senegal tallies. In this chapter I trace these relations through people's various interests in fagara within Dakar's health sectors, both formal and informal, before following the plant to Paris, France, to Cotonou, Benin, to Reims, Champagne-Ardenne, and finally back to Senegal. Despite the attention that many people give to fagara, it is important to understand that its effectiveness is contingent upon social networks that render the knowledge and care derived from this traditional plant variable. This both explains why fagara is seen to "work" in Senegal, while it also accounts for the range of less successful attempts to have the plant accepted and embraced in other parts of West Africa and beyond.

■ **Palliatives for Affective Sickle Cell Pain**

On the day I set out on a lead from a well-known healer to find two of his patients with "sickle cell so mild," in his words, that "it might be cured by now," Dakar was in the path of a Harmattan haze. Wind gusts blurred the air with red-brown granules from the powdery dirt street that lifted to blot out the sky. The usually busy Fas roads were almost empty.

When I discovered the small *cité* of apartments where the patients, who were sisters, lived, I made my way through the earth-colored brick units but got lost in the uniformity of the buildings, since no address numbers made it to the completed housing project. As in many areas, the people living there of course knew their street names and bloc numbers, an indication that intimacy with the locale was the only antidote to an outward sense of confusion. At this point I hardly knew where I was, so I phoned the older of the two women, whom I will call Coumba, on her cell phone. She came down the stairs, still on the line, allowing me to navigate to her voice until we clutched hands in the dark stairwell. She greeted me with laughter, locking my arm in hers, admonishing me that I was "crazy to be out in the wind" as she welcomed me inside.

When we first met in December of 2000, Coumba Mbodj was a thirty-nine-year-old recent divorcée who was looking to start her own textile or clothing business, either by traveling to buy merchandise for the store she imagined, or by working with a tailor to execute designs she had long collected from magazines. As we visited in her apartment we mostly discussed her and her younger sister Soxna's (pronounced Soh´na) sickle cell, but part of Coumba's disease narrative was that she wanted to change careers. Trained in nursing, she had difficulty securing a post in Dakar, as many state jobs required that people relocate to rural areas. But, more importantly, I would learn, she had also become disaffected with biomedicine to some degree, since, in her experience, sickle cell benefited more from certain "traditional" medicines (*la médecine traditionnelle*). Now, seeing all of the small business throughout her neighborhood, Coumba imagined that she could be much more successful in "fashion" or in "business" more generally than in biomedicine. Somehow the prospect of launching her own venture seemed more gratifying than nursing, despite the fact that she was a life-long patient.

After spending the afternoon hearing about what turned out to be the Mbodj women's vivid testimonial of how the botanical *Fagara xanthoxyloïdes* has kept them well, Coumba and her sister slowly drove me home through the sandy fog in their rickety, now unmarked, Peugeot. In the car they began recounting their first forays into selling goods at a small canteen, and then at the boutique of a friend. The gritty air weighing on the city distracted me, but I soon noticed the sisters speaking louder, perhaps afraid that I was not listening, so I leaned forward through the front seats, where we all conversed now, three heads in a row.

The Mbodj sisters were of Peul origin, an ethnicity that many people in Senegal associate with light skin tones when it comes to women—tones that are the envy of many feminine beauty pursuits. In the half-truth of jokes, men often proposed marriage upon first meeting them. In my mind it was the marker of "light skin" (*xés*) that was the initial reason that Coumba began to say that *we* could be related, as our three faces with similar complexions aligned in the car. This happened in a conversation that was initially about her age. She knew she looked much younger than someone approaching forty, who might have children, and, as is customary, begin to put on weight. "It's because of the disease. You can never gain weight with sickle cell," she complained.[2] Soxna, who was then thirty-three, inquired about my age. Since I was younger than both, they pronounced me their "*caat*" (cadet), the last in the family, "long lost," separated by the vast ocean and only to be reunited by the chance of my interest in their blood disorder. They then joked that my homecoming via their disease was "destiny" and that the instant we recognized each other as kin, in the car just now, marked the inaugural moment of the newness of our old connection.

Various Peul, or sometimes friends from the Toucouleur ethnic group, would look for family resemblances in my face. Still other Senegalese, of various identities, upon hearing my last name would immediately understand "Coulibaly," a Bambara name, and declare me a lost "Senegalese." Other iterations of making me "kin" or of "relating" me to them were common. What was initially interesting about this perception of closeness was that this relatedness often eluded the confines of what Americans understand as race. Even if people could imagine me to be family, they could not see me as "black" (*nit ku ñuul*), which is how they saw themselves. Instead, they insisted that I was a "*tubaab*" (white-European, or foreign) despite my attempts to translate my African-American identity for them. Something else was going on for the Mbodj sisters, however. Coumba and Soxna had a precedent of biosocially attaching people as kin—a marker that the other person somehow fit within the intimate cosmology of their illness identity.

The man who had put me in touch with the Mbodj women, a healer named Gaoussou Sambou, practices a form of healing that relies on prayers, incantations to his Diola ancestors, and the dispensation of dried botanicals. The plant concoction that he has prescribed for Coumba and Soxna since 1992 largely consists of fagara. As the two sisters experienced fewer and fewer crises, they attributed their newfound health not only to fagara but to the care afforded them by the healer himself whom they began to refer to as their "husband." Coumba and Soxna met Sambou when they were in their twenties. They have continued under his care into their thirties and now into their forties when women in Senegal are assumed to be married with children. Marriage hasn't worked out for them, however, and Sambou at some point, which neither woman could recall exactly, began to endearingly refer to them as two of his "wives." Coumba smiled as she told me: "Since no one has married us, we don't have husbands, he has married us." This kin reference that both of the Mbodj women and Sambou make is spoken of with lightness and affection. This does not mean, however, that it is somehow actually superficial. They never cast it off at the end of the would-be joke, or attempted to return to a serious or "real" account of causality for their health stripped of this relationship. There is a deep trust that the sisters confide in their healer to keep them well, even in their absences from his clinic when they are "crisis-free."

Both sisters recounted that Sambou's medicines spaced their crises so that they rarely live with sickle cell pain. Yet, other issues emerged that troubled them daily. These centered on their relationships, or, finding a husband to care for them affectionately—and economically. Soxna told me flatly, "The disease makes for an expensive wife." She was in an on-and-off-relationship with a previously married man who was now divorced with several children. Her relationship problems stemmed from the fact that she perceived him to have difficulty making ends meet in his first household, and from the fact that he refused to get tested for sickle cell. For him, the idea of getting tested was culturally jarring. Soxna channeled his attitude saying, "*affair u tubaab la*" (That is something Whites do, not us). She eventually broke up with him shortly after she inadvertently discovered that he "too had sickle cell," when she saw a commonly used anti-sickling pharmaceutical on his nightstand. I later learned that he had sickle cell trait, which he thought made him "tired," but for Soxna this confirmed her fears about his inability to take care of her economically and provide for her health, without "giving her more stress," all of which, for her, went hand and hand.

Coumba ended up marrying "*un Français*," who, it was implied, was not black. As she later she told me, sickle cell "mostly affects Africans, so at least we did not have to worry about passing on the disease to kids, if we had any." She was operating with other assumptions as well, that she would be his only wife, which, in her mind assured her that she would have his undivided attention and care. When she found out that he had a "younger Senegalese woman" in his life, Coumba joked that "he wanted polygamy" and that her conjectures about the cultural location of this tendency were wrong. More importantly, she felt betrayed. At the time that she found out about his infidelity she was also diagnosed with ovarian cysts, which were affecting her sexuality and her confidence in her newfound health. She tried to make the marriage work for a time, but eventually she and her husband separated, and as she sought treatments for her cysts she began to have feelings for her gynecologist. This man had a "first wife," but Coumba knew this before her affection began. Most importantly for her, he listened and seemed to understand her problems. She referred to him as her "friend," and eventually, as family. As they became involved, she initially called him "*ton ton*," an affectionate term for *uncle* that can also signify closeness and simultaneous respect between younger Senegalese women and older Senegalese men. They mutually confided in each other on the phone daily for what would become years. He helped her financially and encouraged her to take care of herself. In early 2007 they began to talk of marriage, but his wife protested. Coumba imagined the woman's complaints about the "cost" of her as a potential co-wife, which a state doctor might not be able to "comfortably afford." It was later that spring that Coumba had the first sickle cell pain crisis that she had had in years. She laughed at herself, stoically downplaying her pain to visit with me when I found her curled up in bed with her cell phone. She finally got through the crisis with fagara, folic acid, and a brief hospitalization.

For the Mbodj women the constitutive order of biology, kinship, and economy *partially* renders sickle cell mild by enlarging relations of care where palliatives of love, surveillance, and health goods, such as fagara, are mediated through different aspects of life's problems. Yet there are clearly elements of their lives around questions of marriage and reproductive normalcy that they continue to experience, in pain. In this case, their actual sickle crises have become less the issue over the years, in part because of fagara and because of their affective ties with Sambou, even if their larger troubles of finding a caring spouse who could assume their "cost" has derailed their well-being in different ways.

Other women I met in Senegal were accused of being "prescription wives" (*jaabar u ordonnance*). This was not in the generous sense of a wife who fills the script of "just what the doctor ordered." To the contrary, a *jaabar u ordonnance* is a wife who, alone, or through the sick children she bears, is perceived as requiring her husband to spend a fortune at the pharmacy. Usually co-wives or mothers-in-law were the ones to level these accusations. They did so when they feared that the wives with sickle cell (or trait) in question would drain their husband's resources, to which, of course, the co-wives or mothers-in-law making the plaint were simultaneously staking claim.

Given this, for Sambou to include the Mbodj women in his family through idioms of kinship (specifically about marriage) touched Coumba and Soxna in a way that went beyond the usual joke of making them his wives because of their light skin. It is in this context that fagara cannot be emptied of a special human significance: that it comes from plants that pass through Sambou's hands. Although different in the details, this broader ethic of care that permits the Mbodj women their health is not unlike the therapeutic economies from which Magueye Ndiaye or Rokhoya Sylla extracted care and a sense of normalcy in the previous chapter. What sets the Mbodj women apart, however, is that their fears of rejection and economic tensions came to define their would-be love relationships more readily, in the end, than the competing assurances of new social safety nets (however imperfect) offered them by their lovers. Yet they still shared broadly conceived notions of kinship that were articulated through their strategies for managing their disease. For the Mbodj women, these ties were not only about human attachments. That is, they explicitly referenced the chemical effects of fagara as part of their biosocial nexus of health causality that solidified other non-birth and non-traditional notions of family kinships of care with Gaoussou Sambou. Their ability to affectively bond with their healer through medicinal plants has provided Coumba and Soxna with a therapy that, as they recounted, "changed" their sickle cell hemoglobin count, lowering it, while raising their protective fetal hemoglobin.

■ Seeking Better Health

On the day I interviewed the Mbodj women for the first time, they talked about what they considered to be a newfound experience of living with sickle cell. Over dark hibiscus tea they put their past together for me, each adding her own details to tell the same story about living life "tired" before their diagnoses, and then living life "frustrated" and in pain before they met Sambou and started on fagara.

Soxna's disease was much more bothersome in childhood, provoking many hospital visits and a sickle cell diagnosis when she was twenty-two, several years before her older sister's. She had been (correctly) first diagnosed with rheumatism at fifteen, which for years was taken to be the sole problem (as the symptoms are similar). The doctors she saw finally clarified that she also had sickle cell when she suffered several serial crises. Her primary doctor then prescribed a medication called *hydergine*, which is an ergoloid mesylate derived from rye that was once a given for sickle cell in the 1970s, but has since proven to be ineffective. It is now sometimes given to patients with Alzheimer's or simply taken as a "smart drug" in the United States. Hydergine's uselessness for sickling was not new medical news when I arrived in Senegal, since researchers began to denounce prescribing it for the disease almost twenty years prior (Roth et al. 1978). Dr. Diagne, at Albert Royer, and Dr. Saliou Diop and Dr. Awa Touré, at the CNTS, were constantly trying to correct their colleagues' errors when patients would come in with the expensive packages wanting refills.[3] Soxna smiled regrettably and said that at least her family "didn't waste *as* much money as other sicklers on the useless medications," since her father's insurance covered most costs because he was a state employee who had been relocated to a rural zone far from Dakar.

Coumba's story about how her disease revealed itself was steeped in references to biomedicine on multiple levels. After both women were diagnosed, they were referred to Dr. Mamoudou Thiam, one of the most familiar and visible faces of biomedical sickle cell treatments at the CNTS. Dr. Thiam, who since 2000 has served as the dean of the University of Dakar's Faculty of Medicine, prescribed not only hydergine, which both women took for several years, but also *pentoxifylline*, which is still prescribed as an anti-sickling agent and to help increase the fluidity of viscous blood. The Mbodj sisters came to consider both not only as expensive but mostly futile. Most people with the disease in Senegal cannot afford to take these medications regularly, nor do CHU sickle cell specialists usually write scripts for them.

During our conversations, Coumba recounted feeling frustrated at the time of her diagnosis, when she was twenty-eight years old. As she spoke, she became angry all over again: "the pharmaceuticals did nothing!" She remembers always having been "weak." Perhaps because of this, she felt nursing was her calling. At one point during her schooling, she began to neglect her health in the usual way that a student might. She never slept enough, skipped meals, and was often overwhelmed by "stress." One day she fainted in the shower. Her mother, who had come to Dakar to assist her daughters with everyday care, and to help Coumba manage her anxieties about school, rushed her to the hospital. That is when they discovered that Coumba also had sickle cell. Soxna told me that she and her sister had been close friends (*ay xarit lanu*). They each understood the other's periodic pains in ways that their other siblings could not. "Perhaps," Coumba told me, "we knew deep down that we both had this thing."

For this sister pair, as with many living with sickle cell disease in Dakar, relatively late diagnoses did not hinder them from recounting their lives through the lens of sickle cell in an effort to make sense of the pain and fatigue that was only later given a name. They told of their periodic aching joints and limbs as children and linked these to their exquisite sensitivity to heat, cold, and temperature changes, such as the subtle shifts in humidity and barometric pressure before it rains. There is a specific term for this weather pattern before the rain in Wolof, which is the state of *xiin* (prounounced *heen*). Other sicklers I encountered mentioned *xiin* as a precipitating factor for sickle cell crises too. On some such occasions, but not all, Coumba and Soxna recounted being bedridden for two to three days at a time. Rheumatism was thought to be the culprit in both of their cases (even though only Soxna was truly affected by it), and ineffective aspirin was given to calm it. Soxna eventually dropped out of school because she was sick too often.

Shortly after her own diagnosis, Coumba feared that her health was deteriorating, and wondered if, like her sister, she would not be able to pursue a career. She began to have sickle cell crises at least twice a month and was desperate for a treatment that worked. She learned about Gaoussou Sambou through an intern practicing at the CNTS who told her that there was a researcher at the *Institut fondamental de l'Afrique noire* who might be able to do something for her. Coumba told me that "as a nursing student," she had been skeptical of "black people's medicine" because traditional healers never measured their doses. She was particularly attentive to sanitation and sterility, and worried that the administration of plants might not always be conducted in the aseptic manner she personally required as a function of her own training. She admitted that she was apprehensive, but went to consult Sambou because a doctor of "modern" medicine had referred her, reiterating;

> If I hadn't taken Sambou's medicines I myself would not have been able to go into nursing. I would not have been able to finish school. Just the pace of our course of study is too much, working in the clinic in the mornings, taking classes in the evenings, not much time in between. . . . If I had been taking modern medicine alone, I would not have been able to keep up. I would have constantly been sick. I know it . . . for sure. I would not have ever obtained my degree.

According to Coumba, the efficacy of the "traditional" treatment permitted her to pursue her career. For her, the informal health sector facilitated her being trained to work in the formal.

The Mbodj sisters still occasionally present themselves for check-ups at the CNTS, but because they feel relatively healthy—Coumba attests that she can now go for years without having a crisis—they no longer schedule quarterly check-ups, as is indicated. At the time of our first interview, both women felt healthy and had stopped taking medications for a while. Whether it was biomedicine or "traditional" medicine, the Mbodj women rarely took palliatives on a regular basis. Their thinking was that "when feeling weak," then they would fortify their bodies. Otherwise, they would try to live "normally," at least with regard to their physical sickle cell pain.

■ The Easy Sale of "New" Cells, Explanations of Better Health

On separate occasions Coumba and Soxna both told me that the first hemoglobin electrophoreses they had done, after starting on Sambou's plants, revealed a remarkable change. Coumba explained that after taking Sambou's medications her electrophoresis showed a "new protective cell, the 'F' cell," referring to fetal hemoglobin. I asked her to be more precise: had she seen this before she began her plant regimen? "No. This F cell appeared only afterwards." When she asked her doctor what this new cell type signified, Coumba recounted, "he said that 'F' is a protective cell, and that when I have an increase in 'F,' my 'S' level goes down." Soxna spoke of a similar change. The first time the sisters saw an electrophoresis where their fetal hemoglobin levels were measured coincided with other life events and the experience of feeling healthier, which they attributed to Gaoussou Sambou's plants. Both sisters logically associated this "new protective F cell" with Sambou's fagara regimen.

Since there have been no conclusive in vivo studies concerning the positive effects of fagara on sickle hemoglobin, fetal hemoglobin, general anemia, and patients' overall health, it is impossible to say for sure that fagara, alone or in conjunction with other plants, raised the Mbodj sisters' fetal hemoglobin levels.[4] A few years after the Mbodj sisters learned about the importance of "the F cell," a group of researchers in Reims, Champagne-Ardenne, France, who were interested in using this plant for treating leukemia, found, quite by accident, that fagara acted to induce expression of the gamma globin gene responsible for fetal hemoglobin production (Dupont et al. 2005).[5] Most often, however, increased fetal hemoglobin and its associative "mild" disease in Senegalese patients is attributed to genetics alone.

If indeed Senegalese sicklers, like Coumba and Soxna Mbodj, had a higher level of HbF, it could be hypothesized that if fagara use is as widespread as it appears to be, then a population-level effect signaling a milder disease may be at work. Researchers in the United States, France, and Senegal have attempted to document the causal relationship of the Senegalese haplotype to this mild form of sickle cell. Most often they found statistical "associations" for only a small percentage of the overall variation in HbF levels linked to the Senegalese and other major haplotypes (for a review see Chang et al. 1997; cf Lettre et al. 2008). Moreover, they have discovered a multitude of other genetic effects, spanning at least four distant chromosomes (two, six, eleven, and the X chromosome) that might contain genes that modify high levels of fetal hemoglobin in patients with sickle cell disease for diverse, albeit mostly unknown, reasons. All of these studies have shown that the story of fetal hemoglobin persistence in these patients is, to use an overly relied upon term, complex. Additionally, researchers who specialize in the molecular bases of sickle cell phenotypic variability have modestly claimed to only be able to account for a fraction of all variation in fetal hemoglobin production observed clinically (Lettre et al. 2008). The source of other causes is not clear. What, if anything, might the widespread use of fagara among sicklers have to do with this? What if anything, might the human relations that push fagara through informal healing circuits that socially function to uphold the formal health sector have to do with claims of mild disease in Senegal more broadly?

The remainder of this chapter details both human and nonhuman relations, concerning fagara, while making the case that the circulation of this aspect of Senegalese pharmacopoeia constitutes an important element of the informal health economic structure, which is also foundationally part of the formal. On a broader register, the plant itself is a node in the social life of knowledge in Dakar where science, medicine, well-being, and global standing meet. Fagara, as a healing product, in some instances, and a scientific object, in others, links actors in research domains that are nominally designated as traditional, biomedical, pharmaceutical, genetic, and clinical. The plant, and more recently in France, one of its alkaloids, circulates in the hands of healers, doctors, patients, and geneticists. I began this story with the Mbodj sisters to illustrate the human relational nexus of care where Gaoussou Sambou's fagara mixture enters into people's lives and subjective health. Sambou, a university botanist, a practicing Muslim, an ethnically self-identified Diola who claims ancestral legitimacy for his practice, not only cares for patients, but he also works with European university professors involved with Catholic Mission health posts and consults for an NGO concerned with health, economic development, and the environment.[6] All of these actors have also implicated themselves in making fagara more pervasive. Additionally, certain biomedical practitioners in Dakar have tried to legitimate fagara, and have also backed away from it, largely due to social perceptions, and relations with their French colleagues who refuse to detach fagara from its relationship to a Beninois healer who began claiming in the year 2000 that his plant mixture, which contained fagara, "cures" sickle cell. Within these many circuits, the fagara plant captures anxieties and longstanding fears about African Traditional Medicine, charlatanism, and North-South jostles for power over the truth of what might constitute a sickle cell cure. All of this begs the question: does a "proper" cure simply entail the eradication of the disease through gene therapy and bone marrow transplants? Or, might the elimination of symptoms, perhaps with fagara, also count as a legitimate remedy?

The controversy over the Beninois' "miracle cure" drew attention from patients and doctors in several French-speaking African countries in the early 2000s. Unequivocal condemnation from many actors in France made several Dakar specialists, who were open to studying fagara, ever more cautious. For several French sickle cell research-physicians, who have some influence over researchers who work on the disease in Senegal, this miracle cure was seen and constructed as a threat to "true" sickle cell medicine. The critics' most trenchant argument was that this botanical composition had never undergone proper clinical trials. They also charged that those who peddled it offered false hope to vulnerable patients who might abandon their current biomedical care. This was the attitude that several of my Paris-based, French researcher-informants held and continue to hold.

As I discuss further on, there is one self-described "rebel" French scientist who has taken an interest in studying an aspect of fagara, though not the whole composition of the said "cure," and not even the whole plant, in a lab setting in 2008 and 2009. He delegated this project to his former student Dr. Lydie Da Costa of Robert Debré Hospital in Paris. In 2009, when I visited her lab, Da Costa seemed interested in resolving the question of fagara's efficacy and told me that, "If the preliminary results look promising in vitro, then the next step would be to plan patient trials using a purified molecule"—or a single alkaloid extract of the plant's roots. That the alkaloid in question could be of use for sickle cell at all was brought to their attention by Dr. Eric Courot, a plant geneticist, who stepped onto the sickle cell scene only a few years after the Beninois miracle cure debacle.

Courot is certain that the fagara botanical, which many see as pervasive, accessible, and already cheaply available in its crude form in Senegal, cannot be sustained for much longer without a targeted environmental intervention.[7] With this pressure in mind, he is attempting to prove fagara's efficacy in order to valorize it and, he hopes, to protect it. He is doing this on a shoestring budget, however, since his current funding is solely specified to figure out how to make grapevines (*le vigne*) resistant to damaging molds for the champagne industry. Meanwhile, through a knowledge-transfer of broad regenerative technologies, he pursues one of his "real passions," which is to teach researchers in Senegal how to grow fagara in vitro through the generation of the plant's stem cells with help from the French government *coopération* in Senegal. Courot's involvement in attempting to validate fagara from afar, include perfecting cell-immortalization methods in his Reims, Champagne-Ardenne laboratory. For him, "Fagara may be ameliorating sickle cell lives, but in the process its own life has become ecologically endangered." The Senegalese state newspaper publicized this concern after the country's first international meeting on sickle cell, where Courot presented his work (Sané 2006). Since 2006, Courot has begun building ties with University of Dakar researchers as well as with local NGOs concerned with valorizing plant therapies. At least one of them, *ENDA santé*, consults herbalist healers, such as Gaoussou Sambou.

■ **Terrains of Knowledge**

Today sickle cell patients in several areas of West Africa beyond Senegal, including Nigeria and Benin, are told by healers, often times by local journalists, and, in some cases, by their exasperated biomedical practitioners that the roots of *Fagara xanthoxyloïdes* will make their sickle cell pain less frequent. I first learned of this botanical on my initial trip to Senegal in 1998, from the very first person with the disease I encountered when I spent several days in the small village of Nianing, near the better-known fishing village of Mbour. The owner of my hostel put me in touch with a local nurse who manned one of the only "health huts" (*cases de santé*) in the area. The nurse, whom I will call Fadel, was in his late thirties. Fadel suffered from polio as a child and now walked with a limp due to a visibly atrophied leg. He was eager to share with me the irregular nature of emergency health posts, the lack of medical staff in the peripheral regions of the country, and his general knowledge about patients "with everything," including sickle cell. He worried that his ability to treat the disease was limited, but, "like everyone," he told me, he prescribed *hydergine* and folic acid. Throughout our conversation he interrupted himself to say that he wanted to introduce me to a local woman with sickle cell. She was in her mid-fifties and (other than high blood pressure and fatigue) she was healthy. He finally stretched up to close the open metal sheet of a window, locked up, and we set off to see her.

We took a hot dirt path to a new section of Nianing that was less inhabited with people but was dense with mango trees and bougainvillea. The woman, Mrs. Cissé, welcomed us in. We all exchanged greetings for a few minutes, during which Fadel asked if she would be willing talk to me about her disease. The interest in someone interested in her disorder was immediate. He then left us alone, explaining that he had to get back to the post. As we visited for the rest of the afternoon, she told me that sicklers were "unlucky" in life, but that in Senegal they were also "blessed." She then reached into an armoire, pulled out an aged black suitcase and handed me a bundle of news clippings with browned edges. Among them was a special edition of the magazine *Famille et Développement* on sickle cell disease in Africa and the use of the *Fagara xanthoxyloïdes* root to stave off symptoms. We looked at the journalistic photos of the plant next to images of bundled, light-colored sticks. I would later come to recognize the tightly bound twigs as medicinal roots packaged for sale in many market places. We continued to talk as we went through the papers. Her message was clear: "there are powerful plants, including this one in, Senegal.

Doctors in Dakar need to be researching these." She then mentioned that she knew of one "*tradi-practitioner*" in Dakar who prescribed the plant in the pictures. She had seen him on television but could not recall his name. She was referencing the Mbodj women's healer-husband, Gaoussou Sambou.

Doctors in Dakar who would become my informants as of 1999 also knew of Gaoussou Sambou, who had indeed "appeared on television," and who, more impressively for them, had "scientific bearings"(*une notion de la science*). Although physician-researchers at both Albert Royer, such as Dr. Diagne, and others at the CNTS adult care center, such as Dr. Touré and Dr. Thiam, knew of Sambou (and in the case of the latter two, have recommended fagara to patients themselves), there have never been collaborative efforts between these actors to research fagara's action on sickling. Instead, university pharmacy and clinical researchers have performed two small fagara studies, while the televised healer, who also held a University of Dakar post in botany before his retirement in 2000, conducts his own observational studies on people who take his plants. Thus, said "healers," and biomedical sickle cell specialists in Dakar might occupy the traditionally charged roles of "modern" versus "*tradi-practitioners*" but, as I stated earlier, this is mostly in name—a dynamic of integral overlap that others have pointed out for realms of healing, in practice and also in concept (Fassin 1992; Langwick 2008, 429; Wedland 2010, 37; Tonda 2001). A need to curb this over zealous division of epistemologies has also been noted within broader movements of economic development (Diouf 2000; Konaté 2008; Tilley 2011). In Senegal, healers' and doctors' pragmatic vernacular sciences often cross over when it comes to fagara but also when it comes to genetic tests. In other words, practitioners possess additive, rather than subtractive, notions about eradicating suffering. (Patients, as we have seen, also tried to amass multiple approaches, rather than delineating one as necessarily separate from another.) Always donning a doctor's white coat, Gaoussou Sambou habitually asked his sickle cell patients for their electrophoresis results. He was looking for the hemoglobin S plot curve in order to confirm the disease. The electrophoresis alone was not a requirement for treatment, but it helped reassure him about what he was treating. Nonetheless, he would also find himself diagnosing the disease based on a person's jaundiced eyes, an infant's swollen hands and feet, or a client's narrative of serial pain in their joints. Similarly, physician-researchers (who of course also wore white coats) in the university hospital system conceived of sickle cell as a genetic red blood disorder and also often spoke of fagara to patients, especially professionals at the CNTS.

Dr. Diagne, the most ambivalent of my scientific informants on matters of fagara for sickle cell care, who also became a friend, was appointed to be the country's Ministry of Health national spokesperson for the disease in 2007. In 2009, he would tell the state-run *Soleil* newspaper, for the first time publicly, that fagara "offered hope" due to several promising preliminary observations, all of which seemed to point in the same positive direction (Sane and Kaly

2009). Despite the general sentiment I witnessed among biomedical practitioners in Dakar that "there must be something to fagara," which were the words that Diagne used with me on several occasions during my fieldwork in his clinical practice, there was never any concerted effort within Senegal to do "something" about this plant for formal sickle cell research. Dr. Diagne, Gaoussou Sambou, Dr. Saliou Diop, Dr. Awa Touré, and Dr. Mamadou Thiam, some of my principal informants within the realm of sickle cell care broadly, worked largely alone at their respective sites. For instance, Diagne has never met Sambou, while exchanges between the CNTS adult care center team and Albert Royer Children's hospital were rare. Nonetheless, fagara itself circulated at each of these three sites, within the city in local market places, and also between patients and healers of all persuasions. Overwhelmingly, patients and families I encountered reported that they had used fagara at some point in their lives, or in the lives of relatives with sickle cell for whom they cared.

I must reiterate that fagara ingestion for sickle cell symptoms constitutes public knowledge. So one wonders how it happened, then, that after the first Dakar-based published study on it (Thiam et al. 1990) there was no sustained public, or private, effort to establish that knowledge more broadly as "scientific" in Senegal. In the larger landscape, fagara is shared between patients as a source of alleviation. Their faith in the plant often borrows from a basic trust and knowledge in the social ties that bind them to the giver or to the healer overseeing their condition. Many patients also incorporated messages from the different healers and caregivers they encountered: they generally distrusted healers who claimed to "cure" the disease, even if some admitted that they stopped listening to critiques of such claims, folded caution away, and, "as believers," hoped for a miracle.

As Coumba's earlier narrative makes apparent, faith in a healer's plant medicine does not necessarily run counter to worrying about how to gauge correct "dosing" when measurements are not clear-cut. This uncertainty among patients about how fagara might enter into a medical logic of precise administration (an attestation to their belief in its potency) mirrors the uneasiness that their doctors sometimes expressed about the lack of quantitatively robust studies on what the plant does in the body and under what conditions. Judging patient testimonies to count for something approaching empirical data, some doctors took people's experiences as evidence of fagara's safety and efficacy. It is not uncommon for biomedical professionals to assure their patients about fagara if those in need voice doubt. It seemed that both patients and physicians accepted, at base, that they did not know exactly how fagara worked. This uncertainty was not about the plant's efficacy, in most cases, but about its actual healing mechanisms. It was also an uncertainty that was not necessarily unsettling.

The obvious question of why more concerted efforts to valorize a potentially promising plant had not taken place among and between patients, healers, and physicians in Dakar plagued me throughout my time in Senegal, especially when patients and medical professionals alike seemed to concede its promise. How can we make sense of the fact that fagara was both visible and invisible, both valorized and scientifically doubted by some, both intimately central to patients' health and, at times, also disparaged by sickle cell specialists in France?

Throughout my time in Senegal I came to wonder if fagara might not be better off maintaining its functional ambiguities, since efforts to dissect it, to "purify" it for modern science (Latour 1993, 30), would inevitably require that it shed its hybrid social ties with sicklers, healers, and certain doctors who rely on its influence to mitigate suffering. At a more general level, within anthropological, political, ecological, and environmental studies circles there has been much anxiety about corporate commercialization of traditional medicines and indigenous knowledge, often referenced as *biopiracy* (Shiva 1999).[8] Yet, what can be said when a plant cannot seem to hold the scientific attention of those who are well placed to validate its properties? Until recently, Senegalese doctors tried, to no avail, to interest researchers in France in fagara.

■ Neoliberalism, Bioprospecting, Bio-outsourcing

In *When Nature Goes Public* anthropologist Cori Hayden argues that with the implementation of the UN Convention on Biological Diversity in 1993, the marketability of plant specimens, in the context of Mexico, has increasingly been linked to botanical research on the part of Northern and Southern university-based scientists who collaborate with market vendors, healers, and other stewards of "indigenous" medicinal knowledge in order to explore drugs derived from plants for the "shared" benefit of all (2003). For Hayden's informants, a clear emphasis is put on local knowledge as "cultural" heritage. In both insidious and genuinely sincere propositions, the researchers that Hayden followed hoped that untapped cures might aid both the pharmaceutical industry and human health globally. They also pitched that valorizing native peoples' knowledge would furthermore bring the labor of the poor into the global market in newly respected ways. In other words, the "inclusive" aspects of neoliberalism might make businessmen and traditional medicine men natural partners in biological diversity.

Deeply suspicious of the win-win situation often presented by her scientific informants, Hayden shows how both peoples and their labor remain vulnerable to exploitation through bioprospecting, but that benefits-sharing arrangements and a neoliberal logic of individual shared responsibility simultaneously allow for common-sense understandings of "public" flows of knowledge. Thus, potential botanical cures are not necessarily "owned" by anyone but rather "belong" to range of actors from peasants to university professors. This set up has immense cultural appeal to global consumers and pharmaceutical players alike.

Perhaps most astutely, Hayden shows that at the center of this "national" valorization process, biological material, in this case plant life, emerges as "a powerful and contested mediator of social *relationships*, broadly conceived" (Hayden, 2003, 22–23). Following from this, what I take from Hayden has less to do with how "participatory" arrangements implicate cultural stewards of knowledge in marketable partnerships, since neoliberalism in Senegal has not yet fully captured something called biodiversity.[9] Rather, as feminist scholars of science practice have shown, certain "biologicals" mediate relationships where references to kinship bonds structure specific social ties, while larger configurations of "inclusion" and "exclusion," or, "legitimate" and "illegitimate" crosses and offspring, mark others (Franklin 2001; Haraway 1997, 52).

When fagara enters into informal economies of health care, it is often because the formal health infrastructure has given sicklers what it can, which is a level of expertise that many adult patients quickly master and then use to treat themselves at home to avoid increasingly costly consultation fees. As I show in the following chapter, the principal pediatric sickle cell specialist in Dakar has forged strong ties with many families who have entrusted their children to his care for years. When they reach adulthood, however, some have difficulty transitioning to the adult center, the CNTS, whose primary order of business is blood transfusion and blood products. The CNTS is also a research center with a high turnover of interns and visitors who often replace the principal sickle cell specialist there when he takes research leaves. Some sicklers, like Magueye Ndiaye, have been able to build relations with their providers at the CNTS, but many who have not may only show up in dire emergencies. Certain more aggressive patients insist on seeing specialists in sickle cell over those in training, whom they deem less competent. Still it is not uncommon that their options are to consult unknowing interns who, not infrequently, know less about their disease than they do.

For certain adult patients, like the Mbodj sisters, as well as several others who belonged to the ASD, biomedical care has been spotty and seemingly futile when, for unknown reasons, they began to repeatedly suffer crises that they could not manage. Many end up in Gaoussou Sambou's care because of this. In these cases, turning to fagara use as an informal medicinal alternative signifies a biosocial relationship between plants and people where economy and kinship make up an "altered grid of relationality" (Franklin 2001, 319). This is to say that, legally, fagara constitutes an illegitimate "cross" with biomedicine, but there are many levels of "inclusion" and "exclusion" that define the oneness of their relation. Within this relation, the kinship ties that the Mbodj women might share with their healer, or, that the healer may draw upon for the future of his family business, are part of a larger epiphenomenon. That is, they are an effect of a structural set up where fagara provides a commonly accessible palliative for many, including biomedical practitioners and those responsible for state health governance, who are "in need" of a sickle cell crisis solution.

Whatever its medical potency might objectively be, patients' and biomedical providers' subjective estimations of fagara's value allow the informal economy of traditional medicine, as concerns this plant, to make sickle cell mild. If people with sickle cell, like Coumba and Soxna, credit fagara for their health, then the very fact that they have at their disposal a palliative that does not detract from the work, time, effort, and energy of their strapped state-hospital providers, is seen as a boon by these same professionals. It is this confluence of factors that we must keep in view when people claim that fagara "works." On a broader register, what we are witnessing is how fagara socially "functions" in an officially *un*official healing economy that nonetheless allows the official health sector to continue with its priorities (cf Langwick 2008).[10] In other words, the general public health infrastructure (peopled with government officials, with whom many sicklers have pleaded to include sickle cell care) structurally outsources aspects of healing to specific *tradi-praticiens* like Sambou, as well as to the forms of plant life upon which they rely.

When I asked Mamadou Seck, the president of Senegal's National Assembly, when he first learned of sickle cell, he told me the story of a family friend with the disease who "thankfully finds relief from local plant called *deni-gi-dëk*." Seck, the third person in power at the level of the Senegalese state, continued, "this plant grows all over the bush of Mbao village where I grew up. Old people lauded its virtues. We weren't sure about all that it did, but we grew up knowing its importance." Seck, who is also the mayor of Mbao, told me that he was personally interested in research that might be able to scientifically validate the plant (which was fagara, to which he referred by its Wolof name). At the time he was not aware of any research on it for sickle cell until I brought it to his attention. He was surely aware, however, that a now seven-year-old bill that might valorize such plants for legal use in health care in Senegal still languishes somewhere in the government bureaucracy to the dismay of healers like Sambou.

■ **Troubled and Illegitimate Relations**

In the summer of 2009, the National Assembly had just began strategizing about sickle cell awareness and the possibility of prenuptial testing after the ASD and their stately Godmother, Senegal's First Lady, made a public plea to Seck and the *deputés* who constitute the Senegalese parliament to do something for those with the disease. Patients within the ASD and beyond have now begun to make it clear to the state that premarital testing is not their main concern. They want free testing at any stage (in fact, the earlier the better). Moreover, they want medical subsidies for sickle cell prescriptions and surveillance testing for the quarterly blood work they are told they need, but that most cannot afford. Seck was straightforward in his assessment when I interviewed him, saying, "At present, state funding has not been organized or budgeted for medical coverage for sickle cell patients." In a follow-up interview on this issue with Abdou Fall, the second vice president of the National Assembly, and former health minister, he told me that the government currently subsidizes antiretrovirals for HIV/AIDS as well as malaria prophylaxis. Funds to do so largely come from WHO and UN development programs that are complemented by bilateral Western-country aid policies, notably from the United States, France, and the European Union (*coopérations*) (WHO 2009a, 40). From Fall's perspective, Senegalese politicians, interested biomedical specialists, and especially patient groups, would have to do much more to make the disease a "public health priority" that might warrant funds for subsidized care.

The prospects are not entirely promising. To date, even the modest budgetary lines granted (on paper) to the ineffectual National Sickle Cell Program since 2005, for education and awareness, have been diverted to other "priorities" that range from election costs to agricultural aid that have little to nothing to do with health. At the time this book goes to press in 2011, the National Program for Sickle Cell remains the only program listed on the Senegalese government's Ministry of Health website that has a live link but opens a blank page, devoid of any information beyond the name of Dr. Ibrahima Diagne, its said "*responsable*" (director). In my conversations with Diagne since the program was created, he routinely lamented that his *plan stratégique* that detailed the minimum needed to get the program underway, dragged somewhere in the ministerial bureaucracy. Thus he too was at a loss as to why the program (and website) remained devoid of objectives, benchmarks, and, crucially, funding lines (Ministère de la Santé 2011).

In this health economic setting, fagara may be collectively valued, but it is anything but officially valorized. This ambiguity must be situated within a history of state engagement and political impasses when it comes to legitimating traditional medicine more generally. In fact, both "traditional" and "modern" medicine have struggled with different legitimacy quests historically: traditional healers have sought official recognition, while biomedical practitioners have fought to convince the populace that modern medicine can address their ills effectively (Fassin and Fassin 1988, 354). This is especially vexing for problems of "spiritual insecurity," liked to issues of hexing or even witchcraft (Ashforth 2005). Yet, it is perhaps equally so for genetic problems like sickle cell, which affect numerous bodily systems, are seemingly invisible to the naked eye, and have no practical cure in the global South, or the North.

Almost yearly the WHO renews its 1978 commitment to promoting and integrating traditional medicine within formal health structures in its publications and reports. Its special focus on Africa in the year 2000 emphasized the problems of poverty, while advancing the idea that traditional therapies were fulfilling the role of essential medicines.[11] Shortly thereafter the WHO published the *Traditional Medicine Strategy 2002–2005*, again urging member-countries to integrate traditional medicinal practices into formal health structures. According to the report, "in Africa, up to 80% of the population uses TM [traditional medicine] to help meet their healthcare needs" (WHO 2002 WHO/EDM/TRM/2002.1, 1). In a *Soleil* interview with the former health ministry bureau chief concerned with traditional medicine, Professor Alioune Aw, a local reporter retraced the history of efforts to legalize and integrate traditional medicine in Senegal, starting in 1985 (Sané 2007). According to Aw, a national forum on traditional medicine that included healers, scientists, and politicians took place in 1998, and set the groundwork for the content of what he thought would become legislation to regulate this sector of the health economy. Regulation was framed simultaneously as a safety issue for patients, as a method for valorizing traditional knowledge, and as a way of controlling and defining effective traditional interventions (Sakho 2008; Sané 2007). The actual legislative document that resulted, however, only achieved the first step in becoming law, meaning that it made it past the bureaucratic process of being "validated" as viable by the ministry. After that, however, it "got caught up in a circuit of visas," the rubber stamps that permit or block passage, for reasons that were beyond Dr. Aw, and that to this day continue to stymie researchers of traditional plants who want to differentiate themselves from "charlatans" (Kaly 2009; Lô 2010; Niang 2009; Sakho 2008; Sané 2007).[12] Because the goals of the bill were principally to better track efficacy, to provide treatments to the majority of the population who could not afford pharmaceuticals, and to police fakes in order to promote "real" *tradi-praticiens*, healers like Gaoussou Sambou and leaders of NGOs involved in plant research (the two most renowned being ENDA and PROMETRA) lauded the idea at the outset (Faye 2004; Niang 2009). Sambou also became politically active within organizations like *la Fédération des tradi-praticiens du Sénégal*, over which he now presides (Sakho 2008). Many healers have complained that the lack of regulation in Senegal has led to an influx of practitioners from other countries, several from Nigeria in particular, who use Senegal's unregulated media apparatus to make wild claims about curing a multitude of diseases that range from diabetes to HIV/AIDS (Faye 2004; Sakho 2008). Healers in Senegal that are classed as working in phytotherapy, or with plants, have been especially vocal in demanding regulation, which would also mean state recognition for them (Lô 2010; Niang 2009).

The would-be law regulating traditional healing, like many laws, seems to have garnered much political attention when it was initially drafted in 2003. Now, however, it simply reanimates healers every August 31, the WHO instituted *African Traditional Medicine Day*. It is not totally clear why Senegalese lawmakers have not passed the "validated" legislation in over seven years. Yet some government officials cite the need for a comprehensive census of healers before the law can go into effect. As of 2005 there exists a partial census of one thousand healers, yet it strangely excludes those practicing in Dakar.[13] Clearly, regulating a *highly heterogeneous* set of practices that are not institutionalized, or organized at the national level, poses a problem at the outset (Fassin and Fassin 1988, 354). The fact that "a formulation of national policies" for traditional medicine comprises part of the WHO goals for "integrating traditional healing into national health systems in Africa" (WHA62.13 2009b, 2) is further complicated by the criteria for classification of healers. Deciding who should and should not be certified and registered could be a political minefield. This is especially true when the criteria used so far to conduct Senegal's partial census were based on a said healer's "consistent presence in one place," "notoriety," "obtained results," and "continued accessibility" to the population in need (Sané 2007). Such loose and subjective standards would do little to separate out those with "real" talents from those with publicity savvy who have been accused of charlatanism. Such sticking points, and state soul-searching, over how to approach the WHO mandates may partially explain the long lag in passing the law.

In a context where traditional medicine is still illegal, yet culturally licit and needed, fagara is referenced by actors who are not explicitly in conversation with each other but who attest to the utility of this plant and its public perception as a palliative for sickle cell anemia. Healers, politicians, and biomedical professionals have placed fagara at the center of an unwittingly complementary relationship for sickle cell care. These actors see fagara as an environmental, even ambient, biological product offered by the landscape. This terrain includes healers' clinics that are accessible in the *quartiers populaires*, as well as more traditional notions of plants growing freely in the "village bush." In this relational topography a certain estrangement of politicians from healers and from biomedical professionals exists at one level, while, at another, patients can successfully establish family ties with healers and, in some cases, rely on their biomedical doctors to recommend fagara to them. Both sets of interactions create a grid of relationality that keeps this botanical mobile as a readily available, unofficial, but culturally legitimate, form of care.

It is within this political health context that Sambou's familial clinic informally provides healing to patients in need. Although sickle cell specialists at public university hospitals, such as Dr. Thiam and Dr. Touré at the CNTS, encourage people to comply with biomedical treatments, such as folic acid, mild painkillers, and, in rare cases, certain anti-sickling agents like *pentoxifylline*, they also believe that fagara "works." Several doctors I interviewed emphasized the point that it works "socioculturally," reiterating that it provides an affordable alternative for the very poor. As we will see further on, in some professionals' minds, however, it also works "chemically" as an anti-sickling agent that may have something to do with fetal hemoglobin production.

■ **Fagara Research: Starts and Stops**

The first studies on fagara's anti-sickling properties were conducted in Nigeria in the 1970s. Since then, studies on the plant's efficacy for sickle cell have been carried out in the Ivory Coast, Burkina Faso, Benin, the United States, and most recently, as of May 2009, in France.[14] Studies of the botanical's action on leukemia have been conducted since the 1970s (Messmer et al. 1972). Most recently, scientists interested in leukemia honed in on the specific genetic action induced by fagara's principal compound, an alkaloid called *fagaronine*. The French researchers who have been interested in fagara for leukemia for nearly a decade recently found evidence that the alkaloid in question incites young red blood cell (erythrocyte) formation as well as fetal hemoglobin synthesis in a leukemia cell line called K562 (Dupont et al. 2005). Diagne and others with whom I worked in Dakar had no knowledge of the leukemia-related research on fagara until I brought it to their attention in 2006. They were well aware, however, of the history of sickle cell clinical medicine—especially with regard to several (now mainstream) pharmaceutical therapies used in the United States and Europe. The general pattern has been that these molecules were first used in leukemia, and then later used in sickle cell treatment because of their ability to induce fetal hemoglobin production.[15] Upon learning that fagara seemed to be following the same pattern, Diagne began to take patients who swore by fagara's effects even more seriously.

Before they learned of the fagara K562 story, researchers in Dakar had only done two early scientific studies on the plant. Both were framed as fagara's "potential to reverse sickling" (Thiam et al. 1990, Wague 1987). The first was a thesis in the Department of Pharmacy in 1987 carried out by a student named Tacko Wague. Wague's thesis was directed by Professor Issa Lô, who headed the *National Pharmacy* under the previous Socialist Party administration, which was still in power at the time of my initial fieldwork. Wague's thesis, under Lô's supervision, had the imprimatur of state approval, yet neither she nor he ever followed up their preliminary experimental results in a larger sample of patients with medical oversight, since, as Wague told me in 2000, they "were pharmacists, not doctors." They also made no distinction between those with sickle cell disease and those with one normal allele, or sickle cell *trait*, a lumping-together that some physician-researchers, especially those in Northern countries, would critique.

For the thesis, Wague and Lô followed thirty sicklers who took regular doses of the plant in a capsule form fabricated by a local pharmacist named Dr. Marie Diallo. After completing her degree, Wague went on to open her own private pharmacy. During our interview in 2000, it was clear that the topic of fagara no longer concerned her and that it was never a subject that she planned to pursue beyond the study to obtain her degree.[16] Diallo also went on to other ventures, namely to start a company that produces natural cosmetics and soaps, which are sold locally at prices that are on par with Western imports. When I interviewed Dr. Lô, he spoke to me of legalities, especially of "medical visas," which had to be obtained to sell pharmaceuticals, as if even this locally grown therapy would have to "emigrate," undergo testing and "purification," and then reenter the local health care market of pharmacy after a double-blind trial in order to be taken seriously and sold legally. None of these steps have yet been taken. Fagara had no "visa" permission in the wider field of sickle cell care, especially in the scientifically-oriented field dominated by French biomedical research scientists, even though many Senegalese within this field have had more than a hunch that the botanical yields therapeutic compounds that aid those with the disease. To prescribe fagara in Dakar hospitals today remains "illegal, strictly speaking," as one CNTS hematologist reminded me in a conversation about how she tells patients that "it works!"

Sickle cell specialists at the national blood transfusion center in Dakar conducted the second formal study on the plant, but in an effort to reestablish usual procedure, they examined its effects in vitro, while acknowledging that Wague and Lô's previous in vivo query produced positive results. This team published their findings in the local medical journal, *Dakar Médical*, in 1990. As concerns methodology, the CNTS researchers added an aqueous solution of the plant to sickle hemoglobin blood that had polymerized due to oxygen deprivation in the controlled environment of the laboratory. They found that the fagara additive reversed the sickling of the cells through previously un-known processes of "oxygenation" (Thiam et al. 1990). Significantly, the fagara solution was said to reverse the sickling of those cells just as well as, if not better than, the standard medication then given, *Torental*. The CTNS study ended with a call for more research, but nothing truly substantive followed it. The persistent interest in fagara has not inspired the empirical studies neces-sary to bring this treatment from the realm of experiential-experimental local knowledge into scientific medicine, even as Diagne has begun conversations with Eric Courot, a key author in the K562 study. Courot passionately believes that there is something to uncover in fagara with respect to its utility in leu-kemia, and now sickle cell.

■ Fagara Chez Sambou

On the day I arrived at the university research unit where Gaoussou Sambou reportedly worked, the halls were eerily quiet. Piles of desiccated leaves clut-tered the window ledge of the main botany lab at the *Institut fondamental de l'Afrique noire*, known to people with an interest in Africa as IFAN. The herbs had been laid out to dry and were almost ready, since the bright winter morning bore no trace of the heavy humidity of the warmer months. Dr. El-Hadji Thalap Sarr, also a botanist and traditional healer, welcomed me into the office-laboratory where thousands more "life preserving" specimens were stored out of immediate sight.

I came to IFAN in an initial effort to contact Sambou—a much more re-nowned, older man than Thalap. Even in his absence, Sambou seemed to command Thalap's obsequious respect. The younger botanist explained that "the knowledgeable Sambou" was "still at his clinic." He then proceeded to present in the most scientific fashion the results of his twenty-five field missions: his own new catalogue of plants, with their Wolof and Latin names, accompanied by artists' renditions of each. He carefully explained, in more detail than I could take in, flowering mechanisms, and new species he had discovered as well as the uses of plants and poisons in every day life "traditionally." "Do you know of any that treat sickle cell?" I asked, informing him of my project. He flipped through the pamphlet and stopped at *Fagara xanthoxyloïdes* in Latin, *dengidëk* in Wolof. Together we read the short entry that he had written in French. I admired the drawing, which failed to impress him. "I must show you the real thing. Alive." From there we walked down the stairs to a dark corner of the IFAN garden where a small but ferocious looking tree stood. "What do you see?" he asked. We both smiled at the plant's ingenious self-protection. It had evolved a complete body armor of thorns. These varied in size, consistently proportional to the density of the arbor's various parts: large and thick on the truck, small and hard down the spine of each leaf, and soft, yet still present, on the leaves' undersides. Thalap then explained, "This plant's very morphology bespeaks its importance for our people. It is clear that our ancestors needed it, and we continue to need it. Its only option for survival is to protect itself . . . from us. We all prescribe it for sickle cell."

Finally, one afternoon a few days later I found Sambou who then invited me to lunch. He had recently retired from the institute, he explained, but still liked to socialize with colleagues over Senegalese cuisine at the IFAN basement "resto." I explained why I had come to see him in the awkward brief dispatch notable of academics' descriptions of their projects. He responded in a manner that is characteristic of Senegalese intellectuals who want to help Americans "eager to learn something about their ways." "*Formidable!*" he kept saying, between spoonfuls of rice and amid a conversation mostly focused on the politics of the upcoming 2000 election with others at the table. He was clearly pleased to let me tag along.

Upon my request, Sambou gave me access to all of his neatly ordered patient registers where hundreds of sicklers' visits had been noted since the early 1990s. All of these patients had been prescribed experimental doses of the fagara plant; the amounts were tinkered with only when people responded poorly, or not at all. They were also prescribed other herbs, such as *Maytenus senegalensis*, *Khaya senegalensis*, and *Calitropis senegalensis*, which were mixed in varying proportions with fagara to maximize its effects, according to Sambou. As one of his sons, who was in training at the clinic, told me, "Especially today, healers need to protect whatever special aspect they bring to the well-known prescription." This knowledge had to be protected from the myriad others who cultivate and prescribe the plant for sickle cell disease in Dakar, according to the younger Sambou. Sambou's sons and other

Figure 3.1 Fagara's thorns are thought to be a testament to its vital importance. Tree trunk detail. Fann, Dakar. Photographed by the author.

Figure 3.2 Tiny thorns line fagara's leaves' undersides. Fann, Dakar. Photographed by the author.

worker-relatives did not know that he had already shared these particular not so discreet "secrets" with me. He mixed in other plants to treat the multisystem disorder that is the disease: "one is added to combat anemia, another to prevent fatigue, and yet another to fortify the spleen and kidneys." Fagara, he was clear, "is used to prevent crises." For Gaoussou Sambou market value did not necessarily lie in exclusivity.

Faced with shelves stuffed with heavy black patient registers, I started in chronological order. Very quickly I came across the Mbodj sisters' recorded visits that dated back to 1992. As discussed earlier, the Mbodj women live in Fas, in an area of the city just outside the small world of sickle cell medicine. The Fann-Hock *quartier* is just down the ocean road (*la corniche*) from IFAN, while IFAN lies only minutes away from the *Fann* hospital complex where Senegalese doctors treat both pediatric and adult sickle cell patients at Albert Royer Children's Hospital and the CNTS (national blood transfusion center), respectively. These sites are within a mile and a half of each other, aligned geographically, slightly inland from the sea (see Dakar-Fann area neighborhood map, fig 3.3). Coumba and Soxna's illness narrative revolved between the two most distant points of this topography of care, the CNTS, where they were seen by hematologists, and Sambou's lower Fann-Hock clinic, where they were treated with phytotherapeutic plants.

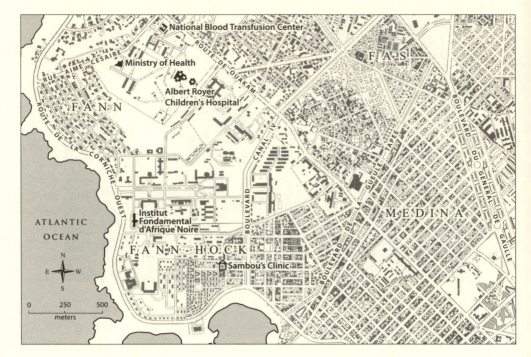

Figure 3.3 Dakar's topography of care: healing sites. Produced by the Harvard Center for Geographic Analysis.

■ The "Human Sense" of the Modern Economy

Sambou's own interpretation of fagara drew from a discourse of biological change that parallels the narrative recounted by some of his patients. In no uncertain terms he told me that "fagara *distances* sickle crises." He made no claim to know how exactly it works, however, preferring to leave the power of its uncertainty in tact. In practice, he contents himself with observing what patients under his care "feel" to be effective, and, in this way, his take on fagara and his patients' testimonies are reiterative. At base, his confidence as a healer, and sometimes as a "doctor," was itself rooted in the exchanges between himself and his clients. He put faith in them and their ability to overcome their ailments, while they seemed to respond favorably most of the time, stoking his ego with positive stories of amelioration, even as they often continued to complain about other life problems. He spoke to people directly and forcefully, often accompanying them out of his office with injunctions to act, saying, "*dégg nga?*" (all right/got it?), followed by an avuncular smile.

I would sometimes see patients from the ASD or the CNTS visit the Fann-Hock clinic. In addition to fagara treatments, Sambou might treat them for problems that they understood to be more "severe" than sickle cell, such as an inability to conceive. Aby Kane visited with hopes that Sambou might help her retain a pregnancy. One day as she was leaving his consultation room, he took a moment before seeing his next patient. "That woman is really suffering," he told me. And it is not her sickle cell." He did not, however, reveal to me her "medical secret." When Ami died from a bad blood transfusion a few months later, one of her doctors at the CHU went to what he thought was her home to present his condolences. He asked for her husband by name. The woman who answered the door confirmed that it was the named man's house, but that he was out. The doctor told the woman to tell him that he had stopped by to express his regrets for the passing of his wife. The woman explained that "*she* was his wife," assuming that he had no other. Sadly, now that fact was true. Perhaps Sambou knew more details about Aby than her biomedical doctors. He seemed to know the inner pain in the lives of many patients beyond that caused by their sickle blood.

Sambou's healing space was also a family workshop where his blood-kin likewise accorded him reverential attention. His position as someone upon whom his sons and the sick relied made him feel obliged to teach his children his trade to assure his healing legacy. He not only brought his sons, who ranged in age from thirteen to the upper thirties, to work under his tutelage, but he invited nephews and other extended family members to become experts in plant remedies as well. Beyond these elements of his planned providence for both his patients and his progeny, Sambou also became adept at enlarging his own network beyond "traditional medicine," his Islamic faith, and his biological kin's family business. His attachments to people who could, in various ways, spread word of his practice and who could reiterate the powers of fagara were far-reaching.

■ I worked in Sambou's clinic during the afternoons, since I spent most mornings at the Albert Royer and the CNTS sickle cell consultations. On Fridays, however, all of the university clinics closed early due to the Muslim prayer. To the surprise of many, Sambou continued his work on Fridays, waiting for patients who were desperate enough to come seeking treatment on a holy day. The healer had even constructed a mosque at his front door so that his family-staff would not miss the 2:00 p.m. prayer. I often found myself at Sambou's on Fridays. I wanted to get through his entire patient registers, and, because the queue was sporadic rather than steady, I could spend more time talking with the Sambous. On busier days the healer's sons and nephews might glance over periodically as I flipped through the large graph-paper pages of the registries. Once in a while they would decipher handwriting for me as I took in the vast number of patients, their ailments, and treatments, which were scrawled over tiny grey gridlines in red and black pen. I was searching for diagnoses of "*drépanocytose*," or simply 'drépano.' When I found them I would write down whatever information was recorded, which was often inconsistent: the number of visits, the patient's personal information, the demographic detail it seemed appropriate to include at the time of consultation, as well as the duration of care.

It appeared that most people visited in spurts, coming many times a year over a few years before slowly dropping out. As I jotted the information that concerned me, Sambou consulted people who were lined up out the door. Those at the head of the line waited patiently next to me on a long wooden bench. I greeted them as they inched up the plank, in order of arrival, as the consultation went on. Most responded briefly, implying that it was best to remain silent in the healing space, as if they were holding their words for Sambou. The room was a windowless, shack-like structure, lit with a blue florescent light—with the exception of a chance skylight created by a missing board on the roof. The booth at the back of the room where Sambou consulted the patients had a small desk-lamp with a slightly warmer feel.

The side of the booth facing out into the room—where the younger Sambous took powders from old juice or *Nesquik* jars and roots from cubbyholes lining the walls— contained a large open window barred by a ratty piece of cloth. After each consultation, the healer would call out the prescription for his family of helpers to fill. The younger men would pour soft piles of green, yellow, brown, and sometimes red, pulverized plants onto large pieces of newspaper, roll them up in a football-sized bundle, and hand them to *le malade*. Patients always thanked the men, and me, before quietly leaving with their remedies.

One day as I was counting cases, an elderly, crisply dressed European came in for an unusually quick visit. He had not gone through the line, but did wait until the doctor had finished with his current patient. As the man left Sambou's booth, the healer instructed his sons to prepare him large quantities of fagara (mixed with another plant called *maytenus*). The man fidgeted impatiently. When his powders were neatly packaged, he skulked off. Shortly afterward Sambou came out of his consultation room to ask if I had witnessed the visit. I told him that I had but before I could comment further, he boasted that the man was a "Frenchmen, a professor of medicine" who, thanks to Sambou, had left the University of Dakar to start his own "traditional healing" farm on the *Petit-côte* near the town of Mbour where I had first heard of fagara, years earlier. The man was a professor of "health sciences" who worked with the NGO *ENDA-tiers monde* (Environment, Development, Action in the Third World), which operates in the Sahel region.[17] Its mission statement declares: "We invite you to integrate yourself in diverse actions toward sustainable development, giving a *human sense* to the modern economy."[18] This modern economy in Senegal included "traditional" and Muslim healers, such as Sambou and his family, French citizens such as the professor in question, and an international group of Catholic nuns who distribute the plants at catholic mission health posts. The catholic sisters receive fagara packages from ENDA. Sambou consults for ENDA, the European professor works for ENDA. All of these actors, as well as the many *malades*

Figure 3.4 Two of Sambou's familial staff filling prescriptions. Pulverized plants in jars and numbered patient registers sit overhead. Fann-Hock, Dakar. Photographed by the author.

who seek care from these various healers, continue to give fagara the benefit of the doubt, and allow it to circulate in a therapeutic economy where belief in its abilities to heal sickle cell crises pushes the plant as a valuable currency for health.[19]

Sambou was deeply aware of the ways that "human sense" was necessary to the microeconomy of his own clinical practice as well. In the same way that he had bragged of the Frenchmen who came to buy his medicines and consult his knowledge, Sambou would often tell patients that he had an "American studying under him" (*moom defay jang sama ginaaw*) to learn how he treated sickle cell. The healer utilized the perceived cultural capital of my own "human sense" as an outsider from one of the world's most powerful, wealthy, and scientifically advanced nations to bolster perceptions of his own power to improve life locally. More importantly, he also had photographs of a former American diplomat in his desk drawer who was said to have been a patient of his during the man's assignment to Senegal. Successful in enrolling, and attaching, various machinations of American citizenship, while reifying my "formal" state persona to boost the "informal" power of his own, Sambou distinguished himself from other healers not so much by what he possessed (fagara) as by what he "did with [his] possessions and attributes with respect to others" (Strathern 1999, 158; cf Fassin 1992, 247–48). He drew from my "American presence" as an added resource to the many human connections (his patients included) that served as testimony to his powers. He did this not only in his clinic but also on public radio, the most common means of information diffusion in West Africa.[20]

Not everyone in Sambou's clinic was entirely privy to his keen marketing strategies, and my role there remained unclear to some family members. One of Sambou's nephews once asked to peek at my notebook to be sure that I was not writing down plant recipes. Surely this move was, for him, an effort to protect the family economy—a shared entity whose interior space was nonetheless perceived differently by Sambou and this member of his family crew as concerned the necessity of perceived outsider endorsement.[21] What became clear was that Sambou was actually less interested in his own "property right" (given that many of the same plants are used in several locales in Africa) than in expanding the relational network of those who could validate the importance of his product. His enterprise has been successfully advertised through radio and television informational programs, wherein he was always presented as "a researcher from IFAN" as well as a "traditional healer," demonstrating that his marketing was about inclusiveness rather than trying to isolate a small domain over which he could be said to reign. Unlike many healers in Dakar, he does not hand out flyers, and his "clinic" has no signage; he does not need to make such obvious invitations to clients. Instead, he carefully deploys the symbolic capital of relationships as currency circulated to advance public confidence in his healing above that of others. On subsequent field trips, and as recently as 2010, I noted that Sambou's patient base was expanding rapidly. He explained to me that his prices have stayed low over the years, at 5,000 *cfa* per consultation [US$10], while other healers in Dakar, who offer the same plants, were charging patients upwards of 40,000 *cfa* [US$80], a fact corroborated by several of my friends with sickle cell. Sambou's prosperity and success is also partially because of his proximity to the two major biomedical sites for sickle cell care. Indeed, I saw patients leave the CNTS and go to Sambou to fill prescriptions of their own volition. In other instances, as with the Mbodj women, more than a few were told directly by their providers to consult with Sambou about fagara.

■ **Politics that Plague the Postcolony**

Borrowing from social studies of science scholars Michel Callon, John Law (1982), and Bruno Latour (1987), Cori Hayden reminds us that scientific "knowledge does not simply represent (in the sense of *depict*) 'nature,' but it also *represents* (in the political sense) the 'social interests' of the people and institutions that have become wrapped up in its production" (2003, 21). In Dakar, what can we make of Steve Woolgar's call that "interest work demands treatment in its own right" (Woolgar 1981, 371)? Here, researchers' interest and calculated *uninterest* mark their engagement with fagara for political and scientific reasons that extend beyond Senegal's borders.

Even though Dakar's spheres of healing often overlap, in terms of interest in fagara's nature, the plant is gaining legitimacy with some biomedical
practitioners, while it is losing their support before they publicly declare it.
This loss has less to do with the plant per se than with biomedical specialists' own personal anxieties about professional legitimacy in the larger, global
circuit of sickle cell science. Add to this the fact that more extensive scientific research on fagara at laboratories like those housed within the CNTS are
structurally limited, since both French and Senegalese researchers alike cite
research-funding constraints that prevent them from abandoning their daily
practical obligations to take up work on botanicals. Perhaps more of an issue
is that powerful northern countries that enter into economic and development proposals with southern poorer ones play a significant role in whether
or not certain forms of cultural valorization and validation will go forward.
I argue below that key French sickle cell researchers' negative reactions to a
purported medicinal compound that contained fagara have somewhat tem-
pered the enthusiasm for and openness to fagara in Dakar's university teaching hospital where most patients receive care.

Notes on a Scandal

In the fall of 2000, I went to Paris to investigate the troubled dynamics of a
new sickle cell haplotype collaboration that Dr. Diagne brought to my attention. When I arrived I first visited Dr. Robert Girot, a specialist I knew well
who had previously allowed me to do fieldwork at the Tenon hospital sickle
cell clinic, which he runs, when I was a graduate student deciding on field
sites. During 1997, I spent seven months working with Girot and his north
Paris team. My hope was that he could introduce me to the researchers who
were approaching Diagne for the new population genetic study.

Professor Girot is a wiry man with an ageless face. With his precisely parted
hair, square framed glasses, and unfailing suit and tie beneath his white coat,
he could easily be from our times, or blend into the past of another era. He
greeted me with his usual warm welcome and generous smile and invited
me into the small meeting area just outside of his office. He asked about my
"time in Africa." He listened for a moment and then impatiently interjected:
"I have something that should be of great interest you!" He then took out a
red file folder and tossed it onto the table in front of me. As it landed with a
clap, he proclaimed: "*C'est un scandale!*" On it was written VK500. Throughout our conversation, a new proposed collaboration between the French, the
Senegalese, and others from the continent on the African haplotypes was
put forward as progress on understanding sickle cell difference at the genetic
level, while, at the same time, one specific use of fagara, in a mix now phar-
maceutically called VK500, was a terrible throwback of "exploitation." With
this unfamiliar new product, of which I had yet to understand the origins,
fagara began to garner negative attention within Parisian sickle cell circles as

a sham therapy peddled by an unscrupulous African doctor who would drain (*ruiner*) the economic resources of hopeful African patients.[22]

VK500 is a concoction of eight plants, including fagara, produced by a Beninois biochemist who is now notorious in Francophone sickle cell circles for what some characterize as "intellectual dishonesty." The doctor in question is Koffi Jérôme Fagla Médégan. Girot's red file was my first introduction to Médégan and the swirl of controversy that had surrounded him since late 1999. On this sweltering August afternoon that now made Paris seem like the logical extension of "French Africa," rather than the other way around, Girot rattled off his frustrations, critiques, and exasperations of this false African power to heal before I could fully assimilate the information in front of me. On the product listing for this strangely named compound, the brochure described VK500 capsules as containing the "traditional therapy" *Fagara xanthoxyloïdes*. Médégan was quoted as distinguishing himself from others who employ fagara since he claimed that the plant alone did not yield the best results. He assured readers that he had worked for many years to devise a more efficacious preparation through the addition of numerous other plants. My first semiotic reading was that this man's last name, Médégan, strangely resonated with *médecin*, or doctor. His second last name, Fagla, was easily associated by the ear with *fagara*. I would later learn that he often dropped the use of his two first names, first Koffi, then Jérôme, and usually went by Fagla Médégan, and sometime Médégan Fagla (which strangely mimicked *Médecin Fagara*, or Dr. Fagara).

I asked Girot if he had ever heard of the fagara plant. He had not. I found this the perfect opportunity to tell him something about "my time in Africa": that many sicklers in Dakar take fagara, the key plant in the "*phytotherapy*" in question. Many report some alleviation, I tentatively offered. Girot continued to focus on the injustice before us in the red file. "It may be used by patients, but it is *not* a cure!" He was right, at one level. The brochure claimed that the concoction "cured sickle cell," which only gene therapy or a bone marrow transplant could do. But surely patients would understand anything that spaced out their crises as some form of a cure, regardless of whether it was a permanent one. Then Girot went on to describe what was "perhaps the most scandalous" feature of the publicity, "trumping even the act of giving desperate, poor patients false hope." That is, Médégan claimed to have proved the efficacy of the medication in "a laboratory in France."

In a newspaper clipping of an interview that accompanied what appeared to be a press kit, Médégan allegedly conducted clinical observations on patients who supposedly took the concoction. He asserted that a well-known professor in Francophone sickle cell circles, Dr. André Orsini of Marseille, allowed him to do this with his own patients. Furthermore, Médégan's printed material stated that Orsini could corroborate his science. In a later investigation, several outraged French specialists, including Girot, ascertained that Médégan had apparently met Orsini, but the details Orsini gave contradicted

Fagla's account. In an exchange of facsimiles initially sent to Orsini and Girot from the most prominent biomedical sickle cell specialist in Benin, Dr. Mohamed Cherif Rahimy, who brought the VK500 story to the attention of the French researchers, the men concluded that Fagla Médégan was "lying" about Orsini's endorsement. Indeed, Orsini had replied to the doctors to say, "I obviously cannot vouch for a medication whose origin I am unsure, and whose nature and effects have never been the object of a rigorous biological or clinical study. . . . I proposed to help Dr. Fagla conduct this indispensable query. At that moment Dr. Fagla disappeared . . . . "[23] The question for Girot and countless others in France and Africa who were reading the same lines as I was as this file circulated—with similar injunctions to "beware"—was that if Médégan had done studies, where were the publications or efforts to share the results?

I made a trip to Benin a few years later in 2004 for the first international sickle cell conference in French speaking Africa, which was held in Cotonou. Médégan had been banned from the meeting because of his previous claims, but he showed up anyway. After he made a confrontational scene, to which I will return below, I sought him out, hoping that I might learn his take on the above events, and scheduled to meet him away from the conference. He invited me to his home for dinner with two doctors from Angola who were selling VK500 to patients there, and who reported favorable results.

Over the next few days, I returned to meet with Médégan at his grandiose home and spacious, but curiously sparse, medical office. When I put the story of the "scandal" to him directly, asking about Orsini, he complained that much of the data had been "lost," but that he was in the process of doing a new analysis in Africa with patients in Benin and Angola. Using this data, he had applied to present his work at the OILD sickle cell congress currently being held in his home city, but which was being hosted by "those against him." And of course Rahimy, the country organizer, was Fagla's compatriot who called him out in the facsimile to Orsini. He told me that Rahimy, "a long-time enemy," was in "cahoots with the French in a scheme (*combine*) against him." Why? I asked. "Jealousy!" "Struggles for power," and "intelligence." "I am smarter than Rahimy, that's what he cannot stand," he barked. Rahimy might indeed be called the darling of one of the most powerful research teams in Paris, led originally by Dominique Labie and now led by her protégé, Dr. Jacques Elion. It was this team that approached Diagne to collaborate on the new African haplotype study. Diagne and the late Dr. Mohamadou Fall, who ran Albert Royer during this time, initially held out signing on to the collaboration because the first study of African haplotypes, published in 1984 by Labie and her students, failed to mention any Senegalese collaborators (a point of tension I return to in chapter 5).

As Diagne and I traveled back from the Cotonou conference to Senegal together on a seventeen-hour flight (due to four unscheduled layovers), he filled me in on the same events recounted to me by Fagla Médégan and the decision to blacklist him, but from the standpoint of the conference scientific committee, of which Diagne was part. During the planning phase, the scientific committee was split on how to deal with Médégan. Half of the group wanted to have him present the VK500 work, which they imagined that they would be able to critique as "unscientific." The others felt that it was dangerous to offer Médégan the podium at all. They feared that his message and visibility would reach both "unschooled" researchers and, perhaps more importantly, *les malades*. The consensus congealed, and the committee voted to censure him by exclusion.

As mentioned above, Médégan showed up anyway. His mission was to make his case clear. He called out "*les Français*" and their "*combine*" against him in a quiet pause during a question-and-answer period after a session on traditional therapies. There, too, one of the researchers was being thoroughly criticized for "not being scientific," for committing "statistical errors," as well as for using *hydergine*, which the questioner complained was outdated, as a control against a plant concoction from Burkina Faso, which also contained fagara, called FACA. Fagla claimed that his invention had better science behind it and that he was being censured at the expense of *les malades*. No one responded to his outburst, and there was an uncomfortable silence and sense of shock among many of the sicklers. Could there be a treatment—an *African* treatment that was being kept from them? Certain sicklers were beside themselves with confusion, and perhaps hope. A break was then called after a few more questions were taken for the researcher on the podium. That is when I went in search of Fagla and requested that we meet away from the conference.

What I learned from Médégan in the coming days was that the "rebel geneticist" mentioned at the beginning of this chapter, named Dr. Gil Tchernia, had been "part of the effort to censor him," but that Tchernia also wanted to give him the opportunity to share his findings in a more transparent fashion within a laboratory setting. By both men's interview accounts, Tchernia proposed a three-pronged preliminary study to determine the veracity of Médégan's claims. These were: 1) to reanalyze clinical observations of sicklers he followed in Africa, and who served anecdotally as references for exalting the plant composition, 2) to do an in vitro experiment with different concentrations of VK500 on its ability to reverse sickling, and to see if it affects red blood cell malleability, and 3) to test the mix of plants on sickle cell transgenic mice, notably one named *Berkeley*, with collaborators at an NIH National Center for Sickle Cell Disease in Oakland, California. Thernia had secured research funding to carry out this third and most important phase. But negative findings on the first two aspects stalled the third. Tchernia posted the series of events and exchanges with Médégan, as well as more details of what followed, to the whole sickle cell community in France and beyond on the *Fédération des malades* website. Concerning the first two (versus the last) steps of the three-step process to test VK500 he wrote:

The analysis of the patient files showed that the results, which were judged favorable [by Médégan], were not based on any serious clinical methodology or objective criteria. When Mr. Médégan came to discuss the results, visibly defeated, he suggested that we probably did not receive a good batch of the product, and [he] then proposed to come back and be [physically] present for a new set of experiments with samples of his product that would be slightly adjusted—to which I gladly accepted. [Following this] I never saw him again and the experiment on the mouse model never took place.[24]

Thernia added: "I am not doubting the possibility that *fagara zanthoxyloïdes* [*sic*] may have an effect on certain aspects of sickle cell disease. This effect [however] still needs to be demonstrated." (*Je ne mets pas en doute l'effet possible de Fagara zanthoxyloïdes sur certains aspects de la drépanocytose. Cet effet reste à démontrer.*)

When Médégan and I met and did a taped interview in 2004, he spoke as if he was preparing to embark on the study with Tchernia on the transgenic sickle cell mouse model. When I interviewed Tchernia in 2006, he wrote off VK500's inventor as a grave disappointment, seeking only to "make money" off of potential patients for life. Actually doing a study on VK500's efficacy may indeed not have been in Médégan's interest. I tried to contact him on numerous occasions by email and phone later that year and subsequently to get his version of things, but he never responded. In my frequent, regular searches, I have found no mention of VK500 or Médégan in the medical and scientific databases, such as *PubMed* and *Web of Science*. Médégan did however appear in the news media, both French and African, in June of 2007 when he obtained a patent for VK500 in Paris.[25] This information sent the Francophone sickle cell email lists ablaze, as Tchernia and other medical providers in Paris, blasted messages to patients as well as their international colleagues and interlocutors, myself included, denouncing the news. Not only did the patent state that VK500 was an effective sickle cell treatment, it also stated that the compound could be used to treat AIDS.[26] Certainly not everyone on the online mailings of Francophone patient groups wanted to rule out all plants in the concoction. The *Fédération des malades* issued numerous statements to the effect that fagara must get a proper clinical trial, but that this was not it. They also provided "testimonies" (*téamoinages*) of doctors, patients and those in the leadership of their organizations that mostly warned patients to be skeptical. The now archived thread carried as its subject heading: Beware, VK500: To Cure Sickle Cell . . . Information or Intoxication?" (*Attention VK500: Guerir la Drépanocytose . . . Info ou Intox?*)"[27] Fagla Médégan was not to be trusted, most waged, and this "plant remedy" was simply another example of a "miracle cure" being put forth by a "charlatan."

In Cotonou in 2004, I saw firsthand how Médégan played on people's hopes when he met certain key Senegalese members of the newly formed sickle cell

disease association (ASD) as we were nearing the end of the Benin conference. Magueye Ndiaye was then the newly elected president of the nascent
advocacy group. Magueye and Touty Niang, the ASD's general secretary, sat
with me in the hotel lobby as we were preparing to check out and travel back
to Dakar. Médégan showed up just as we were heading out to find a taxi. I introduced him to Magueye and the others. With contagious enthusiasm, he described his creation as "a miracle handed down from God for this disease." He
promised that his compound relieved the painful symptoms that punctuate
sicklers' lives and the emotional burden felt by mothers of sick children, like
Touty. I found his claims incredible, such as his pronouncement that VK500
"reduces the size of large hearts," and thus alleviates a whole train of complications. He told Magueye that "within three years of taking the medication
the large organs, the heart and the spleen, would return to normal size" and
that Magueye would gain weight and be able to play sports. Magueye looked
dreamy-eyed and said, "I've always wanted to play soccer." Lastly, Médégan
promised that he "would not die from the disease."

Médégan offered Magueye a bottle of his "older product, only three plants
instead of the eight," at a "discount, 5.500 *cfa* per month" [~US$11]," calling
it "VK500 *Light*."[28] Médégan insisted that "health had no price" and assured
us that he would follow Magueye for free by email and phone from Benin.
Two years later, in 2006, Magueye told me that he still had not taken the pills.
He mentioned them to me again in 2010 when another "doctor," this time in
Dakar, approached him with a miracle cure. Dr. Médégan had never followed
up. The Senegalese patient group, like the French sickle cell specialists, eventually wrote off Dr. Fagla Médégan as "out to profit from the ill."

Discontinuities Regarding Fagara

Once I returned from my late 2000 visit to France, when Girot presented me
with the red Médégan file, Diagne and I continued our after-hours conversations. It was clear that he, like Girot, Tchernia, and many others wanted
some aspect of "science" to resolve the fagara efficacy issue. Although he was
obviously irritated by Médégan's approach, he contended that, "there must be
a positive effect" from the plant, "since people from Senegal to Benin agree
on the same thing for the same problem." He wanted to see "*legitimate*, scientific results" demonstrating the plant's efficacy that might corroborate what
patients seemed to "feel." This would allow him, as a biomedical practitioner,
to formally endorse fagara use. He worried about both patients and doctors
being duped with the promises of "cure."

As Diagne broached the topic of fagara being sold "by African pharmacies
without the proper authorization initialized by a scientific study," he went to
retrieve a folder. The document it contained turned out to be the same letter
that Dr. Girot had given me, although not accompanied by a whole "press kit."
He passed his hand over the thin folder, saying, "nothing has been published

yet to be able to say for sure. . . . " The title read: "*Gellules anti-drépanocytose VK500*" (anti-sickle cell capsules, VK500). At the top of the page was scrawled a hopeful message, which he said must have appeared a few stops before the facsimile reached him, or Girot. It read: "*De la part de L. Aunori, une raison d'esperer, F. Karna*" (From L. Aunori, a reason to be hopeful, F. Karna). Aunori had sent it to Karna, who had sent it to someone else, and so on, until it finally ended up in the hands of Dr. Rahimy, Fagla's rival who had trained with Girot's collaborators in France. Rahimy, whom Fagla regarded as his enemy, sent it to Girot, who sent it on to Diagne.

The pamphlet listing VK500's benefits was accompanied by the following testimonial:

Dear Sir, Representative

As previously discussed, I send you the documentation on sickle cell. We are in the same situation [*sic*], my oldest child is also an SS sickler. With this new product, we have a reason to be hopeful. Here in Niamey, I have a niece who has already taken the treatment, and everything is apparently going well now. She has no more crises. In fact, it was she who sent me this documentation of the product. I send this with my best wishes, which extend to your usage [of VK500]. May God protect us. Amen.

Mrs. K. Mariama
Project sr/pf[29]

It is impossible to ascertain the origins of this letter, given the manner in which it appeared in the files of Girot and Diagne. Its importance lies in its expression of hope. It imparts a religiously inflected testimony, or "witnessing," of the fact that someone's child has "no more crises," and this good news should be passed on, "Amen." For the doctors, it became a testimony of Médégan's reach; Benin, Niger, France, and Angola were all included in Girot's file.

The possibility of false hope (of actually being "cured") inevitably experienced by people who could be duped by charlatans, rightly upset Dr. Diagne. What Girot called *escroquerie* (fakery, swindling) was given a free pass into some people's lives through their desperate need to trust that a miracle cure for their problems was forthcoming. Diagne now, like the French doctors, focused on the fact that there had been no convincing data on fagara's efficacy in humans or animals. This fault was compounded by the claims that the plant could perform scientific feats, like reversing a genetic effect, or healing taxed organs. "It's intellectual dishonesty, pure and simple," Diagne snapped. Through the far-reaching claims of Dr. Médégan, fagara became tainted, and Diagne became less enthusiastic about it than he had appeared in earlier years when he seemed perfectly open to patients taking it as long as they "felt" its powers working in their bodies. This plant had made sicklers like the Mbodj

sisters feel "normal" despite the stigmatizing elements of their lives attribut-
able to the disease, but it now became a risk in and of itself in the eyes of
biomedical practitioners like Diagne. Girot and others in France continued to
denounce the plant for several years to follow, until new research claims, this
time from France, began to shift their thinking.

■ **Fagara Research in France Today**

When Gil Tchernia learned of a Reims team's promising study linking an important alkaloid in fagara, or, *fagaronine*, to a genetic induction of fetal hemoglobin in the K562 leukemia cell line, he began conversations with one of
the principal scientists involved about doing an in vitro study on the *purified
product* in sickle erythrocytes. The scientist in question, Dr. Eric Courot, proposed researching the "brute, whole fagara plant" instead. Going back over
the details with me, in the spring of 2007, Courot explained that he tried to
make Tchernia see that "synergy could not be excluded in this case." We both
agreed on this obvious point, since patients take fagara, not the extracted and
purified alkaloid. I then informed him of the fagara "scandal" that involved
VK500, which consisted of eight plants. He sighed at the complexity of the
fiasco and at the mysterious compound. After a moment of silence, deep in
thought, he feebly offered, "Eight is *a lot*." Courot had no previous knowledge of sickle cell or the political life of sickle cell science between Africa
and France before 2006 when he began looking for allies to boost his case for
funded research on fagara for leukemia. When he learned that the OILD was
holding an international conference on sickle cell in Dakar in November of
that year, he submitted an abstract, which was accepted.

Courot arrived in Dakar for the conference knowing no one, but through a
series of what he called "serendipitous meetings and exchanges," he was introduced to French geneticist Jacques Elion at a cocktail party where four African First Ladies were scheduled to toast the event. Elion warned him of the
minefield that he was about to walk into and said to make sure that his presentation was "scientific," and that he not oversell the plant. At this point, by
Courot's account, he was so startled and left-uneasy by the conversation that
he went back to his hotel room, before the First Ladies even arrived, to re-
organize (and also to nuance) his presentation. He ended up working into the
early hours of the morning. Elion also told him that he himself had no interest
in researching fagara, but that Gil Tchernia might. He introduced the two, and
indeed Tchernia told Courot to be in touch back home. A few months later,
in Paris, when the two met, Tchernia reportedly told Courot that because of
"recent unfortunate events with a certain Beninois named Fagla Médégan and
his product of VK500, which contained fagara, we would not be able to convince our colleagues to work on the plant." That was when Tchernia proposed

to simply study the alkaloid *extract* fagaronine—which, of course, was not the same thing, scientifically, or politically.

Following from this, at the beginning of 2007 Tchernia contacted one of his former students, Dr. Lydie Da Costa of Robert Debré. He interested her in studying the alkaloid's effects on undifferentiated red blood cells in collaboration with Courot. Finally things were starting to fall into place, but a few more hiccups, regarding equipment failure and the lack of available graduate students to help with the unfunded research, would delay the study until 2009. The goals of the inquiry, which finally got underway in May of 2009, were to see if the young red blood cells in question would live at all when exposed to fagaronine, and what dose would prove fatal. Once Da Costa began to approximate the correct dose of fagaronine for actual human cells, which was at most half, or "even potentially a fifth," of that used in Courot's previous study on the K562 leukemia cell line, she then set out to see if fetal hemoglobin induction would be signaled, and how much would be produced. Finally she hoped to determine if the preliminary results would warrant studying the product in patients. Results obtained with different experimental doses of the alkaloid "were not perfect," Courot told me in September of 2009, but "the effect was an increase in fetal hemoglobin." Da Costa did not want to flaunt these results, since "the dose may have still been too high." The issue for her was that in each of the experiments, three at the time, too few of the blood cells remained alive to obtain "the kind of peaks," or signals, that she was "accustomed to seeing" on her real-time PCR analysis readouts. In October 2009, the various study follow-ups began, but they were, once more, being done piecemeal. Again, with little funding to borrow against their main research projects, they lost the graduate student who could do the tedious bench work for the project. As Da Costa told me, she would have to redo the experiments in the spare time that she did not have. In the spring of 2010, Courot reported to me, yet again, that a lack of resources and manpower in Da Costa's lab delayed the next steps of the study, "perhaps until the summer. . . . "

It must be reemphasized that this research has taken place marginally, literally "on the side," in Da Costa's lab since her principal research budget is earmarked for work on Diamond Blackfan Anemia, not fagara. Courot, for his part, continues to grow fagara in his lab, to be able to extract the alkaloid without killing off live trees in Africa for Da Costa, while he economically masters growing techniques. He, too, works on fagara, on the side, since his main work for his university research unit is grapevine plant stress, immunity, and regeneration. Specifically, he experiments on grapes used in champagne, as Reims, Champagne-Ardenne is the Champagne capital of France. The French "traditional" plant of *le vigne* occupies much of his research day but it may also have more in common with fagara than he ever previously imagined. In the spring of 2009 I learned from Courot that a sickle cell research team in Créteil, a suburb of Paris, who could be said to be "mild" competitors of Girot's, had recently approached him to extract *resveratrol*, a chemical compound largely found in red grape skins, and a constituent in red wine, so that they might test whether it has any effect on fetal hemoglobin production. Recently resveratrol has been studied for its antioxidant and anti-inflammatory qualities (see Kundu and Surh 2008 for a review), anti-diabetic properties (Palsamy and Subramanian 2008), ability to increase fat metabolism, prolong physical endurance (Lagouge et al. 2006), and even possibly extend life! (Wade 2008). For the Créteil sickle cell specialists it may be this *French* plant product that turns out to be the long awaited natural cure to dietary induced high fetal hemoglobin in sickle cell (Rodrigue et al. 2001). Courot found the prospect of actually melding his two research worlds exciting. He now imagined conducting sickle cell studies on each molecule separately, as well as with a mixture of the two. When I visited his lab in May of 2009, small branches of fagara roots were growing in petri dishes in the same cool, well-lit temperature controlled room as tiny *Pinot Noir* and *Chardonnay* plants, even if they were on opposite sides of the chamber (see figures 3.5 and 3.6).

■ A Broader Ethic of Care

As Courot puts it, the "human and environmental threat" to fagara prompted him to start a French-Senegalese knowledge-transfer concerning how to grow phytotherapeutic plants in labs for populations who can benefit from them. Courot initiated this effort, which is now funded by the French *cóoperation* in Senegal, with the French ambassador to Senegal when his department chair and university president "dragged their feet," as he said, since it seemed too tangential to their main emphasis on *le vigne*. He has since invited key plant-researchers at ENDA to do training stays in his lab in Reims to learn about his growth and extraction processes. Part of what drives him is his belief that plants like fagara can make powerful interventions to stall or reverse disease processes. He has spent much time thinking about how fagaronine mitigates leukemia (Comoë et al. 1987; Dupont et al. 2005; Larsen et al. 1993). This property leads some to think that fagara may help in other cancers, since fagaronine functions as a topoisomerase inhibitor, or inhibitor of two enzymes (topoisomerase I and II) that control changes in DNA structure during the normal cell cycle for tumors (Larsen et al. 1993; Fleury et al. 2000). Several of Courot's mentors, namely Léopold Comoë, an Ivorian professor of pharmacy under whom Courot worked in Abidjan, were convinced that even brief exposure to the plant could have lasting effects (Comoë et al. 1987).

Today Courot collaborates with ENDA Tiers Monde, which, as stated earlier, has been working with a range of actors, such as Gaoussou Sambou and the Catholic nuns who distribute fagara to sicklers through a series of health posts, notably in Ker Moussa. ENDA also does outreach with Senegalese

Figure 3.5 Plant geneticist Dr. Eric Courot examining Chardonnay cultivated in vitro. Reims, France. Photographed by the author.

Figure 3.6 Courot holds up two petri dishes where fagara stem cells have yielded incipient root structures. Reims, France. Photographed by the author.

school children in Mbour who now grow phytotherapeutic plants in their schoolyard gardens with hopes to conserve them (Arab 2003). In 2007, Courot initiated his planned course of study that he and others at Reims would teach to Senegalese college-level students. The program designed for on-the-ground practicum in Dakar entailed allowing students to earn the equivalent of a bachelor's degree in pharmacy (which is currently reserved for postgraduate studies) that would be focused on plant reproduction. In May of 2008, he made his second trip to Dakar to teach a section of the course. It was on that trip when he met with Dr. Diagne in an effort to reach out to local sickle cell specialists who might be convinced of eventually studying fagara in vivo. Both men reported to me that they talked for nearly three hours, with each of them agreeing that there must be "something" to fagara worth exploring in patients. Diagne began to again imagine a robust clinically controlled trial. The plant would first have to prove itself in vitro in Da Costa's lab, however, with the proper tools and technologies of validation. When we talked via Skype® (with me in Cambridge and Diagne in Dakar) after Courot returned to Reims, Diagne consistently framed the African fagara studies' inability to enter science as a "lack of proper objective tools that might yield formal *proofs*." By this he meant that most African researchers did not have access to genetic technologies that could measure and chronicle red blood cell differentiation and fetal hemoglobin induction at a cellular level.

Diagne rarely lamented the lack of technology for sickle cell treatment and care, however. He wanted to emphasize that research in Africa can, and increasingly does, rely on technology. Care, on the other hand, was a much more basic human task that, thankfully for him and his patients, consists of "low-level techniques" with high health returns, as we will see in the chapter to follow.

CHAPTER FOUR

Attitudes of Care

Nearly all of the biomedical professionals I encountered during my fieldwork spent extended research stays in Paris to obtain higher medical training in hematology, genetics, and pediatrics. These fields are key to sickle cell disease management. When Senegalese professionals return to Dakar, however, a certain realization sets in. The disease looks different in Senegal, they all seemed to agree, while the technologies they mastered in Paris quickly faded into skills learned for training purposes with limited local application. Quite simply, techniques without tools *sur place* come to mean very little. Blood transfusions, neonatal screening, prenatal diagnoses, protein analyses of disorders that are often co-inherited with sickle cell, such as beta and alpha thalassemia, or more specifically, the techniques to properly carry them out, are limited or nonexistent once researchers return home. As concerns a recently acquired piece of *isoelectrofocalization* equipment to carryout such testing and newborn screening at the primary children's hospital in 2008, the once glossy machinery now sits there covered in a fine patina of dust, due to a lack of funds for reagents. Negotiating how the few technologies that they do have, namely "surveillance" and "organization," can function to save lives, and also be recognized as science by their Northern colleagues, often leaves local practitioners relying on rationales of Senegalese specificity to enhance their inventiveness and underwrite their rigor.

When recounting his own return to Senegal after his first year of research training in Paris, Dr. Ibrahima Diagne optimistically explained that he had to reconcile two very different treatment realities. "I tried as much as possible to see what I could and couldn't apply to my own clinic, to the population of children with sickle cell here. Fortunately, for sickle cell, the advantage that developed countries have over us only concerns the ability to do sophisticated charts, tests, and research." He stopped himself, and then added, "These things are not necessary for following patients, or for giving them proper care." Today Dr. Diagne is the Senegalese government specialist and contact person (*point focale*) for sickle cell and the country's principal pediatrician dedicated to the disease in Dakar. Cumulatively, he has spent over two years in Paris and has worked to master a range of technologies from assessing incompatibility risks in whole blood transfusion therapy to assessing protein analyses of hemoglobinopathies, most of which cannot be applied locally.

For their part, many patients were hesitant to undergo the principal therapeutic interventions for sickle cell used in countries like the United States and France, routine blood transfusions and the chemotherapy hydroxyurea. They were seen as simply too risky. When discussing transfusions, people immediately cited the threat of HIV and hepatitis infection. Hydroxyurea was understood to carry the risk of temporary sterility, which could put people's hopes for a future family line in peril. Patients already lived with an existential anxiety about their own life and death. This was part of the hold their biologies had over their bodies when sickle cell pain crises set in. Rather than alleviating their thoughts of death, many patients characterized what they took to be risky treatments the of global North as additionally threatening, in the context of Senegal. They were seen as additive hazards to their health when the blood supply was not fully guaranteed, when hydroxyurea monitoring was too costly, and, most importantly, when this drug would force them to gamble with their fertility. Physicians also understood these technical therapies to potentially create new medical problems that would surely overlay the first. What people did want, at times, however was access to scanning technologies that might reveal minute capillary damage in areas of the brain or the spleen that had been compromised by repeat sickle cell crises.

It was with regard to these more "sophisticated" technologies that Diagne accepted that certain questions would not be answered through high-tech means in his clinic. They would remain open, yet were often assigned assumed answers, after he and his colleagues had discussed their probabilities through other techniques—what he called "*semiologie*," or a science of symptoms as *signs* that intuitive, attentive doctors could use to make informed diagnoses.

Medical semiology, as Diagne defined it, entailed reading the visible signals, and also sounds, of the body with one's own senses (cf Wendland 2010, 93).[1] These readings happened through doctor-patient interpersonal exchange, rather than with complex tools, and constituted an essential aspect of the medical curriculum at the University of Dakar Cheikh Anta Diop campus where most physicians in Senegal are trained. Even as many everyday Senegalese people imagined that certain medical procedures carried out in the United States and Europe could resolve problematic or uncertain diagnoses, such as organ damage or neurological impairment, most could not to travel to these places. In recent years Diagne has begun to implore more affluent patients, friends, or family members who have managed to get care abroad to follow up with him when they receive their diagnoses. Often when people are back in country they will bring Diagne their paperwork, scans, images, or other results gotten overseas. He then makes a point to compare his own diagnosis, based on semiology, with that produced by the high-tech machinery of medicine in wealthier places. He amuses himself with this challenge and comments that he is "usually right, merely by looking at the signs." His simple semiology gives him confidence that he and his colleagues are within an acceptable set of bounds that comprise global standards of medical diagnostics and management, despite their lack of resources. It would be a mistake however to say that he is not a believer in the power of technology. He simply assures himself that he can mostly do without the interventions that he has had to forego due to circumstance anyway.

On another register, in conversations over the years, Diagne spoke to me about "the problems with technology." His unease was a general sentiment: that cell phones were an invasion of privacy, that people were becoming "automatons" with Bluetooth earpieces attached like "appendages to their heads," that machines were not necessarily going to make our lives better. He quipped that soon people would be for sale at the vast electronics section of the *Sandaga* open market in the city center. He laughed at himself just as easily when I reminded him that he could be seen as the epitome of technical achievement in Africa—he was a rarity, as a pediatrician with training in medical genetics on the continent. In his village some people no longer even considered him "African" but jokingly called him "*toubab*." His "modernity" was understood but could make him seem out of touch with his family, who still lived in his deceased father's compound where his brother, who never went to school, remained with his multiple wives and Diagne's mother. Hardly anyone in the family home spoke French. Diagne explained that perhaps it was because he was "from the village," hailing from this "pristine" context, that accounted for his tendency to privilege "the organic" over "the technical." His bias toward the organic in treatments, he assured me, was usually corrected by a conscious attempt to strive for "objectivity" and sound judgment to assess the best course of action for a specific patient. It was this attitude of his subtle bias toward an "organic" approach to life in general that led him also to interpret Senegalese sicklers' increased rates of fetal hemoglobin, and their own optimistic outlooks when faced with this disease, as "natural" causes that alleviated sickle cell complications in this population. It also permitted him his own faith that he and his colleagues could manage this complex condition despite the economic hurdles stacked against them.

■ Cultural *Équipement*

In a discussion about how scientific practitioners often turn out to be their own historical agents of change, Michel Foucault pointed out how ideas from the margins of mainstream knowledge usually become much more integral to present ideas of truth than the annals of science have let on. He writes:

> The successive transformations of . . . "truthful discourse" continuously produce reshapings of their own history; what had for a long time

remained a dead end, today becomes an exit; a "side" attempt becomes a central problem around which all the others gravitate; a slightly divergent step becomes a fundamental break. . . . In short, the history of discontinuities is not acquired once and for all; it is itself "impermanent" and discontinuous. Must we conclude from this that science spontaneously makes and remakes its own history at every instant, to the point that the only authorized historian of science could be the scientist himself, reconstituting the past of what he was engaged in doing? (Foucault 1991, 15)

In this chapter I trace the sites of struggle where sickle cell physician-researchers in Dakar not so much "reconstitute a past" (marked by historical distance) of what they themselves were engaged in doing as science, but rather how they constitute care marked by a spatial and attitudinal distance from certain sickle cell treatment norms they learned in France. "Slightly divergent steps"—their *semiologie*, their acceptance that many patients include fagara in their drug regimens, and their affirmation of a palliative *attitude sénégalaise* (to be detailed much more explicitly further on)—have a fundamental presence in the Senegalese clinic. These aspects of care, or what Paul Rabinow (2003, 11–12) might call Senegalese conceptual "equipment," are also scientifically "impermanent," and often formally understated in a "discontinuous" way. Their impermanence happens not in the sense that Foucault describes above, as being subject to the transformative effect of new interventions. Instead, physician-researchers vacillate between foregrounding these concepts and meditations as important explanatory mechanisms for their clinical successes, while they alternately silence themselves on such mechanisms when it comes to writing in medical journals, or presenting on them at international conferences.[2]

I attended three Francophone international sickle cell congresses in the course of writing this book. The first took place in Paris in 2002, the second in Cotonou in 2004, and the third in Dakar in 2006. At each event, Senegalese physician-researchers engaged with international researchers, mostly French, on "country differences" that concerned the feasibility of administering frontline pharmaceutical therapies, such as hydroxyurea and buterol, in the global South, while several Senegalese biomedical practitioners emphasized the importance of vaccinations, folic acid, and clinical surveillance as key elements of their patients' health. When "cultural differences" were articulated as such, they were usually only in reference to behavioral trends, such as social uptakes of genetic testing and counseling, or of the population's understanding of sickle cell transmission. What I saw at dinners, coffee-breaks, and in other informal interactions between my Senegalese informants and their French counterparts was an almost unrecognizable uneasiness that, at times, overtook the healthy confidence that I came to associate with them back home. In these international settings, even the one "at home" in Dakar, local experts' defensiveness of their "scientific standing" translated to a refusal to explicitly theorize and valorize *semiologie*, to make known their own medical acceptance of fagara, or to cite their belief in a perhaps seemingly sentimental articulation of a palliative national mentality (however problematic), articulated as the "*attitude sénégalaise*."

Publicly, Senegalese biomedical practitioners hesitated to make such cultural equipment part of their present history and practice. In our conversations over the years they often spoke of their inability to delimit, name and quantify these cultural appurtenances explicitly for fear of giving their Northern colleagues, with whom they continuously strive to gain power, a reason to belittle their status and magnify their place-in-the-world, both globally and within sickle cell science. Local research-physicians may simply be choosing which battles to fight for their scientific standing (as will become clear in chapter 5). What can be said here is that they often resigned themselves to a position that elements of their clinical cultural equipment would remain *dead ends* within systematic, experimentally derived scientific knowledge (that which downplays its connection to lived experience and becomes associated with disciplined—quantifiable—experimentation). At the same time, these dead ends could still prove vitally productive on the ground. Even if the intimacy of intuiting bodily signs, accepting patients' choices to take pharmacopoeia, and articulating something as amorphous as a healing "*attitude*" could not be simplistically quantified, they were realities that nevertheless animated an experience of improved quality of sickle cell life as doctors like Diagne observed it.

As will see in the pages ahead, in addition to these cultural effects, certain practitioners utilized the genetic explanation of the Senegalese haplotype ambiguously, as a safe referent, or, simply, in the case of one, to opportunistically avoid specific patients that chronically called on her. She recommended fagara to them quite willingly, perhaps because of her absences, so as at least to leave them with something. Yet this doctor's actions, coupled with those of others who were more present, still reveal how minimal materials partially circumscribed a range of ethical responses and notions of responsibility. Aided by a mild manifestation of the disease, which emerges as a reality for the biosocial and economic reasons seen in the previous chapters, sickle cell science in Dakar spontaneously makes and remakes not only its own "history" but also its own moral possibilities, life standards, and norms. Biomedical actors in Dakar are fully aware of the legacy of colonization that still bears upon them both in the form of constraints and expectations that are simultaneously external and self-imposed. They strive to be less bound by that history and instead to define a reality of care that makes the most sense for them. Certain, but not all, of the local norms that emerge from this process have a feel of necessary exits, or simply "good enough" care strategies.

■ Techniques of Care

I first met Ibrahima Diagne with his Pediatrics Chair, Dr. Mohamadou Fall, in January 1998. I was in Senegal for a two-week visit while conducting field-work in France in two of the hospital services where Diagne had received specialty training to expand his knowledge base. On that initial exploratory trip to Dakar, the two men spoke to me excitedly and openly about "mild" sickle cell as well as other particularities of their patient population, notably the widespread ingestion of traditional medicinal therapies. Professor Fall has since passed away and now Dr. Diagne has become the principal sickle cell pediatrician at Albert Royer Children's Hospital.

As part of the teaching hospital system of the University of Dakar, Albert Royer and the CNTS receive 60 percent of their overall budget from the Sen-egalese state, which allocated only 4 percent of its annual expenditure to pub-lic health care during the years that I carried out the bulk of my fieldwork (WHOGHO 2007a). The remaining 40 percent of the CHU's financial costs are paid for by patient consultation user-fees and, in the case of the CNTS, revenue comes from user-fees in addition to services such as the sale of blood and blood products to private clinics, laboratories, and other hospitals. The overall budgets of both hospitals do not designate funds specifically for sickle cell disease. In the years between 2000–02, before the institution of the now ever-rising fees at the CNTS, several doctors there told me that they "volun-teered" their services to take on sickle cell patients who had "no real home" in the health ministry's accounts and ledgers. When I began my fieldwork in the late 1990s, specialists in hematology complained that their clinical service would benefit greatly if a budgetary line was created specifically for sickle cell. The disease's chronic nature requires extensive monitoring, serial laboratory testing of various biomarkers related to hematological health, and four yearly check-ups. Without targeted subsidies, these costs fall to patients, who mostly cannot keep up with them. Patients, too, complained that their disease was not publicly recognized and that their care was not sufficiently subsidized.

The primary task of pediatricians like Diagne at Albert Royer is to ex-amine the children lined up with their mothers outside the medical offices who present with the range of illnesses defined as "priorities," from malaria to the parasitic intestinal infections that often affect young children in this part of the world (PNDS 2004). Although Diagne tried to manage his sicklers by scheduling them on Tuesday mornings, small patients with fevers, diar-rheas, skin rashes, and other afflictions would insert themselves into the line in emergencies, while his sicklers would show up on days not designated for them either. As if scheduling itself were a feat, he told me, "Management is a key technology for us. If we could only sort appointments out, then already we'd see an upswing in the overall health of our sicklers."

This comment not only referred to organizing his clinic visits and solicit-ing patients' compliance with disease-specific scheduling, it also alluded to convincing patients to pay 3.000 *cfa* [~US$6] for their quarterly visits, even when they felt well. For many, this proved an exorbitant fee for merely "checking in." Yet the money was well spent when they had it. Diagne never "timed" his patient consultations; some office visits lasted nearly an hour. As several described it, he had "no notion of the clock." When follow-up appointments were scheduled, they were made only for the date in question, rather than for a specific time. Most people reserved the entire day to sit with their children in the open-air waiting room. Those who showed up late in the morning, knowing they would file into the first-come-first-serve series of small clusters of mothers with children, complained that the day always vanished and that their homes and family meals would be neglected in their absence. The "queue" consisted of no actual physical line. Bodies simply filled the open courtyard. The mass of mothers and children in search of shade contained its own internal logic and winnowed as child-and-mother-pair by child-and-mother-pair gradually filtered into the doctor's office. The smell of food cooking and the pounding of the mortar and pestle could be heard from the small cinderblock constructions that encircled the courtyard. Diagne's office faced this series of rooms called *le Pavillon des mères* where mothers could stay when their children were hospitalized.

As those seeking care awaited him outdoors, inside of his dimly lit office Diagne would examine each small patient with methodical scrutiny, measuring his or her growth, palpating each child's lower stomach for signs of enlarged and hardened spleens, all the while assessing their overall development.[3] The only tools he used, in addition to his own senses, were a stethoscope and a blood pressure measuring device. As patients entered, Diagne would employ his semiology, looking for signs of sickle cell disease in those who had received other diagnoses. For example, a sick child's sibling came in with her father to learn more about the disease and said that she had "non-symptomatic trait." Diagne diagnosed her with sickle cell by looking at the whites of her eyes, which were yellow from jaundice. His penchant for discerning the body's interior problems as displayed on its exterior extended to simple imbalances as well. Men would come in with their children only to complain of their wives' incessant irritability. "It's usually anemia. So I just prescribe iron without hesitation," he recounted as if such an antidote was totally obvious. He knew, however, that the overwhelming social and economic burden of caring for sickle cell children took its toll on women disproportionately in families.[4] Not infrequently siblings of patients came in with small builds and skins seemingly sensitive to the touch. In all cases, Diagne first made his diagnoses, and then ordered biomedical screens to confirm them when possible. In most instances, his first intuitive characterizations were correct. Like his assessment practice, prescriptions were equally consistent: folic acid. This script was sometimes complemented by antiparasitics, vermifuges, and other supplements besides B9, such as magnesium, if tests indicated the need.

■ Destiny and Health

Dr. Diagne has a curious life trajectory. As he shared his past experiences with me, it became clear that aspects of his own biography have not only influenced his approach to care but have more generally anchored medicine as his "calling" in his mind. Although he was from a poor, rural family where French education was almost unheard of, he was enrolled in a French school at the insistence of none other than the village doctor. Subsequently, he enlisted in the Senegalese Army, which paid for his higher education in medicine and continues to pay part of his salary. Diagne regards these two events as "perhaps destined." In telling me his life story, he recounted the many obstacles that could have barred him from going to school, from passing the necessary *concours* (examinations), and from training for the career without which he could not imagine his life today. He "miraculously" passed exams, despite being hours late because of circumstances beyond his control; he navigated seemingly impossible medical bureaucracies by "coincidentally" finding distant relatives in positions to help him obtain needed tests or documents; and he succeeded in mastering a military education system with honors, without which he could never have afforded to pursue higher learning in the health sciences. Later, as a pediatrician, he found himself assigned to his home village of Khombole, working in the same service where he was born. While there, he once treated Magueye Ndiaye as a young adolescent. Almost a decade later, the two encountered each other again after Magueye was elected president of the ASD. He and Diagne were both on an awareness campaign trail to spread knowledge of the disease to populations who lived outside of Dakar (state centralization of resources in all things governmental still proves a problem in Senegal). Magueye recognized Diagne by his tall stature and his status as a towering uniformed army doctor, impressions left on him when he had felt the opposite, "small and sickly," in the village hospital bed. These and other events have allowed Diagne to borrow the language of "destiny," at least among familiars. As Diagne is a Mouride Muslim, a religious order that emphasizes hard work in achieving teleological ends,[5] he is reluctant to speak of "destiny" in the context of medicine and his fate as a man of science. Writer Milan Kundera, who is equally skeptical of the term's assumption that human actions are determined rather than chosen, preferred the formulation, "as if by chance." As Diagne told me about his life, I thought of Kundera's phrase. I then asked Diagne about the fit of these life events to Kundera's take on fate; he agreed that it seemed to capture his experience.

The life-defining events of education to which Diagne referred visibly marked his ethic of care. A signature intervention of his practice is that he insists that his young patients be enrolled in school. The conversation he would have with parents about this issue was seamlessly threaded through other medical details and injunctions to focus on their child's health and life, rather than on the periodic painful episodes of their illness. In these conversations he framed school attendance as a practical aspect of each child's actual treatment. Many parents hesitated to let their chronically ill children out of their sight and doubted that it was worthwhile to invest precious and scarce family resources in school materials, uniforms, and tuition (as schools are rarely free in Senegal) for a child with a debilitating disease who might not live long enough to graduate. Diagne tried to make his values about education obvious to these parents by telling them that, with the proper care and investment, their children could live long lives. He felt a major sense of factual accomplishment when he ran the numbers and saw that sicklers' in his service were enrolled in school at rates that surpassed the national Senegalese average (Diagne et al. 2000, 22). However, he lamented, this only concerned small children and early education, since many people dropped out of the larger education system altogether, both nationally and in his clinical service, during high school years. Still he did what he could to convince parents to think of their children as just as capable as any other child, often asking about their studies and their placement in the rank system of their classrooms. His interest kept parents invested in making sure that they had good news to report to the doctor on their next visit in terms of their children's bodily health and intellectual progress. Formal scholastics, Diagne insisted, would provide children with an eventual entrée into society and the work force where they could use their minds rather than having to rely on their bodies for physical labor. This economic incentive was further framed in biological terms since those with sickle cell might experience a range of physical problems, such as hip necrosis that requires expensive surgery, which many in Senegal cannot afford to treat. Although such disease manifestations were rare, he made a point of linking educational opportunity to economic assurance, and to future health self-care.

Many parents thanked Diagne over the years as their children would pass their entrance and exit examinations, permitting them to progress to the next level, that mark almost every educational phase in the French system. Yet whether the schools in question were French, Koranic, or bilingual *écoles franco-arabes* was not important to him. His principal ethic was to provide children with a "purposeful activity," to optimize personal and psychological "development" (*épanouissement*), which, he argued, would "reduce the effects of sickle cell disease itself" on the body. Rokhoya Sylla, and her parents' commitment to her education—and an eventual vocational training that inspired in her a certain confidence of creativity to design and then crochet ornate dresses—proved his model patient on this "social" front as well as in "biological" terms. In many respects Diagne exhibits what Annemarie Mol describes as "the logic of care," which, she writes: "has no separate moral sphere. Because 'values' intertwine with 'facts,' and caring itself is a moral activity, there is no such thing as an (argumentative) ethics that can be disentangled from (practical) doctoring. You do what you can while watching out for the problems that emerge—in bodies or in daily lives" (2008, 79).

Despite his insisting, continually inquiring, and counseling parents on the intimate details of their children's lives and livelihoods, Diagne remained professional, and often distant in his relationships with patients and their families. His military training may have shaped this aspect of his demeanor. He was attentive, respectful, and reserved (even after a bond had been formed). His distant style was not a customary way of maintaining relationships among the many Senegalese I encountered in Dakar. Diagne commanded an effortless respect from his patients and their families, but it was also clear that he reciprocated this basic recognition of dignity when faced with those seeking care. Nonetheless families always felt that they could count on him, like family, and were visibly frustrated when he had to travel or take vacation. Some would wait until he returned rather than see an intern or another doctor. They valued him as one of the rare people in the university medical corps who allowed them the time to ask as many questions as they wanted. The doctor encouraged this kind of exchange, while many others in his profession took patients who questioned medical expertise to be impertinent. More than a few biomedical practitioners abhorred inquisitive patients. On one occasion, I even witnessed a patient get expelled from a consultation for inquiring about the effects of prescribed medications on his condition at another site. In many interviews, patients described doctors they encountered as solely self-interested; and as Senegalese people often say, their practices "were not serious" (*caxaan la*).

■ Local Biologies and Social Realities

Dr. Diagne's emphasis on education and measurement was complemented by practices more common among those providing sickle cell care elsewhere. Many approaches to care for this disease are shared between the two Dakar biomedical sites that I studied, as well as those beyond the borders of Senegal. The core treatment that remains consistent in Dakar, the United States, and France is the administration of folic acid supplements to stave off the anemia brought on by the disease. The major difference between protocols in the United States and France and those in Senegal lies in the fact that in the North folic acid is the minimal, basic "supplement" given to reduce anemia, whereas in Senegal folic acid is the major "medication."

Although some modes of treatment and attitudes of care for sickle cell may be specific to Dakar and to Africa, Senegalese practitioners feel increasingly compelled to introduce neonatal screening as well as the possibility of safe transfusion technologies. The ability to test newborns, which would require machines (and a reliable stock of reagents) capable of isoelectrofocalization, and the ability to transfuse repeat stroke patients, which would require a better managed blood supply, where a range of currently untested antibodies and proteins could be known, figured on practitioners' lists of what was "lacking" in their services. Other absent technologies and treatments, such as hydroxyurea, were simply seen as unnecessary, and as "impossible to implement" anyway. Dr. Diagne was reluctant to categorize the effects of unmet needs as arising only from "economic" constraints. In our discussions of the subject, he relied on the familiar discourse of the "Senegalese haplotype" to bypass questions of economics altogether. Rather than emphasize what he took to be an overly exaggerated emphasis on what they lacked, or where they were powerless, Diagne highlighted his and his patients' power, since, "according to the science," they were endowed with a beneficial genetic particularity. Even though he sometimes held the haplotype discourse at a distance, in this context he readily accepted its potential value, claiming, "In many ways it compensates for what is lost due to economic disadvantage." Thus, when needed, the Senegalese haplotype permitted him a kind of professional biosociality whereby this genetic sequence variation made him optimistic that he, as a biomedical practitioner, could help his patients attain even better life outcomes.

This did not detract from the fact that for Diagne the most effective external "technology" that he could hope for was almost too simple: organization.[6] In his mind, sickle cell patients could achieve relatively good health if he and his colleagues addressed their minimal needs in a more coordinated fashion. As he told me in 2002:

> We are lucky enough to have a patient population where the majority of those seen have a form of sickle cell, the haplotype Senegal, which is relatively well tolerated. We aren't faced with the same serious problems that one sees in Central Africa or elsewhere. We don't have the same pressure, if you will, to manage extreme complications. Consequently, our most important activity is simply following, surveying patients [*notre activité le plus important c'est une activité de suivi*]; this is to say, we are concerned with how to utilize the simple things. Clinical exams are available to any doctor. No one needs super-sophisticated material to examine a child. To make and keep regular appointments is a question of organization. If we organize and make ourselves available, because we *believe* such an approach will work, we can do it. The most mundane, but necessary, testing technologies needed are things we do have, hemograms, etc. We possess all of the necessary medication— granted patients don't present real serious complications—folic acid, *nivaquine* [for malaria]. . . .
>
> Our main problems are linked to certain explorations necessary for very rare cases, problems that require going beyond the simple techniques required in our daily practice. But once again, patients who present serious complications are exceptional cases here in Senegal. Another problem regards an adequate structure to treat patients when emergencies do arise, but fortunately, as I said a minute ago, with the Senegalese haplotype we don't have many of these situations. In general,

most of what we are faced with is within our means for treatments, for general knowledge, and the ability to diagnose the major problems of the disease. We recently conducted a five-year study in which we realized that we didn't have a higher mortality rate than those in Europe or in the United States, we didn't have more complications. The haplotype plays a part, but the fact that we utilize what we have, and organize in the way that we do, has allowed us to obtain more or less the same results as the others [French and Americans]. This is to say, financial and technological means are not *decisive* in sickle cell care.

The basic care that practitioners at both Dakar biomedical specialty sites offer is seen as sufficient in most cases, even though Diagne constantly challenges himself to do even better.

The doctor could not reiterate enough that local experts' current inability to fully organize themselves properly is to blame for the desired aspects of care that are still missing. This is especially true for safe blood transfusion therapy.

With regard to fundamental research, we do have problems. We can't actually understand a lot of what is happening, hiding under the surface so to speak, in patients' bodies. But for clinical care, since there is no real therapeutic miracle—it just requires the simple things, to be regular about care, to detect infections, to give folic acid, etc.—we don't have major problems. The only problem, *perhaps*, is the inability to transfuse. First there's the risk of AIDS. Even though Senegal doesn't have a much higher rate than many developed countries, which at most is 1 percent, we still have to be careful. The major problem concerns the fact that we don't have all of the necessary blood products to do blood typing if we wanted to adopt a polytransfusion program. When patients have grave complications, like cerebral infarctions, it is recommended everywhere in the world, in America and Europe, to polytransfuse. In Senegal our hands are tied. We can't blindly throw ourselves into transfusing. Not only do we not have all of the blood derivatives we need, but we can't turn to full blood transfusions either. These require introducing multiple bags of blood. The problem is that the CNTS does not phenotype the blood fully. To obtain the blood reactants necessary for testing all donors would not be that difficult. Some might say and think that this is a financial problem, but it is more organizational than anything. If nothing else, the CNTS should fully phenotype a portion of donors so that the few patients who repeatedly present complications, who would benefit from polytransfusions, would have access to them. The problem is definitely more organizational than financial. With a bit of organization all things will come in time. Less than ten years ago there was no focused sickle cell care; no one knew about the disease. We are the pioneers in making crucial issues in sickle cell care visible, public concerns. It is up to us to make things happen. Even now, few people know or talk about the disease in the circles that matter, where the funding is concentrated. Supply adapts to demand. As we have organized patients' care, the *need* for transfusion technology has arisen. In a few years the CNTS will have to respond to this demand and start supplying blood safe for polytransfusion.

Diagne highlights the co-constitutive process of social and medical organization that has allowed his specific sickle cell care clinic to function at all and that has, by extension, increased people's well-being and led to new health needs. One such need was a potential rise in urgencies for polytransfusions. In these early days, he predicted that the funding structures would have to meet the demands of his successful practice of keeping Senegal's most problematic sicklers alive long enough so that they would constitute a health population that would require technologies, like transfusions, which were previously seen as out of reach, or too rare to demand resources. In addition, with education and organization, more adult sicklers were encouraged to "live normal lives," as we have seen previously. For them "normalcy" meant having children first and foremost. Pregnancy was one period when women with the disease would need regular, safe transfusions. Despite the distance they still have to overcome, Dr. Diagne cautiously congratulated his colleagues and other local researchers on the progress that they have made in articulating sickle cell as a problem that will demand more attention, and resources, as it gains visibility.

■ Fagara on the Hospital Grounds

Throughout my fieldwork at Albert Royer Children's Hospital I would sit across from Dr. Diagne, next to his patients and their parents, in the short row of attached, orange plastic chairs arranged for the doctor's clients in his consultation room. Not infrequently people would bring in samples of fagara to ask the doctor's opinion and to seek his approval for this widely used treatment, which he had not prescribed. On a few occasions I witnessed mothers of Diagne's small patients present the doctor with sachets of the dried and pulverized plant. Some would explain that it was the same *garab* (Wolof for both "medicine" and "tree") that they were using, in the form of chewing sticks (*soj*), to clean their teeth and gums. Usually, however, they presented fagara, not from ENDA, but from "the market place" in the most ordinary form of packaging, in crumpled white notepad paper with the mustard-hued powder of its roots stuck in the creases of the much-used sheets. For some time Diagne kept a small package of the plant, branded with the ENDA logo, in his lower desk drawer. One day as the consultation ended, I brought him back to our earlier 1998 conversation, when he and Dr. Fall thought that they would conduct a study on fagara's efficacy in vivo once and for all. He had backed away from the idea for reasons I found rather unclear, and I wondered why. As if remembering that he had fagara in his possession, he pulled out the small sachet. It seemed that he was keeping it for just this occasion, as a physical reference to the reality of pharmacopoeia used to treat the disease he carefully assesses but cannot cure.

In one of our habitual end-of-the-afternoon conversations, Diagne began to recount how Mr. Samba Diallo Tall, the then hospital director, was concerned about sickle cell patients' frustration with the dearth of palliatives. Mr. Tall one day hastened to the clinic and excitedly informed Diagne of "a potential sickle cell remedy." Diagne had long known about the plant, he had explained, but Tall wanted to tell him that the plant was growing "right here on the hospital grounds." Mr. Tall, like every Albert Royer director before him, was given a house behind the *Pavillon des mères* and Diagne's office bloc. Mr. Tall's stucco abode was hidden from view, across a small dirt field where skinny goats grazed on sparse clumps of wild grass behind a whitewashed cement wall. On the other side of the wall, in Tall's garden, purple and pink bougainvillea interspersed with the greenery of medicinal plants. Apparently, Mr. Tall cultivated fagara as well as other key botanicals from what he considered to be "Senegal's vast pharmacopoeia."

A few days after Diagne first spoke to me about the hospital director, he walked me over to the hospital administrative offices to see if we might find Mr. Tall working after hours. Tall was a jolly man with a roll to his deep laugh. He was exceedingly formal in manner, adding heavy syntax to his Wolof, as *buroom xam xam yi*, or "men of knowledge," characteristically do. Diagne explained my anthropological mission, my interest in sicklers, and, as concerned Tall, their ingestion of fagara. Tall invited me to visit his "garden of remedies" and the prized plant the following day when his wife would also prepare a meal for me, as is traditionally done for "guests" (*gan*).

When I arrived at the director's house, Madame Tall, shrouded in a head shawl, was busily arranging place settings on a large cloth on the floor. She had prepared a "healthy" meal, "not the high-sodium, oily rice, *ceebujen*" (which is the national dish), Tall bragged. Tall asked his wife to cook reduced green hibiscus leaves, which resemble creamed spinach, as well as white rice and smoked fish. He explained that such "wholesome foods" were habitual in the Casamance region, "where healers (such as Gaoussou Sambou) are often from." As Mme Tall continued to prepare the meal, Mr. Tall took me on a tour of the garden. He enthusiastically named the various species in Wolof, Latin, or both. He spent the most time elucidating fagara, explaining that it has long been used as an anti-sickling agent in Senegal. When I pressed him on his sources, he responded: "It is simply general knowledge, but it's good that you're curious (*sop*)."

Tall's tour was the first time that I had ever seen what he called "*fagara*." I took many photos, using a macro lens to capture its botanical detail. As

I learned more about fagara from other healers, especially Thalap Sarr and Gaoussou Sambou, it became clear that fagara, whose name in Wolof (*dengidëk*) narrates its morphology of "thorns" (*dëk*), was not in Mr. Tall's garden of therapies. Eventually I had to tell him that his plant was *Maytenus senegalensis* in Latin, which was often confused with fagara because of its similar name, as well as *its* thorns. To make matters worse, people called *maytenus genegidëk*, in Wolof, and often called fagara *genegidëk* as well, since it sounded so much like *dengidëk*. Healers like Sambou simply mixed the two to be safe. Tall then went on to explain how he himself had been treated with traditional medicines a few years prior for a painful bodily condition, which he thought could have been gout. The doctors he saw were at a loss for a diagnosis however. He finally found a cure for the mysterious illness from a traditional healer. Once he recovered, Tall decided to become a student of indigenous plant therapies. The point of his story was that he was "still very much learning," he explained, as he looked over my photos. He nodded and hummed to himself upon examining the photos of fagara I took at IFAN, compared to his *maytenus*. His assessment: the latter was small bushy, slightly dainty, fine; the former was rougher, seemingly stronger and had "*jiko*" (more personality). Tall promised to find himself a fagara tree for his garden. His principal intention, despite the mix up, was to cultivate a pharmacopoly, manufactured

Figure 4.1 *Maytenus senegalensis.* Note its long thorns that branch, and even leaf. Dakar, Fann. Photographed by the author.

Figure 4.2 *Fagara xanthoxyloïdes.* Note its smaller thorns on the stems and leaves. Dakar, Fann. Photographed by the author.

by nature, which he alternately called "*Yallah*" (God), of all the plants used to heal local diseases in Senegal, right on the hospital grounds. In this way "needy patients could just consult nature then and there, rather than spending means that they might not have at the pharmacy."

■ Side Attempts and Central Problems

Dr. Diagne, like Mr. Tall, was of course concerned about specific practices his patients adopted that could improve their lives. He regarded their ingestion of fagara as "intriguing information." He sometimes noted it in patients' charts but had yet to do so systematically. He intimated at "eventually" doing a study on the issue but also hesitated to ever act. "It would be interesting, one day, to try to ascertain whether or not these patients experience fewer crises," he told me several times over the years. He admitted that the many "retrospective" studies carried out in the CHU were less credible than studies that recorded changes in health status and practices in real time. Only a rigorous double-blind trial of fagara would be robust enough to withstand scientific scrutiny.

Diagne, unlike the medical staff at the CNTS, was at first reluctant to endorse fagara, as a scientist and a doctor. In his characteristically diplomatic tone, when the subject arose he repeated the need for confirmatory in vivo studies before he would feel comfortable lauding the plant's properties. The only studies he felt confident about were those confirming that the plant was not toxic. He told his patients' mothers to continue giving their children fagara if they thought that it was helping but to also continue with the folic acid supplements he prescribed. For Diagne, the most important thing was that the patient experienced an improved quality of life.

■ My initial 1998 conversations with Ibrahima Diagne and Mohamadou Fall centered on two studies in the conceptual stages, one mine, the other theirs. Both men were excited at the prospect of medical anthropology taking place in their sickle cell clinic. For reasons that they perhaps already understood but needed to explain with some formula of "science," most of the families who consulted them rarely ever changed their plans to have children, or to continue having children, once they found out that they were at risk for sickle cell disease (Diagne et al. 2000, Fullwiley 2004). Sickle cell testing did not change their behavior, and most often people simply continued on with their lives. Diagne, Fall, and other specialists I encountered almost always cited "culture" as that catch-all concept that would explain this response (or non-response) to people's knowledge that they carried a genetically transmitted disease. The physicians hoped that getting to some element of culture might somehow clarify the behaviors of their patients, which they described as inscrutable, but also said that they understood them on some level, since children were so important to every couple they saw.

As I sat across from Diagne and Fall in Diagne's office one sunny January afternoon, they threw ideas back and forth, agreeing with each other as if they were transmitting the same thoughts, simply letting the other take his turn in voicing aloud to the anthropologist what was known between them. Even their temperaments and laughter seemed to coincide as they resounded the same themes. They were toying with the idea of studying fagara in vivo, and had been for a while. They had also been waiting for something "like anthropology" to happen in their pediatric service. They wondered if I might allow a thesis student to work with me as a way for them to sustain a focus on "culture" and its intersection with medicine once I returned home. As they contemplated the feasibility of a fagara study, they began to cite the necessity of doing it, and then confided that they were not novel thinkers in launching the idea. Colleagues in the CHU departments of pharmacology, hematology, and pediatrics had discussed the need for a fagara study for over a decade. Bits and pieces, small efforts here and there, have been posited, examined, questioned, and even once published locally, only to be abandoned and later taken up once more (as seen in chapter 3). This continuous interest, yet discontinuous investigation, as they presented it and as it became clear in my own fieldwork, seemed to be another circular, but vital (as in always alive) dead-end.

In our 1998 conversations, Diagne and Fall conceptually outlined a plan to follow patients who already took fagara to compare them with other patients who, by their own choice and practices of care, did not. The physicians said that they probably would not distribute the plant; their patients could get it on their own. This move would make them less vulnerable to criticism from their colleagues in scientific medical circles "up North," understood as France. The experiment would be "natural" in every sense; in their back-and-forth they each kept using the words "organic research." As we talked more about the hypothetical protocol for the study, Diagne commented that they did not want to deprive any "control group" of treatment. Often the standard double-blind "methods," he confided, were at base "unethical" for depriving one group of a therapy for too long. In Fall's mind their more "organic" approach would side-step the usual protocol that patients could neither choose their treatment nor be told what treatment they were receiving. The doctors' ruminations on the issue brought to the fore how easily physicians' obligations of care and scientific researchers' methods of investigation can conflict. It was this conflict more broadly, the act of intervening on a cultural ethos and practice of care while imposing a standard of scientific truth that may or may not capture the palliative source of the plant, that also troubled Diagne. Additionally, he has had difficulty reconciling his subject position as a biomedical practitioner with his stance that this instance of traditional medicine (which is not formally "his domain") deserves a fair clinical trial.

When I returned to Dakar, in the fall of 1999, the fagara study had not yet materialized. Dr. Diagne cited numerous obstacles that blocked him and his colleagues. Most were organizational: they were underfunded and understaffed, and no one had the time to monitor a group of patients who, in any case, usually only took fagara when they felt weak, stressed, or sensed a crisis coming on. Over the years to follow, and as late as 2008 when Diagne again began contemplating a study of this very sort ten years later once he met Courot, he fretted about "formal proof" and "precision," which he understood and wanted himself. Yet, he also feared that a narrow emphasis on these would diminish the value of studies he classed as "organic." Why the continuous interest in fagara has met with so many breaks can also be attributed to the additional social pressures on Senegalese actors to remain skeptical of endorsing this traditional therapy that were detailed in chapter 3. The dramas that ensued around fagara between Paris and Cotonou are coupled in Diagne's mind with a self-consciousness about his and his colleagues' intellectual and scientific worth, which remains highly vulnerable in their interactions with certain French colleagues and would-be collaborators.

■ **Between France and Africa**

Dr. Robert Girot hosted Diagne in Paris in the early 1990s, providing him access to patients at Tenon Hospital and a place on his research team where he could gain more expertise in hematology. Like two other specialists on the disease in the Paris region, who have also hosted Diagne at different intervals, Gil Tchernia and Frédéric Galactéros, Girot had done part of his medical training in the former French colonies. All three Parisian specialists felt that sickle cell was a "marginalized" disease. Girot furthermore qualified it as a "ghettoized *maladie*." Galactéros, in a more poetic locution carrying a clever pun, pronounced the genetic condition a "disinherited disorder." Tchernia condemned France as "a racist country," which, for him, was the basic problem facing sicklers there, while he added that the United States suffered greatly from the same "pathology" of discrimination but that *les Américains* at least recognized the condition. Of consequence, each practitioner felt himself to also be somewhat marginalized within the interconnected fields of hematology and biochemistry for dedicating his career to this problem. Unlike Tchernia, Girot was uncomfortable speaking about race. One of his close colleagues explained his reticence by saying that talk of race was actually "taboo in France."

Nevertheless Girot remembered with fondness being stationed in Africa during his medical military service, specifically in Dakar during the mid-1970s. The doctor had not been back to Senegal since, and barely recalled such details as the names of streets, greetings in Wolof, or any specific incidence of sickle cell. For him the disease surely existed, but had not yet been articulated during his assignment in "*les tropiques*." He insisted that physicians treated each of its symptoms independently. He was not aware that sickle cell trait was one of the final interests of *Afrique occidentale française* (AOF) colonial medics during the 1950s. He was confident that even today serious care for the disease on the continent was sorely lacking.

When I returned to Paris in 2000, during one of our meetings Girot started in on a plaintive about the low standard of care for sickle cell patients on the continent. I then put forth Dr. Diagne as an example of someone who had successfully begun a sickle cell consultation in Senegal with good results. He smiled and referred to him as "a smart boy" (*c'est un garçon très intelligent*). I thought to myself that Diagne, then in his early forties and a husband and father, was far beyond boyhood. The French doctor did not notice the blunder. In the same conversation, as if talking about Senegal transported him back to another time, he referred to Senegal as "French Africa" (*l'Afrique française*). This time he covered his mouth and said, "Oh, if they heard me say that!" and laughed to himself, embarrassed (a bit boyishly). I mention these revealing slips (*lapsus révélateurs*) not to villanize the French doctor but to illustrate certain telling signs of the climate that Senegalese physician-researchers encounter in their efforts at collaboration with their French counterparts. These are small indications (from the hard-working, well-intentioned, and self-described marginalized medical provider that is Dr. Girot) that certain ideas still abound in Paris today and are ever-present in sickle cell care circles. French disease experts still ruminate about the tropics with a certain bias towards their own power faced with another's pathology, which is also now their own pathology (professionally) when it comes to matters of this racialized disease.

In one of our long post-consultation talks, before my return to do more fieldwork in France in 2000, Diagne and I broached the topic of an easily locatable tendency we both felt in Paris within medicine but also more broadly: a "fascination" with Africa as an exotic locale. Many Senegalese equated this exoticism with a form of indirect racism. I recounted how, in the case of a psychologist who works with sickle cell patients in Girot's clinic and with a local "African ethnopsychiatrist" who "heals" those patients in Paris, the mental health specialist often used the phrase "*je suis fascinée!*" (I am hypnotized, captivated) when talking about what she and the ethnopsychiatrist, who was from Benin, referred to as "the invisible world" operative in Africans' daily experiences of rationality. In such a world, which was only truly "*invisible*" to those whose psyches did not partially reside there, objects and spirits inflected the course of action in the "*monde visible*," the world of supposed modern rationality, that purportedly dictated the life courses of most (French) people, in her reckoning. Diagne's experience with French notions of African "exoticism," as it is fueled by both French and Africans, bore traces of the term's original meanings: outside, foreign, extrinsic. They were also less droll.

In a monotone voice characteristic of the late afternoon of his workdays, which in many ways dramatized rather than muted his disbelief, Diagne recounted the following story after I told him about the French psychologist, her collaborator (the Beninois healer) and her fascination with *l'Afrique*.

My experience in France taught me to never underestimate the ways that many—not all—scientists there still continue to treat us as if we exist to service their needs. They don't treat us as equals. They may take an interest in Africa, but at base there is a form of racism there that I don't think they even fully realize. It happens with publications, and collaborations, as if we are here to simply facilitate their work. This has happened to me personally. It has happened with others here in Senegal as well. (. . .) When I was in Paris, in Girot's service, we were working on an article together with a few other people. I clearly wrote up my section, and the methods for the part of the research I conducted, but I had to go back to Senegal before the paper was actually submitted. At some point shortly thereafter, I asked Girot about it. He was clearly bothered [*gêné*]. He said that there was "a problem," but sent me the published text anyway. When I received it, I was nowhere to be found among the authors. Now, if this concerned a European, not an African, I do not think that things would have gone this way. Maybe too many Africans accept this. Someone has to initiate a change.

Diagne was mildly forgiving. As he continued talking, he wondered if things would ever shift to real equality between the North and South. This story then flowed into the next. At the time he was in a delicate situation with a few of Girot's colleagues who were trying to convince him to "collaborate" with them on a new sickle cell haplotype population genetic study.

Diagne, who now saw himself as being in a position to initiate the change that he himself had been calling for, was in the process of choosing his battles. I say this because the timing was such that he and Professor Fall were trying to send a stern message to their Northern colleagues that they were to be taken seriously, and as equals, with regard to the haplotype study, at the same time that the VK500 controversy was brewing in Paris. In other words, his negotiations with his Parisian colleagues on the haplotype study coincided with him leaving fagara to the realm of patient experience for the time being. He could not afford to be tainted by association or by having sympathies with Fagla Médégan's "unscientific" behavior in putting forth a plant "cure." During this period, from early 2000–2002, Diagne seemed content to let patients take the plant but distanced himself from the possibility of a fagara trial until years later.

■ The Senegalese Attitude vis-à-vis the Senegalese Haplotype

What became increasingly obvious was that after the VK500 scandal certain physician-researchers in Dakar cultivated a deliberately ambiguous position on patient-use of fagara. It was quietly accepted in Senegalese sickle cell circles at Albert Royer and received a more open, but calculated, endorsement by specialists at the CNTS. Patients, who were mostly unaware of VK500 until they heard about Médégan's 2007 patent, continued to give fagara the benefit of doubt. Their hopefulness mixed with their realism, since it was one of the only available treatments that, despite the hesitations of Diagne and certain key French doctors, enjoyed a positive association with their disease in public culture. Sicklers often testified to one another about the plant's virtues. Open-air-market vendors also enthusiastically cited its powers. Diagne remained as neutral as possible and never tried to dissuade patients from taking it. He simply maintained that he could not vouch for its efficacy.

As part of an ongoing attempt to problematize unseen biases in language and scientific thinking—where ideas of order blur the lines between the social world and the untidy space of nature at all costs—health philosopher Georges Canguilhem pointed out that humans attain scientific knowledge "by identifying reality and quantity." But, he went on to say, "it should be remembered that, though scientific knowledge invalidates qualities, which it makes appear illusory, for all that, it does not annul them. Quantity is quality denied, but not quality suppressed" (1994, 348). As an anthropologist of science and medicine, I wondered about the relationship of quantification, precision, Diagne's concern with "formal proof," and the *quality* of life that fagara may or may not have offered to people with sickle cell I knew. I also wondered about this same set of concepts as they related to knowledge on the "Senegalese haplotype." It seemed that "quality," as the pedigree of process that yields any specific disease outcome, was indeed being suppressed here. Both fagara and the haplotype were defined as "scientific," or not, in the case of the plant, based on the ability of researchers to deploy metrics of "quantification" that might be assumed to elucidate something about biological end points, or health outcomes. Empirically both objects have appeared in various medical journal articles, each has been linked to better health outcomes by association or through a theorized mechanism (oxygenation of red blood cells and anti-sickling of blood, for fagara, and a link to increased fetal hemoglobin, or simply population differential expressions of illness, for the Senegalese haplotype). Yet neither has been *proven* to directly cause better health. Ambivalence, as well as attempts to ascertain certainty by fiat, characterized many of the conversations I had with doctors and patients who believed in the truth of either fagara, the Senegalese haplotype, or both.

In my discussions with Dr. Diagne, and with those who follow sickle cell patients at the CNTS, they occasionally asked me semi-rhetorically, "Why is it that Senegalese patients indeed do fare better?" The discourse on the effects of a certain physical configuration at the genetic level, or the haplotype, at times appeared attractive, and all Senegalese practitioners specializing in sickle cell care dutifully mentioned it in one setting or another. Yet their references to the haplotype were often qualified, and they consistently interrupted themselves to discontinue this line of thought and suggest others. Although the genetic hypothesis is, for lack of better information on the topic, treated as "verging on truthful discourse," to borrow Foucault's language, these practitioners still hoped to push the limits of the scientific world they partake in by inserting aspects of the social, cultural, and perhaps biological environment specific to life in Dakar. Although he cites the haplotype when it seems fitting, Diagne could not fully accept a logic that assumes that increased fetal hemoglobin (HbF) levels necessarily account for better health when his healthiest patient, Rokhoya Sylla, has always produced very little of this protein. The answers, he acknowledges, are far from clear.[7]

Senegalese physician-researchers offer a variety of possible explanations for the overall good health of Senegalese patients, if "better health" can even be claimed. This assessment is usually followed by many qualifiers. In comparative studies, Diagne and his colleagues found that while their patients suffer less from infections, their levels of morbidity and mortality are on par with cohorts of patients studied in the United States and Europe (Diagne et al. 2000). To claim "better" overall health, given these "equal" levels of morbidity, is in part an attempt to position themselves as guardians of a special population (even if they are not quite sure about the best way to qualify this exceptionalism). It is also an intellectual move to trouble the taken-for-granted emphases put on outcomes without properly taking into consideration the environment in which differential life chances are situated. Diagne's heuristic move that both differentiates and defines Senegalese sicklers is meant to emphasize that his patients confront many more environmental threats from disease-causing bacteria, malaria parasites, malnutrition, dehydration, and other "risks," such as a lack of vaccines and proper newborn screening, many of which he and his colleagues attribute to poverty in sub-Saharan Africa. In publications on the general health of their patients, practitioners in Dakar mention the Senegalese haplotype as a potential contributing factor for better health on the ground. Yet they place their emphases on regular clinical follow-up, acquiring vaccinations and folic acid, as well as scholastic education—all of whose importance they feel has been overlooked in the literature focused on haplotypes (Diagne et al. 2000, 23; Diop et al. 1999, 173–74). Lastly, Diagne and his collaborators theorize that the ecology of Senegal, including climate and general "environment" on the peninsula of Dakar, affords patients "stable temperatures" that also work in their favor (Diagne et al. 2000, 23). In short, doctors in Dakar feel confident that the mild disease they witness is due to multi-layered intricacies. All of this, however, falls within "scientific reason." Notably, they leave out of publications more fluid aspects of their conceptual *équipement* (*semiologie*, an openness to fagara) as they attempt to recalibrate the weight given concepts of genetic causation in the story of sickle cell "moderation."

In putting forward emphases on surveillance and education, Diagne and others felt that they have nonetheless made clear that they are observers of a unique bio-cultural phenomenon. The exact sources and causes of Senegalese health still remained vague, or uncertain, both in their minds and in their conversational attempts to articulate them. For instance, in a conversation about how he did not want to be too generous to the haplotype discourse, by letting it "have everything responsible for mild sickle cell," Diagne articulated a kind of cultural corollary. Even in its grammatical form, this alternative was clearly a retort against the explanatory power of *l'haplotype sénégalais*—it was an "as if" scientific rejoinder that Diagne himself named the "*attitude sénégalaise*."

The "Senegalese attitude" was often articulated by Dr. Diagne and his colleagues in response to the perennial question of why Senegalese patients "fare better." This localized "attitude" serves as a plausible alternative to genetic markers and as a tangible enough explanation of the fact that most patients are healthier than would be expected. Diagne, like many practitioners in Senegal and elsewhere, was wary of overemphasizing the role that genetic information (insofar as we know it) has on health outcomes. This is not to say that he would deny the role of genetics categorically (Diagne et al. 2000, 23). Nor does it negate uptake of a more general idea of "mild Senegalese sickle cell" that he and others in Dakar find to be a useful tool, at times. Yet, as far as a genetic causation is concerned, the myriad relations of DNA, proteomic, enzymatic, and other physiological factors influencing biological cause and effect remain largely unexplored and constitute a vast terrain of unknowns for Diagne and his colleagues the world over. Furthermore, the technologies that might capture these and reveal their relations to sickle cell health are not readily within reach in Senegal. More proximal and evident to him, since it is expressed through the actions of his patients and their families, is an "attitude" that Dr. Diagne consciously attributed, and localized, to Senegalese people. In so doing, he was both playing with and challenging the genetic-mapping logic that named the haplotype of Atlantic West Africa "Senegalese."

What exactly one might mean by "attitude" in Senegal is more encompassing than the term in English. Almost all of my conversations, interviews, and interactions with health care professionals in Dakar took place in French. It made sense that Diagne employed the French term in his clinical setting because of its emphasis on, and implication of, the body. The *Petit Robert French Dictionary* provides the following definition:

> Attitude: 1: The way in which one holds one's body. SYN: countenance, upkeep, pose, position, posture, stance [*station*]. 2: The way in which one carries one's self [*se tenir*], (and by extension comportment) which corresponds to a certain psychological disposition. SYN: Air, allure, aspect, expression, manner. 3) Disposition with regard to something or someone: the ensemble of ideas [*jugements*] and tendencies that lead to a certain behavior or comportment. SYN: disposition, position, comportment, conduct.

Dr. Diagne, while laughing slightly upon hearing himself speak in terms of "attitudes" aloud, explained that the problem had to do with things "quantifiable and not." He asked himself, how could one use such a concept, *attitude*, in his field? How could he possibly write and publish on such an idea in a medical world where things *qualitative* have little place? Recall that Canguilhem suggests that qualitative phenomena are made to "appear illusory" within science generally (1994, 348). Diagne assured me that science would have to go beyond this tendency in order to understand the experience of his patients.

Genetic researchers, such as Jacques Elion and his team, have tried to make the "Senegalese" and other haplotypes into reliable references that indicate some degree of severity. Yet before it was clear that such a diagnostic register was even possible there was already a cultural tendency in Paris sickle cell circles to simply cite population-specific haplotypes as shorthand for understanding sickle cell differential expression. To date most haplotype/population-based research on sickle cell has counted as "scientific"—despite its deep uncertainty about what the sequence changes actually *do*—in part because it was founded on quantifiable concepts in the 1984 study. The "quality," or meaning, however, of haplotype differences remains a missing link. Finding, or defining, this link may dramatically increase knowledge on sickle cell expression and the value of the haplotype-based severity diagnostic framework—or not.

Despite many publications about the population frequencies of African sickle cell haplotypes, not much is known about what these DNA sequence variations actually confer in peoples' sick bodies. This is true for genetics in France, Senegal, and elsewhere. Physicians in Paris, including both Robert Girot and his sometimes rival Dr. Frédéric Galactéros, routinely refer to these markers to classify their patients as having "mild" vs. "severe" sickle cell disease without really knowing exactly what haplotype differences mean in patients' clinical courses. In an interview with Galactéros, who allowed me to do fieldwork in his Créteil (suburban Paris) clinic for six months in 1997–1998, he recounted that haplotype testing was often done and that "surprises were rare." Although he and his colleagues had patients undergo the HbS genetic clinical identity testing, he still safely assumed that those from Senegal had the Senegalese haplotype, which for him also meant that they had a less severe form of the disease.

Beyond aggregate patterns in genetic configurations showing that ~82 percent of Senegalese people tested shared "something," as did most of those tested in Benin, it can be safely said that practitioners who refer to haplotypes when classifying patients do not know exactly what "quality" they are specifying. Sickle cell haplotypes were born of, and continue to circulate in sickle cell scientific circles largely because of, the "quantitative" quality of the original research. These aspects of quantity (population frequencies of DNA sequence variation) were made to *represent* differences in sickle cell quality—observed differential symptom expression and disease courses. The power of quantification has in many ways absorbed a larger preoccupation with differential life and health—qualities that inspired the initial haplotype studies in the first place. Research clinicians admit the fuzziness of their useful HbS African haplotypes concept. The concept is starving for scientific "qualification," but is obviously being fed by other modes of cultural meaning, population grouping, and, for Senegalese practitioners, medical necessity. Even so, Dr. Diagne and other African physicians often felt the haplotype paradigm to be an importation that could not adequately account for many sickle cell realities in Dakar, in Senegal, and across the continent. By contrast, the "*attitude sénégalaise*," which Diagne admitted was less scientific, appeared to be a "local" clue to differential disease severity. This concept is laden with its own problems that also have deep roots in ethnicizing Senegalese behavior but in a different way. Nonetheless, this potential dead end becomes an exit to approach a reality that captures an aspect of affect inherent in people's aspirations for health.

Diagne, many of my Senegalese friends, and other Africans often told me that they felt Senegalese people to be "particular," meaning special and somewhat unique, not only in their homeland but in the social networks they extend throughout the world through travel, commerce, and work, as they have successfully relocated to almost every corner of the globe. It is this particularity, explained from an insider's perspective by someone who feels himself "Senegalese," that Diagne tried over and again to make me see. In an attempt to illustrate what he was getting at he described an ethos that allows one to navigate difficult situations that combines old-fashioned "gumption"—a mix of resourcefulness, initiative, an enterprising spirit, and common sense—with a belief in actionable fate, which trumps individual agency, and inspires a disposition toward positive thinking (known locally as *rafet njort*, or "beautiful thoughts").

This attitude was said to persist even when people were faced with the most desperate situations. Such tactical strategies of positively mentally *making-do* ultimately convey a mode of rationalizing that places the human being in question as secondary, or even tertiary, to fate, to others who may intervene on his or her behalf, and to God. Somewhat relieved of personal responsibility for his or her own health and future, the person who occupies the position of the sufferer is able to take care of the self in other ways. In short, the *attitude sénégalaise* is a disposition that alleviates some degree of Diagne's patients' mental and bodily stress through which their condition makes itself felt. Indeed, "*coono*," a Wolof term that encompasses social stress and physical fatigue, was the principal factor that sicklers charged with bringing on their crises. Despite desperate situations of lack, poverty, and loss, they cited notions of getting by, or making-do with their disease, as Magueye Ndiaye's story in chapter 2 makes clear.

Diagne mused over the fact that the Senegalese attitude would probably not make it into medical journals. He is still trying to make a name for himself as a researcher and is not willing to risk being ostracized by his French colleagues, even if an article on the subject could someday make its way through a review process. He confided that there needed to be a way to talk about such things. If not, the gap in medical knowledge on Senegalese sickle cell, which is obvious to and intuitively understood by Diagne and his colleagues, would remain hopelessly exposed. The haplotype, by contrast, made up in conceptual coverage what the Senegalese attitude left bare. As a biological trait, at the DNA level, localized in people living in Senegal, the Senegalese haplotype has actually been located beyond its national borders to the bodies of people in Guinea, Mali, Gambia, and other countries that make up Atlantic Africa. Nonetheless, the naming of the haplotype as "Senegal" symbolically worked to confer a local impression, when needed, that nature had ruled in both patients' and practitioners' favor. This distinction, and bio-cultural particularity, has myriad near and distant repercussions, both temporally and spatially, as will be fleshed out in chapter 5.

■ Varying Attitudes of Care

Other practitioners in Dakar, just across the way at the CNTS, relied on a belief in the attitude for varied instrumental means. They also used it almost interchangeably with the haplotype to claim certain freedoms from their patients' demands. The fact that Senegalese sickle cell was conceived of as "mild," for uncertain reasons that could be nonetheless theorized, created an ambivalence about the necessity of their own utility as care providers, which at times turned to negligence. Practitioners who subscribed to multiple lines of thought found an opening, "an exit," which leads us back to their acceptance of fagara for patients who may be benefiting from haplotype, "attitudinal," and pharmacopoeia's effects. In interviews with several key providers at the CNTS, I learned that they believed in the healing powers of plants quite seriously. At the same time, they operated within the structures set up by "truthful discourse"—on the tested and accepted therapies for sickle cell—inherited from their French training. As an object of their ambivalence, fagara itself was polyvalent, used as means without a finite, determined end. Fagara was, among other things: 1) a buffer, perhaps softening the blow of living with and caring for a disease for which neither cure nor sufficient palliative treatments exist; 2) a real alternative, as those who cannot afford pharmaceutical drugs are often told by their practitioners at the CNTS to try the plant; and 3) an "out" that allowed some practitioners to abnegate their responsibilities since they have faith that the fagara plant and its "anti-sickling properties" will sustain the chronically ill patients who constantly call on them.

The attitudes of medical practitioners, as well as those of their patients, warrant analysis, since it was physicians who named and deployed the idea of an *attitude sénégalaise* in the first place. Patients sometimes pointed to Islam, their religious faith, their solidarity, and their "beautiful thoughts" as palliative, even sometimes curative forces. But they never ventured a self-analysis that included a generalizing concept like the Senegalese attitude. Their caregivers' vantage point of seeing sickle cell medical reports in a global literature that made their cases appear mild by comparison enabled them to make this assertion. People living with the disease were, by most accounts, symptomatic, and often suffering. They did not share physicians' senses that their relatively "moderate" form of the disease was a special "blessing," as such. (As we saw in chapter 3, some people, like Madame Cissé of Nianing, however, considered fagara a blessing for making sickle cell manageable.) Indeed, few living with the disease were aware that their condition was seen, in scientific terms, to be less severe than in other places, before I brought it to their surprised attention. Explanatory categorizations of this sort are always telling. They reveal, often with great clarity, how one group of people understands and sees another. Yet they may also tell something about those making the claims and doing the categorizing. In interviews and conversations with these practitioners, it became clear that, in practice, the *attitude sénégalaise* had a certain utility. Biomedical practitioners themselves were also operating via *attitudes* that partially fit descriptions they detailed as "Senegalese." Like sickle cell sufferers who saw their condition as a result of forces beyond their control, certain physicians either did not consider themselves to be primary actors responsible for their actions, or their repercussions, or they pointed to a greater force, which required some degree of faith, as the orchestrator of events wherein they themselves served merely as conduits. At the same time, they too displayed a certain gumption in positing, promoting, and practicing particular forms of "care." The Senegalese sickle cell (haplo)type would not only "save" patients, it would also spare practitioners the trouble of doing so.

The CNTS Clinic

In the remainder of this chapter, I present other Senegalese practitioners not by their hierarchical rank, as is wont to do in Senegal, but rather by their varying degrees of visibility in the institutional setting of the CNTS. It is important to restate that the CNTS is a blood bank. For adult sickle cell patients, it is also their clinic, but more importantly, for the staff of the blood bank, it is a blood donation site. Donors are usually processed first, and pass ahead of those who come seeking care outside of the Thursday morning consultation reserved for sicklers. In the late 1990s the center began a "day hospital" service, and a few years later it began to accommodate patients who required hospitalization. Sickle cell consultations were free until 2006 when the center began to charge 2.500 *cfa*, which sparked widespread complaint. In 2010 the fee doubled to 5.000 *cfa*, while a consultation with an intern still runs lower, 3.500 or 2.500 *cfa* depending on how good they are judged to be by the CNTS director. The principal sickle cell specialist at the CNTS, Dr. Saliou Diop, was in Paris on a molecular genetics and hematology research stay during my initial fieldwork, in 1999–2001, and had taken time off to study for his tenure promotion (*aggregation*) during one of my subsequent research stints at the CNTS in 2006. Others were standing in for him during these years. These visiting doctors, when they were not students or interns, seemed to feel as though they were donating time taken out of their busy schedules at other CHU sites that had functioning hospitals and more sophisticated labs, such as *l'Hôpital Le Dantec*. Sicklers were often reminded of this fact when they would cross the path of Dr. Diop's main replacement (for nearly two years, from 1999–2001), Dr. Awa Touré, in the hall on her way out of the complex and on her way to *Le Dantec* at the time of their scheduled consultation. "You should have been here earlier. No one was here so I'm leaving. Come back next Thursday," she would say, often without stopping. Dr. Touré had conflicts with some patients because of what they called "her attitude," including Magueye Ndiaye. He arrived one morning in crisis during Diop's absence. "She was late! And when she arrived she we was simply visiting and carrying on in the hallway. I told her that I had been waiting since 7:00 a.m. I was irritated and she threatened to call the guards on me. I told her to call them, as they all knew me." I walked in as Magueye stormed out. Dr. Touré was angry and unable to calm herself for the rest of the morning. Magueye did not come back to clinic until Dr. Diop returned.

Touré was one of the few women working on sickle cell disease in the CHU system in 1999 and 2000, yet sickle cell was not her specialty, as she told me in 2000:

> What really interests me in hematology is homeostasis, hemophilia, etc. That's the stuff that excites me. But since we're African, we also have to be generalists. Saliou is not here so I have to take over the sickle cell consultation. And I've realized, working on sickle cell, that it does have its interesting points. There are homeostasis problems among sicklers that I can exploit.

She looked forward to working at *La Dantec* to do research after Saliou's return.

Dr. Toure treated all sicklers, young and old, men and women, AS and SS patients. The consultation at the CNTS consisted mostly of a quick interview to determine whether or not the patient was taking folic acid, or had experienced a sickle cell crisis since the last visit. This short question-and-answer period was followed by a renewed prescription for folic acid and *doliprane* (acetaminophen). Periodically, especially when patients complained of pain, fatigue, or crises, Touré ordered a blood test to determine the patient's hemoglobin level to monitor their anemia. There was little contact between the doctor and the patients she had been confided by her colleague. In one interview, she conceded that she covered the clinic mostly to ensure that it did not lose patients during Diop's absence.

More than once Dr. Touré and I discussed issues of research ethics. We initially broached this topic following a discussion on theoretically implementing protocols for hydroxyurea. Hydroxyurea has been approved by the United States Food and Drug Administration (U.S. FDA) and France's *Agence française de sécurité sanitaire des produits de santé* (AFSSAPS) but Touré explained that she and her colleagues "would not prescribe the drug for sickle cell patients in Senegal because practitioners at the CNTS test drugs locally, even if they are approved in the West, before administering them to their patient population." Although others I interviewed, including the then head of the National Pharmacy, Issa Lô, agreed with this claim in theory, it did not seem to hold in practice. Doctors not only prescribed drugs that were approved elsewhere, they also prescribed drugs off label if they needed to improvise a treatment regimen at times. Yet it is on this point of local testing of drugs that led Touré to the topic of unethical research. She reasoned that she and others were especially concerned about a drug like hydroxyurea, a chemotherapeutic with a potentially high level of toxicity. The National Pharmacy in Senegal has approved hydroxyurea as a leukemia treatment, but Touré was not sure that it would be legally permitted to administer it for sickle cell without a proper local trial, which would raise the ethical issues she had in mind. First, because Senegalese patients have been observed both to possess high fetal hemoglobin levels and to live a "milder" clinical course, Toure doubted that they would need such a potent medication. Other researchers in Dakar mentioned social and economic problems that inhibited them from offering this drug for sickle cell in Senegal. A daily dosage costs eight times as much as folic acid. Touré added that it would be unethical to have patients *themselves* purchase such an expensive treatment so that scientists (who usually had little funding for local trials) could test the drug's efficacy in affected Senegalese. Attempting to put the hypotheticals together, I asked her to elaborate on the ethical issues more precisely. She explained:

> What is it in fact that we're looking for in hydroxyurea research? By using hydroxyurea, the hope is to raise fetal hemoglobin levels. We know that the Senegalese haplotype corresponds to a relatively high level of fetal hemoglobin, which isn't always the case, but generally it's relatively high. Those with the haplotype tolerate [interrupts herself] —Would it really be necessary to give Senegalese patients hydroxyurea, given the fact that they already have high HbF levels? . . . We would have to be sure that hydroxyurea [interrupts herself]—Even if we prescribed it from the outset, we would have to regularly do hemoglobin electrophoreses for each patient, and then the numerations and electrophoreses would pose a problem [because of costs], yet we would have to do them to make sure that we are efficacious, at least, and that the drug that we're giving indeed raises fetal hemoglobin levels. We would have to survey the effects. This is not a banal drug. We're talking about a chemotherapeutic agent. We have to be able to follow the side effects, and to do this requires taking repeated numerations. Hydroxyurea will not only act on hemoglobin production, but moreover, it will act on normal elements in the body. It can destroy normal, needed elements. If it were not well implemented, it would be a dangerous treatment.

For Touré, a notion that local bodies produce high fetal hemoglobin levels permits the CNTS practitioners to opt out of a theoretically costly testing procedure, or a specific trial on their population, even if outsiders might see such additional testing as unnecessary, or redundant.

Despite the doctor's claim that she could not oblige patients to purchase the expensive medication for such an experiment, she later revealed the source of her anxiety on this issue. She had actually seen firsthand how such deceptive experiments did occur. She gave an example, careful to avoid revealing principal investigators' identities. She recounted that when she was a student, in the 1990s, she was involved in studies where patients were asked to buy medications, in some cases expensive medications, in order to enable curious researchers to assess their efficacy in Senegalese patients. She felt that studies in which patients not only unwittingly participated in research but also had to pay for the drugs were unethical. Touré explained that doctors' careers often get advanced "on the backs of their patients." We both knew that patients who come to the CNTS, which at that time offered free care, were often among the poorest people in Dakar who could not afford private consultations. She then partially excused these seemingly inevitable practices by adding: "In an underdeveloped country, it is not just the economy, the schools, and the infrastructure that are underdeveloped, it is the mentality, even in medicine. That's what underdevelopment does to people."

"Doctored Neglect" and Pardon in Senegal

On some Thursday mornings, rather than finding Dr. Touré, I would find straggling patients sitting on the small hard benches that flanked the CNTS corridors. Later I would see them standing in the dust on the makeshift sand sidewalk on the *route d'Oukam* waiting for the bus home. These were the mornings that Dr. Toure simply did not show. The receptionist would tell patients to come back the next week. In some cases, it already was the following week. As patients got to know me, they would interrogate me about the doctor's whereabouts and when she would be available to see them. Once when this happened I called Dr. Touré at *Le Dantec* hospital. She explained that she was swamped, and then asked me to tell the patients to come back the following week, or even the week after. Every missed consultation had its own excuse. Most people were accepting and forgiving.

Patients told me that Touré's behavior was not out of the ordinary at the CHU. Dr. Touré and others working on sickle cell would cite many reasons for why it was difficult to give care in Dakar. For her, there were three fundamental saving graces that allowed her to skip out on patients and carry on with her research at *Le Dantec*: the Senegalese haplotype; the widespread ingestion of the *Fagara xanthoxyloïdes* plant; and, curiously, Islam. Dr. Touré's discussion of "why bring hydroxyurea to Senegal?" indicates her reluctance to intervene using serious medications. Relying on understandings of a "less severe form" of the disease, Dr. Toure also takes into consideration patients' use of traditional plants and their strong religious faith, both of which offer her "exits" from medical responsibility. The following was also from our 2000 interview:

DF: What are some of the most felt obstacles facing you as a practitioner in Dakar?

AT: Most of them are . . . socio-cultural. People only come in when they're sick. And then, especially with hemophiliacs, it's often too late. The sickle cell patients are somewhat better. Dr. Diop and Dr. Thiam have established a culture around sickle cell at the CNTS and people are more informed about their disease. But since they have fagara they don't need to come in all of the time. They can just take the plant at home, rather than coming in to get care that they might not need.

DF: Being a doctor, can you recommend traditional medicinal plants to your patients when these plants are not yet approved by legal and pharmacological state administrative offices without suffering legal ramifications?

AT: It's not legal, but, well. . . . This is not a repressive country at that level of things. People aren't yet that cultivated to attack someone because of this kind of thing. But it's not legal, not at all. All traditional medicine is illegal actually. Certain people are working on trying to change this. You know [that] I don't have the right to use or prescribe medications that are considered "illegal." I don't have the right to talk to my patients about it, but, oh well.

DF: If they ask . . .

AT: Of course. I tell them to go and get themselves some *fagara*. It's scientifically proven that it works! [referring to Thiam et al. 1990] If they ask me, I tell them without a doubt to go and get some *fagara*. I myself use traditional medicines, they work!

In a society where patients and doctors alike ingest medicinal plants, and in a clinic where Dr. Touré's colleagues and superiors at the CNTS are the scientists who, in her view, "proved" Fagara's efficacy, she may feel that her responsibility to be present and to follow these chronically ill patients is a waste of time. For Touré, the fact that her patients would forgive her absences had less to do with the fact that they had no choice if they wanted sickle cell "care," than with her belief that her patients were inclined to forgive much more serious offenses. Seen in this light, surely her neglect would warrant pardon.

This issue became most clear when I asked Dr. Touré to elaborate on situations in which Islam, or what she called the "socio-cultural," acts on the course of medical practice and thinking. She replied:

There are so many influences, but most of the time it's unconscious. It's educational [*c'est l'éducation au sens large du terme*] more than anything else. As a doctor, I was still educated, brought up in a certain way. It's social, in fact. Often you have an idea of things that differs with that learned in medical school or that diverges from ideas advanced by the discipline. Sometimes your own upbringing, religious or otherwise, will dominate and influence you in your everyday practice. Now, can this type of thing influence the general direction of medicine? I don't think so. But I could be wrong. For example, it's true that the laws on abortion are totally informed by the religion. . . . And, again [interrupts herself, thinking] . . . Come to think of it, why aren't there more lawsuits here? In Western countries when doctors mess up [*font une bêtise ou une grosse bêtise*], people sue! Here [in Senegal] you can put someone on an operating table, open them up, kill the person, God forgive me [she lapses into Wolof just to say *astafurla*! [*God forbid*], but people will never sue you because of the religion.

I asked her to explain the link between religious belief and the lack of litigiousness.

AT: People . . . say that it's Allah that kills people. . . . For them, it's not the doctor that killed the poor guy on the table, it's God that has decided to pass *through* the doctor and kill the guy because he was *supposed* to die. You see? The religion actually protects us. We're always making ridiculous mistakes and messing up [*on fait plein de conneries*] and then no one ever does a thing. We're protected.

DF: Celestial insurance. . . ?

AT: And it doesn't cost a thing. It just takes giving the Koran out to the whole population!

DF: That's terrible. But true, people here seem to have made a habit out of pardoning.

AT: They forgive so easily.

The *attitude sénégalaise* was thus not just about improving life by creatively and resourcefully making-do, but could potentially also entail a fatalism so intense that wrongful death might be excused. Dr. Touré highlights the extent to which patients are often willing to doctor neglect, to dress it up for the better, not because of a faith in the sterile mask of medicine, but because of a belief in the final word on human existence decided by the holy.

■ Plant Life and Placebo Effects

Professor Mamadou ("Doudou") Thiam currently serves as the assistant director of the CNTS, and as stated in the previous chapter, in 2000 he was appointed the dean of the Faculty of Medicine in Dakar. Thiam was also the first author on the often-cited article on *Fagara xanthoxyloïdes*' effects on sickle hemoglobin published in *Dakar Medical* in 1990.[8] Again, as discussed in chapter 3, the results suggested that an active ingredient in fagara might stave off sickle cell crises. The English abstract, which appears on *MEDLINE*, claims that fagara was just as efficacious as the widely prescribed drug pent-oxifylline, known by French-trained pharmacists as *Torental*, which is costly by Senegalese standards.[9] Curious to know more about this and other plants that had become the subject of many University of Dakar theses, I met with Dr. Thiam to talk about the powers of local pharmacopoeia. Thiam told me without hesitation that fagara works as well as, if not better than, *Torental*. If his patients could not afford the imported drug, he would prescribe the indigenous plant.

Dr. Thiam, like Dr. Touré, held consultations, but unlike Touré and Diagne, he did not see sicklers on a specific weekday. He would see those he knew personally whenever they flocked to the general clinic to wait alongside patients with other blood disorders. He had over twenty years' experience with sickle cell. In his role as an administrator, he periodically dropped in on Dr. Touré's consultation to make sure that everything was operating smoothly. For the most part, in my experience, many patients did not know who Dr. Thiam was. They rarely mentioned him as their physician, although some recalled that he had refused to let them into certain medical trials, which they understood might have provided them with free medications. One trial was for Wague's pharmacology thesis, still remembered by some from the mid-1980s, which remains the only in vivo study of fagara ever conducted in Senegal.

Professor Thiam and most of his colleagues at CNTS are biomedically trained hematologists. Neither the CNTS hematologists nor those at Albert Royer ever mentioned collaborative studies with traditional healers. One of the main questions I had in coming to Senegal concerned such collaborations, since Dr. Diagne and Dr. Fall's early interest in observing the effects of fagara would have been hypothetically based on patients who obtained the remedy from traditional practitioners.

The possibility of bringing to light the geographical, historical, and cultural specificity of "Western" and Senegalese traditional medical practices by joining them collaboratively has a historical trajectory that extends far beyond the current situation facing sickle cell providers at Fann. During the late 1960s and early 1970s, the School of Psychiatry in the Fann hospital complex made an effort to correct a misalignment in then current diagnostic and treatment categories of French psychiatry when applied in Senegal. Local idioms and understandings pertaining to mental pathology were not taken into account by French classification systems, which relied on diagnoses and treatments that privileged the individual as an individual and overlooked diseased social relations as the frequent cause of personal distress (Collomb 1973; Sow 1997). Attention to the social topography of mental illness in Senegal became a more serious endeavor as a new class of "native" professionals began to have some power within medicine, and in psychiatric practice. Yet it was Collomb who highlighted for his field that Senegalese notions of the person and his or her relation to the larger social body were crucial to knowing how to best to ease the mentally disturbed person back into society (Collomb 1973). Concern over the incongruence of Senegalese and French conceptions of mental illness led to the integration of traditional "psychotherapies"—such as the *ndëpp*, a type of spiritualistic group healing—with Western approaches to treating the mentally ill patient. The *École de Fann* school of psychiatry thus brought aspects of Senegalese social life, or "the village," into the clinic (Collomb 1973; Sarr et al. 1997; Seck and Sarr 1997; Sow 1997).[10] I wondered if what had happened in psychiatry in Dakar might provide insight into contemporary possibilities concerning other understandings of, and treatments for, disease. Would there be a time when hematologists with medical genetic experience and training in both France and Senegal might find it useful to bring the pharmacopoeia of "the village" into the clinic?

In a logical, but tortuous way, Dr. Thiam responded to my yes-or-no question so as to render his answers complex enough to correspond to the heterogeneous social reality in which he works. I began by asking if he or other hematologists who believed in the value of fagara had collaborated with the traditional healers who distribute the fagara plant. He replied that these practitioners were unwilling to collaborate with biomedical physicians.

DT: No collaborations exist. They're nearly impossible. The problem lies in the fact that these healers will not give up their secrets.

DF: But you already know their "secrets." You've studied fagara in vitro, and others have isolated the active ingredients. You have the formula, so to speak.

DT: The thing about traditional healers, most of them anyway, is that they possess other bits of knowledge crucial to the plant's capacity to heal. I was raised in a village; I have seen the complex powers of healing with plants. The first thing you have to understand is what I will call "the exotic aspect" [*l'aspect exotique*], which is that factor unexplainable by science. It's the talent certain healers have of just caressing the plants in a certain way [*leur manière de les caliner*], after having cut the roots at a certain hour, at the right angle, etc. There's a total protocol that goes into gathering, harvesting the parts of plants best known to heal. This is what we can not know by simply isolating active ingredients at the chemical level. This psychic aspect [*l'aspect psychique*] is what the healers will not share with Western-trained scientists. These are really two worlds with similar realities. What I'm getting at is no different than the placebo effect. I know that I can lower a patient's blood pressure simply by the tone of voice I use to talk to him. This is a well-known aspect of Western medicine, the placebo effect, which is by all counts "irrational." There's no science to explain it, it just is. The efficacy of plants works in similar ways. Sure, isolating the compound will get us closer to being able to heal with the plant, but the really power-ful element is that *exotic, psychic* one. How to get the plant to react like the patient acting under the influence of placebo? How to get the plant to react to your touch, to your voice? Traditional heal-ers do this with chants, prayers, songs, etc. What I'm getting at is that plants are sensitive to a placebo effect too. Not just anyone can approach the same physical plant and have it perform in the exact same way as the next person who has picked from the same tree. These secrets are what traditional healers will not give up. At the same time, we're always trying to rationalize our science. We actu-ally can't have "exotic" aspects coming in. We wouldn't be consid-ered legitimate.

So I posed the question in another way. "What about a *co-habitation*, where traditional healers would be brought into the Western clinic, where healers from each system would take over aspects that the other could do nothing for?" He began by pointing out that in psychiatry "it took a foreigner, Henri Collomb, to tell us that we should bring traditional healing methods, the *ndëpp*, into the Western clinic." "Perhaps," he speculated.[11]

If someone from the outside was interested in fagara, something would have been done with it by now. After the 1990 publication, I received only one letter from a doctor somewhere in France, I can't quite re-member where. But only one! We don't have the infrastructure needed to carry out all of the studies that would be necessary for legalizing the fagara plant, or to use it in sickle cell care as a legitimate part of medical protocols.

He concluded by remarking wistfully that "we have a plan to build a day hospital here at the CNTS where we would have a greater ability to monitor patients and conduct reliable clinical trials, but as of yet, we're all still wait-ing—always waiting to see if things will happen."

Thiam, like Diagne, hoped to do a clinical trial in a "rational way," with-out the "exotic aspect" adulterating the process. But he also clearly believes that a "psychical" force inheres in healing with traditional plants. He under-scored his own experience with such powers by recounting his awareness of "irrational" practices during his childhood in "the village." For the doctor, the *tradi-praticiens* possess a truth that will forever escape the majority of scientific practitioners like himself. Perhaps knowing that his patients have access to efficacious plants is enough. It could be that Dr. Thiam realizes that he is already part of a dual system of healing, a co-habitation that extends be-yond the walls of the Fann hospital complex throughout the city where tradi-tional healers and peddlers sell fagara to many of his patients. The boundaries between these two systems of healing are rarely clearly drawn, as we saw in chapter 3. Professor Thiam and his colleagues, who are themselves under the psychical spell of plants whose efficacy they have not fully justified scientifically through in vivo trials, continue to suggest that yet another university student embark on a thesis in order to study the effects of fagara on sickle cell disease.

■ Attitudes of African fitness

Lastly, I present, Dr. Lamine Diakhate, the person who held the directorship of the CNTS during the years of most of my fieldwork, until 2009 when Saliou Diop replaced him. Diakhate has been the public figure associated with the blood bank. Almost yearly he would appear on television to encourage people to give blood and to participate in various festivities surrounding public drives. He is not a sickle cell specialist, per se, but he oversees everything that has to do with problems of blood in Dakar. His name appears on articles whose topics range from HIV/AIDS to leprosy, from lupus to blood typing, from sickle cell to leukemia. A hematologist by training, his specialization lies in alloimmunization, or blood typing. Diakhate's MEDLINE presence is partly cultural: medical publishing practices in Senegal often conventionally include not only those conducting the research but, in a gesture of recognition, the person in charge of data sources.

The most challenging aspect of Diakhate's job involves convincing people to give blood, which is a problem in Senegal. Even though those at the CNTS transfuse only when no other option is available, Diakhate says that they can supply no more than two-thirds of the local demand. Here scarcity on multiple registers converges. There is simply not enough blood, while they cannot afford to fully type the blood that they do have.

Whole blood transfusions, or partial transfusions of packed red blood cells, are an essential part of sickle cell care in France and the United States. Repeat transfusion is recommended for patients with "serious" disease, a history of frequent crises, and HbSS women who become pregnant and intend to go to term. Introducing normal adult hemoglobin (HbA) has been proven to reduce sickle cell crises and to prevent some of the most disabling aspects of the disease, especially cerebral infarctions, or strokes, that can cause paralysis. In Senegal, however, blood transfusions are extremely rare, as Diagne made clear above. For Diakhate, the operational philosophy goes like this: "any transfusion that is not strongly indicated is strongly contraindicated!" The risks are too great, since the CNTS does not have the means to do total compatibility tests. They are only able to determine basic phenotypes regarding the A, B, O, and Rhesus systems, that is, which proteins or antigens of these groups are attached to which blood cells. This limitation means their matching is very crude. Solely determining limited blood phenotypes can be dangerous. And in Dakar accidents of improperly matching do happen.

The risks and the material limitations are only part of the story however. In our conversations I also learned that Diakhate felt confident that the local biology of his patients played a role in his conservative approach. In this case, it was not their haplotype to which he referred but something much more general. He spoke of a biological tendency shared by "most Africans" to withstand anemia. He first brought this up when I pressed him to explain why he so rarely approved of transfusions for people with the disease, he elaborated:

> Sicklers *can* eventually be transfused. . . . There are two categories. There are those who live their illness well, their blood does not hemolyze as often, and others who would benefit from being regularly transfused. It is a matter of following patients closely. Here at the CNTS this is exactly what we do, and if in reality the patient's hemoglobin level drops low enough to induce respiratory distress or similar effects, then, we could [pauses to hesitate] make an indication to transfuse. What you must retain, in any case, is the fact that Africans in general—it must be said maybe it's something physiological with them [*chez eux*]—but they withstand extremely low hemoglobin levels. This has everything to do with adaptation. The organism finishes by adapting to every condition imposed on it. As long as someone is anemic, and he is able to live with it [*il supporte bien son anémie*], we will continually defer the transfusion. Transfusions should be carried out only if there are signs of *décompensation* due to an anemic state, when we feel that the subject can no longer endure his anemia. If we see that cardiovascular problems set in, what we call an "anemic heart" brought on by intense anemia that eventually stresses the heart beat, or may cause cardiac spasms that actually bring on pain or a cardiac infarction, then we will intervene. There are also various respiratory problems we watch out for. If we remark that the patient's nostrils start to flutter as he's having trouble breathing, in other words, if we feel that there are signs of distress, then a transfusion is indicated. Often these kinds of symptoms correspond to hemoglobin levels falling to less than 5 grams. In Africa, we have a tendency not to transfuse, even if hemoglobin levels are relatively low, as long as we haven't seen signs of decompensation. In Europe, maybe in the US as well, I'm not sure, they transfuse immediately. When someone has 7 grams of hemoglobin, that there is enough for them—it's a *dramatic* event even—and they rush to transfuse. They are much more interventionist than we are in this domain. We hardly transfuse. We follow patients regularly, and as long as there are no signs of distress or decompensation we will simply give them an anti-inflammatory to ward off the crises, perhaps a vasodilator, as is regularly done everywhere.

Most Western practitioners would consider that allowing a patient's blood level to drop to 5 grams of hemoglobin would be consciously courting death.

Diakhate rationally explains his method of extreme delay by saying that the population he cares for has "adapted" to such situations. Nutritional anemia, aside from that brought on by sickle cell, is a broader and major problem in Senegal. People understood their anemia to be a state of "lacking blood" (ñakk derët) and would sometimes take iron to improve it. Yet many told me that they "did not like taking pills," or "could not swallow them," so they gave up on trying to cure chronic anemia. Diakhate's reference to adaptation goes far beyond the notion of successful physiological survival within a specific ecology of illness, however. His philosophy also includes other axes: the economic—a lack of means to test blood for all possible phenotypic differences important to proper matching; the biological—a purportedly "natural" tolerance for anemia; and, finally, the social—the fact that the doctor actively promulgates the idea of African fitness and adaptation when he is trying to stretch the CNTS's limited stock of blood (and testing reagents), which is also a clear case of medical and economic making-do. The robust "African" body, able to withstand stresses and endure quantitative physiological changes that exceed limits defined as "normal," does however appear to be a "cultural" view that many in Senegal shared, both within and outside of medicine. This generalizing tone, as if "Africans" were a "race" unto themselves, was often used to distinguish "Africans" from "Westerners" in Senegal. In comparing "attitudes" regarding major interventions such as transfusion for sickle cell disease between Dakar and "the West," Diakhate does not hesitate to use such a gross term, although he surely knows the risks of such racializing rationales.[12]

The discrepancies between standards and practices of care between France and Senegal are evident to Western-trained Senegalese physicians in Dakar. In their daily work, various "side" attempts become central problems as they consider how to organize and deliver care for a sickle cell disease perceived as relatively "mild." These strategies range from accepting that there are benefits to fagara, to pronouncing a mediating "attitude," to relying on the Senegalese haplotype, to deploying logics of African fitness. Scandal, skepticism of traditional healers, fear of French criticism, and a lack of resources to carry out a trustworthy clinical trial have all figured as obstacles to freely inserting fagara into biomedicine for sickle cell in Dakar. Clearly some Senegalese practitioners, like Diagne, tiptoe along a paper-thin line that separates ridicule from respect in the international scientific publishing community, especially where medicine associated with African healing practices is so easily slighted as inherently specious. In the end, because of Senegalese practitioners' own attitudes, they let fagara live in a larger topology of care. They do this while accepting its presence on the hospital grounds, in their own consultations, and in their discontinuous interest in ascertaining its efficacy through scientific inquiry. In these ways their ambivalence is clearly functional, as is their economic triaging in most aspects of care at each site.

In the following chapter, I turn to the history within which we must place Dakarois physician-researchers' uneasy references to Senegalese difference and African fitness. This historical past has partially constrained and prefigured their present needs and enforced the extreme range of possibilities that mark their attitudes of care. Certain practitioners were highly attentive to make up for all that has gone missing in Senegalese sickle cell medical history, while others displayed moments of negligent apathy given the same structural absences. Next we will see how the coordinates of these varied responses can be mapped onto the history of racial science in former French West Africa, where the disease itself suffered from a colonial refusal to characterize its aspects of illness in favor of the view that it was a racial marker to measure human difference.

CHAPTER FIVE

Localized Biologies: Mapping Race and Sickle Cell Difference in French West Africa

As French colonialism was coming to an end in the late 1950s, Senegal's future president, Léopold Sédar Senghor, was among the few influential African politicians who held posts in *Afrique occidentale francaise* (AOF)[1] to argue that the newly independent African states should retain the form of a federation.[2] In his tract *African Socialism*, he reasoned, "Wealth springs from the diversities of countries and persons, from the fact that they complement each other. We shall always remember a truth often expressed by Father Teilhard de Chardin: races are not equal but complementary, which is a superior form of equality. *So it is with countries and men*" (Senghor 1959, 4; emphasis added).[3] Together with Modibo Keita of the Sudanese Republic and Mamadou Dia, who became Senegal's first prime minister, Senghor created the Mali Federation with these statements in mind on April 4, 1959. The union was the first iteration of postcolonial political independence for the former French territory.

Senghor imagined this new "French Commonwealth," which he encouraged the other former AOF territories to join, as parallel to the political cohesion of France itself. Showing the extent to which he felt French history to be a reliable model, he wrote: "The building of a state is a long-term enterprise, requiring centuries of effort and patience. France took more than 2,000 years—up to Napoleon's time—to become a nation-state. . . . [W]e were wise to begin at the beginning, with . . . the Mali Federation" (1959, 4). He continued: "In the interest of Black Africa and of France, our aim must be to unite. . . . By so doing, we will only be following the French example . . . to make a nation out of diverse races" (1959, 5).

Senghor's plea for unification went beyond French notions of nationhood however. As he pointed out, his own political imaginings might be French, yet the French design of grouping peoples under its colonial dominion was, in turn, deeply African. In his historical presentation of the rationale for new articulations of a federation, he reminded his audience that "France borrowed, for her own use, the great designs of the emperors of Mali and Songhoi: To link Senegal to the Hausa country and the Sahara oases to the Gulf of Benin in order to group the Sudanese races" (1959, 5) within the AOF. History shows that "ancient Africans," the French, and now Africans anew held a similar vision, he maintained. For him, this vision, and racial ethos, was worth retaining for political and economic reasons. The Mali Federation dissolved the same year it was created, however. Mistrust among its leaders led Senghor to declare Senegal's independence from the pact on August 20, 1960. As tensions were running high, he sent all the "Soudan leaders" in Dakar back to Bamako, the Malian capital, in a locked train (Kurtz 1970, 406).[4]

Senghor's advocacy of federalism was founded in a belief in cultural affinities that were at work long before and that continued well after his political and economic proposals. For him, certain West African peoples who shared "climate, soil, blood, language, and customs, art, and literature" (1959, 4–5) could be united with other races "*not so much as equals but as complements.*" His idea of starting with likeness and then absorbing difference was about "assimilating" groups within "frontiers" that he knew were not "natural" (5; emphasis mine). These notions resembled those of the French colonial authorities, who at different points in history emphasized philosophies to solidify federalism and to encourage "civilizing," while also preserving racial distinction to different ends (Amselle 2003, 86–88).

French colonial ideas of African races, whose malleable or intractable cultural traits were central considerations, became the basis of their policies of "assimilation" and/or "association" during the late nineteenth and early twentieth centuries (Betts 1961). From the 1890s until the First World War, assimilationist ideals of "uplifting" Africans were based on 1789 Enlightenment universal principles of rational self-determination, which prevailed mostly in theory (Conklin 1997, 75). It was actually after the revolution of 1848 when France extended political rights to its possessions and gave the inhabitants of its territory in Senegal the right to vote and to elect a deputy to the National Assembly in Paris.[5] Yet Republicanism, based on individual rights and human universals, also offered rationales for "associationist" approaches to governing, which, resembling British methods of indirect rule, involved cooperation between French and indigenous authorities rather than the wholesale imposition of French norms.

Designed to avoid or mitigate conflicts between colonial authorities and their subjects, this alternative policy was rooted in reaffirmations of native difference, particularly the notion that "traditional elements" should be allowed to continue on and that Africans had to "evolve" within "their own cultures" rather than that of France (Conklin 1997, 75; Ginio 2006, 95). Fears that the privileged "*originaires*" of the four communes—Dakar, Gorée, Saint-Louis, and Rufisque—in the territory of Senegal had, or could claim, too much power were partially at the root of reassessments of assimilation, prompting much soul-searching about whether this universalist philosophy with roots in Enlightenment thinking should prove the basis of French rule (Conklin 1997, ch. 6; Ginio 2006, 96). Both the revolts that erupted in response to forced conscription of

Senegalese men during World War I and the demands made by the African French elites (called *evolués*) for equality with French citizens made it appear to many colonial officials that ignoring precolonial institutions in favor of assimilation had been a philosophical and costly mistake.

According to historian Ruth Ginio, the retreat from assimilation policy during the interwar period and again in the late 1940s was "marked by a wish to reconstruct the old order and a growing respect for all types of hierarchy—social, sexual, racial" (2006, 95). On a subtler note, historian Gary Wilder counters that this simply amounted to "racializing native populations" through new instrumental discourses of valuing difference. Valorizing racial difference was one among many "contradictions immanent within colonial humanism" (2005, 78), which "enabled a (cultural) racism that was *simultaneously universalizing* and *particularizing*" (2005, 143; emphasis mine). Wilder writes:

> The administration's concern with keeping *evolués* tied to village communities, in the name of cultural respect and social stability, became a way of fixing them to their Africanity, which was then defined as irreconcilable with French citizenship. . . . Colonial humanism was not simply universalism. Its antiracism was grounded in an ethnologically informed cultural relativism that recognized Africans as members of different but legitimate societies. In this spirt, [AOF *commandant*] Delavignette ask[ed] rhetorically, "Fraternity in difference, is this so difficult to understand?" (2005, 124)

This newly explicit "respect" or regard for race was especially evident within the territory of Senegal and the commune of Dakar, where putative equality and French citizenship for Africans had made the biggest strides. Now the Senegalese subject could be "exceptional" as a potential French citizen, and still be pegged as racially and culturally deeply African.

Senghor's comments with which I open this chapter make clear just how easily certain Africans with French citizenship were able to assimilate French political rationalities. He, too, deployed specific notions of racial difference in the "associationist" mode in the hope that the "assimilation" of others on the continent into his new federalist fold could constitute a viable unitary African politics. The specific notion of "a superior form of equality," seen as the outcome of a system where races were "not equal but complementary," could readily be taken up by an African with French citizenship from the part of the AOF where special rights had long been exhibited as an attainable norm and where, during the interwar years, "differentialist conceptions of humanity," colonial assimilation and association were structurally integrated (Wilder 2005, 80–81).

The effects of these aspects of power, history, and geography bled into other aspects of social life in Dakar, both before and after 1958. This was particularly true with population studies of blood differences, where sickle cell hemoglobin frequencies in different ethnic groups became one biological frontier through which races were imagined. Colonial Dakar was central to these studies because it was the AOF capital where African military recruits, children enrolled in French schools, and later blood donors could be targeted as serological subjects. Postcolonial Dakar has remained central to more recent studies on sickle cell genetic difference because the colonial central administration left a legacy of health infrastructure, such as the CNTS, *Le Dantec* and *Principal* hospitals as well as the *Institut Pasteur* of Dakar. The latter two would be important for French researchers seeking help with DNA collection and storage for the 1984 seminal study on Senegalese versus other African sickle cell haplotype differences detailed in chapter one.

■ **Mapping Black Purity and Pathology**

The remainder of this chapter examines a crucial site through which the re-affirmation of race in the late colonial era was articulated and localized in a specific technological project: widespread sickle cell testing implemented to detail differences related to blood types and racial distinctions within the AOF starting in 1950. After elucidating this late colonial instrumentalization of sickle cell testing, which took place over fifty years ago, I examine two more recent technological forays into differentializing concepts of African humanity that were articulated through sickle cell science. In joining these recent events to those of the not so distant past, it becomes clear that the positions of power that Senegalese sickle cell specialists now claim for themselves—through the leverage that the "mild form" permits them—cannot be completely deracinated from historical entanglements with French science, or from a past where the disease itself was made into a technology of racial classification that still continues to touch their lives. In the AOF during the 1950s, sickle cell was used as a method of commenting on an array of human types and on racial "purity," notions that in the early 2000s again set Parisian scientists on a quest to capture and contain African sickle cell genetics of, as one put it to me, "pure" population groups "before it is too late."[6] This obsession with ethnicized national purity maps directly onto two seemingly distinct, earlier cartographic projects that relied on frontiers that were less natural than they were political. All three efforts were concerned with local-izing difference through both territorial and biological markers of racialized ethnicity conceived through sickle cell.

■ **The Geography of Racial Purity in Three Sickle Cell Studies**

The publications on sickle cell in the AOF make it difficult to pin the exact motives and political rationales of those who carried out these hematologic analyses for the so-called science of "*raciologie*" directly to what Wilder has called colonial humanism. Nonetheless, it is clear that between 1950 and 1954 a political will to study the presence of sickle cell hemoglobin in African populations in general, and in the populations of the AOF in particular, emerged despite many financial and organizational troubles plaguing administrators and, once it was built, the National Blood Transfusion Center.[7] Scientist-colonial administrators took great interest in mapping inter-African differences, starting in the 1940s, with more general studies on nutritional deficiencies and bodily traits pertaining to size, weight, and bodily morphology (Bonnecase 2009). In 1941 they added blood groups to their measurements.[8] With what they took to be increasingly precise markers of blood, starting with ABO antigens, but then settling on populations' sickling propensities in 1950, the anthropological mission drew up maps to schematize an anatomical picture of the region by literally placing aspects of Africans' measured "biologies" onto the topography of colonial geography.[9]

The bloods were drawn largely from people *within* the commune of Dakar where pronounced French political rights should have made such a query strange if not "contradictory" (Wilder 2005, chap. 4).[10] The mission was furthermore a scientific enterprise that defined the presence of sickling as a characteristic of "fundamentally" (*fonciérement*) black African blood and found its frequency in "mixed" races evidence of their black ancestry (Pales and Serré 1953, 66). It is important to state that sickle hemoglobin testing preceded any notion of sickle cell *disease* screening in the territory, and was used during this period solely to investigate blood differences between ethnic groups who, because of their varying prevalence rates of sickle hemoglobin (HbS), came to be seen, reiteratively, as distinct biological races that were as different as the homelands from which they came. Sickling was specifically framed as a "*pathologie exotique*" that delimited French colonial subjects by race (Pales and Linhard 1952, 53).[11] Subjects' physical differences, as markers of race, were extrapolated to a conceptual order where geography and biology would reinforce each other. In the words of the two key scientists leading the study, who also held posts in the French colonial military, *Colonel* Dr. Léon Pales and *Commandant* Dr. Jean Linhard, "We are purposefully not approaching the pathological nature of the anemia. We think that the first item is to construct a map of the racial and ethnic distribution [*répartition*] of the trait in Africa" (Pales and Linhard 1952, 85).

Sickled cells appeared in the French medical literature for the first time in 1943. Remarking on two individual cases, Linhard admitted that he did not realize the importance of what he and a colleague were seeing in the blood of two anemic yet otherwise healthy African subjects (Pales and Linhard 1952, 55; Leroy and Linhard cited in Pales and Linhard 1952, 55). A tool for mapping, tracking and understanding indigenous blood types and ethnic differences within Senegal in the 1950s, the disease was used thirty years later as a biological marker to delimit "the Senegalese" as a group from others on the continent through the lines of their nation-state boundaries. In 1984, just a few decades after Senegal's political independence, the racialized ethnic groups of "Wolof," "Peul," "Lébou," and others that were central to the 1950s AOF testing all but dissolved into a more global and nationalized notion of "the Senegalese."

The 1984 sickle cell haplotype study demonstrates this conceptual shift. In the mid-1980s Dominique Labie's team provided evidence that the sickle cell gene evolved on at least three separate, independent occasions in human population history. Closer inspection and further inquiry revealed that there were actually five separate appearances of the sickle cell gene in human evolution. In both the 1950s and the 1980s, West Africans were grouped by how the scientists studying them parsed and organized aspects of their sickle cell trait and, later, linked inherited alleles. Sickle cell identity was first marked by serological and then by genetic difference, while each instance of research provided scientists with biomatter from which they made claims about native bio-geography. In the 1950s the researchers in question did not consider the cultural practice of social endogamy as a factor that could explain the unequal distribution and subsequent retention of genetic traits in some groups but not in others. By the 1980s one might have expected researchers to theorize about the differential prevalence of genetic traits in some populations when compared with others in light of the mid-century finding that sickle cell offered a survival advantage to people in settled regions affected by malaria (Allison 1954; Wiesenfeld 1967). Researchers in both eras, Pales and Linhard, as well as Labie and her colleagues, overlooked these aspects that made sickle cell an effect of pervasive social cultural tendencies. (As regards the haplotype studies, one has to wonder if genetic variations in the malaria parasites matter, or if other issues pertaining to the human-parasite-mosquito relational symbiosis in the cycle of infection have any bearing on the emergence of human population genetic variants linked to HbS). Researchers' focus was neither on environments nor on customs that might facilitate the appearance of relative disease *affectedness* among different groups. Instead they seized on the power of assumed natural differences in bloods, for those working in the 1950s, and in genes, for those in the postcolonial present.

As mentioned in previous chapters, in 1999 and 2000, Dr. Diagne and Dr. Fall were approached by several of their Parisian colleagues to participate in a new major haplotype study. As I interviewed researchers in France about the study in 2000 and 2001, it became clear that their conceptions of sickle cell grouping were being modified by other trends that can, like the first two, be called "naturalizing." They readily drew from the perceived differences between the social and ecological contexts of France and Africa in order to tease out a new assimilating force for recent African migrants to Paris: "the environment," qualified as a milieu of transplantation. Their proposed collaboration between French and African sickle cell specialists now consciously included this notion of the comparative environment, specifically between France and locales such as Dakar, Senegal, as a factor that might influence population-specific sickle cell gene expression. These were some of the same geneticists who established the existence of the original haplotypes for sickle cell. For these contemporary French researchers, African sickle cell difference continued to be largely based upon its bearers' place of origin. But as concerned sicklers who now lived in Paris, difference was theorized to manifest in new ways. One geneticist I interviewed about the most recent study confided that "transplanted" sicklers were "interesting," due to the potential "effect" that their emigration to Paris may have on their disease, and even gene expression. This was one of several reasons cited for comparing Senegalese (and other Africans with specific "African" haplotypes) in Paris with those still living on the continent. Although a systematic comparison of genes might eventually shed some light on the fact that researchers should look beyond them to the environment, or vice versa, (if these can even be completely teased apart) what was particularly intriguing about the study design from the outset was that it maintained an emphasis on populations as bounded national-biological entities first and foremost.

Despite shifts in the political rationales that gave way to the naturalization of ethnicity in the AOF, to statehood in the postcolonial period, and to the power of environment on the "displaced" subject in Paris today, one thing has remained constant in the studies I examine: language about biologically "pure" populations figures centrally in all three. Geneticists I interviewed in Paris could not dispense with the concept, since comparatively speaking— that is, compared with "the Americans," as one put it—they have a "pure population of Africans" whose genetic particularities they must detail before "globalization, with its increased migration and mixing," finally deprives them of the opportunity.

■ **The Nomenclature of Human Difference in the AOF**

On April 5, 1950, the AOF *directeur général* for public health sent circular no. 1358 to the service's local directors in the Ivory Coast, Guinea, Mauritania, Niger, Chad, Mali, and Senegal telling them to prepare their doctors for widespread population studies on *sicklémie*, or sickle cell trait, throughout the *fédération* (Pales and Linhard 1952). In Dakar the letter was sent to the director of the local Pasteur Institute, who then shared it with *médecin-colonel* Léon Pales, the recent "ex-chef" who still wielded most of the power in the French Anthropological Mission in West Africa. Traveling between posts in Dakar and Paris, Pales was also the assistant director of the *Musée de l'Homme*. Pales and his hematologist colleague, *médecin-commandant* Jean Linhard, were responsible for the most extensive sickle cell trait population studies in French West Africa, which were conducted in Dakar between 1950 and 1953.

Pales and Linhard screened 2, 370 Senegalese "blood donors," mostly students and military recruits, for sickle cell trait in the first year of the study, grouping them by age, sex, and ethnicity.[12] In their template map, Pales was especially concerned with the contours of local ethnic groups as "areas" to be charted as he superimposed ethnicity, indicated in bright colors, over the lines of regions which, at least pictorially, became secondary (see figure 5.1). The template was the guide for Pales's various "raciological" studies, including blood groups, ailments such as gout, measurements of stature, head size, and nutritive assessments, all of which constituted a larger project that he called "*biologie comparative.*"

In retrospect, the most curious aspect of this science is not that within Senegal a notion of biological race was extrapolated from ethnicity, but rather that sickle cell trait frequency, as it was found to differ from one group to another, was the index by which biological difference would be localized internally, in bodies, and also externally, between geographical social spaces. Race was qualitative difference cemented by traits that varied in quantitative frequency. Notably, while differences in the proportion of a population showing sickled cells were used as a proxy for racial distinctions, for example, between the Wolof and the Toucouleur, the trait was not equally shared among all said to belong to the "race" of Wolof, Toucouleur, or any other group under examination. Effectively, sickle hemoglobin frequency was a metonym for group distinctiveness. In the 1950s, the borders of what was then the territory of Senegal, which included the immediate fluvial areas of Mauritania, contained much human variation (in today's parlance). Yet, through the scientific nomenclatures of anthropologists and hematologists, Pales and others sought to elucidate how each group might be conceived of as more or less pure. This was the case even though researchers acknowledged that people of said groups often mixed with one another through migration and intermarriage. Still, the bounds of ethnicity were judged to be the lines that contained biological difference. Indeed, researchers testing for sickle cell first found that among the Wolof sickle hemoglobin (HbS) frequency was 6.2 percent. The Peul averaged 11.0 percent and the Toucouleur, who were categorized as separate from the Peul, had the highest rate, with an HbS incidence of 11.4 percent. That the Peul and Toucouleur are known historically to be nomadic, closely related, and have some of the highest rates of consanguineous marriage in Senegal, and elsewhere in West Africa, was never mentioned.[13] Conducted by the *Anthropological Mission*, this research claimed to be "anthropological," despite oversights and assumptions that, if scrutinized, might have yielded other conclusions, or still other scientific questions to pursue.[14]

The Shorter Oxford English Dictionary on Historical Principles provides two sub-definitions for the term "nomenclature" that highlight the meaning French colonial medics working in West Africa were trying to make of disease, geography, and ethnicity by means of sickle cell trait. Under the third definition, "The system or set of names for things, etc., commonly employed by a person or community," there follows "b. the terminology of a science"

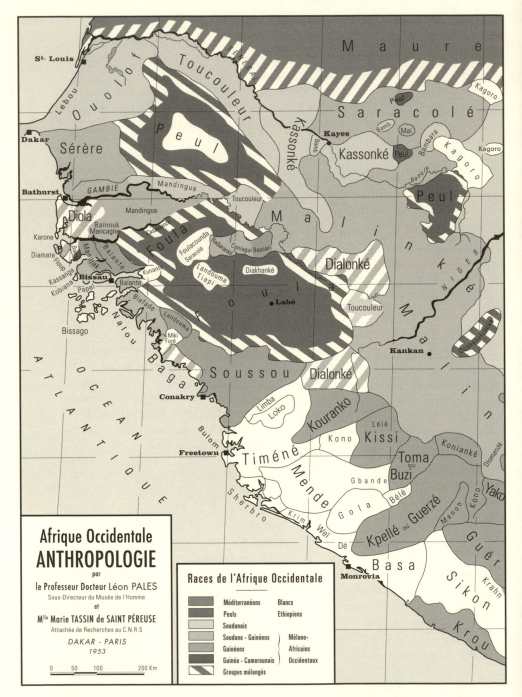

Figure 5.1 Pales and colleagues' "West African Anthropology: Races of West Africa" map. 1953.

and "c. the collective names given (or to be given) to places in a district or region." In 1950s Dakar, men of science in the capital of the AOF were working toward an anthropological assemblage that incorporated all three.

Between Two Continents: The Norm and Its Double

Pales and Linhard's conceptions of sickle cell as a racial proof lends itself to at least one significant cultural comparison of the "same" science from the same epoch, but from across the Atlantic. Much sickle cell research in Africa was inspired by the early scientific literature on the disease in North America. Interestingly, researchers in both the United States and Imperial France made use of the troubled scientific notion of race, but to quite different ends. In the early twentieth-century United States, sickle cell was seen as a marker for "blackness," a *general* category assumed to include all persons of African descent. In America the grid onto which differences were mapped, starting in the 1910s and continuing into the 1950s, dealt with two peoples as poles of normative distinction: white and black, the normal and the pathological. As anthropologist Melbourne Tapper has shown, by the late 1940s when various Italians, Greeks, Cubans, Arabs, and a white Native American with Scotch-Irish parentage were found to have sickle hemoglobin, every effort was made to ascertain "pure" genealogies so as to rule out—or prove—racial hybridity as the cause (Tapper 1997, 83–85). Even when "white patients and families extensively accounted for their family pedigrees and found no black members, it was still assumed that a Negro strain was somewhere present" (90). Classification concerning sickle cell disease in America took on an explicit form to express "discrimination of qualities in conformity with the polar opposition of a positive and a negative" (Canguilhem 1991, 240). In the French West African colonies, however, values concerning sickle cell trait frequency were conceived of almost entirely differently.

The French carried out studies in West Africa not on black peoples as a unitary race but on Africans as multiple "ethnicities" which, it was thought, could be placed within what they called the larger "races of West Africa." In practice such large races were described as "Guinean," "Sudanese," "Peul," yet also "Guinean-Sudanese," "Guinean-Cameroonian," as well as "Mediterranean" and "Mixed." The idea was that all West African "ethnic subjects" ("Lébou," "Peul," "Wolof," "Sereer," etc.) could place within a tableau of demonstrated serological characteristics that defined each group and that, taken as a whole, each ethnicity would neatly fall within the races that were assumed to contain them. Thus, within the AOF, knowledge of sickle cell disease was structured not through the relationship of the "normal to the pathological" but rather through the construction of a *range* by which differences could be displayed. If, as medical philosopher Georges Canguilhem states, "the normal is at once the extension and the exhibition of the norm" (1991, 239), then the situation here focused on the extension and the exhibition of the pathological as a *particular* kind of norm. The sickle trait, which was seen to extend geographically across West Africa, was studied for the express purpose of exhibiting—literally, on Pales and colleagues' maps—the degree to which the presence of this blood irregularity could serve to demarcate groups, none of which could be cast as fully normal referents. For the French Anthropological Mission, the emphasis was not so much on the "normal norm" but rather on its double, the "pathological norm" —a vision of pathology as a certain state of order through which sickle cell trait emerged as a marker of *native* normativity. In this way, it bears repeating, that the status of sickle cell was not one of an affliction warranting medicine, as it was instead a *pathologie exotique* whose medical aspects were specifically *not* studied (Pales and Linhard 1952, 85). This may have actually precluded the possibility that sickle cell could figure as a disease warranting care at all. In the yearly reports on health in the AOF, and even in the local "*Rapports de santé*" for Senegal, I found no mention of sickle cell in the annual surveys and summaries on diseases affecting indigenous populations for these years.[15] A colonial accent on HbS pathology, which bracketed disease, in this case, differentiated sickle cell mapping from other racialized approaches to actual disease management in the AOF. In more classic cases, colonial anxieties about control provided rationales for interventions on natives' health, "hygiene," and temporally deferred but progressively proximal "civilization."

Most historical accounts focus on this latter aspect of colonial medicine where West Africa was an environment that the French administrators saw as populated with innumerable biological threats,[16] and where pathologies proved an obstacle to successful colonial ordering of space and territory. This was especially true in the cities, where blacks and whites lived in relatively close proximity, such that race and ethnicity were furthermore markers of native living conditions in need of hygienic reform (Conklin 1997, 48–50; Echenberg 2002, 119–20). Various segregating policies were undertaken to protect the European population from contagion, in Dakar and elsewhere, as scientists and Africanist specialists touted decorated General Hubert Lyauté's refrain that medicine in the colonies was the administration's *nerf du succès* (lifeblood for success) (Bado 1996, 151; cf Keita 2007, 100–101).[17] Historian Meghan Keita puts a great deal of emphasis on the role of French health care interventions within the AOF medical corps as a weapon of power and as a racial technology of quarantine to manage African populations who, it was feared, were "disease carriers" (2007, 99, chap. 5). Perhaps because sickle cell was not seen to affect Europeans, and because it was not contagious but rather viewed as located in the nature of African blood, disciplined health care as that arm of colonial power that sought to control disease and its spread did not extend to sickling. The study of pathology with regard to racialized sickle blood did not explicitly raise concerns about native behavior, culture, or French attempts to display medical prowess over African healing methods. Rather, it focused on biological differentials in human *being* quite literally.

On a broader level, blood-based notions of racial "mixing," a menace to white supremacy in the United States during this period,[18] had other connotations for French colonial enterprises that, as we saw earlier on, ostensibly operated through ideas of partially "regenerating" or "civilizing" indigenous populations (Amselle 1996; Conklin 1997, 77; cf. Coquery-Vidrovitch 2001). Therefore French and African *métisse* classes were often granted political and economic status from which black Africans were barred (Conklin 1977, 151–52). Similarly, Africans with "Moorish," "Ethiopian," or "Mediterranean" "blood" were also perceived as having higher potential than blacks.[19] In this way, ideas of regeneration, or civilizing, played certain groups against others by ordering them in a hierarchical system based on perceived differences, while perhaps reinforcing culturally anchored or colonial economically-created differences between them (see Dozon 1999). Concepts of "uplift" and "regeneration" were structurally linked to the idea of human universal, natural progress—Africans' potential for sameness—as well as to racial and linguistic classifications, which served as constant reminders of difference in the colony. The tension inherent in this attitude ultimately served to distance all groups in their degrees of Africanity from the French universal ideal, where the normative potential for political and intellectual self-rule was perpetually beyond reach. In short, the possibility of actually obtaining French citizenship status was exhibited before, but rarely fully extended to, African peoples regardless of where they lived (Conklin 1997, 110; Coquery-Vidrovitch 2001; Wilder 2005, 134–39).

■ The Dubious Powers of Serology

The original sickle cell studies undertaken by Pales and Linhard were later complemented by collaborative research they led with others: Jacque Bert (*Médecin-Capitan*), René Fourquet (*Médecin-Lieutenant*), and M. André Serré (*Chargé de la section de la Mission Anthropologique de Haute Volta*). The ways in which these men made race and biological traits into "natural" underpinnings of ethnological differences pervaded earlier trends in scientific racism more globally, which, in the early twentieth century, narrowly examined population characteristics through serology broadly. Serological optics allowed for ways of seeing difference by parsing humans into groups via blood proteins measured and compared between populations. Scientists would often corroborate the resultant trait frequencies by borrowing from felt notions of human difference situated within the bounds of culture (Hirshfeld and Hirshfeld 1919). The problem with this technological approach was that imagined correspondences did not always comply with protein frequency differences empirically. Yet, even in the early 1950s this science in the AOF was not yet out of place for its time. In fact, the drafters of the first UNESCO statement on race, who attempted to explain surface physical variation in humans through patterns of migration, adaptation, and cultural practices rather than as frozen notions of biological difference, were forced by physical anthropologists to revise this nuanced view. Subsequently in 1951 the panel of scientists reconvened. This time it mostly consisted of physical anthropologists who wrote a second statement that explicitly asserted the scientific reality of population-based races, which, they claimed largely overlapped with geographic continental divides. This was the same period that Pales and Linhard set out to map sickle cell as the racial proof of ethnicity in the colony, which for them might reveal microcosmic examples of this general idea that human essential difference could map onto geography.

Post-war 1950s marked a critical moment in twentieth-century scientific thinking on race. On the one hand, the international community was trying to grapple with the eugenic atrocities of Nazi Germany, while, on the other, many physical anthropologists desperately wanted to rescue the idea of race and thus detach it from societal politics altogether. The UNESCO physical anthropologists hoped to insulate biological definitions of race, such as the existence of subgroups within the human species that might be genetically distinct, from any "social end—whether it be totalitarian or egalitarian" (Reardon 2004, 31). Consequently, at this specific moment, colonial scientific evidence of distinguishable "African" blood in 1952 had much broader implications for thinking about the human species as a whole—or not.

By way of background, the ABO blood group system, discovered at the turn of the century, was one of the first tools used to explain what many took to be deep differences in the nature of physically and culturally different people who exhibited surface, or phenotypic, variation. Shortly after the "Great War" began in 1914, scientists began to measure the presence of three different blood substances (A, B, and O) and quickly identified "types" that were mapped onto preexisting "races" throughout the world.[20] In a schema that clearly registers Eurocentric notions of white superiority, early racial charts divided humans between "Europeans and Others (Afro-Asians)," which were then divvied up into "European, Intermediate, Hunan, Indo-Manchurian, Africo-Malaysian, Pacific American, and Australian" (Marks 1995, 128). To the dismay of some researchers, however, many groups did not conform to ABO frequencies consistent with others perceived to belong to the same large racial group. Several populations assigned to one "type" actually had ABO frequencies that fell within the ranges of other types. Conversely, some seemingly different groups had an uncomfortably similar distribution of markers, producing unbearable inconsistencies: the peoples of Senegal, Vietnam, and New Guinea ended up together, as did those from Poland and China (Snyder 1926, 244). With such obvious overlaps in the peoples of the world, the use of blood groups for racial classification was abandoned by many scientists as early as the 1930s (Marks 1995, 129). Yet, in the AOF, Pales and Linhard's studies on sickling curiously took them up again as additional variables of interest.

How and why ABO remained possible markers for racial and ethnic differences in the AOF after the 1930s may be an example of what Anne Stoler calls "epistemic confusion." Here, the move to "coherence," or the will to make sickle cell do what blood groups had failed to do, was in this case the result of what Stoler terms "discrepant stories" (2009, 185). On the one hand, race was seen to be located in blood and, on the other, history had shown that this story had not panned out. Discrepancies in science practice, from a historical vantage, are useful nonetheless as they "provide ethnographic entry into the confused space in which people lived, to the fragmented knowledge on which they relied, and to the ill-formed and inept responses that knowledge engendered" (Ibid., 185). It is possible that in the confused space of serology in Dakar, Pales and Linhard attempted to redeem the shortcomings of ABO racial distributions with sickle cell hemoglobin—a seemingly deep African trait—by correlating the two. In the end, however, no correlation between sickle cell and ABO frequencies was found (Pales and Linhard 1952, 79).

■ Methods and Their Pitfalls: The Interior Space of the Studies

In their first mass survey of sickle cell in the AOF, Pales and Linhard recuperated primary markers used in racial studies at the time beyond ABO, such as Rh, and MN blood groups, to possibly link them to sickle cell trait. Secondarily, they wanted to examine the possible connections between sickle cell (which would now carry other blood proteins back into race science) in analyses of HbS frequencies and West African ethnic groups.[21] The study sample on which their first article was based was not random. Although it primarily drew upon healthy military men and school children, the subject pool also included "laborers" (*manouvrières*), hospital workers, and even hospital patients (Pales and Linhard 1952, 61, 64).[22] Later studies, conducted after the transfusion center was built, drew specifically on blood donors. Women were underrepresented, since they generally did not give blood, join the military, or go to school—yet sex was still one of the correlates used in the analysis.

In the section of their 1952 article titled "*choix et identification des sujets*," Pales and Linhard laid out the necessity of careful identification and meticulous notation of subjects' ethnic identities. The categories of racial-ethnic classification were to be strictly adhered to, and subjects were to always be "correctly" assigned. Ethnic identifications were taken as they were given by the West African subject himself, with strong caveats to the research assistants to be "beware" of subjects' own misclassifications. French ethnologist Jean-Loup Amselle claims that, for West Africans, ethnic identities were "onamastic emblems" to be appropriated and abandoned in an aleatory fashion according to political contingencies (Amselle 1998, 43). Although I am skeptical of such a sweeping assertion, it is clear that prevailing French understandings of self-proclaimed identities as pure versus impure categories were difficult to institute in practice. Ethnicity in Dakar was often used to designate a "relation" rather than a fixed phenomenon; it had social, economic, and locational meanings.[23] Yet in an attempt to empirically fix this fluidity, Pales and Linhard used race, tribe, and place of origin to structure their map of the West African world. They hoped that by measuring the incidence of sickle cell trait they would retrace, biologically, the indigenous ethnicities that were already linked to land and geography differentially, if not naturally. They wrote:

> In the heart of black Africa, variations in frequency of the sickle cell trait from one population to another seem to be significant. . . . *These variations, their breadth, their meaning even, will markedly appear the day when a map with ethno-anthropological divisions of this hereditary blood characteristic is drawn up.* To achieve this goal, it is necessary to carefully class the subjects of study. And we think *that it is at least as important to identify the race, the sub-race, the ethnic group, the tribe and the place of origin as to specify their sex and age.* (1952, 61; italics in the original)

Their collection methods were thorough, envisaged to track those who possessed *sicklémie* (sickling) and decipher their pedigrees, as well as to make their sickle cell status part of their "civil files." The disciplining act of mapping the territory thus overlapped with surveillance of the field through specific (and necessarily partial) genealogies of the "natives." They continued:

> The preliminary work therefore consists in determining race and ethnicity. The *état-civil* [marital status] information must also be carefully specified: it will then be written up and given to the proper professional authorities. For each subject, it will be necessary to find out:
>
> —the race or the ethnic group of both father and mother:
> —the place of birth (village, canton, subdivision, and circle);
> —sex and age.
>
> Finally, whenever the test detects a sickle cell [hemoglobin] carrier, it is of utmost importance to go through the family pedigree to the sources, meaning to examine all family members so as to establish the genealogical tree then and there.
>
> As for the samples of school children and military men, the personal identification information will become part of their general dossiers (61).

The primary goal of the study, to construct a racial map of sickle cell incidence, most likely was never completed, however. Maps of gout, stature, "cormic index" (sitting height), and the other aspects of comparative biology undertaken by Pales and his collaborators appeared together in a packet printed by the *Anthropological Mission* a year later (Pales and Tassin-de-Saint Pereuse 1954). Curiously, sickle cell was not among them. This might have been because they failed to realize this most detailed biological proof of their vision. Ethnographically, the interest in sickle cell trait frequency studies at this time constitute less an event than an instructive *non-event*—an unrealized and improbable plan—that nonetheless highlights the problematic of race in the colony (Stoler 2008, 106–7).

From the beginning, Pales and Linhard confronted numerous complications and were at a loss as to how to read their data, which changed from study to study. Nonetheless they pressed on. The first signs of difficulty came with the initial classification of subjects. The authors were, in the end, only able to use half of their original target population since they ran into significant problems of racial-ethnic "mixing." To their frustration, they found that in mid-century Dakar nearly 60 percent of school children reported to have parents who belonged to different ethnic groups (1952, 62). Apparently only five ethnicities presented more than one hundred subjects whose mother and father belonged to the same group (1952, 71). Despite this substantial ethnic mix, most of Pales and Linhard's subjects were later classed in the "sub-race *Soudanais*" and then compared with the "*Guinéens*," on whom the British had done similar studies. Expressing their exasperation with the difficulty of finding "pure" subjects, Pales and Linhard warned their colleagues at other AOF sites to exercise vigilance concerning the racial information that their respondents were providing. The first line of reasoning about "correcting" the problem was based on the assumption that the natives could not be trusted to report honestly. Many Africans tended to self-identify with certain ethnic groups over others when they had relatives belonging to more than one. As Pales and Linhard warned:

> The African families in Dakar that have one Wolof somewhere in their pedigree gladly reclaim him to define their ethnic group, even though the other members may have a different origin. The Lébou, and many other inhabitants in the capital, identify as Wolof in much the same way that in France people from Provence living in Paris will call themselves Parisians. The racialogical study must be careful of these pitfalls [*embûches*]. (1952, 73)

The "Wolof," the majority ethnic group in Dakar, indeed emerges as the largest sample by far.

In this first study, the serological characteristics of 623 Wolof, 416 Lébou, 108 Bambara, 175 Toucouleur, and 109 Peul were subjected to "correlation." As we see in tables 5.1 and 5.2, the ABO blood type frequencies for Pales and Linhard are also linked to sickle cell frequencies, which do vary. Frequencies are relatively low for the Wolof and Lébou, slightly higher for Bambara, and significantly higher for the Peul and Toucouleur. In examining relatively small groups of different sizes, random factors might bias the results. For the authors, however, the real "problem" of their findings laid in the fact that the Peul and the Toucouleur, whose "long faces," "lighter skin," and "straight noses" made them resemble the more "Caucasoid Ethiopian race" (1952, 74), were found to have higher rates of sickle cell trait. This relatively elevated incidence appeared "paradoxical" to the authors, who noted that British research on "Guineans," who were seen as "real blacks," showed them to possess high frequencies as well. How to explain the similarity in sickle trait levels among groups who were phenotypically "so different" from one another and the relatively lower levels among groups who were phenotypically and similarly "black" (like the "Guineans") stymied the French nomenclators. They wrote:

> Compared with other West Africans (the people of Guinea from this study and the Black people in the British territories), these levels of sickle cell trait are relatively low. Now, the Wolof, Lébou and Bambara are specifically Negro. Their extremely dark skin tone is the basis on which they are called "the blackest of the Blacks." This is also the case for the Lébou. Our results thus seem paradoxical, especially when we compare them against our findings for the Peul and the Toucouleur (73).

Such paradoxes would not be easily resolved.

The last point of comparison in the 1952 article focused on the sub-races *Sudanese* and *Guinean*, two categories that are not clearly defined, but that very much reiterate the common understandings of human difference of the day based on geography. Observing the higher prevalence of the sickle cell trait among "Guineans," but not among the "Sudanese" groups, Pales and Linhard sought to explain this outcome, with the following reasoning: "Anatomically, the two sub-races are distinct . . . In brief, the Sudanese are men of the savanna; the Guineans of the forest . . . Sudanese and Guineans, who are distinguished by geographical environment, mode of life, ethnic characteristics and anatomic racial characteristics, are also differentiated by their hematological characteristics: blood group frequencies and incidence of sickle cell trait" (75–76). Pales and Linhard go to great lengths to mark a distinction based on minute differences; the ABO blood trait distributions are more similar than not. Their environmental explanation for the substantially higher rate of sickle cell trait among "the Guineans" makes sense, even though they did not have the tools to spell out the connections. If, in fact, these two groups differed in their recent origins as being from the "savanna" versus the "forest," the relationship between malarial environments and sickle cell trait would come into play. (The sickle cell–malaria hypothesis was first proposed in 1949 and was just gaining traction).

Linhard subsequently published a new series of observations in *Revue d'Hematologie* later in 1952. This second article begins by explaining that the research conditions in which the two articles were based were entirely different. With the recent construction of the *Centre fédéral de transfusion de l'AOF* (French West African Transfusion Center, which is now the CNTS), the researchers had access to many more people. Over fifteen months, they were able to examine the blood of 3,403 new subjects, which greatly increased the

Table 5.1
Pales and Linhard's Findings of Sickle Cell Trait Levels Cross Tabulated
with Blood Type for Wolof, Lébou, and Bambara Populations.

Blood group	Wolof		Lébou		Bambara	
	BG %	HbS %	BG %	HbS %	BG %	HbS %
A	23.4	6.8	26.9	5.3	28.7	3.2
B	17.0	5.6	17.7	8.1	17.5	10.5
AB	3.5	4.5	2.6	27.2	6.4	14.2
O	56.0	6.3	52.6	4.5	47.1	9.8
Total HbS %	6.2		6.0		8.3	
(n)	623		416		108	

Table 5.2
Pales and Linhard's Findings of Sickle Cell Trait Levels Cross Tabulated
with Blood Type for Toucouleur and Peul Populations.

Blood group	Toucouleur		Peul	
	BG %	HbS %	BG %	HbS %
A	24.5	6.9	24.7	7.4
B	18.2	9.3	21.1	0.0
AB	3.4	16.6	6.4	14.2
O	53.7	13.8	47.7	17.3
Total HbS %	11.4		11.0	
(n)	175		109	

number of ethnic samples that were large enough to analyze with confidence. In this later article, the author was forced to rectify the sharp distinctions that he, with Pales, had previously found concerning sex differences and, most importantly, racial differences and sickle cell frequencies.

The subjects we have examined are presumed to be pure from a racial point of view. In fact, we usually noted the approximate place and date of birth, the race of the father as well as the mother in our donor files. It appeared to us that mixing between the races was pretty rare [this time]. In the two studies, we find the percentages to be more or less identical where the Wolof, Bambara, and Lébou are concerned. But on the contrary, our second set of statistics are markedly less elevated than the first concerning the Peul (8.5% vs. 11%), while M. SÉRÉ, in the Ouagouya region of Upper Volta, found 14%. Similarly, for the Toucouleur, the percentages went from 11.4% to 5.3%. These differences may be related to the question of a subject's race. It is possible that

Table 5.3
Pales and Linhard's Findings of Sickle Cell Trait Levels
Cross Tabulated with Blood Type and Overall Trait Frequencies
for the Sudanese and the Guinean Sub-Races

Blood group	Sudanese		Guineans	
	BG %	HbS %	BG %	HbS %
A	24.4	5.7	26.4	12.2
B	19.5	8.1	27.0	4.0
AB	3.8	11.4	3.7	14.2
O	52.0	6.8	42.7	20.2
Total HbS %	7.0		16.2	
(n)	1,568		185	

the Peul of the second study were blacks claiming to be Peul, when in actuality they were not, or vice versa. Similarly, it could be that certain Toucouleur in these studies did not have any infusion of Peul blood. (Linhard 1952, 563)

The differences among the ethnic groups studied are now leveled, or relatively the same. By asserting that subjects were perhaps wrongly categorized due to their own (mis)identification, Linhard again attempts to make stories, and histories, that were seemingly discrepant cohere.

Although sickle cell frequencies did not vary much among ethnic groups, anthropological researchers in Dakar continued to hold onto assumptions informed by French rationales of race, ethnic identity, and purity. Despite the rectifying tone of Linhard's second 1952 report, sickle cell trait levels remained the focus for other studies in subsequent years (Pales and Serré 1953; Pales et al. 1954). In a 1953 article that Pales co-authored with M. Serré, but where Pales's name alone appears on the interior pages of the text, he takes up the "Peul paradox" again. Unlike Linhard, who assumed that subjects claimed the wrong identities, Pales puts the issue back onto "fundamentally" black biology. He writes:

That the Peul Ethiopian base has suffered a Melano-African (to whom they are juxtaposed) personal impression, which varies according to region, is a legitimate hypothesis. . . . However, while they have conserved a certain non-Negro anatomical personality throughout their mixing with the Black peoples, their sickle cell rate highlights, exalts in a sense, an opposite blood personality, which is more Negro at base (if one admits that sickle cell trait is a foundational characteristic of blackness). (1953, 66)

In other words, the surface impressions that made these colonial serological findings seem paradoxical could be rectified by concepts of "ancestry." Purity was lost, but sickle cell could reveal its roots. It may have been that the very issue of mixture that the Peul sickling frequencies put before these researchers thwarted their project of constructing a cartography of race through HbS. Again, the planned sickle cell racial-distribution map was never completed. The racialized groups that Pales and his colleagues had assumed to cohere as bounded entities were in fact marked by disparities, variations, and cultural exchanges that made identity a fluid concept in the colony, much in the same way that they knew it to operate for people who had relocated to Paris from Provence. Subsequently, a lull in this type of research ensued. For decades it appeared that French scientists gave up trying to forge a correspondence between race, deep ancestral biology, and sickle cell—that is, until the question reemerged, differently articulated, in the 1980s.

■ **Haplotypes and the Nature of National Biological Identity**

In the early 1980s when French geneticist Dominique Labie and her team first landed in Africa, they were equipped with new technological means that made no reference to the old rationales of race in the AOF. Informed by the 1978 finding that loci on the hemoglobin gene differed in American subjects of "African origin," Labie and her team set out to isolate, localize, and name those differences in various sickle cell populations. Again, the racialized trait-frequency model so popular during the final years of the AOF was mostly abandoned and replaced by another system of scientific correspondence that lumped all of Atlantic West Africa under the ensign "Senegalese." What continues from the old study into the new, however, is the idea of sickle cell *relative affectedness* concerning different populations.

It was by following "the logic of the map," as Labie put it in an interview with me in 2000, that she and her team localized the sickle cell haplotype variants in blood that they, or usually their collaborators in Africa, collected in capital cities, such as Dakar. They then "simply," and through a certain postcolonial sensibility, "named" them after the broad geographical locales such as "Senegal" that contained these cities. The nominal geographic locus of *les villes* then came to stand in for much wider territories of "West Africa," which even extended to "parts of Morocco." This dramatic shift in sickle cell nomenclature—with newer politically discrete territories now understood via "ethnic" sameness, rather than difference—was partially an effect of nominal African political independence. Yet the totalizing move to "*englobe*" (as can be said in French) the territory of West Africa under any ensign clearly has historical lineaments that are "French" and, as Senghor reminds us in the opening pages of this chapter, also "African."

As I show further on, in these newly biologically federated territories, the Senegalese scientific professionals with whom I worked are still politically at odds with other Africans (scientists) on the continent, whom they claim are "prisoners of the old system." By this they mean that today too many of their African homologues willingly serve as mere "blood sampling assistants" (*envoyeurs de sang*) and "facilitate" research for Parisian scientists on new genetic studies on sickle cell differences, despite past practices of unfairness.

■ Genetic Variations of African Origin

In 1978, Yuet Wai Kan and Andrée M. Dozy of UC San Francisco Medical Center discovered a curious genetic polymorphism adjacent to the beta globin gene responsible for sickle cell anemia. Their methods, which ushered in new technology for differentiating DNA base pairs, amounted to a landmark finding:

> Restriction endonuclease mapping of the human globin genes revealed a genetic variation in a *Hpa I* recognition site about 5,000 nucleotides from the 3' end of the beta-globin structural gene. Instead of a normal 7.6-kilobase (kb) fragment which contains the beta-globin structural gene, 7.0-kb and 13.0-kb variants were detected. Both variants were found in people of African origin and were not detected in Asians or Caucasians. The 13- kb variant is frequently associated with the sickle cell mutation. . . . Polymorphisms in a restriction enzyme site could be considered as a new class of genetic marker and may offer a new approach to linkage analysis and anthropological studies (1978, 5631).

Kan and Dozy's work not only provided the first evidence that the sickle cell gene arose independently at various times in African populations but also posited a new possibility for population genetics linkage studies.[24] With the discovery of the various beta globin Restriction Fragment Length Polymorphisms (RFLPs) in their sickle cell "populations," one of which had a consistency rate of 87 percent, the authors closed their seminal article with an invitation to the scientific community to exploit the utility of their discovery: "The preponderance of the *Hpa I* variants in people of African origin suggests that restriction endonuclease mapping, in addition to the conventional method of analysis of structural protein variants, may also prove useful for anthropological studies. . . . Within Africa, the distribution of the 7.0 and 13.0 kb variants in different regions is of great interest" (Ibid., 5634).

When I met Dominique Labie years later, she referred to Kan and Dozy's closing comments as the source for her inspiration. Leading a predominantly Parisian team, Labie examined blood samples taken from three sites in West and Central Africa to localize markers associated with the sickle cell gene. At the same time, Kan and Dozy's finding led American researchers to map

Huntington's chorea by linkage to an RFLP marker (Gusella et al. 1983; Wexler 1995). In 1980, Kan and Dozy themselves published an article regarding differences in East and West African populations, reporting that the *Hpa I* endonuclease enzyme cutting site differed in the two groups. Yet it was Labie's team, working in collaboration with two Americans in New York, Ronald Nagel and Gregory Mears (Mears et al. 1981a, Mears et al. 1981b), that first found *Hpa 1* polymorphisms in three geographic locations on the continent. These researchers, with the French taking the lead, then decided to examine eleven polymorphic sites on the beta globin gene cluster instead of one, which gave their science a quantitative advance. After testing populations in Senegal, Benin (and Algeria),[25] and the Central African Republic, Labie and colleagues saw an overwhelming prevalence of three distinct sickle cell haplotypes, one in each geographical site.[26] It was then that the team published their seminal article, "Evidence for the multicentric origin of the sickle cell hemoglobin gene in Africa," in *PNAS*.

In the earliest studies based on linkage disequilibrium (LD), the sickle cell gene "exposed" its various markers found in African populations, rather than the other way around. Kan and Dozy's finding confirmed thinking that DNA polymorphisms with no clear "function" could be followed as Mendelian alleles. This idea was corroborated and advanced as a possible approach to mapping the whole human genome, as the first successful linkage maps to isolate genes in small populations or families were appearing (Cook-Deegan 1994, 37). Although genetic linkage mapping did not grow into the Human Genome Project, the hope that it might, at the time, was a testament to the excitement around the potential of this approach within science—with sickle cell once more establishing itself as a first in pushing genetic knowledge forward.

■ Scientific Reasoning, Scientists' Rationales

The idea of three distinct haplotypes in or around the beta globin gene incited two ongoing debates in the world of sickle cell science. The first concerned the multicentric versus unicentric origin of sickle cell trait; the second took seriously the meaning of differences in sickle cell manifestations and whether or not these newly discovered "markers" could provide evidence that other biological factors impressed upon the lived experience of the disease, or "phenotype." Labie, a geneticist whom her associates, such as Dr. Girot, characterize as "ready and willing for any challenge," mobilized her students, several of whom later became her colleagues, to take on both questions.

Labie is a small, sprightly woman who appeared to be in her seventies when I first met her in 2000. Her spirit and energy belied her frail frame as she led me into her small office at the Cochin hospital in Paris. As we sat down she pointed to the many envelopes containing information about potential research subjects on her desk. One was festooned with colorful stamps and a

Middle Eastern script. "This one claims he is a descendent of the prophet Mohammed!" she mused. "It's from Tehran." She explained that she must get "the Senegalese DNA for the study on haplotypes and HLA," commenting, "it's still confidential. We have a paper under review right now." When I asked her what was holding up her "collaboration" with her Senegalese "partners," she hesitated. I then informed her that I had just been in Senegal and that I was working with Dr. Ibrahima Diagne. "Ibrahima"? she inquired, as she had been dealing with Dr. Fall. "I'm not sure what the issues are; maybe you could help *boost* (in English) the relations?" After mulling over Diagne's name again, she said that the problem could stem from "cultural differences, because they are Muslim." In the same conversation, through various digressions, she referred to "the Japanese" to "the Indians" to "the Africans," all in the singular. Suddenly self-conscious, at one point she stopped to assure me by saying: "I'm not a racist."

Labie attributes much of her vision about sickle cell in Africa to "a Jewish doctor" who was residing in Germany but was forced to leave at the start of the Second World War when he went to England and was recruited by the British army. According to Labie, "the British couldn't station the man on a front to fight against his former countrymen, so rather than assign him to Germany, they sent him to India where he first encountered sickle cell disease." The doctor, Labie's premier reference, was Hermann Lehmann who, with Alan B. Raper, actually worked in East Africa before going to India and published an early paper on sickle cell trait frequencies among groups that were lumped by racialized labels such as "Hamitic-tongued tribes," "Nilotic" and "Bantu" in Uganda (1949). Labie recalled that, given Kan and Dozy's finding, she remembered that Lehmann was one of the first doctors to observe that sickle cell disease differed depending on where it was found when he, with Marie Catbush, began work in India (in 1952). She confided that she was interested in this sort of "anthropology" and that she wanted to see if the RFLPs on the beta globin gene had any bearing on the puzzling question of varying clinical manifestations of sickle cell disease.[27] According to Labie, Lehmann noticed that people living with sickle cell in central Africa often did not live past infancy, whereas in India and West Africa those with the disease could live well into adulthood without ever having serious symptoms that would warrant a diagnosis. Labie herself had worked extensively in India as well.

In our interview she emphasized that when Kan and Dozy showed that there were clear inherited markers linked to the sickle cell gene, she put the two together and called on her medical contacts in Africa.

> This was at a moment when . . . [interrupts herself] well, the arrival of African immigrants in Europe goes back a bit, but it has increased dramatically since the War. We said to ourselves, we have all of these people here from different places, and that it would be interesting to go and see [people in their place of origin]. The logistics were simple.

I just needed to find money and we needed to find places [in Africa] where we would work. The money came from industry, it was Sanofi[28] that paid for the trip under the pretext that I was going to Dakar, no, to Abidjan, for a pediatrics conference, and that I would be going to Abidjan and other sites we had planned to look at. At each place we needed correspondents, possible interlocutors. It is permitted for a doctor to go to a pediatrics conference, no? I knew that in Abidjan, the city itself was extremely mixed, which quickly presents the problems of our megapolis. The population is very mixed. I addressed people in Dakar because they had a Pasteur institute, and the Pasteur Institute is a place where we could work. I called people in Cotonou and Lomé, especially Cotonou because there was one of our own there who was an intelligent boy, and . . .

Struck by Labie's unself-conscious use of the racist diminutive, I asked the doctor if the man she described as "one of our own" was an African. She responded:

Yes, an African, African, but who directed a transfusion center in Cotonou and who consequently was an intelligent and trained interlocutor. We worked a little in Abidjan, and then in Bangui because there was a Pasteur Institute. The Pasteur Institute there was mostly concerned with virology, but they had equipment, centrifuge machines, and refrigerators. We couldn't just work with ideas, we also needed material.

Once the contacts were established and the functioning of the centrifuges affirmed, the rest went relatively smoothly. A number of patients and controls would undergo testing, and their blood samples would be taken back to Paris.

Labie and her team found telling differences in the genetic patterns taken from the populations they considered. The samples were small, but the finding aggrandized them. They were mostly consistent in typing, yet only 82 percent of the "Senegalese" had that haplotype, while nearly everyone else tested in Dakar had the Benin haplotype.[29] More problematically, Labie said, the Senegalese subjects were often "not from Senegal, nor [were they] Senegalese in origins." Others, too, were not "pure" but "mixed." These points were nagging but ultimately proved unimportant for her since she defined people by their haplotypes in the end. She considered the population genetic markers to be an "anthropological" index, despite the fact that the appellations—Senegalese, Benin, and Cameroonian—are qualifiers that are normally reserved for conceptions of the person as a national or civil subject rather than a biological one. Labie's tendency to conflate haplotypes with location is evident in the following excerpt from our interview.

We were surprised to find a strict geographic specificity, very strict, and a high percentage of homozygotes with the same markers on each gene, which you don't find in America, so these populations were relatively endogamous, and they had geographic specificity. This geographic specificity, we then compared it to . . . [interrupts herself] It was surprising, impressive even. We then compared it to work done by I think it was Cavalli-Sforza who had done a widespread inventory on epidemiological tendencies for all of Africa at the phenotypic level, with electrophoresis, etc. They then drew up a map, a computer-generated map, and we then saw that the specificities that we had seen were largely in the middle of high-frequency epicenters, and that consequently we were onto something extraordinary. From there we looked even further and found that we had a certain correlation, with many exceptions, but still statistically valid, between certain clinical characteristics and the haplotypes we had just come across. This was the first step, which took place between 1982 and 1985.

I asked Labie to explain what pushed her to structure the research in this way, based on high-frequency (capital city) centers within geographic areas. She responded:

We felt like we had a seam [*un filon*], as in a mine, we had to exploit, we didn't know what it was, but a seam nonetheless. So this part was published, we had a paper in the *PNAS* and in the *NEJM* and then we were looking to go a bit further. We then entered into a collaboration with a group in Lyon and we started to see that polymorphisms of regulation in promoters also existed. All this was further developed in the years to follow, and we reworked and improved our maps. When we made the maps we saw that the Mediterranean [population] was entirely what we can call of the Benin region. From there we tried to do a certain number of controls. But it's much harder to take blood from healthy Africans than from sick ones. Africans don't like to have blood taken. So we had some problem with controls, but I got results that were more or less satisfactory. . . .

At that point, Labie and her colleagues engaged in a historically European exercise of mapping Africa.

As she continued her account of their work and their search for collaborators on the continent, I realized that her main stops, and especially those where she was able to cull DNA, were locales that had previously been part of Francophone (French and Belgian) Africa. She recalls this history by lamenting the loss of an old map.

I had a map of Africa I would like to have shown you, but I don't have it anymore. In any case, we were in Dakar, we researched a bit everywhere, we were in Burkina, in Ouagadougou, and especially in Bobo Dioulasso because there was a French ORSTOM center there. We were in Abidjan a bit, for logistical reasons, the layovers etc., the sicklers aren't interesting there, they're all too mixed, like the Americans and the West Indies. We were also in Lomé and Cotonou—I was also in touch with people in Nigeria. I was also in Youande, that's where we got the Cameroonian samples. I was in Lumbumbashi, in Calvosh [*sic*], there aren't many people who go touring around [there]. We went to Congo, to the *République*, said to be democratic, of Congo, which wasn't all that democratic, but anyway—we have a remarkable collaborator there. We received samples with no problem. In all of these places, there are certain people who have stayed homogenous, and others who have proven to fall into sub-groups. It's all very complicated.

To test out my perception that she and her team were, with a few exceptions, effectively retracing the territories of the former French colonies, I asked: "How did you decide to call the haplotypes Senegal, Benin, and so on?" She replied as if it were obvious: "Well, by looking at the map!"

Not all of the names that Labie used for haplotypes signified colonial geographies, however; the most peculiar, "Bantu," refers to a term for the peoples and languages of Central Africa, while it also carries racial-apartheid connotations because of its use in the South African regime to separate white rights from black. In our interview, she asserted that, despite the reigning preference in the United States for "Central African Republic," the haplotype for those in this zone should indeed be called "Bantu." Here she harkens back to Pales's cartographic reasoning in which race was an "area," a people, and a measure of physical traits to be charted. In fact, she was trying to be culturally sensitive in doing so.

DL: And naming them after their geographical location posed a problem, because those from Bangui, we called them accordingly because in Bangui the people are Bantu. And when we talked to our friend Dr. Chebloune from Congo, he confirmed that they are Bantu! I also bought large tomes of the *Anthropology of Africa*. I've got entire encyclopedias at home, and they use the word "Bantu." There are the Bantu from the north and the Bantu from the south. Perhaps they are different. In any case, I don't know why, but the Americans didn't like the word "Bantu," as if it was pejorative. They wanted to call the haplotype "Central African Republic." Now when we go to Congo, this is no longer the case, these are Bantu! This is a race of Bantu. It isn't a dishonorable word to be a Bantu.

DF: Well, in the South African context . . .

DL: Well, when I talk to my African friends, they say "we are Bantu."

DF: Ok, now let's go to Senegal, a country where you have many different ethnic groups that . . .

DL: Well these aren't the most pure people, given their history. We only got 85% homogeneity in Dakar, in Benin it was 100%, and in—with the Bantu we got 95%!

Labie unconsciously corrected her choice of preposition, shifting from "in," designating a place, to "with," designating a people, for "the Bantu." But she seemed not to notice the connotations of her usage of the term "race." Her protests about "my African friends" who call themselves Bantu, and her use of the concepts of "pure" and "mixed" races, are aspects of her contemporary thinking that echo the *raciologie* of her late colonial predecessors. Labie then traced the haplotype regions on the map of Africa that she did have.

> DL: Oh, this map!—I gave my good one away. Well, we tried to find the limits of all this. Now when we map the limits—see, here is Dakar [pointing to the black dot on the coast]. We were also in Mali [traces her finger over Senegal to Mali]. Ok, everything along the Senegalese river is Senegalese. People in Western Mali, those farmers near the river, are Senegalese, anthropologically speaking. The same thing goes for the Mauritanians, and Guineans.
>
> DF: The Guineans? [asking to which Guinea she was referring . . .]
>
> DL: They are Senegalese. . . . So the ensemble of Senegal encompasses Senegal, and without a doubt, Gambia, but I've never seen Gambia. . . . Guinea, maybe Sierra Leone, but no one goes there, because there are better things to do than to go to Sierra Leone right now, and a part of Mali (the western part).
>
> DF: And part of Mali. . . . Interesting.
>
> DL: [continuing, as if on a roll] And probably some of Morocco.

Labie and her colleagues were, and still are, interested in finding genetic factors that are connected with the differential lived experience of the disease. Shortly after their first publications on the discovery of sickle cell haplotypes, they had to speak with caution since they recognized that "many exceptions" existed in the clinical setting, while the sample size of their study was extremely small. Members of her team went on to publish more articles on the likelihood of the various polymorphisms bearing on regulatory factors that influenced disease severity and lived experience. Key U.S. researchers heralded these ideas not only as clinically valid but also as valuable with regard to making prognoses of organ damage and other complications and indicators of severity (Nagel et al. 1985; Nagel et al. 1991; Powars 1990, 1991a; Powars et al. 1990; Powars and Hiti 1993).

Labie and Jacques Elion, her former student who over the years has become one of her closest colleagues and co-authors, have nonetheless tried to temper the genetic determinism that many read in her team's initial findings. Eventually they became skeptical of the wholesale oversimplification of the role of the polymorphic markers grouped as haplotypes and they themselves began to raise numerous questions of epistasis. In a ten-year review of the literature discussing minor breakthroughs on the question, Labie and Elion commended the progress in thinking that had been made since their initial work, while raising doubts about some of their earlier hypotheses relating

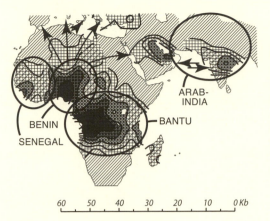

Figure 5.2 An early map indicating the various foyers of the different HbS haplotypes. First appears circa 1980. Reprinted from Marie J. Stuart and Ronald L. Nagel, "Sickle Cell Disease," *The Lancet* 364 (October 2004): 1344, with permission from Elsevier.

disease severity to distinct haplotypes (Labie and Elion 1996, 344). Reexamining the known linkage markers in and around the various haplotypes that may affect disease phenotype, as well as other markers and microsatellites that had since been found and that may be nowhere near the gene (such as the alpha-thalassemia allele) but that still act in conjunction with it, they called for more detailed studies.

Shortly after they wrote the review article, they themselves began preparations to follow up on the early 1980s haplotype results much more extensively. Labie went to Dakar, and Elion later went to Cotonou, in an effort to secure contacts and to ensure a long-standing research partnership with sickle cell specialists in key sites to facilitate this project.

■ **Ethics of Universal Inclusion Through National Particularity**

In a 2002 article titled "*Infectious complications in sickle cell disease are influenced by HLA class II alleles*," the team in Paris, now led by Elion, with Labie still active largely behind the scenes, posited the role of HLA haplotypes in mitigating infections in sicklers with various African sickle cell haplotypes (Tamouza et al. 2002, 194–95).

In the piece, the Paris-based team reiterates the earlier idea of various "determinants" of HbF, emphasizing that the haplotypes may only be partially responsible. The authors explained their claims in light of findings from a small pilot study in Paris in which they saw that those from the region known to have the Senegalese haplotype (now called "West African" in the paper, since Diagne was still pondering contributing Senegalese DNA) often have "protective" HLA haplotypes. They note that confirming and extending this promising small study would require more research, and, consequently, more "collaboration" in Africa (Tamouza et al. 2002, 198).

Participating geneticists whom I interviewed in Paris gave me the impression that the study would not be restricted to HLA haplotypes as these correlate to sickle cell haplotypes and infections. As mentioned earlier, examining these "genetically homogeneous" groups in two different settings would, they hoped, enable the French researchers to analyze discrepant clinical manifestations in genetically similar patients residing in Paris and in Africa, isolating the difference made by environmental "transplantation." Elion also hoped that this study would shed light on pharmacogenomics, or how particular individuals or groups responded to certain drugs for sickle cell, which was an axis of one lab's funding in the collaboration on the French side.[30] New efforts were made to embark on an improved population genetics study in Cotonou, Benin, Kinshasa, Republic of Congo, and Dakar, Senegal, to address these questions from the late 1990s into 2001.

This French-francophone African collaboration was funded by the French Institute for Scientific, Health, and Medical Research (INSERM) and by the American March of Dimes Foundation, which partially financed Elion. As the principal actor on the French side responsible for enlisting the cooperation of sickle cell doctors in Africa, Elion explained the importance of having access to larger, relatively "purer" populations than were available in Paris. The problem as he saw it laid in the fact that there were many West Indians among the Parisian patient population, and because, as he said, "of the history of migration, slavery, and mixing," these "*Antillais*" would not lend themselves to genetic studies that targeted sickle cell and co-inherited factors. These co-factors would have presumably remained in linkage disequilibrium only in populations who had conserved what he called their "biological integrity" and geographical location. Furthermore, he confided that "a certain researcher" in Paris at the largest sickle cell center in the region would not "share" his patients with Labie, Elion, and their team. These local obstacles were framed by larger pressures both global (i.e., migration) and globalizing (or the fact that Africans are, in his thinking, only now becoming "mixed").

Today in Paris an observant traveler often hears people expressing their fears about American globalization. Overhearing strangers' café conversations, walking past a news stand, surfing television channels, talking with a waiter, attending a university lecture, or daring to discuss "politics" with friends or the bus driver constitute some of the everyday activities where these anxieties make themselves known. Freud taught us that fears take on many shapes and sublimations; so do "global" threats in France. Labie and Elion present their current study of the genetics of sickle cell and its associated alleles in patients who have remained relatively "endogamous" as both an advantage they enjoy over "the Americans" and a race (*course*) against an immanent human deadline, since the visible African immigration and "mixing" going on around them in Paris seemed to be an omen of what is to come.

I was surprised by this tendency to see Africans in Africa as static in time and space, genetically fixed rather than migratory with the possibility of bearing children with people "unlike them," while those in France, and America, were characterized by movement and the potential to change. Yet for Elion, "pure populations are on their way out." He envisioned their study as the last of its kind, as he told me:

> In Paris we essentially have an African sickle cell population. We really have a historical opportunity here to try and determine the variable relationship between the environment and genetics. Thanks to our collaborators in Africa, we have access to populations that are homogenous from a genetic point of view. This homogeneity is particularly based on their haplotypes. They are homozygous for the Benin haplotype if we look at those in Cotonou, etc. We have these genetically homogenous populations who live in the African environment, and in Paris we have the same populations. Genetically we can show that those in Paris are really the same as those who are living in Africa, but who all live in a climate and an environment of the Parisian region. Thus, we think that what we have here are non-mixed populations that permit us *tools*, which give us a complete advantage over our colleagues, competitors, and friends all the same, *les Américains*, who, on the other hand, have a completely mixed population. They can no longer isolate important [genetic] differences....

He goes on:

> When one has a homogenous population, which has not undergone much mixing, clearly the haplotype lets us measure the homogeneity of the population in question. For example, if in Benin the subjects are exclusively, or 90%, homozygous for the Benin haplotype, this means that this population has not mixed [with others] because if it had mixed, it would have picked up, or incorporated, other haplotypes coming from surrounding places. These are simply genetic markers that tell us that the populations we are looking at are populations that are genetically homogenous, and if this population [in Benin] is genetically homogenous [carrying one HbS type] then it is different than the population that we have in Dakar because the latter can also show that it is genetically homogenous, a little less, but [homogenous] concerning the haplotype Senegal. So, there are two things going on here. The first being that such an approach allows us to work with constant factors, which are the haplotypes. We have already normalized these, and we know that these are factors in disease variation. Secondly, we use the haplotype as a control that tells us that we are working with genetically homogenous groups. The Americans, on the other hand—[interrupts himself] . . . Even if [their patients] are homozygous for the Senegalese haplotype it is not because there have been marriages [mating] between Senegalese ever since slavery brought them to America. It is because *chance* had it that two chromosomes with the Senegalese haplotype found each other

in one gamete, the child in question. Those patients that are homozygous for the Senegalese haplotype in New York will have normalized the
haplotype aspect, but that does not mean that two individuals who are
both homozygous for the Senegalese haplotype are homogeneous for
the rest. Because for "the rest" the black American population is totally
mixed. The Afro-American population has incorporated at least 15%
percent of Caucasian genes in particular. So, even if the Americans succeeded in grouping their patients according to homozygous haplotypes
for the Senegalese haplotype—actually there are very few Senegalese
haplotypes, the Afro-Americans are mostly of the Benin haplotype—so
if they succeeded in grouping their patients who had the Benin or the
Bantu haplotypes, which the Americans call Central African Republic,
that would only give us one normalization on one variable of the genetic
expression. On the other hand, to be able to work on African populations in Africa, either in Africa or here in Paris, the haplotype allows
us to determine the homogeneity of all the other genetic material, the
genetic base [*le fond génétique*], and to be able to say that this or that
fond génétique is homogenous and that those in say Benin are not the
same as those in Senegal.

There is a subtle but noteworthy shift in emphasis as Elion presents their
thinking. Initially the haplotypes are interesting to him as an object of study
to theoretically serve as a control for the environment. The idea is that Beninois patients in Paris could be compared to their haplotypic equivalents
in Cotonou, and, through methods of deduction, any general differences in
disease outcome that emerged would be due to the environment since their
genetics would be matched. This idea—which surprisingly pits genetics and
environment as distinct bloc concepts and realities that do not interact—is
then absorbed by a kind of focused anxiety about human genetic purity and
isolated population groups that are always passing from the scene.

■ **Contacts and Contracts in a "New Era" of Collaboration**

Labie and Elion viewed their study as the last of its kind. When recruiting
African "contacts" to provide them with samples from patients assumed to
have the Senegalese haplotype, both with and without infections (information crucial for the study on HLA alleles), they were forced to reevaluate the
finality of this claim. To their frustration, this effort at new research in the
global South (*les pays du Sud*) was actually the first of its kind on another register. It was the first time in their collaborations that Africans would insist that
the French researchers formally agree to abide by two "ethical" conditions: to
include their African collaborators among the authors of their publications,
and to keep them informed of where the genetic materials went and how they

would be used or disposed of. The targeted, but troublesome, potential collaborators were Dr. Fall and Dr. Diagne of Albert Royer. The same trends that are partially responsible for the large numbers of African immigrants in Paris and other parts of the world—movements, that for some geneticists, spoil the possibility of certain types of future research and make Labie and Elion's study an endangered breed—also incite certain Africans who have stayed on the continent, or returned to it after training and conducting research in Paris, to demand "respectful" collaborations.[31] Senegalese sickle cell researchers have made it a point since the early 1980s haplotype studies to redress what to them are now unthinkable acts after witnessing what they called "normal" research collaborations between parties in "the North" (*les pays du Nord*) and "abnormal" ones across the "North-South" divide. The ease of obtaining samples and publishing without including their African "contacts," as was done in the first haplotype study, sowed tensions regarding this new research in Senegal. The Senegalese haplotype was indispensable to the current study for Elion and Labie, given how their ideas about severity and difference were fundamentally tied to the map that was so central to Labie's every point during our interview. In this way, the haplotype's value gave researchers in Dakar the leverage to exact certain demands, or, in Diagne's words, "to apply certain ethics."

"So It Is with Countries and Men"

Diagne remained uncertain about what the Senegalese haplotype meant, or if it accounted for the diminished severity of disease in his patients. While some of Labie and Elion's later publications warn against easily attributing a given sickle cell phenotype to the nominal haplotype configurations, they often came across to Diagne as believers in the genetic determinism that some of their American colleagues pursued as well (Steinberg et al.1995; Powars et al. 1990; Powars 1991b). With patients such as Rokhoya Sylla in mind, Diagne kept discourses on the haplotype close by, but also actively sought out other explanations, particularly the *attitude sénégalaise*. Nonetheless, he found the preliminary results on HLA alleles of "intellectual interest."

Pediatricians working on sickle cell at Albert Royer had been contacted by Labie or Elion about a potential collaboration on several occasions starting in late 1999, and in late 2000 Diagne finally agreed—given certain terms and conditions. With contacts long secured in Benin and Central Africa, Labie and Elion were not pleased when the physicians whom they targeted in Dakar eluded them, became evasive, and then, in the end, got confrontational. Diagne explained his and Fall's concerns:

> Besides what everyone knows about how people were treated and how illnesses were learned about in the colonial period, in the initial period after decolonization there were not many native doctors or researchers in Senegal, or in Africa in general, so research continued to be done by

Europeans, and by the French in particular. And as Senegal did not have any structure worthy of calling an ethics committee in place, or any sort of "stop lights" to avoid, or rather to oblige these people to do ethical research, there were lots of abuses, notably concerning work on liver cancer and research on vaccines. . . . I'm primarily talking about abuses of patients here [not physician-researchers]. This state of mind has long existed and still does.

Even if we are no longer talking about French researchers working in Dakar, many of those now working in health institutions were trained by the French who were here, and in many other African countries. Many of these [African] doctors continue to work in this vein, to be utilized as, let's say, "collaborators" in research initiated abroad. This often means that someone somewhere else wants to research a certain domain and he or she knows that in Senegal there are many patients, much opportunity to do research without having to go through all of the necessary, complicated formalities posed by committees in their own countries. They realize how easy it is when they have a contact on the ground. They often do not offer anything in exchange.

Now, certain of us—I think the term was coined by my boss [Dr. Fall]—talk about being "blood senders" [*envoyeurs de sang*]. [Diagne then assumes the voice of someone calling for blood from Europe] "Could you send me a sample of x . . . " or sometimes they come to you with a list of "I need this many blood samples, from this kind of person, with such and such complication, etcetera." Many times the patients were never informed of what was going on for this research, which benefited neither the local health structure nor the patients. Some of the local doctors who facilitated the material needs of those researchers did so in good faith, thinking that they would be included in the [results of] studies, or that there would be some benefit to patients, vaccines or something. It often went like this. . . .

Now many young doctors have understood that this kind of thing cannot continue. Such a complete change in thinking is mostly due to the fact that they have sojourned in Europe or have been partially trained there. They saw how collaborations happened in Europe between two countries that respect each other. This younger generation no longer accepts that people come here to practice what they cannot do in their own countries. We are just as scientifically rigorous and serious as those they enter into real collaborations with, so there was no reason not to include us in the publication process as is usually done. Things are changing. What was "acceptable" ten or twenty years ago cannot be done here anymore. This is the case in Senegal anyway. Generally speaking, many people in other African countries still let themselves [reformulates his phrase]—are still prisoners of the old system.

With a distancing style characteristic of someone who wants to remain objective, Diagne presented this narrative in both the first and the third person. He himself is one of the younger generation who has "sojourned in Europe" and seen how mutually respectful research takes place. For Diagne, it is up to the Senegalese to free the "prisoners of the old system." Yet perhaps only the Senegalese hold the power to negotiate through the biological "advantage" of their patients. They are moved by a historical remembering of how Senegalese DNA was utilized in the 1984 study, while patients and practitioners alike were forgotten. In setting their own terms, Diagne hoped to establish new rules for future collaborations between, to use Senghor's phrase, "the countries and men" of France and Senegal in the form of a new ethics. At Albert Royer Children's Hospital, he says:

> We have become really hesitant about just sending blood samples without knowing what will become of them. For a few years now Dr. Fall has inculcated everyone here with this culture [of hesitancy], to avoid falling into "facility". . . . From now on, each time that we enter into collaborations, we define a minimum framework by which the work will take place, saying: this is what we are looking for, this is what we'll do, this is the method, and finally this is how we will exploit the results *together*. We are trying to inscribe ourselves in this process [*démarche*]. And, unfortunately, it is a way of doing things that, quite often, does not correspond to the ideas that certain research teams—for the moment I can only speak of French teams, since they are the ones that I know—have of Africa. They have habitually—in other countries, or at other moments in history—done research without having given anything back. They have even published the results of studies [carried out in collaboration] where not one African name figures among the authors. When we read the methodology of these works, we see that all of the data, the blood samples, were taken from African patients, and there is not one African author listed. Manifestly there has to have been collaboration with at least one African person. But no African names figure among the authors, and there was not even a thank you in the acknowledgements to a clinical or hospital service that helped them. We have many examples of this, of data that have been published in the literature, that have often times served as references that everyone uses. This research has taken place in an African country, but that was never made evident, neither was the collaboration, or the participation of African researchers.

Diagne and Fall were particularly upset about the 1984 study, which Labie led. They have clearly read the papers, seen the author lines, and read the acknowledgments. For the seminal haplotype study there are two people acknowledged in Dakar—they are just not Africans, nor are they people who have a public history of taking an interest in sickle cell.

Diagne was not totally comfortable speaking out like this. He did not want to alienate his colleagues. Nonetheless he and others were clearly bothered and were not going to remain silent. But he furthermore wanted to make the point that he was not one to generalize unnecessarily. By this he meant that one of his best research interlocutors was also French. When Diagne was in Paris on his first research stay, he spent several months as a resident in a pediatric service with Gil Tchernia and often spoke of Tchernia's anti-racist efforts in France and even in Africa during his younger years. For Diagne, Tchernia's experience in Africa where he engaged "*with* Africans," faced with colonial politics while there, formed a different set of principles. It was Tchernia who invited the maligned Dr. Falga to prove his point about fagara in the Berkeley sickle cell mouse model. Diagne and other Africans saw this openness as a significant move on the part of "the French." He treats friends like Tchernia as hopeful exceptions to what he nonetheless sees as a French pattern.

> This isn't to generalize, because next to teams that behave like this we also have the experience of having worked with others in real sincere, serious collaborations. For the most part the latter were constituted of persons who had lived in Africa at some point, and who came to know Africa, maybe they even feel themselves to be a little African somewhere in there, but in any case they know that it would be disrespectful to work like this. This is to say, there are people who collaborate perfectly well with us, with fair co-responsibility without the least attempt whatsoever to utilize the results for their own benefit. But there are others who think that they can continue to exploit African data without respecting even the most minimal ethical conditions, or put quite simply, morality . . . Often times it is after things have already appeared somewhere when we come across them in the literature, after the fact. It is only then that we realize that we have been played [*dribblés*], if you like. Now we want things in writing before engaging; that way if the collaboration is not respected we can present them with what they signed and agreed upon.

Diagne's rationale for asking "the French," specifically Dominique Labie, to sign a contract is framed by the way the "original" haplotype study was authored and whose contributions were—and were not—acknowledged.

I then asked Dr. Diagne to describe the initial contact with the French research team that sought his participation in the study of HLA haplotypes and to discuss how their collaboration developed. Significantly, instead of detailing the current project, he returned to the history of unequal relations.

> For years now, ever since people realized that genetic aspects could modulate the severity of sickle cell disease, or that during some of the very first research efforts on the question, a specific haplotype was dis-

covered in Senegal that was associated with a relatively good tolerance of the disease, . . . people have been interested in Senegal. And what's more, the very first research on this published in the 1980s goes back to what I was saying a minute ago. Here at the *Principal Hospital* in Dakar, a team came through. They took samples from patients at Principal, and most likely at other hospitals as well, and they obtained a certain number of samples that permitted them to identify, with certainty, a characteristic of Senegalese sickle cell, now called the Senegalese haplotype. This study was among the seminal first studies to speak of the Senegalese haplotype showing that 85% of Senegalese sickle cell patients carried this haplotype. I am forever bothered that among those listed and signed as authors on the study, there figures not one Senegalese name. The proof is right here [referring to published papers on his desk]. Since sickle cell is the textbook example for genetic research, everyone who learns about sickle cell reads this article. Since this initial publication many people have become interested in Senegal. Everyone wants to have a foot in the place famous for this curious haplotype.

Diagne did eventually come back to my question and at that point simply said that he hoped that Labie, through Elion, might "update" her practices this time around.

On all counts, Senegalese participation in the current study is more crucial to the French team than it is for those at the CHU in Dakar. Diagne considers the potential information useful, but ultimately "intellectual," meaning that not much will come of it that will benefit his patients in the here and now. In debating the merits of interesting questions versus pragmatic knowledge he can act on, he predicted that sickle cell and HLA haplotype knowledge, although scientifically interesting, would do very little. "I cannot change who does or does not have the protective haplotypes, or the protective HLA alleles," he told me, adding that he is not sure if these are even the right questions to be asked. A better one, might be how can he actually prevent patients from getting the infections that compromise their health, rather than documenting a genetic pattern that may correlate with them. For the French scientists, the study could not be done without the cooperation of Diagne and his Senegalese colleagues. In our interview in Paris, I asked Jacques Elion to explain the roles of the French and African collaborators:

DF: For the current project, how will you work in Senegal?
JE: The idea is that the samples come here. [. . .]
DF: So, do you envisage doing this study for all of the known haplotypes?
JE: Yes.
DF: And with the same system where the samples come here to Paris?
JE: Yes.
DF: But unfortunately, as you say, there was a problem with Senegal?

JE: Yes there was a problem with the biologist at the Children's Hospital in Dakar [CHU]. But I get along quite well with Mr. Fall and Mr. Diagne and I think that we will be able to restart things. [. . .] As it stands, the Senegalese haplotype is said to be less severe; I would like it if we could test this seriously. The way in which this has been established, studies on Senegalese in New York [with Ronald Nagel's patients] or other studies where they had very few people with the Senegalese haplotype [Labie's early work] are not sufficiently convincing in my opinion. In Paris, we have these three haplotypes, and to be able to compare them in African environments will be very important when comparing them with those living in Europe. We are sure to have interesting results—to take two identical populations, at the level of their genes, in two different environments—that will prove very interesting.

Apparently the biologist in question was a person who Diagne and Fall hoped could do a research stay in France to learn techniques and benefit from the collaboration that way, but the details were difficult for both sets of researchers to agree upon. Diagne felt that there was a sense of "shock" and perhaps even outrage that may have stalled the negotiation. For him, however, the most important parts of the agreement had less to do with knowledge transfers and training per se than with a true collaboration. More forthcoming on the issue than Elion, he told me:

When this same [Labie's] French team approached us at the end of 1999 and in 2000, I was asked to give my opinion to the team here as the main sickle cell specialist. The kinds of things I was asking for go without saying for a normal researcher.

But these reflections were not warmly welcomed when we heard back. Let's just say all of this irritated those with whom we were supposed to do the new collaboration. It irritated them, probably because this was the first time that anyone had ever spelled things out in this way. They felt "*accused*," but they ended up accepting the essentials, meaning to put the nature of our collaboration on paper. We wrote up an agreement where we would have the same responsibility as them and where we would exploit the results together. And that's where we are now. The base is laid, now we are in the first phase of the study.

■ Down with Delegated Democracy

For the most recent haplotype study, the initial expectation that Senegalese and other African specialists would simply send blood samples up North was not met, and French researchers had to renegotiate the terms of the collaboration in order to enlist practitioners in Dakar. This all happened as public discourses about democracy were an audible feature of daily life for most Senegalese throughout 1999 and 2000, which may have played a role in how Diagne and Fall tried to reorder North-South relationships. Specifically, this was a period when the opposition Democratic Socialist Party (PDS) was demanding a change in power from the Socialist Party that had held onto power since decolonization through tactics often regarded as unjust. Dr. Diagne and his colleagues, like many Senegalese, constantly engaged in talk of "power change" and "righting wrongs." The PDS came to power in February 2000 and now it, at its turn, has retained power ever since.

Since the first haplotype studies, indicators both biological and cultural have presented French researchers with the need to refine the initial studies to take the complexity of the "environment" into consideration and to adopt fairer ways of collaborating with their African colleagues. Elion characterized the new study as "ambitious" because of its geographical reach and its promise to shed light on the question of gene-environment interactions. From a different vantage, Diagne also saw the study as ambitious. For him it signified a political feat of setting a new tone for engagement that would benefit Senegalese and other African scientists as well. Refusing to be a prisoner of the old system—which mirrors what French sociologist of science Michel Callon and his colleagues have called a "delegated democracy" (*démocratie délégative*) (Callon et al. 2001)—that reigned for much too long, Diagne strove to establish its alternative, or "dialogic democracy" (*démocratie dialogique*).

The understanding of how the genetic material of the current study could be exploited by both teams "together," as Dr. Diagne insisted, lay in these practitioners' ideas of, and interests in, genetic and medical technologies and trends. In the end, the Senegalese team agreed to the collaboration on the basis that they might ultimately benefit from increased knowledge about infections. The French group presented the research to the Senegalese as a study on HLA haplotypes as these differ in the already established foyers of the sickle cell haplotypes. Among themselves, however, Girot, Labie, and Elion discussed reinforcing, or possibly disproving, aspects of their first studies, while looking for manifestations of the disease that could be attributed to "the environment." Elion even mentioned the pharmacogenomic implications that the data might yield. The discussion in Senegal, by contrast, was limited to HLA and infections. This discrepancy over how the information could and would be exploited mimicked other "divisions of vision" (Canguilhem 1998[1965], 11) between actors in the two locales. Given significant technical differences, but more importantly the value of population genetics and a preoccupation with genetic homogeneity as a "tool," as Elion phrased it, it is clear that—contract notwithstanding—the stakes of this research may not fully translate across the North-South divide. As researchers in Paris imagined pharmacogenomic outcomes, the French scientists explained the study in Senegal in terms crucial for any African doctor: infections. Even armed with the power that their "mild" sickle cell affords them, the Senegalese researchers were not fully equipped to equalize their chances for exploiting the results while at the negotiating table. Despite their ambitions and their healthy patients, it is clear that "superior forms of equality" are, in fact, rarely born of inequality no matter how "complementary" the countries or men.

CHAPTER SIX

Ordering Illness: Heterozygous "Trait"
Suffering in the Land of the Mild Disease

In early December of 2003 the newly formed Senegalese Association for the Fight Against Sickle Cell Anemia (ASD) convened for the first time. The form of the forum was to be a dialogue between the principal member of the nascent group's scientific advisory counsel, Dr. Diagne, and the mothers of his small patients. Diagne addressed the essentials of sickle cell care in Senegal: details of "crisis" prevention and assuaging the hallmark symptom of the disease, pain. Shortly into the discussion, one of the mothers seamlessly left the topic of her child's pain, broaching that of her own. Her concern, quite naturally—or so she thought—was how to care for her child when she herself was in "sickle cell crisis." The doctor quickly corrected her by pronouncing her a sickle cell carrier (*un porteur sain*), meaning, he reiterated, that she was healthy. In differentiating "AS," or sickle cell trait, from the disease, "SS," those with the trait, he professed, "were *not sick*." Several of the women looked to each other in defiant solidarity and protested. "With all due respect," they insisted, the doctor had it wrong. He, however, held his ground and pleaded with them to see their own "health" compared to their children's "disease." They refused. Outside as the women parted ways, they reran the highlights of their personal experiences of pain aired in the discussion. Nonetheless, a meddling realization escorted them home in their disbelief. Had they achieved their years-long struggle of establishing a patient interest group with this local specialists only to have him potentially dissolve one of their most subjective "interests"— that of their own pain? Was it possible that modern science could allow them to be labeled *drépanocytaires AS* (HbAS sicklers), but would not allow them to suffer with the pain that they understood and lived as central to this condition?[1] Had they "mis/recognized" themselves (Haraway 1997, 50) in the cross threads of a familiar discourse that was now becoming strange?

In the world of sickle cell, specialists in the United States and France agree that, under normal physiological circumstances, sickle cell trait is a "benign" condition (Sears 1994) of "asymptomatic" character (Benkerrou, Denamur, and Elion 2003, 296; NHLBI 2002, 10). In this Western literature on sickle cell trait, the designation "HbAS," signifies the heterozygous phenotypic state, or the "sickle cell carrier." The "A" conveys normal "Adult" hemoglobin (HbA), while the "S" stands for "Sickle" hemoglobin (HbS). This combination (HbAS) is thought to code the carrier as one who quantitatively possesses blood with up to 50 percent "S" hemoglobin, with the potential to sickle, and 50 percent normal hemoglobin, thought to compensate for, and stabilize, any disease effects. Despite these percentages, those with HbAS in North America are said to be "healthy-carriers." They may feel little to no bodily symptoms, but depending on the genetic status of their partner, they can pass the sickle cell trait or the disease onto their offspring.

Yet, like the women of ASD and others to be presented here, some Americans experience their status as "healthy carriers" as all too hyphenated since there have been periodic reports that people there suffer dramatically from symptoms that both differ from and greatly resemble those of sickle cell disease (HbSS) as well (see Kark 2000 for a review). In the United States, evidence of sickle cell trait suffering may be garnered from seemingly fleeting anecdotes described in sports medicine, clinical military journals, and congressional testimonials for early sickle cell testing legislation.[2] It could be that such cases are statistically too rare to warrant real attention, while many of them seem to be the result of physical exertion, heat exhaustion, or other "*non-normal*" physiological conditions. The scarcity of this reporting, however, might also be understood in light of the *lack* of a cultural "option" to be sick with sickle cell trait in the United States.[3] Here I am referring to the negation of the possibility that was instantiated by the social-political work that went into making sickle cell trait a "non-disease" (Hampton et al. 1974) amid "the sickle cell controversy" in post–civil rights era America (Gary 1974), which was provoked by a National Research Council (NRC) investigation of the trait. Despite the fact that the NRC committee "concluded that data on the topic of pathologies associated with the carrier status were inadequate," it nonetheless recommended that all recruits for basic training in the military be screened for both the trait and the disease (Duster 2003, 26). As sociologist Troy Duster points out, this and other studies set up sickle cell screening only to block, not to further, empirical inquiry on the question of whether and why sickling could occur in American carriers (2003, 29). What then ensued was a set of understandably anxious responses from some black Americans who felt that they were being unfairly tested and consequently unfairly denied opportunities on the basis of the presence of sickle cell trait, which most felt to be benign in their population (Tapper 1999, 120; Wilkinson 1974).[4]

A very different socio-medical consensus had already cemented in most people's minds across the Atlantic in Senegal, however, both before and after this key moment in American minority right's history. There, almost everyone I encountered, in both medical and lay settings, understood the heterozygous condition of the sickle cell trait to be a *disease*, a source of suffering, and a cause for redress if not for cure.

As we saw in the previous chapter, since the inception and articulation of a phenomenon called sickle cell trait (HbAS) in Dakar, in the 1950s, those affected have been categorized alongside those with HbSS as diseased.[5] In the late 1970s, when sickle cell disease became an interest for post-independence Senegalese medical professionals, the physiological manifestations of the disease and the trait came into clinical focus. Lamine Diakhate, the recent director of the CNTS until 2009, and one of Dakar's most renowned hematologists, was a student and eventual colleague of Linhard who, with Pales, conflated the trait and the disease for their own engrossing cartographic anthropological science. The legacy effect of this conceptual conflation of trait and disease leaves many generalist practitioners within the University Cheikh Anta Diop, Faculty of Medicine, diagnosing patients with "the disease of trait" into the present. Thus still today, sickle cell trait and disease are seen as varying degrees of the same potentially debilitating phenomenon in Senegalese society, while both may, or may not, require intervention.[6] But as the first ASD meeting tensions portend, change is afoot.

In the last decade, clinician-researchers working on sickle cell disease in Dakar have undergone genetic and medical training stays in Paris, France, and have returned to the University of Dakar, Faculty of Medicine with the view that sickle trait should no longer be classed as an illness. Such a stance is an entirely new way of seeing HbAS in Senegal, and in many parts of West Africa, where this trait has long been understood to be a "lighter" form of sickle cell anemia itself.[7] In this chapter I examine multiple determinants of sickle cell trait suffering. In so doing, I hope to show that illness in part hinges upon the cultural and ethical forms of a particular society (Good 1994, 34), while the options and naming of those forms may be varyingly shared with and influenced by actors beyond the locale in question or under study. In this case the thing named is sickle cell trait, while "the option" refers to the power of this trait to induce experiences of disease in its carrier. Despite the power and presence of North American and French influences on one medical aspect of sickle cell trait understanding locally (that it is genetic and requires a molecular test to determine), once they are diagnosed, many Senegalese people choose to ignore the principal medical characteristic of HbAS in American and French biomedical descriptions: that it is benign. As concerns sickle cell trait sufferers' claims to an illness category in Dakar, there is little in the way of "commonalities of diagnosis" (Geertz, 2000, 257) with those in the United States and France. Rather, it is their divergence, or *un*commonality of their symptoms as a disorder, that proves instructive.

■ **Ordering Illness**

In the *Normal and the Pathological* Canguilhem famously described health as "organic innocence." "Like all innocence," he wrote, "it must be lost . . . so that knowledge may be possible" (1991, 101). Following from this, we might ask: what knowledge can be learned of lost health, or from affliction, that is not *supposed* to be experienced as such? What can we derive about medicine, bodies, and the purported universals of science when faced with a disorder that is not necessarily a lack of "order" in all places at all times by those doing the categorizing? The willingness, or cultural option, to suffer from this "disorder" in Dakar can be analyzed in light of philosopher Henri Bergson's idea that "order" is the "mind finding itself again in things . . . [even if] the mind can go in two opposite ways" (1998 [1911], 223). This act of finding (*se retrouver*), for Bergson, largely refers to life fitting new knowledge to recognizable norms, and vice versa. Thus, rather than speak of disorder per se, one might simply speak of *orders* in the plural. In short, I argue that "sickle trait suffering," seen to be abnormal from the point of view of Western science, serves as a function of expression that is quite normal as order where not only the mind but also the body "finds itself again in things" in this cultural, economic, and environmental context. Various elements of sickle cell trait, an entity implicated in a hereditary disease that affects the blood and that has been articulated as "genetic," find and fit themselves to expressions of social stress, religious fate and fatalism, and enigmatic physiological suffering in Dakar. In other words, the historical trajectory of North American medical science that actually led some to call sickle cell trait a "non-disease" in the 1970s United States (Hampton, Anderson, Lavizzo, and Bergman, 1974) happened through stakes very different than those that named it a marker of human "exotic pathology" in colonial Senegal.[8] Both trajectories anchor present-day perceptions of sickle trait in each locale, even as certain blood specialists are attempting to reshape the popular—both medical and lay—notion of HbAS, or sickle cell trait, in Dakar.

The "mild" case of Senegalese sickle cell disease that has been problematized throughout this book does not refer to those with the single trait, and with the exception of Mr. Seck, does not refer to people with heterozygous HbSC, which is often taken to be less severe than homozygous sickle cell anemia itself (HbSS). Given its seemingly comparative insignificance on health, trait suffering demonstrates how people in Senegal resource their biology to give precision and order to multiple instances of pain and life difficulty whose origins made little sense for them before their diagnoses. "Trait patients" struggled with ordering life's disorder through this biological, physical element, and, in so doing, they constructed new norms by which life became manageable, or, for some, simply possible at all. People with both sickle cell disease and sickle cell trait in Senegal order their lives, physical disease, social stresses, and economic constraints by giving order to the disordering effects of certain biological kinship expectations, while finding meaning in an illness identity that is shared in biosocial connections of kin more broadly through solidarities built through publicly speaking out on behalf of themselves and other people with their illness (c.f. Nguyen 2004; 2005). Unlike the different ways that sickle cell patients often reexamined economic constraint by triaging aspects of care, or drew upon biosocial kin to share burdens, the people who suffered from sickle cell trait in Dakar were often totally overwhelmed with poverty and had lost aspects of family that they often could not recover. What marked sickle cell trait "sufferers" off from those with the trait who felt healthy was that economic difficulties for the former were associated with loss generally, while they sensed that doubts and uncertainties exist in everyday life, but, that for them, "the worst happens every time" (Das 2007, 134). Both dramatic and quite ordinary setbacks plagued them and, in the process, to go on living an ordinary life was often no longer possible. Certain trait suffers were finally able to emerge from their suffering by rethinking and redefining life's setbacks, and by reworking debilitating economic limitations. Others were not.

■ Sociosomatic Genetics?

How and why the phenomenon of "somatization" differs across the globe was an early question for medical anthropology and cross-cultural psychiatry (Kleinman 1977, 6). One aspect of this literature focused on how suffering could be understood through "idioms of distress" having to do with liminal, newfound "vulnerabilities" with which people find themselves confronted in times of political, economic, and social change (Nichter 1981). This work, shuttling between somatization and psychologization of psychiatric symptoms, was largely concerned with cultural inflections on anxiety, depression, and other forms of "mental illness." These early cross-cultural studies critiqued biomedicine as unduly biased toward physiological symptoms that it assumed were universal. Not surprisingly, researchers in this field called for a reexamination of culture in relationship to depression and to illness in general (Kleinman 1977, 9). Rooted in these seminal calls for cross-cultural psychiatry, medical anthropologists have more recently documented the ways that social and political strictures become unmistakable idioms of pain and suffering in multiple political, and often tumultuous, social and cultural contexts (Becker 1998; Das 2007; 1991; Kleinman 2006; Kleinman, Das, and Lock 1997; Scheper-Hughes and Lock 1987). Still, few have explored the interrelation of physiological human differences and universalized medical norms and nosologies on a given disorder and its symptom expressions, or "local biologies" (Lock 1993b, 38–39).

Despite the obvious inroads that anthropological inquiries have made in broadening our understandings of mental health, we must do more to grasp the somatization of bodily facts that are taken-for-granted as unquestionably "physical," such as genetic anomalies. We would be gravely mistaken to assume that genetic points of difference like HbAS are immune to getting embroiled in people's struggles to negotiate personhood, bodily health, and social stress.

Genetic traits, like myriad other ailments that stir people's identities and concepts of normalcy, are acted upon by individuals who aspire to find a sense
of order that might acquit them of some aspect of suffering. Often, ironically,
this begins by naming their suffering as a concrete biological entity in order
to fully inhabit the symptoms associated with it. Today, the many Senegalese
trait carriers who complain of a boundless array of bodily complaints make
clear that the possession of HbAS can result in illness expressions, and also
in changed physiology. Thus, instead of ascribing different health outcomes
globally to variants of genetic traits in different populations, we must explore
the possibility that somatization as a cultural process might be at work in differential expressions of genes, such as heterozygous sickle cell trait, as it is with
"mental" health disorders. In other words, if we are to fully sort out the cultural
phenomenon of somatization, then we need to get out of the "mind," as it were.
I argue that in the case of sickle cell trait in Dakar, social suffering enunciates
itself through a physical gene anomaly, a single allelic manifestation of this hemoglobin variant, "carried" and experienced in the bodies of some Senegalese
people. Borrowing from Paul Rabinow (1996), on the one hand, and Arthur
Kleinman, Veena Das, and Margaret Lock (1997), on the other, such an amal-
gam might be thought of as *biosocial suffering*.

■ Splits in the "Medical" Mind

Others who have researched "elusive diseases" (Moss and Teghtsoonian 2008;
Palca 1991), such as chronic fatigue syndrome and chemical sensitivity disorder, have noted the overwhelming gender bias of such suffering, as it largely
affects women (Frame 2000; Greenhalgh 2001; Lipson 2004; Ware 1992). This
dynamic is doubly vexing as treating physicians, often male, label the symptoms these women present as "psychological" rather than "physiological,"
which further layers denied suffering with the stigma of a mental disorder
(Ware 1992, 351; Greenhalgh 2001). Often in the absence of any clear biological
or biomedical measure to differentiate those who suffer and those who do not,
larger cultural stereotypes of weakness and malingering work to "delegitima-
tize" sufferers' symptom "realities" in the doctor's office and beyond (Lipson
2004, 207; Ware 1992, 352). In Dakar, where women also disproportionately
make claims to sickle cell trait symptoms to a largely male medical corps, patients are often told that they are "not really sick." Although physicians rarely
directly call people's suffering "psychological" during the medical encounter,
many patients nevertheless understand this to be the message. Statements
imparted by doctors, such as "simply forget your 'disease,'" or, "your sickle
cell isn't serious" (*c'est pas grave*), are seen as dismissive and minimizing. The
belittling nature of such comments is sometimes confounded by physicians'
partial acceptance that patients are indeed suffering from sickle cell trait. The
quantitative aspect of this partial acceptance matters in that trait suffering is

not wholly rejected. Rather, it proves *diminutively* physically possible, in the most literal sense. Such diffident scientific recognition surfaced in various doctor-patient interactions, such as when one vocal trait sufferer and member of the ASD was told by her physician that he indeed believed that she had "mini–sickle cell crises" (*crisettes*), but that they could be managed at home, not at the clinic.

Despite such medical concessions in practice, most specialists still hoped to disabuse patients of the idea that they were sick with sickle cell trait. They repeatedly asserted that "trait suffering" was a psychological, or "psychosomatic," problem. Nonetheless, the problem of sick trait-carriers continues to grow, especially after late 2006 when sickle cell finally registered as a problem warranting government attention. In September of that year Dr. Saliou Diop told me: "I'm going to be completely honest with you, these AS patients are annoying us! (*ils nous embêtent, quoi!*). They show up on general consultation days, and they aren't really sick! It's psychosomatic." Nevertheless, Diop consults and follows sickle cell trait patients and they constitute not an insubstantial part of his patient roster. When I pointed out this inconsistency he said that he schedules sickle cell *disease* patients (*drépanocytaires SS*) to come in four times a year, and that he only makes appointments with trait carriers (*drépanocytaires AS*) twice a year. This is further evidence of a quantitative acceptance: that "mini-crises" warrant a "mini–care regimen"—which is a care regimen all the same.

In an attempt to "reason" with a patient population that in most cases has clearly decided to ignore, and in some instances contest, the newfound medical prescription increasingly diffused in informational settings that "sickle cell trait is not a disease!," physicians in Dakar who wish to impart this message do not unduly blame patients. Rather, they fault the many generalists, nurses, interns, and other ancillary technical staff in the majority of hospitals, health centers, and health posts throughout Senegal who also see "trait" as an illness. It is often these "non-specialists," who are most accessible to the general population, who increasingly test and continue to diagnose patients with the disease of trait.

Today the small number of hematology professionals who are attempting to redefine sickle cell trait in Dakar are operating within a context where the medical norm of what it means to have HbAS itself still has wide consensus in larger medical circles outside of Dakar's two sickle cell clinics. Yet even within the structure of the National Blood Transfusion Center, where the adult sickle cell clinic resides, a clear generational divide exists. As the younger, more recently trained, hematologists look for ways to divert AS sufferers away from the clinic, their superiors, the most notable of whom, Dr. Thiam, is now the dean of the Faculty of Medicine at the University of Dakar, willingly consult HbAS patients: as this public medical figure assured me in 2006, "*Drépanocytaires AS*, they are sick! (*Ils sont malades!*)" Thus, in contradistinction to other cases of elusive disease cited above, sickle cell trait suffering as a medically reasonable disease category is not actually perceived of as "made up by patients" but, rather, is known to be conferred on them by diagnosing physicians (usually, but clearly not always, by non-specialists). Faced with this new knowledge, patients often come to recognize prior pains—inexplicable fatigue, mysterious swelling and aching of the arms and legs, intense headaches, insomnia, and a host of other less consistent symptoms, ranging from heart palpitations to "boiling" bodies—as part of their recent sickle cell trait diagnosis. Their bodily disorder is finally made sense of, as are certain elements of life's other disordering effects, via an attribution to what they see as a source of biological precision, or the sickle cell trait.

Those who make "the disease of trait" diagnoses are members of the "legitimate" medical corps in Dakar (as opposed to traditional healers) who test people for sickle cell when one's child is diagnosed with HbSS, when women come in for prenatal care, or simply in the context of failed attempts to explain patients' persistent, perplexing symptoms. Thus, is it not only patients but also learned medical professionals who, following from Bergson, find and fit the new knowledge of HbAS in patients' medical work-ups to a previous series of disordered and disordering experiences. In this case, such a process of ordering disorder is shared by both medical professionals and the populations who consult them—all involved contribute to the biosocial production of this disease entity. This, as well as the fact that HbAS is seen to be quantitatively, if diminutively, proximate to sickle cell disease itself, lends sickle cell trait suffering a biomedical, legitimating anchor for some. This same process is largely absent in accounts of other so-called "culture bound syndromes," such as the widely disseminated notion of *nervios* in the anthropological literature (for a review, see Lock 1993a, 141–44). Sickle cell trait suffering in fact flourishes in the space of ambiguity left open when the larger medical corps and a new class of specialists diverge on what counts as sickle cell trait disorder, i.e., when the collective medical mind (*esprit*) goes "in two opposite ways."

■ **Economic (Dis)Order and Its Sublimation**

As we saw in chapter 2, poverty and its perceptions can motivate people to care for the self and others in ways that, for people like Rokhoya Sylla and Magueye Ndiaye, partially account for the attitudes that keep them well. Rokhoya's father's networks, familial training, and management of the family's tight economic resources to make sure that she had all she needed might be compared to how Magueye, on the other hand, made use of economic lack to train his body for minimal need. The ways that people engage their economic situations, and larger life slates of self-assessed defeats, also entails how they draw from these struggles to make sense of physical ailments to start on a process of self-repair. For one father of two, whom I will call Noah, the diagnosis of his teen-aged daughter's sickle cell disease prompted him and his wife Agnès to notice their own symptoms. The couple also assumed that their son, and first born, probably had the disease of trait, like them. All three were active vocal members of the ASD in 2006. Noah was adamant about telling Dr. Diagne that HbAS sufferers did indeed experience pain. As we will see in other cases to follow, many people with AS who are parents of children with full-blown sickle cell come to relativize their own illness. In the case of Noah's family, however, the disease instead became both a medium to share suffering and a concrete source of that suffering. The plight of shared illness came into focus for Noah only after he and his family became educated on the disease, even though his life trajectory seemingly set him up for it.

In recounting their story, Noah centered it with himself. He began by telling me how despite years of hard work as a young man, he was made to leave the university because of what he called "jealousies" that people in his natal village harbored toward him. He was from a Diola Christian village in Casamance where many parents wanted their children to be French educated, but as each phase of schooling in Senegal requires difficult testing, and culminates in the baccalauréat exam, few actually succeeded to go on to higher education. For Noah, his fellow neighbors' jealousies were tied to his "leaving them behind." He named the people, flipping through memories of them in his mind. Some were actually relatives, second and third cousins, who were once close, but because of their envy they began to "work" (*ligéey*) on him, eventually "hexing" his body. He ended up with a condition that resembled debilitating gout, but which apparently did not respond to the standard medical treatments for gout. After spending much time searching for how to quell and then finally excise the spirits sent to afflict him, with the aid of traditional healers, Noah realized that he had lost too much time at the university to catch up, so he started on a new path and began vocational training in law.

It was just a few years later, however, that he was expelled from the vocational school for organizing strikes for better conditions for students. Although this social justice work was not in vein, as the school administrators ended up yielding and giving the students better grant subsidies, Noah was still asked to leave for being a rabble-rouser. Confused at the injustice of having been the one to set things right, only to be forced out, he decided to quit school and begin working. Subsequently, he bounced around from job to job, all of them well below his qualifications, before spending most of his employed life as a retail stockperson and salesman in a sports store. When the Senegalese storeowner sold the business to a Lebanese family, Noah complained that the working conditions became harsh, and the pay less. He still held onto the job, however, until finally they phased out him and most of their other African employees. After periods of unemployment, in 2000 he campaigned to get Abdoulaye Wade support in his prefecture, motivated by the prospect that he might get a government post. The people who had once promised that he would at least get an interview forgot about him once Wade was elected, and they never returned his many calls. Finally, Noah began toiling as a night guardian, a lowly, but commonly held job for men in Senegal.

In his economic decline, members of Noah's larger extended family began to avoid him and Agnès out of fear that they would ask to borrow money. When I met the couple they had become so indebted to the kiosk store on their corner that they were no longer on friendly terms with the owner. For Noah the merchant ceased to have patience and sympathy. Noah was working all night, and hardly sleeping, in order to earn enough to pay off the debts and live simultaneously. When I arrived at the house, two folding chairs, a wood bench, and a card table were the only furnishings in the open living area. Noah and Agnès apologized and explained that they had to sell all of their furniture, and that luckily they had paid off their house before the sports store, where he worked for nearly twenty years, put him out. The chairs were hard and Noah would often get up as we were talking to massage his back. When he did this, he spoke about how sickle cell manifests itself in his spine, his wrists, knees, and ankles, all the while grabbing and rubbing each part vigorously as he mentioned it. He also told me that because of his night schedule, which was sometimes followed by a day shift, his sleep had gotten so irregular that his mind did not know when to tire. He would sneak in naps when he could but he said his mind "could never rest." For him the problem was that he was sick with sickle cell trait, and also profoundly stressed with economic burdens, which made the trait "worse." For Agnès, these issues were not meant to be separated. As we spoke in Wolof, she used the exact same word, "painful" (*metti*), to describe both their economic situation and the sickle cell trait in their bodies.

The crux of the issue here, as in other people's lives throughout this book, is not simply whether or not people are poor. Rather, of essence is how they perceive of their situations, their ability to better them, and their prospects for, as they say, "getting on top" (*ci kaw*) of life's problems. Self-perception of their own power, will, and social mobility largely affected how people did or did not make their symptoms central to their person and identity. These social framings overlaid the possibility of biological difference at work in the bodies of sickle cell trait sufferers and trait non-sufferers. Indeed, in a multi-disciplinary pilot research project that I eventually carried out, in 2006 and 2007, with doctors and immunologists in Dakar, local practitioners were able to examine a range of sickling, immunity, stress, and possible parasitic infection biomarkers in light of the sickle cell trait complaints I observed in my ethnographic work. A preliminary analysis of this unpublished data, in conjunction with in-depth interviews, taken from some of the HbAS sufferers whose stories, in the case of Noah and Agnès, are presented here, indicates that those who complained of "trait illness" had an increase in inflammation markers that epidemiologists use to measure physiological changes brought on by undue stress (Brydon et al. 2005; Steptoe et al. 2001; Yamakawa et al. 2009). In our pilot study, among twenty-four cases (trait sufferers) and twelve controls (non-sufferers with trait), the two individuals with the highest levels of the cytokines IL-6 and IL-1 were Noah and his wife Agnès. Given their situation, to what exactly might this spike in inflammation be attributed? Equally important, how does making items like biomarkers matter—by considering such variables in my analysis at all—both add and subtract from an anthropological emphasis on the social processes and cultural understandings of distress in Noah's family illness narrative? In this case, these biomarkers add to a fuller account of the slippery concept of stress and its real effects, while prompting health professionals who privilege the quantifiable to perhaps follow the thread presented by our pilot research on inflammatory cytokines. This should not subtract or detract from the ethnographic analysis that provided the conceptual entrée for such a query to begin with. People in Senegal, once coalesced in ASD, demanded to be taken "seriously" and examined biomedically, and so with several local doctors, including Dr. Diagne, we did just that on a small, pilot scale.

The cytokines IL-1 and Il-6, along with IL-8 and TNF-alpha, are also generally elevated in people with sickle cell disease (for a review see Pathare et al. 2003, 33). With the exception of IL-8, which we did not study, these are the three pro-inflammatory cytokines that were generally elevated in the trait sufferers who took part in the multidisciplinary pilot study that stemmed from my earlier fieldwork (unpublished data). This trend in raised cytokines signaled to doctors in Dakar that some physiological aspect of disorder may be brought on by a single HbS allele in people like Noah and Agnès. This signal may be the effect of economic stresses, or an interaction between social stress generally and hemoglobin S somatized. Such a signal is an initial sign that something physiological has transpired in those who were in unquestionable pain when probed and examined both ethnographically and clinically. HbAS sufferers like Noah and Agnès systematically complained of pain in the same areas of the body (wrists, ankles, backs, and knees), and nearly consistently spoke of life stresses and insomnia coupled with these.

As we brought our pilot study to an end and noticed the clear differences between the trait sufferers and trait non-sufferers, Diagne conceded, cannily in private, that "inflammation might be an issue in HbAS." Yet, even so, he reasoned that the problem could be resolved if people simply took an anti-inflammatory, such as aspirin. His fear was that people would make such an "ordinary" event—as "we all have some inflammation quite regularly"—"into a disease." He continued, "Every one has soreness and swelling coupled with pain, even myself. You do not have to have sickle cell trait to get everyday pains." The remedy, in his mind, was equally "ordinary," again, the most basic medications that most households already have, mild painkillers. If these HbAS sufferers lived in a home where someone had sickle cell, then they would possibly already be acquainted with such treatments.

Diagne was willing to concede that Noah, Agnès, and the others in the pilot study who presented with the same symptoms might "actually" be suffering from the trait itself. Nonetheless, these study participants were not people who suffered inordinately, or enough to warrant an illness label. Other specialist doctors, such as Saliou Diop, agreed. Both men were afraid that people would become debilitated upon learning about their trait, and would then come to see all of their problems as linked to a physiological condition whose gravity the doctors equated with the everyday minor aches and pains of life, both for "normals" and trait carriers.

In the remaining cases to follow, I present trait suffering from more amorphous causes. In each case, doctors intimated to me that they would never believe the trait to be the "real" cause of these people's suffering because of the many "possible confounding factors" they present. In these stories, people enlisted HbAS to order both physical and social suffering, in ways similar to Noah and Agnès. Themes of social demotion run throughout. People cite the chaos of having their social statuses abruptly undercut, losing spouses to out migration, or worse, to madness. Here too, economic constraints inured people to the fact that their suffering was a broad and natural fact of their lives and life trajectories, and because of its expansive reach, they tried to narrow its effects. In the process they attempted to streamline, and locate, their bodily symptoms within a framing of a monocausal agent, or sickle cell trait. In several cases, co-morbidity with hypertension and heart disease, and an eventual ability for people to relativize their own trait vis-à-vis their children's sickle cell disease, made Diagne and Diop distrustful of these people's claims of "physiological" sickle cell trait pain.

■ Economic Public Order and Image

One of the global effects of Senegal's struggling formal economy is that it has spawned many informal monetary networks that are driven mostly by semi-literate "business men." Especially in the last decade and a half, since the devaluation of the *cfa* franc, Senegal has seen record numbers of out migration, both legally and often illegally, of people, mostly men, who leave the country in order to tap into richer nations' buying power in order to reconstitute some of their own. Economists, political scientists, and anthropologists have become quite interested in the phenomenon of Senegalese traders (locally called Moudou Moudou) who emigrate to the world's largest cities in search of capital to send home to families and sometimes to build infrastructure on the ground (Carter 1997; Diouf 2000; Ebin 1992, 1996; Stoller 2002; Stoller and McConatha 2001).[9] What this massive and largely uncharted emigration has meant is that many urban Senegalese households have a husband, brother, or son living abroad. These absent men and the families they leave behind have become part of a national order that has created newfound pressures on both men and women. Men who stay in country worry that the economy will not spare their jobs and wonder about better possibilities elsewhere. Women are increasingly relied upon to work outside the home to augment the family's earnings.

Many of the products that male and female traders introduce in large quantities into the local market are beauty aids, such as skin lightening creams and hair extensions, as well as textiles. It is as if the dark aspect of economic struggle, for women, is addressed by being dressed and by lightening the self (or one's skin), which the outer world sees. Regardless of their class, women often publicly don a message of competence, if not wealth, through fashion. This literal stitching together of one's image of course not only involves the material threads of cloth, but also, and more importantly, it is concerned with obtaining and maintaining successful husbands of both health and financial stability, and of keeping their children well. If these various orders of women's worlds begin to unravel, the response is often to find order for distress and pain in other orders where suffering easily fits. In many instances it is in medical explanations; in others, it is through religion, but even more frequently, order is found in a mix of cultural forms characterized by discourses of fate, destiny, and God's will.

Sick with AS, but Burnt from Xésal: The Beauty Pain of Awa Ngom

Awa Ngom is a highly symptomatic middle-aged woman with HbAS whom I met at the adult sickle cell clinic where she is seen by doctors who are skeptical of her complaints. Her medical work-up, performed at a local clinic, revealed sickle cell trait, as well as hypertension, for which she is being treated. In Awa's mind, the hypertension warranted little discussion. It was potentially controllable. Sickle cell trait, on the other hand, was "written into" her being by God, was part of her destiny and family line.

For years Awa was an important woman in her social circles, mostly because of her marriage to a magisterial Colonel who held an important position at "the Ministry" during the Socialists' regime—publicly understood as one of the best possible salaries in Dakar. With the change of political power in February of 2000, the Colonel was demoted. This shift in status and in financial security proved a major shock to Awa and their teen-aged daughter, who now also insists that her HbAS status is becoming "painful" as well.

As I entered Awa's house on the day of our interview, loud koranic music filled the courtyard. It was the first day of *Kor*, Wolof for *Ramadan*. A few months had passed from the time of our first meeting at her doctor's office to the date of our interview. The first thing I now noticed was Awa's face. The area surrounding her eyes was severely burned. The skin above her eyebrows was light pink. That of her high cheekbones was scarred black and brown, and then the side of her face was still another shade. As I settled into my chair across from her, I noticed that her mouth area was white with spots of severely dried skin, surrounded by various colors of brown, and black. I had come to recognize this patchwork of lesions and uneven tone as evidence of the toxic skin bleaching, practiced by many Senegalese women, called *xésal*.[10] Her body was fully covered by her white gauze clothing and she was wearing a head shawl, appropriate dress for the religious period of self-denial and fasting. Her hands were busily rotating a string of prayer beads.

Awa began to tell me about her "disease" and as she spoke stories of her symptoms and injuries were punctuated with details about all of her social obligations—public events of naming ceremonies (*ngentes*), women's meetings (*turrs*), and marriages. She lamented that the preparations were tiring, that she lacked the force she once had. As she may have felt me looking at her face, she said "even powdering my face before the event (*xew*) can make me go into a sickle cell crisis." I asked her how many social obligations she had that month. She started naming off dates, "the 5th, the 14th, the 20th. . . . " before interrupting herself, saying there were many. She paused to seemingly say that she was tired and incapable of counting. Occasionally, when she got excited she would lift her heavy arms, and then suddenly drop them listlessly. One such moment was when she confided that she wanted to reduce the number of events she had to attend. She then sat silently before explaining that if she stopped going her friends would be angry. Now, with the ending of *Kor* celebration (*korite*) in sight, as well as Christmas, New Year's, and the regular *turr* she attends on a monthly basis, Awa says her sickle cell trait has rarely been so painful.[11]

Awa is in her late forties, a period of life that has its own aesthetic of feminine beauty in Dakar. Most urban women, after marriage, begin to gain weight, to don large robes called *boubous*, to creatively deploy their head scarves, and decorate themselves with gold (genuine and not) in efforts to fit an image now called "*dirianke*."[12] The dirianke is a woman who is both classy and excessive. The term conveys a feminine *bon vivant*, while it is simultaneously one of mockery. *Diri* in Wolof literally means "to drag along," thus the dirianke is a woman who drags her feet out of slowness, due to her heavy girth, and her sex appeal.[13] Several of my doctor informants recounted how they felt that this image of beauty was unhealthy. Dr. Diagne told me that dirianke women often used illness, some disease, or symptom—hypertension, diabetes, sickle cell trait, general pain, and fatigue—as reason to "drag" themselves. Complaining of symptoms is a common point of conversation for dirianke women when they accompany their children to the pediatric sickle cell consultation, or when they find the sympathetic ear of a physician, or even of the anthropologist. To be sick, fatigued, or at least to seem so, is part of this beauty ideal.[14] When I first arrived in Senegal, women advised me to slow down. To walk fast, or to seem determined in one's gait, they counseled, is "unattractive and unladylike." The dirianke characteristic par excellence is the constant presentation of the self at public events (*xew yi*).

DF: You were explaining your many social obligations, ngentes, and turrs?

AN: Yes, but I've cut a lot out, I say it's my illness, I've cut things down. You know, women—the time it takes to get dressed, to put on your face, even when I put make-up on I fall ill [*danu*]. I get sick from the make-up, the face powder and all that. As soon as I put it up to my face, that's it. My head gets pained, because of my eyes, and the smells. When I get to the event [*xew*], I'm there laughing and socializing and then the fatigue of it all makes me fall ill. . . .

DF: How many events do you have on the calendar this month?

AN: Ah! As soon as the month has begun, it's over for me. Ah, so many. The month is here, and that's it, over. But you know yourself, and when you're feeling all right. In any case, I will go and contribute my part of the needed money and what have you so that nothing is missing from the fund. I just manage things the best I can. I tell them that I'm sick from sickle cell, or that I've got something going on somewhere else, or that my mother's sick [she has sickle cell trait too] . . . It depends on my health, I take care of it this way, but after a while this is no good either.

Later in the interview Awa tells of her continuous fainting and other symptoms that she attributes to her sickle cell trait. She begins by explaining how she, like many women of the *dirianke* aesthetic, fills her room with incense smoke so that the aromatic fumes might permeate her clothes. As the smoke filled the room one afternoon, she felt increasingly light-headed and when she got up to leave she fell down and fainted. She woke up to her husband bringing her to. As she regained consciousness, he filled her in on the details of how she ended up on the floor. Awa now simply prefers to stay home, as her body, despite its social obligations, refuses to participate in the rituals and events that have proven crucial to her identity for much of her adult life. With the Colonel publicly demoted, and Awa's face badly damaged from excessive *xésal* treatments, she relies on the sickle cell trait to provide a new ordering mechanism—if instrumental excuse—to refrain from the *habitudes* of a previous life where she has lost face on two too many counts.

Other Trait Symptoms: Insomnia, Insanity, and Heartache

The next series of cases to be presented have common points of overlap. Several informants complained of insomnia, while one desperately inquired: "is insomnia a normal symptom of sickle cell trait?" Heart problems also surfaced multiple times. Both symptoms were recounted in interviews with people diagnosed with sickle cell disease (SS) as well. Then, there was one severely affected trait-suffering man with whose case I became familiar through his wife and his young son's doctor. I will call him Demba Gueye. Demba became so distraught at the time of his toddler's diagnosis with HbSS that he first, according to his wife, "suffered from insomnia for almost a year before his mind went bad." He was eventually institutionalized at the psychiatric hospital in Thiaroye, a suburb of Dakar.

Detrimental Diagnostics: Demba, Sukeyena, and Little Papis

Sukeyena Niang is a poor villager who does not speak any French and has never gone to school. She, like many villagers, does not know her age, but guesses that she must be shy of thirty. When asked how long she has been married, she paused and again guessed, saying sixteen years. She and her family have always struggled, but she has never had to work until recently. Her husband was a driver, which brought them a decent income, by their standards. But now, he has stopped everything due to a severe "crisis," which required that he be hospitalized indefinitely in the Thiaroye psychiatric ward.

On the day of our first meeting at the children's hospital, the nurses were backed up and told Sukeyena to wait, or to come back in an hour, at which point she came to see me and we began to discuss her situation. During the interview Sukeyena hardly spoke of her son Papis's disease. By all counts he was fine—he was five years old and was learning to recite the Koran. He was mentally quick (*yewu*), and had always recovered from his sickle cell crises. Sukeyena and her husband, Demba, had already lost two very young children, one at three years and three months old, and the other at just a month old, before Papis was born. She says that she and her husband still do not know what their children died from. She suspects that the older one died from measles, but that neither displayed the same symptoms as Papis. She then explained how Papis was visibly sick as a toddler, and that her husband suggested that they take him to Dakar to see what was wrong. There he was diagnosed with sickle cell disease. When explaining to Sukeyena what her son suffered from, the health care provider she first encountered in Dakar informed her of her sickle cell trait status and cautioned her to stop having children. Sukeyena, like many Senegalese women, thought that such a prescription sounded unnatural and wrong. During a separate session with Demba, the practitioner also told him about "his disease," and that his wife should take birth control to prevent further pregnancy. Demba also lacked formal schooling. As with many uneducated villagers, they both felt that they had no choice but to trust the doctor, although the advice contradicted their usual proclivity to simply let fate, through their faith, take its course. Sukeyena became distressed recalling the details of that day of familial diagnosis and returned to her nagging inability to sleep. This then precipitated the question she had desperately wanted to ask all along: what was the cause of her husband's relentless insomnia that eventually conquered his body and spirit?

[During a discussion of what befell her husband]

DF: Does your husband have sickle cell disease, like Papis, or not?

SN: He, he has that one kind of sickle cell, what's it called? [Thinks to herself and answers her own question] AS. AS is what he has, AS is what I have too.

DF: And he thinks that it's because of his sickle cell trait that he can't sleep?

SN: That's right, he can't sleep. He wanted me to ask you if sickle cell trait could keep him from sleeping [*teye ko nelaw*]? I don't sleep either. When I lie down I just stare out until daylight comes. Sometimes, I may sleep a bit at dawn. . . . Insomnia has affected me for a while now.

DF: How long? Have you always had trouble sleeping?

SN: No. Ever since I started—ever since Papis was born it seems. I never used to be this way. . . . Insomnia [*ñakk a nelaw*] started to affect my husband, until he became sick from it. That's why I have to ask, does sickle cell trait prevent people from sleeping or not?

DF: I do not know . . .

[After some discussion of how her husband understood his son's condition in relation to his own, I ask] Why is your husband in the hospital?

SN: Why is he in the hospital? Because of a significant lack of sleep, that's why. When he didn't sleep his body would be hot, feverish, and it would just get hotter and hotter! [*yaram bi defay tàng, di tàng, di tàng!*]. He was so hot, it seemed as though this fever was doing something serious to his body. . . . It was like he was so sleep deprived that his head—his brain was no longer any good [*xel bi defa neexatul*]. Do you know what I'm getting at?

DF: I think so . . .

SN: His brain, his mind itself was no longer any good. When he—[interrupts herself], I don't know if it was from the disease [sickle cell trait], from the insomnia—the doctor said that maybe this lack of sleep is why his mind ended up, ended up this way.

Although Sukeyena did not state it explicitly, the onset of her husband's insomnia corresponded with the moment when he learned of his son's illness, of his own misprognosis, and of the fact that they were to stop having children.

DF: How did Demba react after talking to the doctors?

SN: He said that this thing, this disease was beyond him. He said, "You are at a time in your life where you should be having children." This was extremely difficult for him—the fact that they told us that we should stop having children [*baña amati doom*]. On top of that, he worried about the disease. He saw that Papis was always worn out fighting his way through these crises, and this depressed him. One day before Demba got sick, when Papis kept having sickle cell problems, he said to me, "One thing really scares me, my own illness here, if I myself end up dead, what is going to happen to Papis, all of the medications, the care he needs, who is going to provide for him?" He thought about it all the time.

After my interview with Sukeyena, I spoke with Papis's doctor to see if he knew who had first received the couple at the hospital. He said that they saw someone somewhere else before coming to Albert Royer. According to Diagne, whoever they saw told Demba that people with "the disease" do not live past forty years old. The practitioner in question did not distinguish the trait from the disease. Even though a life expectancy of forty is not necessarily true for sickle cell disease patients, it surely is not the case for those with trait. Nonetheless, according to Papis's doctor, Demba was quickly approaching his fortieth birthday at the time of the diagnosis. Soon after his first encounter with the doctor who gave him the news of sickle cell trait, he began having the fateful sleepless nights.

Sukeyena, whose young son has sickle cell disease, says that she is stressed and worn down by her own long-standing relationship with insomnia. However, she also feels that her husband's "condition" has surpassed, and even diminished, her own. She admits that her anxieties sometimes at least let her sleep at dawn. She devotes her waking hours to the care of her young son, who has become her priority and confidant in her husband's absence. Papis, for his part, was clearly an exceptional child. On our second meeting at the hospital, as I began writing notes as Sukeyena spoke, he eyed my activity carefully. When Sukeyena revealed things that he thought were important, notably how much he helped and supported her, (and I wasn't note taking) he would command: "write that!" (*bindal!*) Sukeyena laughed and told him to mind his business, but for him this was his business.

Sukeyena's discussion of her own symptom of insomnia was constantly punctuated by the question of "does sickle cell trait cause sleeplessness?" Such a questioning bespeaks a larger process of negotiating whether or not her symptom could be attributed to this trait, or if it was simply a normal effect of all that she came to endure. For the moment she has found some semblance of order in attributing her insomnia to sickle cell trait as it places her affliction in a familial nexus patterned after both the suffering of her husband and her young son.

Disorder upon Disorders as Order: The Case of Khady Tall

Khady Tall is a poor mother of four who found out that she had sickle cell trait during a routine prenatal check-up when she was pregnant with her now three-year-old son. Her other children are older and either live with their father or stay at her mother's home, not far from her single room in the Medina of Dakar. Khady is presently in her second marriage. She divorced her first husband just a year after the birth of their last child. Khady never wanted to go into details about the marriage, but it was clear that it was the source of much frustration. At the time of our interview she had been newly wed for a only month to a man she spoke little of, except to say that he was a "good man," and that he had emigrated to work in France. The couple was married during his last visit to Dakar, but he was now abroad again with no clear return date. Displaying no sign of emotion, Khady intimated that her husband' had other wives and that he only spent some of his time in Dakar with her in the rented room that houses her and her small boy. The space was in a noisy block of similar rooms. Outside, children were screaming, and the neighbor's *mbalax* music flowed through the walls of Khady's small quarter. There were no windows.

I met Khady through her "doctor," a traditional healer, who knew that I was interested in talking with people who had sickle cell. I explained to Khady that I was curious to know how Mr. Sambou's plants worked for her sickle cell disease, before asking her what form she had. She assured me that she indeed had the disease, and that she had "AS." She said that she had multiple other conditions—heart palpitations and tingling in her limbs due to spasmophilia, rheumatism, skin rashes, yearly bouts of malaria, little sexual appetite leading to extreme dryness during intercourse, and an inability to orgasm—as well as sickle cell trait. She said that Dr. Sambou's medicines have helped all of her conditions, but that her "heart doesn't like the traditional plants, even though they are good for it." She complained that the plants and herbs got lodged in her throat, making her chest and heart "heavy and prone to spasm." Mr. Sambou, like the many biomedical practitioners in Dakar mentioned earlier who lump "SS" and "AS" conceptually, made little distinction between sickle cell disease and trait, except that the latter was simply a "lesser degree of potential pathology than the first." Khady who had sickle cell trait, was classed in Sambou's clinical registry simply as a "drépano."[15] Ms. Tall had a similar, but more convoluted understanding of her condition. She talked of SS as being worse than AS, but that to her knowledge sickle cell was "a heart disease"—a disease that taxed the heart in any case—and that given her spasmophilia, rheumatism, and frequent malaria (*sybiiru*) she now had a quite serious case of a compounded condition, a situation that has recently gotten worse. She, like the couple in the previous section, also suffers from insomnia, foregrounding it as the chief nuisance of her symptoms. Khady articulates insomnia as the conduit for her violent sickle cell crises, which "attack" both her body and mind. Her sleeping space, her bed with large headboard, was crowded with medications, both traditional plants and pharmaceuticals, which, as she explained, "spent the night with her" (*fanaane*). These included *Calcibronat*® (Calcium bromo-galacto gluconate, a hormone that balances calcium levels in the body, and a cardiac sedative), *Passiflorine*® (passionflower extract, a sedative) and *Hydergine* (the drug mentioned in chapter 3, which was once a medication given for sickle cell, but has been proven to be ineffective for the disease and is now used by some for Alzheimer's and as a "smart drug" in North America.)

Khady recounts her story of her crises in terms of a healthier past.

> AT: My sickle cell wears me out, it tires me [*defa ma sonnal*]. Well, at first [before the diagnosis], I used to be able to work all of the time, I had energy, but now I can no longer work. I get tired.
>
> DF: How long ago is "at first"?
>
> AT: Well, before he [points to her three year old] was born.
>
> DF: So, did you know that you had sickle cell trait at the time?
>
> AT: I didn't know. When I was pregnant with him they tested me, and that's when I found out. . . .
>
> DF: So you were saying, before your AS diagnosis, you used to work. . . ?
>
> AT: I was able to work all the time with no problem. I would wash clothes, iron, cook, everything and anything. Now, I can't manage the slightest thing. Even my room, whenever I attempt to simply sweep it, my room [referring to its small size], I'm exhausted. If I were to wash a load of clothes today, tomorrow, early morning, I'd be sick. It's shocked me badly now three times. 2:00 a.m. It's always 2:00 a.m. that it attacks me. I may sleep a bit until around two in the morning and then it's like you took a hammer and hit me in the head. It's as if my head were splitting open and dispersing its pieces everywhere. . . . When it attacks, it's like my head, I tell you, my head is all mixed up and confused. . . . It's like the mental illness God gives some people. . . . I have to get out and go for air. . . . Then I'll come back and take some sleeping pills and go to sleep. . . .
>
> DF: Have you ever had your children tested for sickle cell?
>
> AT: I haven't had them tested because that would just add to my problems. I don't want anything to bring me more trouble than I already have.

What became immediately clear when talking with Khady was that she specified "my sickle cell" over and over again. She told me that she has known cousins and other relatives on her father's side of the family who had the disease and suffered from more prolonged crises. She seemed to be quite aware that her form was somehow differentially personalized and idiosyncratic. She had talked to other sickle cell sufferers who did not quite have her same symptoms, explaining, "I have this heart condition on top of it. That's why it attacks me in the way that it does." Also, the mere diagnosis of sickle hemoglobin is powerful here, since she fears that having her children tested could somehow increase her load of "troubles"—as if a positive diagnosis in them could worsen things for her.

Khady's case can be compared to Sukeyena's above. Both women have "lost" their husbands, one to divorce and emigration, and the other to psychiatric internment. Both are also left to themselves on a daily basis, their sole companions being their small sons. On the question of suffering and disorder, both also order their suffering within an order of other afflictions. For Sukeyena this order is achieved by placing her own suffering at a logical interstice between her husband's symptom, with which he associated sickle cell trait, and her son's sickle cell disease. Khady, on the other hand, orders her sickle cell trait suffering within a long list of other disorders only she experiences. It seems that even though now remarried, she is quite alone, save for her toddler and her many afflictions and medications, which literally accompany her to bed on a nightly basis.

Disheartening Sickle Cell Trait: Undoing Years of Diagnostic Damage

The last case is distinct from the others in that it treats a happily married woman who has an enviable economic situation, a present and caring husband, and a small "successful" son with sickle cell disease who has now surpassed her educational level. In this case, the prescribed fate of sickle cell trait (as a disease) was imparted by this woman's childhood doctor. Unfortunately, she recounts years later, he took it upon himself to give order to an evasive disorder that left her hospitalized for months by naming sickle cell trait the culprit.

The woman in question, Uli Mbeng, was diagnosed with "the disease of trait" when she was seven years old (in the mid-1970s). Dr. Diagne, her son's pediatrician, recently told me that he "un-diagnosed" her in the sense that he "lifted away" her lifelong association of this trait as a disease. By both of their accounts, he told her to find an activity and to stop ingesting the boxes of pills she was consuming in the name of "calming her sickle cell."

Uli's case raises many questions that have been reiterated above. She, like Khady, claims to have "a heart problem" although she was not quite sure of the medical name for her condition. During her childhood hospital stays, her heart palpitations were discussed, but the doctors did not know why they occurred. In hindsight, she felt that the doctors were at a loss concerning what she suffered from, and when they saw sickle hemoglobin revealed in her blood work, they claimed it as the cause. As she grew older, however, she wondered about the extent of her disease, since she did not feel "that sick." Later in adulthood, shortly after her firstborn child was diagnosed with sickle cell disease, Uli found herself psychologically, physically, and emotionally exhausted. Dr. Diagne told me that Uli broke down crying in his office one day and asked him what she could possibly do to care for her newly diagnosed sick son when she herself "had never had real peace because of the disease." He told her that sickle cell trait was not a disease and to leave her pouches of pills once and for all. He ended their conversation by telling her to finally implicate herself in the world, from which she had been prescribed away for the last twenty-six years.

UM: So, Dr. Diagne called me into his office one day after that first conversation [about her trait]. He told me, "You don't have any-thing to worry about." I told him that I was exhausted. I was always sick, always tired. I told him that I can't get well, I'm always treating this thing but that I've never actually gotten any better. He said, "The doctor who first saw you as a young girl, he's the thing that's making you sick. He should have allowed you to go to school, to do everything in life that any other child gets to do." Then the doctor asked me, "What do you do now? Are you involved in anything, striving for anything?" I told him as it was. I did nothing. I had never done anything. I have a husband. I did get married, and, of course, I had Omar. Dr. Diagne then said . . . "You must lift the dis-ease out of your mind. What you have is AS, your boy has SS, that's the serious form. But look at him, he's even going to school. So you should know that you could have gone to school too. Now, stop taking all of those medicines. That's probably what's really making you sick." And you know; now I no longer suffer from anything. I don't feel anything any more.

DF: Nothing at all, really? . . .

UM: Yes, well sometimes now, I do feel pain in my legs. Then sometimes I wake up in the morning and I wake up with soreness in my legs, but I take it for what it is, and as the morning wears on, the pain disappears. I don't let myself take medicines anymore. I also some-times wake up and just feel really lazy, like I don't want to get up, or I'll have heart palpitations. I just tell myself to get up, and when I do, those things also pass as I get going about my day. AS shouldn't be made into a serious thing. When Omar started to get sick and we found out that it was sickle cell, they asked my husband to come in and get tested. He did, and he too has AS. I then realized that his AS has never made him sick. He didn't even know he had it. It's never caused him suffering, or laid him up. It must not really be that serious. Omar is the one with the serious disease.

Uli now attests that she no longer suffers because of her AS condition. That is, she no longer allows her sickle cell trait to limit her both physically and emotionally.[16] She continues, however, to feel pain, fatigue, and a certain unwillingness to face the day that she previously associated with this trait. Yet, presently, she refuses to fully acknowledge this pain as "serious" and says, "I just forget it (*dama koy fatte rekk*), like the doctor told me to do." Yet, nev-ertheless, despite her reeducation on the matter, her pain persists. She, like

Sukeyena, concludes that she cannot afford to be sick, while she situates her own suffering as relatively insignificant in light of her child's actual sickle cell disease.

Biosocial suffering—the way that societal and physiological distress is articulated through one's possession of a genetic trait—plays itself out through various means for the trait sufferers presented here. As all are trying to restitch elements of life that circumstance has unraveled, the conditions and constraints that shape each person's present dilemma prove both subjective and transpersonal. There are surely collective cultural forms that people share with regard to the importance of children, spousal status, the cultural permit to suffer, as well as religious fatalism as it merges with biomedical diagnoses of a genetic trait in one's family. That said, the individuality of the person, their biological profiles, their phenotypic variability, and particular attitudes toward life and their lot yield the differential "bodily contexts" in which this trait diagnosis is made. Socially, some people are economically better off than others, but aspects of their family's prospects are grossly out of place, and order. Physiologically, others fall ill with various additional diseases, and live the effects of environmental stressors ranging from potential malaria infection to self-imposed bodily disfigurement and intoxication from skin bleaching products.

In most instances the experiences of life disordered are furthermore marked by economic privations, seared in the collective memory as an effect of structural adjustment and the World Bank's affront to their social and economic health. In their detail, such privations are somehow linked to the uncertainty that characterizes people's futures, as well as those of their spouses and children. Their grief unfurled (faced with absent, demoted, or sick husbands, and the shock of children now diagnosed with disease) finds ways to count as order on various registers of suffering, all of which become mediated through the sickle cell trait. That Senegalese trait sufferers respond to their "disordering contemporary world" (Kleinman 1997, 317) with a mode of expression that objectively counts as disorder should not distract from the fact that disorder can in fact prove a form of order. That said, the forms to which people make their afflictions fit are not limited to illness experiences, as attempts to restore order do, for some, eventually manifest a refusal to suffer. The knotted nexus that comprises the sickle cell trait suffering experience consists of many crossed threads that seem daunting (and are thus often dismissed) at first blush. If nothing else, knowledge that one possesses this trait indeed has varied meanings—biological, social, and, as mentioned at the outset, biomedical. Thus in disciplines inherently weighted toward the social, anthropologists must do more to understand and describe how such diagnoses are not immune to physiological interpretation, and to realize that like sickle cell disease, sickle cell trait is not immune to enculturation.

Other processes of enculturation, through the actions of patient advocates on an international scale, would begin to make political authorities consider sickle cell disease itself as worthy of much more sustained medical attention. This happened with the help of trait carriers and, more importantly, with populations affected by diverse hemoglobinopathies, as we will see in the next chapter.

CHAPTER SEVEN

The Work of Patient Advocacy

In 2001, sickle cell patients and researchers in France and in Francophone Africa met with a force that inspired them to act in concert to attempt a new kind of politics. The singular motivator for this emergent collective was a woman living in Paris, but originally from Congo Brazzaville, named Edwidge Ebakisse Badassou. Several of my French informants described this politically astute mother of a child with sickle cell disease as "indubitably persuasive." Others, with less tendency to be emphatic, simply admired her ability "to get things done," even if her commandeering demeanor could be offensive, or off-putting to some. Whatever the appropriate set of defining characteristics most fitting for the current "First Lady" of the Francophone sickle cell advocacy world, Ebakisse Badassou created an infrastructure through which resources and, most importantly, attention to sickle cell disease would be raised through the theme of "North-South" development collaborations. This thematic became reality when Ebakisse Badassou organized the first International Congress of the International Organization to Combat Sickle Cell Anemia at the United Nations Educational, Scientific, and Cultural Organization (UNESCO) Headquarters in Paris in January 2002.

Successfully exploiting the terms *Nord-Sud* for actors on both sides of the global divide, Ebakisse Badassou's mission was to bring multiple states, research centers, and people with varied expertise together. This meant convening researchers, physicians, patients, and patient advocate groups, as well as local government bodies and development agencies. To unite, coordinate, and sometimes whip up the interests of each around sickle cell, she created the *Réseau francophone de lutte contre la drépanocytose* (Francophone Network for the Fight Against Sickle cell Disease, or RFLD) in 2001. Subsequently, in a motion to internationalize and gain broader reach, the RFLD dropped the "Francophone" qualifier and instead became *l'Organisation internationale de lutte contre la drépanocytose* (OILD) in 2003.

Ebakisse Badassou, as president of her NGO, invited several African First Ladies to attend the 2002 UNESCO meeting as representatives of "Member States" that were affected by the problem of sickle cell. As mentioned in the introductory chapter, each woman was named a *marraine*, or "godmother," of the sickle cell organization and its cause. Today Antoinette Sassou N'Guesso of the Republic of Congo and Madame Viviane Wade (who did not attend the 2002 event but who was enlisted in 2003) have remained the OILD's two official sponsors. As Ebakisse Badassou told the audience at the 2002 UNESCO event her "goal was to make sickle cell disease a global public health priority so that the disparities she witnessed traveling between Paris care sites and those in Africa might be addressed." Reflecting on the murmurings that could be heard in patient advocacy circles in Paris and beyond, she spoke about trying to find a way to insert sickle cell into the growing string of illnesses that the United Nations and the World Health Organization had made health priorities for global development. If global attention was preoccupied with HIV/AIDS, tuberculosis, and, most recently, malaria, Ebakisse Badassou wanted to "find the ways that these affect sickle cell, and vice versa," as she told me in 2004 in Benin at the first OILD meeting held on African soil. A conceptual link with such familiar public health risks would have to be forged, however. Sickle cell was not an infectious disease, nor did it threaten large portions of the global South—or could it?

There is a dearth of actual data on sickle cell births, morbidity, and mortality globally, yet there are different statistics that meet and meld in the lacunae left open by this precise lack of knowledge about the global picture, especially in sub-Saharan Africa (Weatherall 2010, 4331). Familiar with the proceedings of science, Ebakisse Badassou became "a master of the reality of what science did not know" for certain (Petryna 2002, 28). Global official "ignorance" on the disease functioned as a kind of "positivized negativity," where, as Adriana Petryna points out in a different context, "scientific indeterminacy" could prove to be a curse, *or, a point of scientific leverage* (2002, 28). As noted by epidemiologist Nancy Krieger, public health data has historically been "made" through political choices and social preferences for "valued" kinds of data (Fr. *donnée*, or "givens") (1992, 412–13). It would not be long then before savvy people who themselves embodied understudied data points, and who personally valued their own inclusion into global public health problems, would enter into what Alan Desrosières has termed "the politics of large numbers." The aim of OILD's engagement with uncertain health statistics would be to make "their [sickle cell] collective hold" through "aggregates of individuals," and also of diseases (Desrosières 1998, 103).

Only two years after the Paris UNESCO meeting, Ebakisse Badassou and other patient advocates around her began to cite various WHO spokespersons and UN documents that were emerging—with their help—on the disease. A version of the following statement, "of more than 300,000 newborn babies suffering from sickle-cell anemia, as many as 50% die before the age of five years in some rural areas of Africa," became a popular refrain in OILD advocates' cultural vernacular. This very phrasing even made it into the UNESCO "Records of the 33rd session of the General Conference," which, for the first time in 2005, through resolution 22, recommended to the "Director-General

to bring [a] resolution [on sickle cell] to the attention of the Member States."
In this same document an official invitation was extended to the "Director-
General to submit . . . at its 34th session a report on the implementation of
[a] resolution to combat sickle-cell anaemia and its consequences worldwide"
(UNESCO 33C/22, 2005, 58).

Later, in August of 2006, the WHO published Fact Sheet N°308 on "Sickle-
cell disease and other haemoglobin disorders," namely the thalassemias. Here
it became clear that the earlier citation of three hundred thousand births was
based on an aggregate number that encompassed several red blood cell disorders. In this instance the Fact Sheet used language to *disaggregate* the large
number of three hundred thousand yearly births in listing the different diseases in the count. Specifically, in reference to sickle cell and various forms
of thalassemia (alpha and beta), it states "It is estimated that each year over
three hundred thousand babies with severe forms of these diseases are born
worldwide; the majority in low and middle income countries" (WHO 2006c).
The plural "diseases" here is important, as is the key detail that "severe forms
of these" are said to lead to the deaths. The phenotypic, clinical, and life variability for most genetic disorders is vast. Sickle cell and the thalassemias are
no exception. These emphases and nuances did not make their way into the
advocacy vernacular of the OILD, however. Lastly, the Fact Sheet made no
mention about under-five deaths as deaths from sickle cell specifically (since
the number does not exist). This conflation of under-five deaths in populations with these three hemoglobinopathies *as deaths due to these diseases*
would arise in other documents, however. This first happened through infer-
ence, which later passed for certainty.

In the actual WHO resolution on sickle cell, which was published in May
of 2006, the drafters referenced the "conclusions" of the first and second congresses of the OILD, the first in Paris in 2002, and the second in Cotonou,
Benin, in 2004, to preface the WHO's "concern at the impact of genetic diseases, and of sickle-cell anaemia in particular, on global morbidity and mortality, especially in developing countries." A few lines further in the text, the
WHO committee emphasizes the "insufficiency of relevant epidemiological
data" on the prevalence of the disease (WHO 2006a WHA59.20, 26). Just
one month earlier in April of 2006, however, the first "Report" on sickle cell
by the WHO Secretariat (which was marked as a "provisional item" for the
next assembly) stated that even as there were "no firm data on the survival of
patients with sickle-cell anaemia on the African continent," estimates could
be "derived from the age structure of populations attending clinics." From
these numbers it could be inferred, the thinking went, "that half of those with
sickle-cell anaemia have died by the age of five years usually from infections
including malaria and pneumococcal sepsis, and from the anaemia itself"
(WHO A/59, 2006b, 2).

Many sickle cell care centers in Africa have traditionally been for children,
since the disease has often been understood to limit life to childhood. Coupled

with this, in my own fieldwork, I witnessed some older sicklers progressively abandon regular care when it was time to leave their pediatric facility after puberty, such as Rokhoya Sylla. Others, such as the Mbodj Women, came to manage their disease outside of clinics, since they saw biomedicine for sickle cell as offering them paltry treatments that were often unhelpful. Without pervasive newborn screening technologies in most places, and an admission in several WHO documents that there is inadequate public health monitoring infrastructure on the ground, the April 2006 report's "derived" assumptions raise more questions on the 50 percent death count than they resolve.

Nonetheless, in June of that same year, the WHO Regional Director for Africa cited the "50 percent" death-rate figure in the Executive Summary of its report *Sickle-Cell Disease in the African Region: Current Situation and the Way Forward*. In the introduction of the report, the regional committee acknowledges having reviewed yet another document, the report from "*Les premiers états généraux de la drépanocytose* [first global consultations on sickle-cell anaemia], from a meeting in Brazzaville, Congo in June 2005 attended by experts and first ladies from five African countries." This was in fact the third massive action of Ebakisse Badassou's OILD, convened after Cotonou. According to the WHO Regional Director for Africa, the OILD Brazzaville meeting made his committee "take cognizance" of the importance of the disease. In his summary the Regional Director asserts: in most African countries, "Basic facilities to manage patients are usually absent, systematic screening for sickle-cell disease is not common practice and the diagnosis of the disease is usually made when a severe complication occurs. As a result, more than 50% of the children with the most severe form of the disease die before the age of five, usually from an infection or severe anaemia" (WHO AFR/RC56/17, 2006d, 1). Despite the emphasis on severe cases here, it was in this back-and-forth of the OILD echoing the powerful WHO and UN utterances, and vice versa, that a concept formed of sickle cell as a disease that not only affected hundreds of thousands of Africans but that it would kill half of those affected by the time of their fifth birthday.

The urgency of the problem, from a global health perspective, would be even further cemented in the public mind if the productive but ambiguous thread on malaria's relationship with sickle cell disease could be convincingly argued. On this count, the *Secretariat* offered:

> Although a single abnormal [HbS] gene may protect against malaria, inheritance of two abnormal genes leads to sickle-cell anaemia and confers no such protection, and malaria is a major cause of ill-health and death in children with sickle-cell anaemia. There is increasing evidence that malaria not only influences outcome but also changes the manifestations of sickle-cell anaemia in Africa. (WHO 2006c, 1)

The fact that malaria affects sicklers' life chances while the HbS trait is protective against malaria in carriers was potentially confusing (since, as we saw previously, many people understood SS and AS as the same condition with different degrees of intensity). Then the claim that malaria actually changes sickle cell manifestations is without reference, leaving one to wonder what this could mean. With these ambiguities another opportunity to tie the disease to a successful WHO health priority presented itself.

Edwidge Ebakisse Badassou and the OILD's work finally paid off when, on December 22, 2008, the General Assembly of the United Nations unanimously adopted Resolution A/63/237 recognizing sickle cell disease as "a public health problem." This was the first step in "encouraging" international institutions and development partners to support "funds and programmes" to raise awareness and improve the lives of those with the disease. Ebakisse Badassou herself emerged in many people's minds as they read the document, which cited the reports of the OILD congresses as providing impetus for the resolution. More to the point, there are two clauses in the resolution that linked sickle cell to other global health heavyweights. One was HIV/AIDS, the other malaria. In this order, three of the preface lines to the actual seven points of the resolution read as follows:

> *Recognizing* that proper management of sickle-cell anaemia will contribute to an appreciable decrease in mortality from malaria and in the risk of HIV infection,

> *Recalling* the Abuja Declaration on Roll Back Malaria in Africa of 25 April 2000 and the global "Roll Back Malaria" initiative,

> *Taking note* of the reports of the first, second and third international congresses of the Sickle Cell Disease International Organization [OILD], held in Paris on 25 and 26 January 2002, in Cotonou from 20 to 23 January 2004 and in Dakar from 22 to 24 November 2006, respectively, and the report of the first global consultations on sickle-cell anaemia, held in Brazzaville from 14 to 17 June 2005, [The General Assembly] recognizes that sickle cell anemia is a public health problem. (United Nations A/Res/63/237 2009)

In addition to the principal item that the UN would hereafter consider sickle cell to be a problem of "public health," the General Assembly also "urged Member States and the organizations of the United Nations system to raise awareness of sickle-cell anaemia on 19 June each year at the national and international levels," while promoting research and care through international collaborations. During the June 19, 2009 press conference commemorating the celebration of the first "World Sickle Cell Day" subsequent to the resolution, Ebakisse Badassou reiterated the statistics of three hundred thousand sickle cell births a year, repeated that 50 percent of sicklers in Africa would die before age five, and then, most ambiguously, emphasized the "relationship between sickle cell and malaria," in a string of repetitions, without ever stating what that relationship was (UN Webcast 2009).[1] The ambiguity was important. It did not solely represent a negative state of knowledge, rather it facilitated the chance that sickle cell would stick as an illness that merited global attention somewhere within the open sphere of uncertainty around it.

By the time the United States ambassador and permanent representative to the UN, Susan E. Rice, generated her press release, also on June 19, 2009, the figures had again changed. One might say that the ambiguities thrived, actually nearly doubled, when stamped with the American seal. Now the news was:

> While sickle cell disease still poses serious health risks here in the United States, it is 10 times higher in African countries. The disease contributes to a higher infant mortality rate, in fact, studies suggest that 98 percent of children born with sickle cell disease in resource-poor settings die before age five.[2]

The politics of large numbers had just greatly expanded.

■ **Sickle Cell Advocacy Prior to the UN and the WHO**

When we first met, in Paris in 2001, Edwidge Ebakisse Badassou appeared to me as a tireless but seemingly exasperated mother of a child sick with sickle cell. A heavy woman with a serious face, she seemed hardened, yet nervously alert, which could sometimes be mistaken for openness. It was not that she was closed to ideas, especially if those ideas involved enterprise or promotion of the organization, as any president might be. She especially made time for politicians and industry sponsors, as patients often complained that they rarely had direct access to her. Over the years her visibility at the OILD international events waned. In the beginning, she was present at every turn, engaged with patients and participants at the first two international meetings. Oscillating between donning the manner of a good hostess, who must make sure that her powerful guests connect, and that of a discrete power broker, who may not want to show all of her options to onlookers, she possessed a range of smiles and degrees of engagement. At the Cotonou and Dakar meetings she further managed how much she would engage with her members and the public by checking into the hotel under a false name. In Dakar, she rarely appeared in the meeting halls, unless she was touring the site with *les Premières Dames*.

In the 1990s, Ebakisse Badassou and her husband relocated to Paris from Congo Brazzaville for work and soon became immersed in, as she told me, "changing the political future of sickle cell disease." When I met her, she was working for Johnson & Johnson in Paris. Her training was in biochemistry, but she was doing administration. She yearned for more, and a certain "void" inspired her to create *Sud Développement*, an NGO dedicated to aiding countries in the southern hemisphere. She had a specific vision for *development* politics.[3] As a Francophone African, she was also keenly aware of France's strategy to stake territory pertaining to the needs of its former colonies. She put both experiences to work to advance the state of sickle cell awareness, while building on and enhancing whatever structures were already in place, despite their problems.

Two such structures were the rival Parisian sickle cell patient advocacy groups, of which one was initially more "African" in identity and the other more "Caribbean." In their years of bickering, the exact lynchpin of their difference proved a moving target, and their inability to unite became a source of frustration for researchers and patients alike. Many within the ranks of both groups wanted to establish a single forum to air their grievances, together, rather than having two forums to simply attack each other. The groups were at an impasse. Capitalizing on this rift, as well as on a desire that would surface from time to time for French and African researchers to create a Francophone research network for sustained conversations across the North-South divide, Ebakisse Badassou proposed a vision beyond France, beyond the Caribbean, and beyond Africa, where actors from each place would have a role in promoting knowledge on the disease.[4]

These local issues, compounded by the then linguistic dearth of French language activity on the internet (as the web really took off in the mid-1990s and early 2000s) and by a larger silence on the disease at the level of the Chirac government, convinced Ebakisse Badassou and countless others that the RFLD was long overdue.[5] All too aware that the politics of *la francophonie* operated quite visibly within the world of sickle cell research, she put this reality to work for the nascent organization as well. While she and many other French patients and families wanted to connect with the "Anglophone" sickle cell world, they realized, in this very desire, that a "Francophone" space for the disease was strangely missing. Her sentiment met with that of several scientists who read in English, but who nevertheless had spent their careers eking out their own French sickle cell domain. Thus patients and families shared the attitude best described by Jacques Elion, in chapter 5, that the Americans were their competitors (and friends); only for patients, this had to do largely with web-based chat rooms then dominated by Americans with the disease who had established a vibrant virtual cultural sphere around sickle cell.

The politicization of the issue as one of cultural diffusion and "French language," when openly stated, secured her the support of the *Agence de la francophonie* (which is not meant to be translated). Again through politics familiar to someone working in development, this last move made concrete sense: sickle cell awareness, sponsored by *l'Agence*, would become another area where the French language could regain a cultural foothold. Like always, Ebakisse Badassou was working on multiple levels to appeal to multiple publics. She reasoned that the French cultural ministries in the global south would appreciate any efforts to treat French as a "universalizing" language, in this case, of a potentially, if she was successful, "global" genetic disease. Furthermore, Edwidge, like many affected in the Paris region, heard key specialists cite figures that the prevalence of sickle cell in the *Ile de France* made it the most common "French" genetic disorder. Research physicians I encountered also told me that sickle cell was the most common genetic illness in the *Ile de France*, the French *département*, or state, where Paris is located. The point that they wanted to drive home was one of injustice, based on research dollars that were allotted to diseases that were "representative" of the larger population. A brief excursus into the politics of disease advocacy in France in the 1990s is necessary to fully understand how all of this played into the work that Ebakisse Badassou was eventually able to achieve.

■ Patient Groups in the Metropole

During the late 1980s and 1990s, the French public got educated on a then newly emergent problem in France—the genetic disorders called the dystrophies. The work of families affected, specifically of Bernard Barataud, a father who lost his son to a dystrophy disorder, changed conceptions of what patient advocacy could accomplish at the level of the French nation (Barataud 1992; Callon et al. 2001; Rabeharisoa and Callon 1999). Through the *téléthon*, borrowed from the United States, and inaugurated by the American Jerry Lewis, the *Association française contre les myopathies* (French Muscular Dystrophy Association) was thrust into the public eye. "*Le don*," or "the gift," given through the *téléthon* on the part of public viewers, consisted of small donations, sums that amounted to an average of ~50 million dollars annually, beginning in the late 1980s and early 1990s. The money poured in from all over France. A culture of competition between *les départements* joined with a spirit of Christmas giving, since the live event aired annually in early December. Interestingly, these funds were from the public but *not* from the state. In this way, the citizens of *le République* funded the AFM and gave the essentially private, family-founded, disease-based association unprecedented autonomy to shape genetics research in France (Rabinow 1999, 40). Most of the research that the AFM financed was on the various muscular dystrophies, which, even when taken together, were much less common than sickle cell in France (Bonnet 2009, 11). The AFM also funded aspects of studies of other genetic diseases whose research questions they deemed important.

During this time, and since the early 1990s, there were two sickle cell patient advocacy groups in the Paris region, the APIPD and SOS Globi.[6] Each entity was created by heads of sickle cell clinics at one of the two hospital sites where adult sicklers in Paris obtain care. Doctor Frédéric Galactéros sponsored SOS Globi, while APIPD relied on Professor Girot's advisory role. During my fieldwork in Paris in 1997, people at both sites and patients in both groups felt that the very existence of two associations for sickle cell disease was divisive, and that it obstructed patients from gaining strength and influence.

SOS Globi is a sickle cell and thalassemia patient group that, at the time, was led by a lab technician of Caribbean origin at the Henri Mondor hemo-globinopathy polyclinic named Max Petit-Phar. Although he was president of the association, Petit-Phar did not have sickle cell himself. His identity en-trée to the group was that he was from Guadeloupe and thus represented the "Caribbean family," or population, in the *Ile de France*. Beta-thalassemia has always been included within SOS Globi, which, rather than promote itself as a sickle cell disease group, has long emphasized its commitment to these two hemoglobinopathies in a show of "union which makes for strength" (*l'union fait la force*), as their newsletter advertised. Such unity was a gesture toward enlarging their ranks, even if it meant going beyond any one disease proper in efforts to define itself in opposition to the APIPD. The APIPD's tack was to focus solely on sickle cell disease. Furthermore, it has always been headed by families directly affected by sickle cell. This detail of focus and leadership incited some of the disagreement between the two groups.[7]

When I met with the APIPD's administration in 1997, the group's leader-ship was made up of two families—one from Madagascar, the other from Guadeloupe. The two couples divided the main administrative council titles among themselves. Most importantly, no hospital staff person was directly implicated in the group's management body. In the early 2000s the Malagasy couple returned home and the APIPD named Jenny Hippocrate-Fixy, mother of a sick child (and from Martinique), its president. Even with the "origins" disputes out of the way, as both leaders were now from the French Caribbean, the APIPD found fault with SOS Globi's close proximity to Henri Mondor, accusing the group of existing as a mere extension of a sickle cell medical care unit, rather than as a place made for and by patients and their families. The APIPD, for its part, continued to heavily depend on Professor Girot for meet-ing space, for educational materials, and even to promote Mrs. Hippocrate-Fixy's eventual book on her lived experience of mothering a child with sickle cell disease (for which Girot wrote the preface).

■ **An Umbrella Association for Genetic Diseases**

In the early 1990s, the AFM touted itself as a vast infrastructure that would act as a representative of rare genetic diseases. This gave hope to sickle cell families who assumed that France and its departments would gain familiarity with sickle cell and that, at the very least, the disease would enter into French public discourse, rather than remaining relegated to a few circles of African and Caribbean communities (those primarily affected in France). They also imagined that curative research—as there was much talk of gene therapy in the AFM—might be forthcoming. In 1996, SOS Globi "represented" sickle cell disease by setting up a booth at the annual *téléthon*. The following year, during my Paris fieldwork in 1997, patients and medical professionals working on sickle cell claimed not to have seen any direct funding from the AFM. They then complained that the increasingly powerful umbrella association had used their presence in the *téléthon* to raise money from people who might not otherwise have been interested in the dystrophies as such but donated "for sickle cell because it affects their own communities." For people from the DOM-TOM,[8] and nearly all of SOS Globi members were, sickle cell was "used" to get those in the Caribbean to donate for the dystrophies.

Unbeknownst to most patients, the AFM had granted one scientist, Professor Yves Beauzard, previously based at Henri Mondor, three million French francs (at that time, approximately US$600 thousand) to help create a gene therapy laboratory at the *Hôpital Saint Louis* (where there is no sickle cell clinic). Years before, Professor Beauzard was part of the team that built the biochemistry laboratories at Créteil. He also shared the same "intellectual father"—who was a renowned French biochemist named Jean Rosa—with Dr. Frédéric Galactéros. Beauzard and others told me that despite the lack of attention his AFM funding received from sickle cell patient groups, he did make it public by publishing news of his award in the SOS Globi newsletter in 1996. When I arrived in 1997, both patient groups were highly vocal about their resentment toward the AFM and the perceived unjust cause for the association's "rejection" of sickle cell disease. Admittedly, Yves Beauzard works on transgenic mice not people.[9] This may partially explain why, despite Beauzard publicizing the AFM's role in gene therapy for sickle cell, people with the disease constantly chided the AFM as a self-centered organization that claimed to represent rare diseases, but that had no interest in theirs. I traced patients and practitioners' resentment back to the AFM's refusal to fund research on sickle cell *patients* submitted by the team at Créteil. Professor Galactéros revealed the source of the sickle cell public's frustration to be the AFM's "wretched" rejection of his own proposal during our 1997 interview.

> FG: For the moment there is no real interest in Sickle cell . . . Recently we applied for money from the AFM and INSERM for a genetic study. They replied: "Does not fit the subject requirements: sickle cell is not a 'rare' genetic disease." Period. This was the only justification of their refusal. We know very well what this means, this means that the AFM and INSERM, on this question, do not care about sickle cell. Theirs was a silly pretext, that sickle cell is not a rare genetic disease. Of course if we only look at the Paris region, by the definition of a rare disease, which is 1/2000, sickle cell is not rare. It is much more common than that in Paris. . . . It should be for the whole of France, and then we would be clearly within the definition. . . . It is as clear as day. When we see bad faith, so on the mark, we realize that it's an excuse and that sickle cell is a disease that does not come from France, that does not affect the

French, and that subsequently "*we*" will not study it, "*we*" will not finance it.

DF: What was the program that you applied to?

FG: It was a program interested in research characterizing aspects of rare genetic diseases. They specifically wanted projects interested in taking DNA samples and immortalizing them, all the while following a phenotypic aspect, and the possibility of finding markers that could explain phenotypic aspects by doing genomic studies. Sickle cell lends itself *perfectly* to this kind of study. The only thing missing is the funding. Sickle cell is a marvelous case for this kind of project. The probability of getting results, working from a well-defined group of people with a disease, who are phenotypically very well studied and observed, is considerable. What's more, the results and the findings would benefit many, not just those with sickle cell disease. But oh well. I think they were just making excuses and that at base the AFM has closed the door once and for all on sickle cell. [He pauses] I find this wretched [*minable*], there's no other word. This is a disastrous attitude. . . .

I then brought up Beauzard's funding.

DF: In my research I've heard complaints from the sickle cell patient group here regarding the AFM, . . . the fact that they finance many researchers working on rare genetic diseases but not sickle cell. Yet when I talked to Dr. Yves Beauzard at St. Louis hospital who works on sickle cell, he explained to me that it was the AFM who financed his research.

FG: They financed it *because* it was a project on gene therapy and certain approaches and methods had things in common with gene therapy approaches for muscular dystrophy. It was in *no* way for hemoglobinopathies. They always say that those monies went towards sickle cell there, but they didn't. It is so hypocritical. Yves Beauzard will not say the contrary; he clearly cannot spit in the soup of those who fed him.

The AFM's refusal to fund Galactéros's study that fit within the bounds of their call for proposals fuelled a wave of anger throughout the ranks of those working on sickle cell at Tenon and Henri Mondor, as well as in both patient groups. In interviews with the heads of both sickle cell patient groups in 1997, rejection from the AFM served as a wake-up call to unite in the face of "French" (the AFM's) bias against sicklers as "other." When Ebakisse Badassou came onto the scene a few years later, her larger vision of inclusion and research for this "African diasporic" disease appealed to all parties who were looking for a way out of the impasse that bound them—a situation that they had partially created for themselves.

■ Life and Politics in *le Sud*

On the African side of things, and in Senegal in particular, the immediate vision of unity that the then RFLD imagined had less overt divisions to mend, fewer extant elements to bring into concert, but many more domains to develop and grow. Ideas and good intentions allowed for many starts, for instance "protocols" that the two care sites of Albert Royer and the CNTS were able to establish in the form of consistent follow-up. Yet formal structures and programs dedicated to sickle cell would have to be pieced together. As for the politic of patient advocacy, Magueye Ndiaye and others were maneuvering a breakthrough, an event that culminated in the *Association sénégalaise de la lutte contre la drépanocytose*, or the ASD. This was happening independently of the fact that the RFLD would require that Senegal, like any of its "Member States," have its own local patient advocacy group in order to join the international umbrella organization that would become the OILD.

Sickle cell care in Senegal, nonetheless, did have its own series of problems and tensions that actors involved did not necessarily want featured in public discussions. One was a tension, like that between the two primary care sites in Paris, between the two principal sites in Dakar. From my observations, this stemmed from the fact that patients, locally, and researchers, internationally, called on Dr. Diagne as *the* specialist on the disease in Senegal whenever a "point person" was needed. His colleagues at the CNTS, some of whom were older, and, given the social weight of hierarchy there, much more powerful within the university system for which they all worked, did not fully appreciate this. The attention others accorded him was not Diagne's doing, however, and he, as a careful diplomat who wanted to offend no one and live by his humble values, tried to downplay the many interpellations. But with the arrival of the OILD, Diagne could no longer deflect the focus on him when it came to Edwidge Ebakisse Badassou and, eventually, to Madame Wade. The Senegalese First Lady was enrolled for the OILD cause in Paris, in June of 2003, at the UNESCO sponsored "*l'Appel international des femmes pour la lutte contre la drépanocytose*" (International call to [influential] women). The purpose of the event was to solicit the public commitment of African First Ladies who would become the organization's official sponsors.

By the accounts of some who attended the 2003 *Appel* event, Viviane Wade was "set up" by Ebakisse Badassou, or, more kindly, invited to agree to more than she might have envisioned upon accepting to come to the Paris *rencontre*. The OILD president reportedly caught Mme Wade off guard when she asked her if she would be willing to host its third international conference in Dakar in 2006. The question was put to Wade in front of a large audience with three other powerful First Ladies in attendance. As the public awaited her response, Mme Wade, who later admitted on Senegalese state television that the June 2003 meeting was the very first time that she had even heard of the disease, politely said yes. When she returned to Dakar she hurriedly deployed her advisors, called "*techniciens*," to find her the most knowledge-able person on the disease, and fast. They found her Ibrahima Diagne. In fact, Diagne had been in the audience when Wade was committed to sickle cell. It was there, after the "announcement," that Ebakisse Badassou introduced him to his *Première Dame*. Wade, perhaps shaken by the ordeal, did not put it all together until she returned home. She then began to call on Diagne regularly, to ask for briefs and to solicit his help in organizing this massive international conference for a disease that did not so much as have a file at her husband's regime's Health Ministry. All of that was about to change, however. She and Diagne had two and a half years to make it happen.

■ **Concurrent Movements**

In defining the goals of the RFLD for me in her Paris apartment living room one Sunday evening, with her little boy demanding more frightening bedtime stories involving a wolf, Ebakisse Badassou outlined a very structured, hierar-chical schema of the political dynamics of her newest NGO effort. The orga-nization's tiered structure would demand "respectful" collaboration and mu-tual recognition between three imagined spheres. North-South hierarchies and histories of power so obviously at play in chapter 5, were not explicitly discussed here. "We must proceed in good faith," she said. She did express, in other settings, such as at a dinner I was invited to with her friends from Brazzaville, that there was certainly "racism" on the part of "the French" to be dealt with, but that the building of the organization had to come first.

The idea of the *network* was to "serve as a link between three poles of actors throughout the Francophone world of sickle cell," Ebakisse Badas-sou recounted sternly as if delivering a board meeting report. Each pole was strictly conceived as (1) scientists and doctors, (2) patient groups, and (3) "the public." Each would possess a unique domain of expertise that, in certain in-stances, "should remain theirs." Yet the hope of cross-fertilization of ideas was also built into the framework, within the spheres. I then pushed her to think more democratically about this. My insistence was born of my recent visit to the AFM in the Paris suburb of Évry. There a street called *rue internationale* encompassed a modern science and technology village. It was through the AFM, *les malades*, and their families that an infrastructure for genetic disease research never before known in France (the *Généthon* laboratories) was con-ceived. Specifically, this highly vocal and active patient population created a space where it could have an interested voice in research. AFM families enlisted doctors to work on questions important to them. They became fluent in aspects of molecular genetics, and became experts not only on the science, but also of funding politics (see Barataud 1992; Callon et al. 2001; Rabeharisoa and Callon 1999). This relatively new form of civic genetic engagement, where citizens' needs, activism, and science inhered, happened around a disease that

Edwidge and others understood to be much less common than sickle cell in metropolitan France. Ebakisse Badassou listened skeptically to my description of all that I witnessed in Évry and then repeated her own vision of the hierarchical structure of her creation, reminding me that she had to work within certain political confines to succeed.

DF: Most [sicklers] know their disease quite well. Aren't you starting out with the assumption that they will not understand science?

EB: . . . What I said earlier is that the scientific counsel can advise patients.

DF: But the patients cannot advise the scientists? This is not a two-way street.

EB: No. . . . I can tell you right now that the barrier is a tough one in our case. Those on the scientific advisory committee will let you know right away when you've overstepped your boundaries and begin stepping on their toes. They put you back in your place quickly, "No, no, this is no longer your domain. It is the domain of science."

Often when I brought up the case of *les myopathes* with sicklers in France, or with the two Parisian-based patient groups, people responded that the difference between the work that the AFM was able to do, in contradistinction to that of sicklers, laid in the fact that those affected by the dystrophies were largely "white-French." This was as opposed to African, Caribbean, or Arab French. Nonetheless, *les drépanos* in Paris wondered aloud when their "AFM" would come. They too wanted an open conversation, and open lines of communication, with their doctors. They also desired more information on the state of science and research that could never go forward without their participation, so why, they reasoned, would it not be made more available to them? They mused that to be invited to a scientific meeting would be an honor, and that they probably would stick it out even if the subjects were inaccessible to them.

In Senegal, although the case of the AFM was not the referent, sicklers also wondered about a forum, or space, to advance the state of their disease. The paternalism inherent in Ebakisse Badassou's hierarchical arrangement would never have permitted the AFM its success. Although no one knew it at the time, it would however permit her the success she imagined for the OILD within the discursive global coordinates of North-South. The WHO and UN resolutions on sickle cell exemplified the disease's nominal success on the world stage in the context of Africa, even if actual funds and interventions would still have to break through massive bureaucracies once the political will emerged. Yet this was a beginning. It all felt very official and promising. To be "official" has massive cultural appeal in many parts of Africa. Here, in the very language of the OILD and other sickle cell associations in Senegal, leaders trucked in the specific rule-bound formality and culture of international bodies, such as the UN. They referred to their sickle cell organizations and associations as having, or being, "Member States," while large meetings beyond the National Congresses were called "General Consultations," with important sessions referred to as "General Assemblies." For Africa, much aid and many partnerships among large bodies of finance and investment come through these multilaterals. This—coupled with the display of materials, jobs, and conspicuous equipment, notably white four by fours—makes many in the global South experience a certainty of power by simply being associated with, and surely represented by, the UN. Such international bodies are also seen as larger than African states, which, in the case of Senegal is often critiqued for reneging on its promises of good governance, political change, and general better life that the opposition pledged in 2000.

■ Mobilization in Dakar

As Ebakisse Badassou continued apace in Paris, various constellations of patient networks were attempting to establish a coherent base in Dakar. Diagne had long been in contact with one man, Colonel Abdoulaye Diaw, who single-handedly ran a patient group since the mid-1980s, but who, in his undemocratic, highly paternalistic handling of his "members," soon found himself alone on the membership roster. In 2000, when I met Diaw, the retired colonel pleaded with me to take over his association, saying: "it's up to you reanimate it!" Shocked by the quasi order I simply reminded him that as an American anthropologist who had a clear return date to the United States, his proposal made little sense. We talked about the "importance of anthropologists," the "Americans," and his presence at a UNESCO meeting concerning Gorée Island and the trans-Atlantic slave trade. Finally circling back to sickle cell again, I agreed that I would introduce him to people who were ready to heed his order, and gladly. I first introduced him to Touty Niang. Touty and a dozen other mothers of Diagne's small patients were intent on creating a support group and advocacy forum at the same moment when Ebakisse Badassou was developing a structure that, once in "the South," would require that each "Member State" commit to reproducing the three-tiered structure of the RFLD locally. This new series of events would also coincide with Diaw's desire to pass on his baton—or so I thought. From my discussions with Diagne and others who were "convoked" for a meeting on the issue at the CNTS, independent of Diaw, Dakar would have to have a functioning sickle cell association to occupy that crucial middle point in the OILD hierarchy. In 2003, it did not.

In 2000 Diaw's *l'Association sénégalaise d'assistance aux enfants drépano-cytaires* (The Senegalese Association of Assistance to Sickle Cell Children), or ASEAD, was, in the colonel's own words, "defunct." Yet, as I would soon learn, independent of my actions to find mothers like Touty Niang help Diaw

reanimate his association, a group of young sicklers in Dakar had been trying
to convince him to confer the entity to them, so that *they* could "reanimate
it." He had never mentioned these interested parties to me. Perhaps he figured
that they were too young and inexperienced to get anything done. To his defense, they approached him when they were still in high school. One of the
youngsters in question was Magueye Ndiaye.

A few years before my first visit to Senegal, when Magueye was an active
student rallying to publicize the problem of sickle cell, he and his friends
formed a "sickle cell club." By Magueye's account, most of those interested
were simply impressed by his vision and his passion but did not have the
disease. Others had the trait and felt that they too were implicated in sickle
cell as a "problem" that needed an "association." The culture of associations in
Senegal does not easily translate to the North American context. If more than
two people have an interest, or as the law states, "agree to join their knowledge," then it is not uncommon for them to obtain a permit to convene legally
and to declare the constitution of their arrangement an "association" to be
recognized by the state. Almost every neighborhood in Dakar has various "associations" for sports, for women, or for religious interests through the same
law. The tendency of a few citizens to create associations is inherited from the
French, who instituted the practice in the *Law of Associations of July 1901*. In
1901, French law was also Senegalese law. This is one of the many aspects of
French legal culture that remain in place in Senegal today.

In his high school years, Magueye was empowered by the fact that he had
diagnosed himself after hearing about sickle cell in a natural sciences course.
One of his teachers then informed him of Colonel Diaw. Many people knew
about Diaw, some calling him Dr. Diaw since, for a time, he would give out
medications. The colonel's ASEAD was helped by a state-employed journalist,
Fara Diaw (the colonel's nephew), who wrote a full-page spread on sickle cell
disease in the state-run newspaper *le Soleil* in 1986. According to Magueye,
when he and his group of interested friends went to see "old man Diaw" he
made them many promises. He told them that his own sickle cell affected
children had received grants to study abroad, in France and in the United
States, because of their disease. He also told them that he was working to establish this kind of support for Senegalese sickle cell students more broadly.
He had already succeeded in getting a legal code established for sickle cell
school-aged children. The code entailed exemption from physical education
and other benefits—such as scholastic grants and the option to repeat grades
without being failed out of the strict French schooling system—for students
of all ages with the disease (Diaw 1986, 1–3). These codes existed, but no one
applied them or even remembered them in most instances, which clearly
meant they were not enforced. This legality, "of reality on paper only," as Magueye complained, seemed to be a theme with Diaw. Teachers generally were
not aware that sickler students had any kind of special rights, and parents had
to make their cases that exceptions be granted to their children (such as being

able to drink water all day to stay hydrated, or take extra bathroom breaks) on individual bases.

Magueye recounted that the sickle cell club's meetings at Diaw's house were a space "to dream," in the beginning, which later turned into a frustrating game of deception. According to him, Diaw kept them waiting for a transfer of the legal papers to the association, which, as Magueye now complained, "he never planned to pass on." The students asked for the papers on numerous occasions, as Diaw also repeatedly complained of his age, of his ailing heart, and the need to leave the association to the younger generation. "We were the younger generation!" Magueye told me in 2004. When Magueye one day grew impatient and confronted the Colonel on his doublespeak, the older man took him to be insolent and disrespectful and told him to simply wait until he convened the "General Assembly," presumably so that the extant members could vote on the matter. Magueye recounted this period for me, starting with the small efforts he organized at school.

MN: In high school we had a club, a club of sicklers and we would organize information sessions . . . We also undertook a census of sorts. We sent information sheets to counselors at several lycées. And they helped us by telling us the number of cases they knew of in their schools and their type of disease. The first big project I did, I targeted five high schools—we were associated within a complex of lycées. . . . It was through my 'studies,' if I can call them that—that I first began. Many people knew me through this work. . . . little by little I developed a taste for organization, for solidarity . . . We presented ourselves as a group *chez le vieux* Diaw one day. We sat and talked with him for hours. He made us believe that we were the future leaders [*détenteurs*] of the association, of ASEAD. . . . Then every Wednesday evening we would go and see him. We would talk for hours. I really thought that one day I'd be someone who would help people with this disease. That was what was motivating me . . . He told us that, in all honesty, he would call a General Assembly and that he was going to hand the association over to us because he was too old. . . . I lived in *Colobane*, he was in *Bopp*, so it was nothing in terms of distance. I went to see him often . . . I went by myself in the beginning and he told me 'since you're in high school, you should start a group, try and get the maximum number of people involved in order to advance things. You will all be part of my association.' He gave us advice. We were very, *very* young. . . . It took me a while to get it, but one day it finally donned on me that I would have to start another association. He led me on [*il m'a traîné*] for years making me believe that there would be a General Assembly. . . .

DF: This recurring idea of the *assemblée générale*—there was all of this formality and you were waiting . . .

MN: *Voilà*, too much, and the wait was too long. And another thing—I would always talk to Dr. Saliou Diop about what was going on with the old man. Finally, one day [after talking with Diop], I went [to see Diaw] with no other intention than to tell him what was on my mind. I told him 'listen, we are organizing meetings and conferences at school with social workers and counselors. We are trying to organize, so *when* exactly is this general assembly going to happen? [*à quand l'assemblée générale?*] Then, he said: 'Well, a General Assembly does not just happen like that!'

Magueye continued to talk with Diop and others at the adult sickle cell center. The staff and research corps at CNTS all knew Diaw well. They respected his status as a once powerful colonel, and perhaps more importantly, as a customs officer. They too told Magueye to be patient, and to be careful not to disrespect the much older man. Magueye tried to abide by expected codes of conduct that put age and status above most else, but he had a short temper. In his own words, his "capriciousness" was a trait that he "inherited from his disease."

Elsewhere in Dakar, other people were looking to organize. In 2003, Dr. Diop of CNTS informed Magueye that several of Diagne's patients and families were strategizing about how to approach Diaw to "reanimate" the association. At the time Magueye knew neither Touty Niang nor Diagne (or so he thought. As it turned out, he and Diagne were from the same village). Both would later become two of Magueye's closest allies in the fight against sickle cell disease locally.

When members of what would later be referred to as the "Senegalese delegation" returned from the Paris 2003 UNESCO *Appel des femmes* meeting, Diagne, Touty Niang, several mothers with AS, and doctors (at both CNTS and Albert Royer) were slowly beginning conversations about the potential for a national sickle cell program. They were not optimistic that Senegal had the resources to fulfill its RFLD "Member-State" obligations. Nonetheless, they called a meeting in Dakar at a WHO-sponsored health prevention center. Diaw came, as did Magueye, as well as various research-physicians from both sites. Previous (disappointed) members of ASEAD showed up as well. Magueye confronted Diaw about the association. "Who are its members? What is it doing? "*À quand l'assemblée générale?*," he publicly pleaded. Diaw simply responded that he "considered everyone there a member of ASEAD." Magueye was incensed. Dr. Diagne and Touty also sided with Magueye and asked the Colonel to be reasonable. He said that he might consider the request to hand over his association, agreeing that he was too old to carry ASEAD forward. The Colonel imagined some sort of formal transfer of power, where he would be recognized for all that he had done. This seemed to be as good a setting as any, but he continued to hold out. In discussions with other members of what is now the ASD, Magueye learned that the problem was not as difficult as he had imagined since high school. Soon thereafter, at the suggestion of the others, he inquired at the appropriate ministerial office and learned that two associations of the same nature could in fact exist, a seemingly wasteful move that he had never before considered. The only stipulation was that the two groups could not have the same name. Magueye obtained the necessary paperwork and created the *Association Sénégalaise de lutte contre la Drépano-cytose*. He was later elected its president, Touty was named the *Secrétaire gé-nérale* and Drs. Diagne and Diop, were appointed its scientific advisors.

The ASD's launch aired on state television (RTS) since Madame Wade had recently announced that she was sponsoring the cause on an international level. Most Senegalese sicklers I knew understood, quite logically, that she would also be sponsoring the local association (an assumption that did not always pan out in the early days). The "public," that third tier of Ebakisse Badassou's imagined structure, was learning of sickle cell on state television for the first time. They were witnessing the First Lady alongside Magueye, a then twenty-eight-year-old SS sickler, while being made "aware" that an association where sicklers could convene would begin its meetings at the CNTS every first Wednesday of the month. Sickle cell had publicly begun "to happen" (*xew*) in Dakar.

■ **Sickle Cell in the Public Sphere**

Magueye became a sickle cell star overnight due to his RTS appearance with Madame Wade. He merited the attention regardless of the First Lady at his side. He was young (but old in local understandings of sickle cell years) and spoke ardently of his cause, unlike many of those who often passed across the television screen to inform the public of the sick but who were visibly removed from the pain of sufferers. He was of the "*fleau*" (calamity) being addressed. He also had too long been "ignored." He, like the many with neglected diseases, "had waited in pain as doctors flitted by him in hospital corridors." Many of these "so-called professionals," as he referred to them, had no idea how to treat his disease and "prescribed useless and outdated medications." It was time not just to educate "the public" but it was also the moment to train the medical corps throughout the country, since surely Dakar was better off than most rural areas, denoted as "*les régions*."

In its initial period, the ASD was largely comprised of parents of sick children, mostly mothers who themselves felt ill and, as it turns out, were there to learn what they could do for themselves as well as their children, as we saw in the previous chapter. Most of this membership was already informed about sickle cell complications, "prevention," and where *they* could go to seek care, since their children were followed by Diagne. Thus, from the earliest days, "AS sufferers" constituted the majority constituency of the ASD. As the group would perform local awareness campaigns and radio spots, even as they often differentiated "AS" from "SS," they rarely downplayed HbAS. As time went on, the number of vocal AS sufferers, now mostly young women without children afflicted with SS, increased. These were women who, most often, had been to see multiple doctors, had undergone many tests, and were found to be "healthy" despite their complaints. ASD provided them a forum wherein they could connect with others like them, others who had lived the same confusing diagnosis for a disease that was increasingly being dubbed a "*non-maladie.*"

Like those with HbAS, many of the ASD members with full-blown sickle cell disease were sicker than most sicklers I encountered in Dakar outside of ASD. At meetings I listened to complaints and testimonies from people with various forms of sickle cell, with HbSS disease, but also people with HbSC disease, all of whom were concerned with some vexing complication. They often also looked visibly ill, malnourished, underweight, or physically handicapped. The "severe cases" were starting to make themselves known in (disproportionately) larger numbers. In this context, it seemed that the CNTS team, led by Saliou Diop, initially may have offered too low of a figure on severe cases and complications for sicklers in Dakar (Diop et al. 2003). Their early efforts to make country-specific assessments now seemed to only partially tally a reality that researchers had not yet empirically known or fully appreciated. Then there was awareness.

Many of the severe patients who began to flock to the ASD had not been to the CNTS, perhaps had never been referred, and thus had never been counted. In fact, they were not followed, or regularly treated, anywhere. One thirty-year-old, who was five foot one and 110 pounds, in addition to his extremely stunted growth, was grossly afflicted with open leg ulcers that would not heal. He had undergone two skin grafts to no avail, which got seriously infected. He had endured his battle with the ulcers for seven years when I met him in 2006. Sometimes his wounds would scar (a positive sign of recovery) only to reopen, reinfect, and again send him on an expensive quest to consult specialists and surgeons. Only recently had he come to the CNTS for regular follow-up by Dr. Diop and the interns he trains. On some days he was confident that with surveillance and regular care he would now be able to finally heal. On less hopeful days, he spiraled into depression. In one of his bouts of hopelessness, he claimed to all present at an ASD meeting: "No one, none of you, has known pain like I have. There are degrees of sickle cell, and none of you come close to my misery." Touty quickly darted her eyes around before telling him that he could not make a statement like that. "You have no idea what other people have gone through. Everyone here has suffered. Everyone has a life situation that can not be relativized." But the man held his own, and continued: "No matter what amount of pain you've had, I've suffered worse. I'll stand by my words." He went on to first talk about the open sores at his ankles. The wounds were hidden under his large cotton pants, but he raised his cuffs so as to show people the thick gauze that encircled his legs. He then spoke of his larger social ills. Over time he had become so costly to his family, because of his disease, he said, that they now preferred to pretend that he "didn't exist." He was able to live with a sister for a while, but only if he paid rent. His relations with his family were tense, and he complained that he was alone. He had heard about the ASD from a nurse with whom he worked at a bottling plant. It was this work that required that he spend hours a day on his feet. This was likely the reason that his leg ulcers formed, and now could not heal, and why the surgery probably would not take. Clearly the man was frustrated, but moreover he frustrated the group. Nonetheless, Magueye reminded them all of their link that was solidified in their family of shared blood, after which he then promised to put the man in touch with a social worker at the CNTS to see what might be done. Magueye, himself, eventually accompanied the man to meet different specialists whom he knew in Dakar and rarely ever left him to seek out care alone from then on. In future meetings, people asked the man about his progress, and began to help him research his problems. There seemed to be a small task force forming around getting him information, proper care, and most importantly a resource of other people with whom he could share his pain.

Similarly, other cases, in which people suffered debilitating bodily break-downs, became flash points that compelled others to action. Several hobbled in and out of the meeting hall, their pelvises atilt. They suffered from badly de-teriorated upper-femoral mass, or necrosis of the hip, that could only be rem-edied with hip-replacement surgery. In Senegal the procedure costs 1.5 million *cfa* [~US$3,000]. Others in the ASD were also suffering from varied symptoms of "severe disease" that would benefit from surgical interventions. For these sicklers the costs of such procedures was usually far beyond their means.

It was in this way that AS sufferers and visibly ill SS sicklers became the essential base of the ASD. These two groups of *malades* positioned themselves as most in need of the help of the state, of the medical corps, and of their com-rades in the fight to raise awareness. Thus the "type" of life most visible in the ASD as sickle cell went public was not that of the "mild" sickle cell patient that had long been associated with the disease in Dakar. Within the ASD, sickle cell life became articulated through long-ignored experiences and a new, in-tensely graphic form of suffering. Both led to the ASD's unequivocal demand that the state subsidize a portion of medical costs for this chronic disorder, which became the first explicit politic of the group. Limping, and often emaci-ated, these "severe SS sicklers" no doubt anchored the image of sickle cell in the public mind as a cause neglected when they appeared in television spots. It was not a conscious effort by Magueye to garner support by featuring those most deformed by the disease, however. The desperate sicklers put themselves before the cameras because they had finally found a medium through which to access the state. As members of the ASD, but also as individuals, each wrote letters to Madame Wade, to "plead" that she find the means to secure their surgeries. Through their visibility, they also publicly made their own plea to the larger society to assure that sickle cell would have a place in the articulation of local, official public health problems.

The ASD was capable of airing multiple messages, however, and the range of sickle cell debilitation, including health, was also inserted at every turn. Magueye and Touty had their own politic, as the group's leaders, that sicklers were not to be stigmatized, seen as unduly weak, incapable of marriage, and necessarily prone to die young. Magueye was known for his age, now approaching his thirties. For him his survival achievement served as "proof that others could live life to adulthood and pursue their goals." This overture was both a move to encourage parents to enroll their children in school, despite the often-cited concern that their education would amount to scarce resources poorly invested, and an affront to all of those Dakarois who took it upon themselves to make early prognoses for his ASD family members.

Just before the November 2006 OILD congress in Dakar, the *Association Sénégalaise de lutte Contre la Drépanocytose* boasted seven hundred members.[10] They had also started satellite groups in Richard-Toll (in the North of the country), in Kaolack (in the center), and in Ziguinchor (in the South).

■ **The National Program**

The personal stories that gave life to sickle cell on the airwaves in Dakar were surely also being heard by government higher-ups who in 2005 decided to create a budgetary line for a national program. Yet, as most of my fieldwork took place before the enrollment of Madame Wade in the OILD, I saw firsthand that it was not ignorance of the issues that accounted for the sickle cell void at the health ministry. Many people I met who worked for the government knew about the plight of sicklers and its utter absence as a public health priority. They, unlike Mme Wade, were not hearing of sickle cell for the first time in the 2000s. When I first visited the reading room of the WHO Dakar office, in 2000, which is partnered with the Ministry of Health, I found not one brochure, report, or printed material of any kind mentioning the disease. The librarian readily admitted that the void was strange, given that the majority of publications that affect the Senegalese population were deposited there. Could it really be that there were not any? He then went on to tell me about actual cases of sickle cell in his family. Similarly, the principal archivist of the National Archives was befuddled when together we could not find historical documents pertaining to the disease. He too could relate instances of people he knew who were affected. As one *conseiller technique* to the health minister would tell me in 2006 regarding the sudden public visibility of the problem, "When it interested Mme Wade, it interested us!"

The government of Senegal's first announced budgetary line for sickle cell anemia, of 42 million *cfa* [~US$95 thousand], was in response to research-physicians' drafted action plan to educate doctors and to set up the most minimal types of laboratory facilities in cities and towns outside of Dakar. Dr. Diagne primarily authored the project proposal, in which he also envisaged working with the ASD to tour regional high schools, to field questions, and to aid in the spread of sickle cell awareness on a broad "population" level. For their part, he and other specialists would focus on training the medical corps in *les régions*. The RFLD model was fully integrated into his imagined execution of the program. Diagne had only a few months to ponder this particular dispensation of the funds, however. As the series of government bodies required to vote on the budget approved the line in February of 2006, with the funds said to become available in May, the entire budget was then diverted away from Diagne's plan to finance the establishment of an office (*secrétariat*) for the Dakar 2006 OILD Congress. In a matter of days, it seemed, the funds morphed into four computers, a photocopier, two telephones, and their billed *unités* for calls, monthly cell phone calling cards for the organizing staff, gas for the two hired secretaries to be chauffeured to the ministry, paper reams, and notebooks. Diagne and the ASD were assured that some of the "materials" could be used for the national program once the conference was over and that this expenditure was an investment of sorts. Still, their basic needs, such as their own office in which to place their new "investments," have yet to be met.

The ASD leadership, namely Magueye and Touty, were initially disappointed that the plans for the national program would now be on hold, "sacrificed," as they initially saw it, for the conference preparation. They had been to the Cotonou OILD congress in 2004, and in 2005, they went to *les Premiers états généraux* in Brazzaville, which repeated some of the same elements as the OILD larger meetings. Magueye worried that their precious lost funds were now being used to finance a "scientific exchange" that might not have direct benefits for the many Senegalese in need of physicians who could be trained and educated on the issues most crucial to their disease. He imagined that Diagne's plan, "to go to the population in the rural areas," would be more effective than any notion that they might all flock to Dakar to learn all that they would need to know by listening to conference presentations on how to best treat the disease elsewhere (as many of the presentations would be about care in Europe).

Allowed to still possess and sometimes express their reservations, both Magueye and Touty were quickly brought into the ministry's planning. Touty, who was trained as a secretary, but was unemployed, was hired temporarily for the conference. The ASD was also promised resources to directly involve its members and promote its mission: such as a budget to carry out an awareness campaign before the conference. Still, throughout the last phases of intensive planning, Magueye, disillusioned at the pomp and unimaginable sums that were being invested in the conference through the OILD, wondered if this was the best use of his time. He, as the ASD president, was on the conference planning committee's smaller board. After several of their meetings held at the Health Ministry, he left feeling dejected. As I ran into him on the *route de Oukam* leaving the ministry one afternoon, he complained, "I'm torn on whether this is about helping us, or not. The association has so much work to do, and our resources have been diverted for this meeting that might easily forget the population itself." The conference was planned at the five-star resort hotel, *le Méridien President*, located in the ultra-rich *les almadies* suburb. It would be held in the wealthiest and one of the most remote areas of Dakar (both distance-wise and in terms of economic access) as concerned most Senegalese, sicklers or not. The planning sessions took place at the glossy new Health Ministry that was recently built in Fann, another wealthy neighborhood where many foreign embassies are tucked away in between large villas. The new ministry building was financed by the World Bank and USAID, and as the conference date drew closer, certain logistical meetings were held at the *Méridien*.

Magueye would leave these spaces that bespoke global power and the capacity of money, as these were arguably two of Dakar's most obvious symbols of outside wealth (the *Méridien* was built with funds from Saudi Arabia), and return to his small rented room that contained his life's belongings in an eight-by-ten-foot space. Every paper he had ever signed his name to, his medical analyses, his high school notebooks and reports, all of the medications he had accumulated "here and there" for various conditions that he never took, or only partially completed once he felt better, were stored in a locked wardrobe. These ranged from penicillin for an abscess to various analgesics to the VK500 from "Dr. Fagla" in Cotonou. In the heat of the rainy season, he had only a small desk fan to break the still air. He imagined one day buying a larger one, but joked that his "*ventilo célibataire*" (bachelor's fan) would have to do for now. Dr. Saliou Diop would address him as the honorable "*pauvre président*" (impoverished president). Both men would laugh at the absurdity of the couplet. It was a way to soften the stark display of so much wealth surrounding the meetings as it contrasted with the daily reality of the local sick. The awareness day, however, would be held in a *quartier populaire*, a "people's neighborhood," near *Colobane* where Magueye had spent part of his teen years.

Dr. Diagne held a more optimistic and, at base, diplomatic view of the event and did his part to keep all parties on board to make the meeting a success. They were all now "hosting the meeting," he counseled. Soon, a certain pride, a notion that Senegal could do it "better than Benin," began to circulate as a rallying point around an initially upsetting redirection of funds. As the state-appointed *point focal*, Diagne also had a broader vision for the impact that the conference would have not only on the public but also on the

powers that be. Diagne, like Magueye, was also thinking about the population. For him, however, the strategy to advance sickle cell public knowledge
had to do with securing the media's attention, getting as many people as
possible at the Health Ministry involved in making the disease one of their
talking points, and engaging the many specialists of medicine who could
intervene in the multiple problems presented by this multisystem disorder
(from hematology to pediatrics to surgery to optometry). His goal was to
amass human resources and to create a sustained state interest—even at the
level of the president of the Republic himself. Only acts like these would
guarantee the National Program a future. Initially, Diagne seemed to trust
quite willingly, despite the fact that his "comrades" in the ASD skeptically
observed how the events were unfolding.

■ **The Promise**

In late 2004 Ebakisse Badassou made a special trip to Dakar. Diagne was
invited by the OILD president to accompany her to Brussels for a meeting
with representatives of UNESCO, the UN, and the WHO with the aim of establishing sickle cell as a public health priority globally. If these international
organizations would back the cause, funds to states to implement programs
locally would also follow. Diagne, Madame Wade, and a few other interested
parties from UN member states, would join the OILD president to make their
case. As Diagne was preparing his trip to Europe, Ebakisse Badassou flew
south in order to make the voyage with her Senegalese partners. Later it became clear that her business in Senegal also entailed a meeting with President
Abdoulaye Wade. Diagne was also invited to meet his president and to inform
him of the state of sickle cell care and the present needs in his own backyard.
Ebakisse Badassou's thinking was that before asking for support and funds in
Europe, they needed a promise from African heads of state, and who better
than President Wade, a successful opposition leader. According to Diagne,
Mr. Wade told him that before the First Lady's engagement with the disease,
he, like her, had never heard of it. Wade was a lawyer by training and had
spent the majority of his life battling the Socialist Party. Now in his eighties,
he was steeped in politics more than ever with little time for much else beyond
his knowledge base. This was not "his domain." He gave a similar disclaimer
to the public at the opening ceremony of the 2006 OILD conference, over
which he "presided."

According to Diagne, the Senegalese president made his two visitors a
promise that day. It was a promise that, for them, signified a crucial step in the
progression of sickle cell care that would be based in Dakar, but that would
benefit sicklers throughout the region. He promised them 200 million *cfa*
(~US$453 thousand) for a sickle cell disease reference center. The idea of such

a center was to establish a place where any and all testing could be performed, while special needs would be addressed (such as surgeries and transfusions) on an incident-by-incident basis. Physicians could also send samples to be analyzed in Dakar, while their patients could still receive care in their home regions rather than making the long and often arduous journey to the capital. Eventually, the center would also be able to conduct neonatal screening to monitor sicklers from birth to assure their extended lifetime care. Again, follow-up and surveillance were the most effective of all technologies in Diagne's view. This *centre de référence*, Diagne imagined, would both further centralize certain aspects of care and expand the "impact" that Dakar's specialists could make for the whole region. In a conversation where he enumerated for me the many things he hoped for the National Program, Diagne began with neonatal testing to emphasize the extent to which the terrain was in need, technologically and organizationally. Yet the first step in achieving this crucial testing episode in the lives of young sicklers, for Diagne, would be the establishment of a dependable central testing site, which would also coordinate care and promote research. He then circuitously ended up where he started, at the idea of the reference center. The circle of his logic clearly demonstrates his belief that good care only follows from early diagnosis—which at its earliest means neonatal testing.

> One major prerequisite that needs to be in place before we can do neonatal testing is to have a sickle cell reference center. It is important that not just anyone performs testing in any old way, with various kinds of materials and tools that give false positives or false negatives, etc. . . . We need a trustworthy system in place. To have reliability in a country such as ours, we will need a reference center that will guarantee quality control—that a sample from Tambacounda[11] can arrive in Dakar and will be guaranteed a correct reading—[For this] Senegal has to have a reference center. In our conception of the center, there are three aspects. One is about care . . . In fact the *centre* would serve as the central node for the region to work through a network [based in Dakar]. All of the doctors trained in the rural regions would have a way into specialized care located here. [He explains the hypothetical case of someone in Tambacounda who develops necrosis of the hip and needs surgery]. . . . If there are no specialists who know the proper course of action there, then the local doctor can decide: "I will send this case to the Dakar reference center so that they can assess the situation and indicate what needs to be done. . . . " In any case, those who are better positioned in terms of means, technology, experience, etc., can assess the situation, recommend the treatment and help in resolving the issue. . . .Thus, the care aspect would be about taking charge of difficult cases from wherever they come throughout the country. . . . The second aspect is that of research. . . . we can begin to centralize our

data and analyze what in fact are the characteristics of the disease in Senegal, clinically, epidemiologically, biologically. . . . That will have an enormous impact on sickle cell in Senegal nationally. . . . Then there is an aspect, within the axis of research—actually, I'm not sure if it should be in research or care, but this concerns neonatal testing. Locally, there has to be a center that *coordinates* and *manages* this effort. There has to be a center for neonatal testing where the coordination of the maternity wards takes place, a site where knowledge about who runs each ward and who our interlocutors are at each site—we will need to know the same things for *les régions*, who is in maternity in Tambacounda? Who is dealing with the blood draws, etc? . . . As we wait for care and training to happen throughout the country, at the very least we need a laboratory in place that does nothing but neonatal testing, a central structure of this sort.

Touty joked that the plan for a center was "Diagne's baby." We were all waiting for the diagnosis indicating whether or not it would actually thrive. At the meeting with Ebakisse Badassou and President Wade, Diagne was promised a lifeline through a commitment of funds offered by the president himself. The promise would later be reiterated by Madame Wade who spoke to an amphitheatre peopled with global sickle cell specialists and groups of patients at the Brazzaville meeting in June of 2005. In Dakar, several health ministry technicians, and eventually even the then minister himself, repeated the plan to Diagne in private. One went as far as to show the hopeful doctor the piece of land, an empty grassy plot between the Fann hospital complex and the glossy new ministry, where the center would be built. He could be nothing but optimistic.

ID: So for the reference center, it's a story that concerns Edwidge [Ebakisse Badassou]. The president of the Republic had us over. He said "Oh yes, when Madame Wade spoke to me about this issue, I decided to authorize that 200 million francs be allotted in 2005—no 100 million in 2005 and 100 million in 2006—in order to finance a feasibility study and get the architectural plans underway to build a sickle cell *centre de référence*. . . . "

Incidentally, a couple of days before, we had a meeting at the Ministry of Foreign Affairs with various ambassadors to discuss the launch of the congress, now this was in 2005. Issa Mbaye Samb, who was then the Health Minister, came . . . and in his speech he made an announcement. He said I am taking advantage of this *rencontre* to inform you that the Senegalese state has decided to earmark 200 million *cfa* francs for a sickle cell center. It corresponded exactly with what Wade told us a day or two later. I was even shown a budgetary line at the ministry. Taiwan had made a donation to the state for health in Senegal. Each year they finance things. So, the administration had taken a portion of the Taiwan funds for the center in 2005 and 2006. This is what was planned.

DF: So, what happened?

ID: At the end of 2005, or the beginning of 2006 [his voice tapers], I happened to be at the Health Ministry and Dr. Noba who is in charge of all of these types of things said "Diagne, I need to see you. . . . Yesterday we decided that with all of the problems with the farmers in the interior regions that the funds that were earmarked for sickle cell are going to now be diverted to the agricultural campaign [silence] . . . And we'll see if we can't find some other means for . . . . " [He cuts the story there.] . . . You see?

DF: Why, because of protests by those in the agricultural sector?

ID: No, not in particular [voice tapers off] . . . It was just politics . . .

DF: . . . Have you brought it up again with Madame Wade?

ID: We talk all the time.

DF: But about this particular project, and the fact that it was promised, sunk, and that there were other "priorities"?

ID: [Shaking his head] . . .

DF: Have you spoken with her frankly?

ID: Last year, the *États généraux de la drépanocytose* was in June of 2005, I think. In Madame Wade's very own speech she announced to everyone that Senegal had committed to building a *centre de référence* and that she had already reserved 200 million *cfa* for the project . . . Now, we are, in fact, back at square one . . . she is fully aware of the need.

In the subsequent years, and especially during the 2007 presidential campaign when Abdoulaye Wade was seeking reelection, it came to light that the majority of the Taiwan funds had been "siphoned off," or could not be traced to a paper trail. There was no accounting for a significant portion of the funds (totaling US$15 million) and a massive corruption scandal followed (Ndiaye 2006). Diagne was incensed and defeated all at once.

During this same period, in 2006, thousands of Diagne's countrymen were also defeated by less personalized state promises that were broken. Despite Wade's 2000 campaign pledge to put the youth to work, to give them a future and a sense of purpose, unemployment rates remained high, and the only way that most families survived was to have a son, husband, brother, or kin of some sort living abroad and sending remittances home. When Abdoulaye Wade came to power, largely through the most destitute classes, he promised them a government overhaul. His opposition party's slogan was, in fact, "change!" (*soppi!*). Six years later as the economy worsened many began filling their small fishing boats, not fit for the high seas, with men and boys who dreamt that if they made it in their precarious *pirogues* (canoes) to Europe then they might in fact know a life of change. They anticipated actually partaking in, and benefiting from, the global order that they increasingly confronted through media, donor aid, and their own aspirations for a better life beyond Senegal. This was imagined to be a life beyond the confines of southern borders that seemed to continuously push them to the bottom of the world.

Economic and Health Futures amid Hope and Despair

In 2006 the global economy had already begun its downward spiral. When the fibers of the U.S. housing market began to give, a cascade of bankruptcies of large financial institutions in the United States and Europe followed. Before the huge losses, very early on, the flow of money gradually began to go from housing to commodities, namely oil, resulting in a commodity price bubble that drove up petrol prices from US$35 a barrel in early 2006 to US$140 in 2008. From the beginning, the small ripples that would culminate in the global crisis of 2007–2009 were already making large waves in the daily lives of people in Senegal. Hours-long blackouts became the norm in 2006 due to the increased costs of energy, which the government could not afford, while the surging price of food, namely rice, was felt by nearly every Senegalese family I encountered. Throughout my years in Dakar, I would occasionally be asked by a mother in need if I could help her buy medications, and sometimes school supplies, for her sickler child. In 2006, I would be asked for the first time to help someone buy a sack of rice. What would become the global economic crisis of the 2000s was a new wrinkle in the longer economic crisis that most Senegalese had been living since the 1994 devaluation of the *cfa* franc. Now many people's balancing act of forcing ends to meet became a much more precarious walk of the tightrope.

During this same period, thousands of Senegalese villagers on the Atlantic coast were discovering that their livelihoods of fishing were no longer sustainable. Chinese, Japanese, and European fishing companies, who for years used massive trawlers, dramatically overfished the Senegalese waters, gradually putting many locals out of work. In 2006, West Africa, but Senegal in particular, saw an unprecedented spike in illegal attempts to migrate to Europe, via the Mauritanian waters, in overstuffed fishing boats. As survivors proclaimed, their boats were their only resource now that there were few fish to be had. If they could not generate revenue by filling them with fish, then they would fill them with the many able-bodied men who were now languishing from lack of work at sea, as well as with other economic migrants seeking a passage to Europe. Their destination was Spain.

2006 saw record numbers of Africans arriving to the Canary Islands, 31,678 according to the Spanish Ministry of the Interior (Statewatch 2008), nearly six times the number of people who arrived in 2005, and far more than any other previous year (Kitamura 2007). It is estimated that of the 31, 678, nearly 6,000 people either went missing or died as these *pirogues* ("cayucos" in Spanish), often capsized. Nonetheless people continued to take the risk to emigrate, saying, "*Barça* (Barcelona) or *Barsax* (Wolof for "the hereafter"). It would be Barcelona or death. In 2007, both Spain and the European Union established several initiatives (namely Frontex and its surveillance programs of Hera I, II, and III) to expand international relations with African states on immigration control and to patrol the waters both in Africa and Europe. With increased EU attention to the matter, the numbers of illegal migrants who attempted and reached the Canary Islands by boat fell in 2007, but still a surprising 12, 478 made it (Statewatch 2008). Many of these desperate émigrés were Senegalese (Kitamura 2007).[1]

In September of 2006, as the Senegalese state was preparing for its first international congress on sickle cell, the media covered the hopeful moment for sicklers amid a more general sense of state and public crisis because of daily reports of Senegalese emigrants dying in their boats. In what became a source of shame for many, international news organizations began extensive coverage of dehydrated, defeated, and demoralized Senegalese migrants who had barely arrived alive to the Canary Islands. Hundreds were arrested by the day. Despite their attempts to fool authorities by refusing to speak their mother tongues, so that they could avoid identifying their country of origin and forestall repatriation, it was they who were tricked in the end. The joke was on them when they agreed to board planes, believing officials who said that they were being flown by the Spanish state to work in Europe, all the while they were in the process of being flown over the Sahara back to Senegal. Between early September and mid-October of 2006, nearly four thousand defeated Senegalese came home this way. A general feeling of global rejection and frustration with their hopes for the future sparked a national conversation about global interdependence, and how the government needed to do more, while Europe and richer countries should finally offer real solutions to their "partners" in the South. After much diplomacy, in December of 2007, Spanish Prime Minister Luis Rodriguez Zapatero promised that over the following two years, four thousand Senegalese would be allowed to work temporarily in Spain. Earlier, in 2006, a promise of the equivalent of US$27 million was made to Senegal by Spain to create work opportunities and to fund job training. Nonetheless the public, and especially the men who had risked their lives, did not trust their government to apply the aid to help them (Kitamura 2007).

This was the general climate to which I returned in early September of 2006, when I found Dr. Diagne, Magueye, and other members of the ASD staked out in a borrowed conference room at the newly constructed Ministry

of Health complex. Diagne, Magueye and Touty Niang of the ASD were discussing the pre-conference "sickle cell awareness" day. It was to be held in *la
Place de l'obélisque*, a local square, at the intersection of the *quartiers populaires* of Colabane and Fass. The ASD would set up information stands so that
the population could talk with sicklers themselves about the disease, while
learning about their own possible risks. Staff from the CNTS would prick
people on site and give them their Emmel test results, which would tell them
only whether or not they possessed the sickle hemoglobin protein. Further
electrophoretic testing would be required to distinguish sickle cell disease
from trait.

On the day of the actual event, 510 people presented for testing, and 202
tested positive for hemoglobin S. Saliou Diop of the CNTS figured that the
sample was biased. "People who came to the awareness day were already somehow thinking that they were affected by sickle cell," he reasoned. "We can't take
these figures at face value. Half of the Senegalese population is not affected."
He then added, "This *has* to be a selection bias." But for those few hundred and
the many others who passed through the ASD's educational displays, a strange
hope mixed with uncertainty. For some, long suspicions were confirmed. Now,
potentially sick, they were nonetheless part of a larger social movement, which
seemed to mushroom overnight in what appeared to be an issue of stately importance. Surely they would not be left uncared for.

Madame Wade, accompanied by the First Ladies of Congo, Mali, and
Benin, as well as by several government officials, came to the ASD's educational stand to be briefed by Magueye and other members about the nature
of the disease, its transmission, as well as what sickle cell actually meant for
them personally. The news media, both local and international, flocked the
stand while Magueye directed the First Ladies' attention to the various graph-
ics, translating their meaning with his very presence as an SS sickler. Despite
the obvious excitement of having such attention to their disorder, people
could not help but feel hope mixed with skepticism. *Radio France International's* Claire Hédon soon began broadcasting her renowned program, *Pri-
orité santé*, in real time to the French-speaking world as she interviewed Dr.
Ibrahima Diagne and Dr. Saliou Diop, along with French specialist Dr. Galactéros about the disease. A few meters away, local media continued to track the
every movement of the African First Ladies. The square was crammed full of
people, mostly women and children. They were all taking in new information,
as well as a new public health message. The events of the day should have been
spread out over a much longer period so that all that was said might sink in.
Everyone was exhausted by the end of it, especially Magueye who kept half-
joking to me that he was "going to have a crisis." The opening ceremony for
the congress was the following day, however. The prospect of the event, which
he critically needed to assess, kept him going.

Several months later, in March of 2007, Magueye told me that he had been
keeping a recorded diary during the time of the congress, including the day

of awareness. Indeed, too much was happening too fast and he needed to find a way to reflect, to record, to retain what he was witnessing and feeling. One of the French journalists let him borrow her digital recorder and he would talk into it, usually late at night, when he could not sleep because the buzz of the day's events kept rattling in his mind. He lost the battle in quieting his thoughts that would play over and over, prompting him to comment, as if he were still being interviewed by the press. We talked about his reactions to the events, and his ongoing sense that he was waiting for actions to follow the state's words of now taking the disease seriously. Magueye gave me the recordings to add to my recorded conversations with him, all the while warning me that they "might get [him] in trouble." He then laughed and reasoned, "Who cares?" (*peu importe*), and that the recordings contained "the truth." He later burned me a CD with fifteen tracks of his thoughts, some as short as twenty-five seconds, others as long as twenty minutes. They were mostly calm, poetic ruminations on his frustrations with his encounter with the state, with the promises offered during the congress, and with his general feelings of being totally divided on his hope for the future of his disease.

■ Productive and Not-So-Productive Encounters

At the end of her book on the generative global encounters she calls "frictions," Anna Tsing undertakes a meditation on uncertain global futures. She writes: "Since we don't know how things will turn out, it's worth attending to states of emergence—and emergency. Here hope and despair huddle together, sometimes dependent on the same technologies" (2005, 269). In their encounters with the global, members of the ASD, as well as specialists on the disease, saw the invisibility of sickle cell as a kind of public knowledge crisis, or emergency, while the state's attention to it marked an emergence of possible recognition and care. Yet in their frictions with a globalizing awareness effort—in the form of the OILD's politic of bringing together researchers, state actors, and patients from the global North and South in one setting for the third time for the 2006 Dakar event—the ASD gained visibility and enlisted state promises of attention, as did local sickle cell specialists like Diagne, that would not be met anytime soon. In the years to follow, actually even before the conference was over, their hope mixed with despair. Technologies of state-led "awareness" threatened to make a mockery out of sicklers' plights, if, once aware, the state simply politicized another "need" on the ground for donor entities to ponder, while doing little to prioritize sickle cell in the here and now. The use-value of such promises was incredibly short-lived.

On the evening of November 21, 2006, the day preceding the Dakar congress, when the ASD informed the public of their disease at *la Place de l'obélisque*, Magueye recorded the following thoughts shortly after 3:00 a.m.:

Deep down I'm worried—worried for what? Instead, I should be happy. I received a *great* lady today, a great lady surrounded by her entourage. But unfortunately, what I feel is sadness, deep sadness because I saw something in her, something *else* in her. I didn't only see these officials come and visit our stands, come to inform themselves of our condition, but rather I sensed that these were officials who wanted to show something off—to show that they were part of what we were doing. . . . They wanted to show that they got it, that they were on the way to conquering this thing. Unfortunately, they remain on the outside of the real issues. I'd even go so far as to say that they understood nothing [*ils n'ont rien compris*]. They didn't belong there. It's not simply about coming and taking a tour of our lives, listening to things that have already been said, or about being encircled by the media. No it's not that. It's not about being seen on television to speak of the illness. No. It's not about that. I was deeply disappointed somewhere inside—disappointed to see a future, which I'm sure belongs to no one but me. These officials who thought that they held the monopoly on this mobilization don't realize that it's not merely a mobilization. It's an ensemble of our pains, a collection of dreams.

Much of what I have described in this book is about people who are committed to getting by with sickle cell anemia and who often make-do within larger networks of kin and biosocial relationships of care—both because of and despite economic scarcity in their lives and within Senegal's health care infrastructure. Yet as of 2006, it became clear that hope for government help set up specialists and patients for frictions with the state. Mme Wade's aspiration to take sickle cell global, to the UN, was a strategy of eventually dealing with the local problem once international partnerships could be secured. It is not that ASD members and specialists in the medical corps did not also want UN–level attention, they did. The problem was that they simultaneously expected their state to show up, to take cognizance of the publics they had brought into view, and, most importantly, to then make good on promises to engage the problems of these publics, rather than trucking in symbolic gestures of good intentions that were devoid of consummate action. When government promises were dashed almost as soon as they were articulated, people felt defeated and angered. When vowed declaration after vowed declaration proved vacant, it was as if the "ensemble of pains and the collective dream" of sickle cell itself went into crisis. In this anger, which I palpably felt in conversations with members of the ASD after the conference and in the months to follow, the disease itself became more severe.

Already in September of 2006, I began to witness this shift. It took shape against a general sense of desperation in the larger society, which was also tied to discourses of dissatisfaction with the opposition government of Abdoulaye Wade. "Crisis" and "severity" were terms that were echoed in the back-and-forth of the ASD members' exchanges on the disease as they wondered about government subsidies for sickle cell health care (*une prise en charge*). At one ASD meeting, I witnessed women, and men, with sickle cell trait complain of pains, both physical and emotional, that were somehow linked to ideas of their expectation for state intervention. For instance, a young woman reported being ridiculed at the CNTS. She was not only told that she was "not sick" but was also informed that she and "others like her were making the work of the CNTS difficult because doctors were increasingly overwhelmed with 'real sicklers' ever since Mme Wade became involved in awareness." On a different issue, a young man with HbSS had reported coming all the way from the city of Kaolack, a day trip for him, since he wanted to start a chapter of the ASD there to get around the eternal problem of all care and knowledge on sickle cell being centralized in Dakar. Others echoed this sentiment and spoke of the seriousness of the strain that continued state centralization was causing them (a problem that government funding and political will could address). One mother, who suffered from HbAS herself, traveled from northern Senegal to bring her eighteen-year-old son who has SS to Dakar for consultations. The boy looked extremely pale and tired. She said that it was because he had been "fighting off a crisis, which the harsh trip in a rickety minibus only aggravated." The distance and the problem of a dearth of specialists in the periphery were adding to the body in crisis.

People took their turns to respond to previous complaints heard, while airing their own. Sicklers who were there for the first time, introduced themselves and told something of their plights. Many peppered their introductions with stories of ill-informed medical personnel and long journeys to Dakar. It was everyday difficulties like these that Dr. Diagne and colleagues' five-year strategic plan sought to address. The plan enumerated what it would cost to implement state-subsidized care for hospitalizations and essential medications, while it also aimed to expand training and equipment to doctors in the hinterlands. As of March 2010, *le plan stratégique* still awaits approval and the official stamp of the government health appointee who oversees noncommunicable diseases.[2] It was these social and bodily issues of "severity," "crisis," and the state's potential role of aiding those in need that the ASD began to reference in larger audiences, where, as of the November congress, state officials themselves were sometimes present.

After November of 2006, Mme Wade scaled back on her work with the OILD and began to concentrate on diffusing a discourse on sickle cell throughout Senegalese society through her NGO, *Association éducation santé*. Because of her clout, the ASD was invited several times to speak on radio, and periodically on television. On most occasions they brought up the need for government subsidies for surgical interventions for the "severe" cases that required costly care. Rhetorically, these more severe cases now merited a minimum baseline investment on the part of the state, since the cost of such surgeries were well beyond the reach of most Senegalese. The ASD cited cases of acute handicap in addition to making the obvious plea for vaccines, anti-inflammatory drugs, painkillers, and malaria prophylaxis more generally. Most importantly they wanted hospitalizations covered. In other words, in the aftermath of the First Lady's adoption of sickle cell as one of the concerns of her NGO, people started to expect real action on the part of Mme Wade and her husband's regime. The expected results have been extremely slow to materialize to the extent that they have.

In 2008 and 2009, the First Lady and ASD members, accompanied by Dr. Diagne, made a number of visits to various ministries in an effort to raise awareness for the disease. During these years the principal cultural work that specialists were able to achieve was in fact educating government ministers about sickle cell. The primary tool used was a UNESCO-Dakar financed film of a touching Senegalese drama interspersed with documentary footage about the difficult social and economic plights of patients, called *la Bonne Décision* (The Right Decision). Now with a powerful awareness technology in hand, Diagne and a small group of patient advocates presented their case to sections of government as varied as the Ministry of Health and Prevention, the Ministry of Education, the Ministry of Youth (*de la Jeunesse*), the Ministry of Sport (*Ministère des Sports*), and also less obvious ones, such as the Ministry of Transportation (*Transports Terrestres*). Their efforts spawned ripple effects, such as a follow-up plan on the part of the *Ministre de la Jeunesse* to organize summer camp and youth scouts (*vacances citoyens*) education themes around sickle cell in 2009. The transportation minister, strangely enough, held a sickle cell fund-raising event for "Madame Wade's cause." (Yet, according to those present at the ceremonial public "gifting," only five million [~US$11,000] of what they counted to be roughly forty-seven million *cfa* [~US$98 thousand] raised, was given to the ASD for education in the end).

Viviane Wade also used requests that others made of her to speak at celebratory events, where "thought leaders" on women's issues might be gathered, to make the same plea. In this way she reached several thousand of the country's female entrepreneurs by speaking to the associations of women in microfinance and to female teachers. These events were sponsored by still other government ministries, such as the Ministry of Women's Entrepreneurship and Micro-finance (*Ministère de l'entreprenariat féminin et de la micro-finance*), The Ministry of Social Action and National Solidarity (*Ministère de l'action sociale et de la solidarité nationale*) and the Ministry of Family, Women's Groups and Early Childhood (*Ministère de la famille, des groupements féminins et de la petite enfance.*) All of these state ministers were in attendance when Vivian Wade and the ASD's governing body attended the twentieth anniversary of the micro credit agency *Crédit Mutuel du Sénégal* (CMS).

People would later report to Touty Niang that they had seen *la Bonne Décision* in the CMS waiting room. Some women became so engrossed that they forfeited their turn in the queue in order to follow the film's narrative. In the story a young, modern, beautiful woman with HbAS is about to marry a successful, attractive man, who does not know his HbAS status, and who initially refuses to get tested. The film ends with the man finally agreeing to test, and coming to terms with the importance of preemptive screening. The film seamlessly pulls the reality of sicklers in Senegal into the fictional content of the drama of the young woman and her fiancé as an effective sympathizing mechanism in practice. The woman is supposedly a journalist, whose boss assigns her to do a story on sickle cell. He is secretly harboring his own concealed disease, as he gives her the president of the sickle cell association's telephone number. She is to go to an ASD meeting and record it for state television. She reluctantly accepts the assignment and is conflicted since she wonders how to confront the pain of sickle cell in her reportage when she is already personally overwhelmed with trying to convince her fiancé to simply take the test. We, the audience, feel that she does not want to know what people suffering with the disease confront. Then, in a narrative condensation of life and fiction, the script has the woman interview real people with the disease in Dakar. They speak about their pain, about medical negligence of sickle cell broadly, about the economic difficulties that people, especially women with sick children, face. By far the most engrossing narrative came from a highly intelligent young preteen girl who described the lack of social understanding that she experienced at every turn, from neighbors, from friends, and from teachers who publicly ridiculed her for "pretending," or malingering. She looked young, healthy, endearing, even vibrant, as she confidently invited the state and the public to act on her condition on film. In real life, the young girl died of a sickle cell complication for which she was hospitalized in 2008. Her outwardly "mild" looking disease had "severe" repercussions.

Shortly thereafter, the ASD made one of its highest profile "visits" with Mme Wade to Senegal's National Assembly. Modeled after the French system, Senegal has a bicameral Parliament comprised of the Senate (100 seats) and the National Assembly (150 seats). In conversation with the First Lady, the president of the National Assembly, Mr. Mamadou Seck, decided on a particular strategy of awareness—one that focused on government leaders as points of information diffusion and as sickle cell spokespersons. This meant that rather than physically going to the population itself, in Mme Wade's mind, the best strategy would be to go to, and by extension through, legislators and politicians. For her, the parliamentarians (députés) both constituted a representative link with the public and were the very people who both knew the laws and, ostensibly, could make new ones (Mme Wade's strategy was also published in the state newspaper le Soleil [see Niang 2009). Her hope was that sickle cell awareness information would pass through a "parliamentary caravan" that would make its way through the families of these state leaders to their children and simultaneously to their constituencies and the public at large.

This was a curious assessment of the National Assembly's societal placement and power, however. As noted by key political scientists of the country, the patrimonial politics and personalization of power that has marked the office of the presidency since independence has worsened with Mme Wade's husband, who actually weakened the legislature despite campaign promises to the contrary (Beck 2008, 225; Gellar 2005, 158–59). Sheldon Gellar describes the current situation as one where "Most Senegalese deputies have little attachment to the National Assembly as an institution and have dedicated more time and energy to increasing their perks—salaries, vehicles, and other benefits." Gellar argues that the National Assembly remains "a weak institution with poor attendance and little will and capacity to check the powers of the president or to initiate legislation of its own" (2005, 159). Linda Beck reminds us that the "National Assembly's alias in the public mind is *chambre d'applaudissement* (the house of applause)" since it was "a rubber stamp for the laws and budgets proposed by the president, though he frequently legislated by decree" (2008, 55). When I asked people who worked within the National Assembly specifically about this perception, they pointed to recent changes in law, under Wade, that actually increased transparency in his aspirations to court an image of "good governance," especially as concerns the National Assembly. Of course most people of the current government are pro-Wade and are careful with criticism. Nonetheless, they countered my suspicions by pointing to a law that allows the chamber to raise issues with the president and other branches of government, issues which supposedly directly affect the concerns of their representatives. They insisted that this was a novel consideration, and what is more is that these concerns must be heard and discussed. Yet, as concerns the *députés* and their direct relation to and voice for their people regarding disease awareness, this was an innovation that they could not quite explain beyond the image and power of Mme Wade and her interest in it. Was indeed the National Assembly so receptive to sickle cell, which the Health Ministry has yet to really fund, as a "favor" of sorts to their head of state's spouse? I put the question to Seck indirectly. "Since when," I asked, "have the parliamentarians themselves gotten into the business of canvassing as disease activists?" What exactly was going on here? He admitted it was rare but diplomatically said that after Mme Wade's visit, the chamber recognized the disease's importance.

In a separate interview with the second vice president of the National Assembly, and former minister of health, Abdou Fall, he offered a more blunt interpretation of the caravan idea:

> Don't kid yourself [*il ne faut pas se faire des illusions*], the Assembly cannot—the Assembly, simply gives visibility to an issue. Now, it is up to others to do the real work. This is the work of the disease associations, it's the work of communications networks, of medical professionals, but it is not the *députés* who will go around raising awareness on the ground—that is not even in the mission of the parliamentarians in any case. They can and do implicate themselves to launch issues. As

political leaders, they can replicate the work that our leaders, President Wade and Madame Wade, are doing for the disease at the national level but on the local level—on the condition that there are people to do the work, the disease associations, etc, on the ground. But to wake up and say, "*voilà*, let's tour the whole of Senegal for sickle cell." No *député* will do this" [*personne le fera*].

In actually citing President Wade and Mme Wade as state leaders who had taken on sickle cell within the state, this was the first time that a politician admitted to me an explicit collapse between the First Lady's NGO and her state role. Fall also made it clear that the branch of government called the National Assembly was comprised of politicians, not disease advocates.

Given this power setup, it is plausible that parliamentarians could be enlisted to speak about a disease on which they had just been briefed, and support, even draft, legislation on the issues. In response to Mme Wade's call for the caravan, the *Soleil* reported that: "Despite a charged agenda at this time ... the parliamentarians made a point to reply *en masse* to Vivian Wade's call" (Niang 2009).

In recent years Touty and one of Mme Wade's assistants, who was intimately involved in the planning of the 2006 conference, became very close friends. One day as they were discussing the launch of the caravan over lunch in a government cafeteria they learned that the office of noncommunicable diseases was planning to kick off diabetes and hypertension awareness events by having the parliamentarians themselves tested for these growing afflictions. They then had the same idea for sickle cell: to publicly test the members of parliament would send the crucial message to the population that "everyone should know their sickle cell status," no matter how powerful or powerless. The eventual awareness event took place in a closed setting, with staff and specialists from the CNTS briefing the politicians about the disease in May of 2010. It was followed by another event a month later in June, where Mme Wade, the minister of health and prevention, and the National Assembly announced a new prenuptial-testing law for sickle cell. They also announced the creation of a special commission that would draw political actors from the Senegalese Senate and the National Assembly to investigate the legal matters related to such a policy, and to discuss anti-discrimination precautions as well. These would constitute the state's actions for now. The media attention that followed both events featured the work of Mme Wade and lauded the attention she had given the "neglected" disorder. The press spoke hardly at all about the issues that concerned patients and doctors. Diagne and others still continue to fight for subsidized care and a *centre de référence*.

Considering the above, what can we make of Mme Wade's ceremonial awareness strategy, especially if almost every concrete promise (a sickle cell reference center, medical social security to cover urgent costs) that the state has made to Diagne, the ASD, and the public at large on sickle cell has gone unrealized? Might her reasoning be that ample discourse and attention would serve as productive bases for social capital, given local conditions of scarcity, or at least, of more "pressing priorities"? To whom might the population turn if the government instituted testing before marriage for a disease that is framed as costly and chronic, often invisible in carriers, which nonetheless may affect their unborn children? Would everyday Senegalese be able to react to their government leaders and ask for help, armed with new awareness and a sort of guarantee of the First Lady's interest in them? In his interview with me, the president of the National Assembly admitted that, with the new law on prevention, rather than care, they are raising a host of ethical questions, as well as increasing the need for even more education, and that the issue was sensitive (*délicat*).

During these years I noticed that both members of the ASD and political actors in the government felt the need to put a *cfa* amount to the disease to rationalize demands. The ASD wanted subsidies; therefore they needed to detail the costs of maintaining a healthy life lived with sickle cell (which included the appropriate medical controls, check-ups, medications, hospitalizations). They calculated 500,000 *cfa* a year [~US$1,000], in a context where the per capita total expenditure on health is ~22,000 *cfa* a year [~US$54] (WHOGHO 2007c). The state deployed this figure to deflect their responsibility, as Mme Wade publicly stated that the international multilateral institutions would have to take the lead since the Senegalese government could not afford to. Until this happened, the state would advance the cost containment strategy of "prevention" through plans for prenuptial testing.[3]

With this, both the government and the population will find themselves in a hard position. To even actualize the caravan, the deputies would have to find resources in the state's budgetary lines in order to be effective. No matter what the outcome, the population would be faced with strange new duties to fulfill, to stay healthy in the face of this newly articulated state health interest, and potentially to rationalize their reproductive partner choices, with little real knowledge about what it means to "carry" or "possess" sickle cell trait in this setting. On the day of *la Place de l'Obélisque* screening effort, I saw people begin to cry when they got their test results. The busy CNTS staff who took people's ticket numbers in exchange for their results told them that it would "be OK," and that clearly, "since they had not been sick, they did not have the 'mean form'" (*la forme méchante*), or SS. Many people left the event in distress. The feasibility of screening en masse in Senegal is not simply about the costs of testing people and their loved ones. It also entails confronting the social and medical public confusion about sickle cell trait itself, as we saw in chapter 6. Lastly, even as the government is now promising to cover the cost of prenuptial testing, several members of the ASD reminded themselves that sickle cell "state" funds often got rerouted to more pressing problems. If this happened now, the deputies would not be the only state actors to shuffle on the issues.

In 2008, the most promising meeting (*rencontre*) by Dr. Diagne's account, later confirmed for me by Touty and Magueye, was their interaction with the then prime minister of Senegal himself, Cheikh Hadjibou Soumare. On the day of their visit to Soumare's office, Senegal's health minister and several of her staff joined in. To initiate the discussion, Mme Wade showed Soumare and his cabinet the *La Bonne Décision*. Magueye then took the floor and spoke about his life experience with sickle cell anemia. He went into detail about how he struggled as a young boy, especially after his father's death. His disease was not helped by his dire economic situation, but, despite stiff odds, he had lived to thirty-one years of age without so much as a suggestion of aid from the state. All of his care was the result of scraping by—of "making do." As Magueye continued his story, Diagne said that the prime minister was so moved that he shed a tear, and then another, and another. "We realized that he was crying," Diagne told me in disbelief. "It was not the reaction we expected, the whole room continued to act like he was still composed."

Magueye had then recently begun his strict politic of demanding subsidized health care for sicklers whenever he had the opportunity. He told me how he emphasized to his prime minister that people's suffering was felt in terms of what they could not afford, given that even the quarterly consultations at Albert Royer and the CNTS were a burden for most. An actual hospitalization usually meant throwing a family into debt. He drove his point home by saying that most of the sicklers he meets at the CNTS, whose numbers were increasing by the day, were in fact "welfare cases" (*cas sociaux*) but they only garnered minimal benefits through constant negotiation and pleading. This was becoming the general population profile. The health minister then took over the podium and avoided making any concrete promises by saying that she and her cabinet "would reflect on the issues, to see what can be done." Without warning, Soumare interrupted her and declared that enough time had been lost and that no more reflection was needed. He then promised that he would "take on the health care of sicklers—no matter what the cost." The room broke into a blast of applause.

According to Diagne, Soumare excitedly directed specialists to quickly compile a document that would detail costs of basic care as well as more expensive interventions that might be needed on a case-by-case basis. Diagne remembered the "sense of urgency" that his prime minister imposed, pressuring him and his colleagues to work long hours to get the document to him the following week. In a series of meetings, local specialists decided on the essentials, and then calculated the costs of the quarterly consultations, the prices of needed malaria prophylaxis, folic acid, painkillers, the costs of vaccines, the occasional hospitalization in times of crisis, and reserves for the rare events of hip necrosis and other surgeries. The highly conservative total to cover sicklers throughout the whole country amounted to one billion *cfa* a year [~US$2,266,009]. They submitted the overview in April of 2008, elated and hopeful. One can imagine that it was more than a let down when they never heard back. They waited, and inquired, waited, and asked again, but were given standard responses each time that "it would be assessed." At the end of 2009, deflated and frustrated, as a different prime minister took office, the ASD all but gave up hope that "the state" would make good on this public pledge.

I wondered with Diagne about the politics of Minister Soumare's emotion. Could such affective sincerity merely be the type of political maneuvering that Magueye sensed from "the officials" at the ASD's educational stand "taking a tour of their lives"? Or, could the prime minister have been overtaken by a feeling that a responsible state should take care of its sick (sickle cell) children—a trope of family and care that often surfaces in political imaginaries in Africa and elsewhere (Bayart 2005, 173). Yet as political scientist Jean-François Bayart points out, such imaginaries are nourished by ambivalences (often contradictory priorities that can hang together in the same mind), which routinely form the "fuel of political enunciations" (2005, 168). It is this mix of priorities, aspirations, and state (in)capacities that compromise the bonds and duties of familial care and fidelities within the everyday acts of governing. The theater of the state stage compelled various degrees of performance where people tried hard to please Madame Wade. Diagne dubbed this "the Madame Wade effect." For him, it was not that his prime minister was dishonest; rather, Soumare's promise was a political enunciation that—in and of itself—constituted a serious social act. It signified what an accountable state *should* do. By extension, the minister's feckless abandonment of the sickle cell advocates at the foot of his podium crystallized for Diagne and the ASD that, at base, perhaps they had no state.

Touty Niang would, however, later come to Soumare's defense, explaining to me in 2010 that a different prime minister had been appointed by Wade shortly after Soumare made the promise, and that he was sincere in his pledge. The problem, again, was the constant turnover within the government. Touty felt as though she and the ASD, with the help of Drs. Diagne and Diop, were always making inroads with certain officials only to have those officials soon replaced. Touty, unlike some of the others within the ASD or within the CHU care structures, made it clear that, for her, Soumare's open and empty promise was not devoid of intention. Rather, its openness was a structural effect of a wasteful system of human resources that she began to witness first-hand once she herself entered the inner corridors of the state. She was careful not to criticize anyone directly, and in fact was extremely hopeful in the spring of 2010, as she got a post within the National Assembly itself. For her, this National Assembly, under Mamadou Seck, had taken the ASD's and Madame Wade's call-to-attention more seriously than the Health Ministry ever had.

Touty's employment at the Assembly was a result of Mme Wade's office making a targeted gesture of *individualized* state aid. It chose two people to do the work of sickle cell education and to push awareness among politicians and the population. Touty was the first since she was the mother of a child who had sickle cell, while she herself had HbAS and could therefore appeal to the majority of the affected population.[4] Magueye was chosen as well, since he was a self-assured, active patient who, it was now publicly understood, lived his life for the disease. A paid post was created for each within Ministry of Health and Prevention budgetary funds. Their jobs would be based on yearly contracts with the possibility of renewal, a possibility linked to power changes, surely, or "even to shifts in philosophy," as Magueye understood things. For his post he was offered pay for the work that, for the most part, he already did at the CNTS anyway. Because of his deep concern for patients, he also lobbied to be able to work as an assistant to Dr. Diop. "Even if it is arranging patients' medical files and sometimes discussing cases with the team, I will learn more. And then I will be able to *do* more," he reasoned. His hope was to be involved in patients' care from within biomedicine, in addition to his work within the ASD, which was a kind of social and economic therapeutic double to formal medical intervention.

Touty's employment under Mamadou Seck served to elevate sickle cell within the National Assembly beyond an awareness campaign for "the people." When I interviewed Seck, Touty briefed him beforehand, and she also accompanied us for the duration of the conversation. He often looked to her for answers on disease facts, or, even on the historical legal precedents that might shape how the idea of prenuptial testing might be addressed. He was comforted by all of her knowledge and told both of us that the National Assembly would become "implicated." He admitted to me that he had "no idea about the "severe" form of the disease, until Mme Wade's visit to the assembly with the ASD and Dr. Diagne," when he saw, and was "touched by," the film. At Touty's suggestion, Seck began to work with Dr. Saliou Diop to organize the testing day for the *députés* themselves. That did not mean that the politicians would be obliged or even expected to divulge their results to the public, however, which the ministers have not done. As I sat with Touty and Seck, it was clear who held the real knowledge on sickle cell. Yet behind the closed doors of official government her knowledge was being transmitted to power. To her chagrin, however, ideas of prevention or sickle cell control would take precedence within this power structure over care. She, like Magueye, would continue to insist that, as she told me in frustration, "Preventing new births may be fine and good, but what is more important is to take care of people with the disease who are here now."

■ Structural Adjustments on Life and Health

One afternoon I sat with a group of Senegalese young men who were brewing a strong pot of sugary gunpowder tea (called *chine* in the local slang) near my house in the *Amitié II* neighborhood. The men were talking loudly about changes in their country's political landscape. None of them was older than thirty, but strangely they seamlessly went from the fact that they were all unemployed, and disappointed in Wade's "entourage," which was "enriching itself on the backs of the people," to an earlier time when "life was better." I assumed that they were talking about life before the year 2000 and the change of administration, but as they continued, it was clear that they where going much farther back on the historical horizon. For some, this was a period before they were even born. One of them interjected, "They used to come around my neighborhood and call out, *"Kai leen liggéey! Liggéey . . . "* [Come work! Work . . .], to solicit people to join some force or project or to fill some need. The young man's story of ample employment was recounted to him by his father who had always worked throughout his life, even retiring with a pension. But the twenty-eight-year-old's understanding was that things had changed, and that this change, under which he had grown up, in the 1980s and 1990s started with *"la crise économique"* that took a chokehold on people's livelihoods in 1994, with the devaluation of the *cfa* franc. What is interesting about this memory recounted is that aspects of this narrative surfaced in conversations and interviews with families affected by sickle cell. Often stories of a person's current limits and economic difficulty were prefaced or punctuated with a reference to a better time, when things were "more manageable," when food was "less expensive" (*moo gëna moins cher*), and when life in general was "easier," which, in Wolof, also means economically accessible (*yomb*).

I often wondered about the need for Senegalese people to go back to a historical juncture located not too far in the past, since they wanted to avoid wishing for colonialism. The short space between independence and the here and now was merely forty years. The 1980s, as a point in time, was both a fair target—half an independent history ago—and a realistic reference for when life on the ground actually underwent seismic transformations. This is in reference to the 1979 IMF policy of structural adjustment, of which Senegal was the first African example. As we saw in chapter 2, this period of austerity resulted in an especially hard hit for government civil service workers, and for social security subsidies for agriculture, education, and health care.

It will be an exercise in making narrative "associations" broadly, then, to conjoin the stories of the young men drinking tea with those of other Senegalese people I encountered who recounted a general belief that life before the 1980s was "still good." They are joined in their opinion by political economist Nicolas van de Walle who, in assessing the impact of structural adjustment on the country at the turn of the new millennium, ventured that "the quality of life of the average Senegalese has probably declined in the last twenty years," despite a pick up in prima facie growth indicators (van de Walle 2001, 3). Many of my interlocutors and friends remarked that this was a period when Senegalese people were also "still good," when outside influences were fewer, when scandalous soap operas from the West were unthinkable, and when the population at large had a deeper reverence for "wholesome values." Not far from my interlocutors' reflections were my own thoughts of people's comparative assessments about life just prior to the 1980s—a time of perceived "living well" in Senegal—as also a time of innovations in genetic science. This was the same period when *Restriction Fragment Length Polymorphism* technology was utilized to differentiate sickle cell genetic types, a technology that reiterated French ideas of African population differences. These RFLP's permitted Parisian researchers to travel to Dakar and other African capital cities to investigate the "genetic underpinnings" of what they took to be different "phenotypes" of Africans' quality of sickle cell life. Could these two phenomena, "better life" in recent economic history and "sickle cell distinction in Senegal" as "mild," be linked? Could it be that the period before the retrenchment, when health care was better subsidized as a state social service and when families had more purchasing power in other realms of life, entered into the picture of mild disease? If so, then it was after the retrenchment and austerity measures were instituted for good that people increasingly relied on medical making-do, living well with sickle cell in the face of economic scarcity and formal biomedical absences. Now more than ever they would be forced to muster their internal resources with those of family, healers, plants, and fellow sicklers to mitigate their suffering. In the process, the professionals who cared for them began to collate their biological outcomes to the (then) recent genetic findings that posited a better fate for those with "Senegalese" genetic mutations around their sickle cell gene.

On yet another register, what I was witnessing in Dakar in the first years of the Wade administration was a progressive loss of faith in the social sphere due to an increased pessimism that the state did not have the population's interest in mind. This was compounded as poverty did not seem to be alleviating itself, while, as of 2006, the economy and a general social malaise dramatically worsened. During this time, which coincided with the Dakar OILD congress and increased state discourse on sickle cell with Viviane Wade's commitment, the disease picture was now being repainted as increasingly "severe." Political neglect and socially articulated needs now converged and "associated" to form a lived construct of sickle cell as a serious disorder. The interface of biology, economy, and health care scarcity was furthermore reiterated in the OILD's emphasis that sickle cell be thought of as "a major cause of death in Africa." The OILD's "data," which made the "severe" lived construct cohere internationally, coordinated many populations, diseases, and risks, politically. The OILD leadership established this renewed and empowered disease entity on an international level, but the hope was that UN funding streams would benefit the OILD's local "Member State" associations, such as the ASD, on the ground in Africa.

The actual social processes that inhere in the production of sickle cell lived "outcomes," as data points, are one and the same as the life stories on strategies of survival, biopolitical advocacy, and power plays to advance various forms of expert knowledge that I have detailed throughout this book. As I have argued, we must ask what specific lines of cultural action converge to form the different *pedigrees of process* that have resulted in the perception of different disease pictures in Senegal today? Clearly many of the lines that join in the two representations of the disease share traits: one can see the family resemblances between sickle cell as "mild," in some instances, and as "severe," more recently. Both outcomes are the result of cultural choices, health care priorities, and political actions. In other words, actors affected by the disease (as well as scientists who study it) have both built and lived an ontological reality of mild sickle cell anemia, as well as the possibility of its double. For instance, Magueye Ndiaye and Rokhoya Sylla draw upon biological family ties and idioms of these that expand the nature of relatedness in order to give their lives, and biology, a sense of normalcy. Neither of them would deny that the relationships they have built with their personal doctors, Dr. Diagne for Rokhoya and Dr. Diop for Magueye, are key to their well-being. It is not always elements of these practitioners' training in biomedicine that touches their patients. Mostly, it is their care beyond medicine and the clinic proper. Patients and families, like the Syllas, take this disease as seriously as they take the life of their children. In the case of Mr. Sylla, he manages his daughter's illness with economic precision. In the process, the family generates new bodily thresholds and norms that have kept her healthy and that she now passes onto others within the network of the ASD after joining its governing body.

In a similar vein, care in informal health economies of traditional healing raises the pervasive issue of plant remedies in Senegal and how patients and families resource the environment to fill the breach that biomedicine often leaves them to navigate. For Coumba and Soxna Mbodj, the roots of the fagara plant yield both a chemical substance, a molecule that changed their biology and perhaps increased their fetal hemoglobin, and a material economic good that allowed their "husband-healer" much of his success. Patients in the clinic attest to the virtues of fagara, even prompting local researchers to study it on a few occasions in recent history. Yet the plant animated global frictions between perceived "croc healers," outside of Senegal's borders, who claimed that the plant cured sickle cell, and French researchers who conceptually always considered sickle cell first and foremost a genetic disease, which plants could not "cure." The plant as a needed unofficial therapy suspended indefinitely the subtle oppositional forces of "modern" and "traditional" health care that, like two poles of the same magnetic pull, often seem to repel each other even as they continuously drew from and supported each other structurally, as we saw in chapter 3. It is not that physician-researchers in Dakar do not believe in traditional healing. Dr. Thiam who serves as dean of the Faculty of Medicine made the point clear enough in chapter 4. He and others at the CNTS were raised believing in what he called "the psychical and exotic aspects of plants." Yet, Thiam, like Diagne, drives home the crucial point that Africans trained in biomedicine have to establish themselves as able scientists who should be taken seriously by their colleagues up North in order to begin to erode an image of their inferiority in this postcolonial global setting.

They also saw an urgent need for measures to demand respect, as we saw in chapter 5, when Diagne entertained collaborating with French geneticists on new sickle cell haplotype studies. During the period of negotiation doctors at Albert Royer imagined the specter of being unfairly associated with opportunistic "healers," which made them hesitant to openly embrace fagara, even as they continued to believe that the plant should be studied scientifically, and given a fair (clinical) trial. Certain practitioners in the Fann hospital complex considered fagara to be a productive cultural product that partially alleviated their patients' disease, as well as their own workload and accountability to patients for whom they could do little with biomedicine. More often, however, they relied on the ways that their patients managed what Magueye called the "capriciousness" of the disease, its uncertainty that often forced him into a dance with "her," "*ma maladie*." He told me that, as with his fellow ASD adherents, he has "also come to love sickle cell" who, he went on to say, "lives with me, in my blood, giving me no choice but to do this life together."

As we saw in chapters 6 and 7, disease constructs are not fixed, but are porous and open to change. Yet there are certain events that set disease ontologies into motion anew. In the case of mild sickle cell, this began with the opportunity of a new disease politic in the creation of the ASD, with new material realities of scarcity, with the plummeting economy already entrenched in crisis, with medical doctors' frustrations about comparative spending and competition for diseases (other than the major infections that dictate the budget lines for Africa), with the formation of international alliances (however troubled), with the securing of funds through those alliances for an international conference, with the persuasive power of advocacy unions to enlist the help of the First Lady, and finally with the tirelessness of the ASD to secure the sympathy of the public. Through these processes, sickle cell disease finally made its way into the formal documents of the WHO and the UN, where another aspect of its phenotypic variability, now its picture of its severity, was freeze-framed.

■ **International Pulls and Interdependence**

Recent anthropology of Africa has stressed an ethic of global interdependence (Fassin 2007; Ferguson 2006), all the while calling out denizens of the richer countries of the North to realize that we may share our world but, as Didier Fassin reiterates, "we share it unequally" (2007, xv). Ethicist Solomon Bentar has declared global health disparities to be the primary ethical concern of our time (1998). As these scholars of Africa point out, our common humanity is not glued to a trajectory of essential differences, biological or otherwise. Following from this, Elizabeth Povinelli's useful insight about discourses and material institutions of liberalism might also be extended to scientific discourses of genetic haplotypes that were used to explain sickle cell mildness within a specifically ranked range of health outcomes for the first genetic disease in the global South. She writes, "Though these discourses may not have had any substantial hold in many places to which they initially referred, over time the actual material and discursive conditions of places change to meet and mirror the presumptions of these discourses. What was at first a misrepresentation becomes an accurate description. Instead of asking, where are the discourses? We might ask, what is being done to produce the world in their image? The dynamic transformation of facts on the ground is not merely a transformation of social values, economy, and political institutions, but the transformation of life forces, of ecology and environment, of disease trajectories" (2006, 15). Yet this is not to overlook the fact that discourses are written into material realities, including human bodies, ecological landscapes and global health economies and priorities for Africa. In other words, "the ground itself is [also] extraordinarily dynamic with multiple rhythms and complex coordinations" (ibid.), which in Senegal, could be seen in doctors' uptakes and interpretations of sickle cell "mildness." Senegalese physicians drew from but also went beyond genetic notions of haplotypes, while many patients often reiterated local medical and broader societal expectations that they focus on health and well-being.

Inequality and histories that have entrenched stratification into our global existence need uprooting from the conceptual ensembles that link lived disease outcomes to biologically based "population differences." Clues about how to undo this knotted nexus are often clarified for us when we experience life outside of the comforting norms that allow us our own health and happiness. Through truly living together, in the same world, we might begin to disrupt assumed givens and explore how the making of biogenetic data and statistics reductionistically parses and packages aspects of the lives of others, often in contradistinction to our own. We must examine our own footing in the foiled reflections that continuously refract realities on the ground in Africa, displacing them, slightly skewed, in this case, from Senegalese people's own experiences and aspirations for survival.

■ Currently in Senegal, people feel that the world is so desperate for its democracy, which at first was awarded exemplary status in the region in the early 2000s, that much of its poor governance goes largely unnoticed. This also fuels their desire to leave and experience "real democracies," as the young men drinking tea also pitched. I heard similar sentiments from doctors. During one of my interviews with Dr. Diagne about the National Sickle Cell Program and the broken promises with which he has had to come to terms, I tried to encourage him to see all that had changed around sickle cell in recent years. I pointed out that the increased visibility had to count for something. I, nonetheless, could not ignore the effects that empty pledges and vacuous performances on the political stage had on him and others. Diagne confided that he still possessed a "measured optimism," while he assured himself that his daily interventions on the ground would continue apace, as always. It was clear that his hope was tightly associated with despair as he recounted these reflections on his own life and work:

ID: In the meantime, I will just continue to live my little life. I will try my best to do my best until the day when I decide to find myself a mini pirogue that will take me away.

DF: Where to?

ID: [Laughing] Well, *Barça/Barsax* of course. . . !

DF: With all of your patients trailing behind?

ID: I don't know if there will be any sicklers in this story, but in any case, the next time that you come back, someone will tell you the whole story about how "he took off to Barça, or to Barsax."

DF: Alright—in a few years time.

ID: In a few years, when you come back, there will be someone else who will talk to you about all of this. You'll say, oh I worked with Diagne, and they'll say "No . . . ooo! . . . [sigh] . . . You knew him? Oh yes, Diagne—the one who drowned in the Mauritanian waters. . . . What a sad case it was." And you'll say, "but do you know *why* he undertook the suicidal mission?" And the person will say, "No, but he went completely mad." And you will tell them that "it all harkens back to the broken promises, and the promised *centre de référence* that never came." It will be you who reveals the effects of this sad truth.

This was in 2006. In 2007 when I returned again Diagne was still working away, harder than ever, finding joy in the progress of his small patients and in their smiles when they would proudly announce a prize won at school, or be able to recite prayers from memory. In 2010, now "a few years time," I happily found him once more, still threatening to emigrate, but firmly rooted on Senegalese ground, or rather on the tiled floor of his medical office. When I stopped in one morning the caring space was crowded with a mother, her two healthy, quite animated children, who were there for a check-up, and three young doctors who were being trained to expand Diagne's service. As he visited with me, they took over effortlessly as he proudly looked on. The reference center was still an unrealized dream, but he was doing what he could to train a small group of new doctors and interns at the Children's Hospital on sickle cell in the event that it might one day come to fruition.

The year 2010 was the hundred-year anniversary of sickle cell anemia's discovery. In Senegal, the ASD organized an event on June 19, International Sickle Cell Day, to address the history of the disease, which largely focused on the problems and progress of the United States, from the politics of race, such as issues of mandatory sickle cell testing for African-Americans in the 1970s, to the many sickle cell specialty centers where care and research combine. Dr. Saliou Diop and several other providers joined patients for this event, which was hosted by the CNTS, to emphasize a need to lobby the government for a sickle cell reference center.

In a press interview that day with the nonstate newspaper *Walfadri*, Diop told reporters, "A hundred years on, and still there's no treatment available to cure the disease definitively. This makes one realize the extent to which sickle cell is a neglected condition." The article went on to say, "According to Dr. Saliou Diop, this neglect is fundamentally linked to the fact that it is a disease that largely affects people in developing countries where research dollars are limited."[5] After the meeting Touty drove home for me the extent to which people were shocked by the "long" history of the disease that affects them, a hundred-year history that, for many, was also marked by the place of its discovery, the United States. The United States for most people in the global South is associated with economic power and also, for many Senegalese, of problem-solving and learning. They could not believe that more had not been done to actually treat, or cure, the disease beyond interventions that were too risky to be of general use, such as hydroxyurea and, increasingly, bone marrow red blood stem cell transplants.[6] Their realizations were both disheartening, and, well, slightly heartening. Yes, it had been one hundred years, but, as Touty pointed out, "It's only been about ten years in Senegal that people have started to learn about sickle cell, recognizing what it is, and with Diagne and Diop we *have* seen some progress."

Four days later, Mme Wade's NGO *Association éducation santé* held an awareness event in the Dakar suburb of Médina Gounass, Guédiawaye to now make a public plea to the population, especially to the youth, to get tested before marriage. Some press reports insisted that she "pointed the finger" at parents for bringing a child with sickle cell into the world without first knowing whether or not they carried the disease or trait. She was accompanied by the current minister of health and prevention, the Dakar representative of the WHO, and also by Touty Niang and Magueye Ndiaye of the ASD. Magueye, as the president of the advocacy group, gave a testimonial speech on the struggles of living with sickle cell and echoed the sentiment of his doctors and allies, Dr. Saliou Diop, Dr. Ibrahima Diagne and Touty, in saying that free prenuptial testing was a start, but that "attention needed to be given to sicklers in the here and now, living with the disease." He then again lobbied for the promised *centre de référence* and for medical social securities for costly care items that were beyond the reach of most people he knew. The postday press mostly emphasized the new legislative result that would be submitted for a vote at the National Assembly, that of a law for prenuptial testing, as well as attendant protections against discrimination after testing, following earlier legislation for HIV. The ASD and sickle cell specialists left the event disappointed. The proposed health legislation was "political," Magueye complained. It was clearly based on the philosophy and economy of prevention, rather than on the health care that he and others felt their state should provide.

■ African Genetics and Anthropology in the World Today

As I was completing the final pages of this book, on June 22, 2010 the United States National Institutes of Health and the United Kingdom's Wellcome Trust announced thirty-eight million U.S. dollars for *The Human Heredity and Health in Africa Project*, designated as "H³Africa," over the next five years (NHGRI 2010). The goals of the vast new project are many: a better understanding of the genomic aspects of disease in African populations and deploying methods that range from full genetic scans of coding regions (exomes) to eventual full genome sequences for both common infectious diseases as well as noncommunicable ones. Of particular interest is the project's "focus on both genes and environmental data in the expectation that it will lead to an understanding of how the interaction between both influences health and disease." The directors rightly emphasized that, "Environmental factors could include more than just nutrition and pollution, but also include cultural, religious, political, and other social factors that may influence health." At the press conference announcing the project in London, Dr. Francis Collins, the head of NIH, attempted from the outset to assuage fears that these richer countries were exploiting African research subjects by stressing the world's global connectedness, and the importance of Africa for human genetic diversity:

> The US recognizes that the global is not the opposite of domestic, and domestic is not the opposite of global, we live in a global world and if we want to understand the causes of illness, we need to investigate them all over this globe, and Africa is a special place to carry out those kinds of studies. There's more genetic variation there than anywhere else on earth and Africa is the cradle of humanity, and things that we learn there will undoubtedly have broad implications for peoples in all other parts of the planet.[7]

The ultimate item on the H³Africa FAQs page actually concerns *researcher* exploitation and equity. Until the proper storage facilities can be constructed on the continent, the NIH promises that "samples only will leave Africa for the purposes of collaboration with other researchers; [while] African researchers will always be involved and will retain responsibility for the samples." Finally, "Samples will not simply be collected and shipped out for others to use."[8]

Also at the press conference announcing the project, the South African doctor Bongani Mayosi, chairman of the H³ working group on noncommunicable diseases, explicitly reiterated the importance of avoiding past practices of (post)colonial science. In terms that echoed those of Dr. Ibrahima Diagne in Senegal, he told the world, "I want to point out, as a person working in Africa, that [H³] indicates a very, very important shift in the way science is done in Africa. Up until now, I think we have been operating almost in a colonial mode of doing science, people from the outside have been coming to collect samples, processing them outside and publishing papers and advancing the careers of people outside of Africa." He continued by linking the prospect of Africans conducting science to the needed changes in Africa's economy, the development of the continent's intellectual capital, and the advancement of biology for the global community at large.[9]

■ In conclusion, I can only hope that this book demonstrates the increasing importance of involving ethnographers in efforts to broaden understandings of genetic medical causation and biological outcomes, which are often reduced to DNA base pairs for many conditions. The H³Africa project will consist of many studies, some of which will require ten thousand subjects each. Globally speaking, for human genetic diversity, this is a massive study effort, the first of its kind. The program's two main thrusts, infectious and complex diseases, will be headed up by African geneticists and also involve the *African Society of Human Genetics*. The NHGRI's emphasis on including "cultural, religious, political, and other social factors that may influence health" for H³Africa will surely also require anthropologists' specialty knowledge. At stake is our ability as ethnographers to use our intimate understanding of how the people with whom we work actually live in order to repopulate the terrains upon which biological renderings have often been localized, sometimes, paradoxically, in isolation from life on the ground.

As H³Africa and other like projects get underway, even with the best of intentions, they will also add to the rise of genetic explanations for health outcomes generally. It is clear that we are in a moment where medical anthropologists and ethnographers of science must now more than ever learn to speak to how scientific categories and social phenomena *respond* to one another and in so doing are often made to *correspond* biologically in association studies and through imagined "cultural" associations more broadly. As I have shown for sickle cell in Senegal, it is within and between these arrangements, that specific lived experiences, bodily forms, and—tautologically—scientific concepts that report on those experiences themselves often congeal in medical norms with varying capacities to anchor local beliefs about the sources, or causes, of variable disease manifestations and susceptibilities. Especially as regards the massive effort to now understand African genomes, environment, and disease, anthropologists are uniquely placed to broaden population genetic categories and understandings of peoples' health difficulties and disease expressions which cannot be decoupled from issues of material constraint and economic uncertainty in the current global order. For their part, if doctors and scientists truly want to understand the "environment" in Africa, they will have to also incorporate into their conceptual frameworks economic inequities that mediate how health and a will to survive are expressed in people's illness idioms, in their therapeutic economies of solidarity and care, and in the symptoms of their physical and spiritual bodies, in addition to their genetic makeup.

At its most general level, I have tasked this book with unraveling how biological data, as genetic sequences of import for sickle cell science, once emerged as some of the most visible, and often favored, facts to explain the nature of the disease's variability. Through their visibility, the genetic variants around the sickle cell gene in Senegal were made to interact with material realities on the ground, including bodies, economies, and environmental ecologies. When doctors and scientists found it convenient to do so, they allowed genetic markers to subsume much larger processes of medical "making-do" in Senegal that characterize one local normalization of sickle cell in this global context. In the initial studies, haplotype data was correlated with a social medical reality and theorized to explain differences in sickle cell lived experiences. Yet this data often morphed into something much more concrete: overly generalized "findings" about causality, or biological endpoints as due to DNA. The connection between genetic findings and some aspect of sickle cell biological expression has hardened in many people's minds, albeit to different degrees, as we have seen throughout. When they chose to do so, my doctor-informants' engagements with such scientific closed concepts risked obfuscating more complex pedigrees of process—that is pedigrees of poverty, pedigrees of informal health economies, pedigrees of care and of health that have come to constitute sickle cell anemia and its "difference" in contemporary West Africa today. When people on the ground survive despite those very processes, and often do so with stoicism and wells of patience, it makes us painfully aware of the human determination to live in the face of threatened mortality and economic uncertainty. It also makes us confront the fact that living well despite the odds through medical "making-do" is an unenviable feat that no one, in Africa or elsewhere, should be forced to achieve.

NOTES

Preface

1. For an account of scientists' continued engagement with this classic article in medical education, see Strasser 2002, 83–84. William Eaton provides a detailed account of Pauling's insights in this classic paper even though it was Vernon Ingram who discovered the exact amino acid substitution that results in the disease (Eaton, 2002, 112).

2. In *The Biology of the Negro*, physician Julian Herman Lewis wrote: "Sickle cell anemia appears to be one disease in which there is a more or less complete *racial segregation*. If those people in whom there is a probability of an immediate or remote infusion of Negro blood are excluded, it is doubtful if there is a single *genuine* instance of sickle cell anemia in a white person (1942, 249; emphasis mine). Analyzing various medical reports from this era, historian anthropologist Melbourne Tapper notes: "What was ultimately at stake in the inquisition of the "white" body in which sickling was found was not sickling (the clinical entity) but the racial purity (the degree of nonblackness) of these bodies" (1999, 16). For a review of the many instances in twentieth-century American medical literature where sickle cell was used to diagnose racial distinctiveness, see Tapper (1999), chapter 1, "Interrogating Bodies: When a Caucasian is not a Caucasian."

3. See Ruggles Gates (1952) for an obvious example of this rationale. Other earlier accounts complicate this picture slightly, since many physicians found the disease to occur at higher frequencies in black Americans who were said to be "admixed" with either "white" or "Indian" blood. "Admixture" itself, in these cases, was hypothesized to be pathogenic as far as sickle cell prevalence was concerned (See Tapper 1999, 41–46; see also Diggs, Ahmann, and Bibb 1933). In other words, the moral message underlying this science was that race mixing posed a dysgenic threat for the offspring of "pure racial types," or for "mixed-race" individuals and populations. Along these same lines, Philadelphia physician John Hodges was inspired to do his own study after "Diggs, Ahmann, and Bibb found that sickling occurred more frequently in 'light' Negroes than in 'dark' or 'pure Negroid' types." Accordingly he wrote: "Such a trend, that is, the transmission of the disease or the increase of its frequency in the lighter Negro and possibly thereby its projection in to the white race, suggested itself as a possibility" (1950, 804). Hodges's own study indeed corroborated that of Diggs and colleagues, as he concluded, "the results show that the incidence of sickling increases with the dilution of the 'pure' Negro by small amounts of white and American Indian blood" (1950, 809).

4. The caveat here is that they did distinguish between types of U.S. blacks, as discussed in note 3. For instance, when physician-researcher Hodges attempted to discern admixture for sickling rates, he first did a survey of "the true Negro" in Africa to make a larger point about African original purity in the United States before admixture. In other instances, U.S. physician–researchers occasionally tried to compile comparative charts of sickling frequencies in people based in different geographical areas in the United States. Generally, such studies set out to discern something about the incidence of the disease without any special emphasis on the local populations' degree of African ancestry, or of white "admixture." For a table of "Incidence of the sickle cell trait" in the United States by locale and principal investigator, starting in the 1923, see Lewis (1942, 235), for a later similar chart with studies and observations up to 1950, see Neel (1950, 148).

5. Regarding sickle cell disease prevalence rates, practitioners in Dakar offer estimates of 10 percent, although no formal epidemiological studies have been undertaken to precisely answer this question. Several University of Dakar Faculty of Medicine sickle cell specialists who were informants for this book directed a thesis wherein a student conducted newborn screening for sickle cell prevalence based on 518 births. He found sickle cell *trait* to affect 10 percent of those tested, while the trait in the double dose, or sickle cell disease, affected 1 percent (Kete 1998). These results were later published in the local medical journal, Dakar Medical (Mbodji et al. 2003). As we will see in chapters 5 and 6, sickle cell trait is also considered a form of the disease itself in Senegal. Epidemiologists estimate that sickle cell trait frequencies vary from 10 to 25 percent for most West African populations. See Bowman and Murray (1990).

6. I use the term *sickler*, a translation of the French *drépanocytaire*, which people with the disease in Senegal use to identify themselves [as in *je suis drépanocytaire*]. To refer to oneself as a drépanocytaire was never about describing one's full identity, however. Therefore unlike in the American context, *sickler* here should not be read as a deterministic label that unjustly defines a person and limits his or her being and becoming to illness.

7. In order to have homozygous sickle cell disease a person must inherit two alleles that code for hemoglobin S, one from each parent, or one on each of their eleventh chromosomes, making HbSS. People with one S coding allele, or sickle cell trait, are usually designated as HbAS, and called heterozygous. Here the A signifies the usual form of "Adult" hemoglobin. Another form of actual sickle cell disease is also a heterozygous form where the sickle hemoglobin allele and another allele for a different hemoglobin variant, HbC, or one of several beta thalassemia mutations, combine. The patients and affected families who appear in this book have HbSS unless otherwise noted.

8. Other scientific attempts to account for biological difference and sickle cell "mildness" along a spectrum of severity have to do with the discovery of multiple forms of hemoglobin that could combine with sickle hemoglobin, resulting in several ultrarare heterozygous forms of the disease. These hemoglobin molecules were often named after the places in which they were discovered in patients, such as "Portland," or "Memphis." In *Dying in the City of the Blues: Sickle Cell Anemia and the Politics of Race and Health*, medical historian Keith Wailoo recounts how in the 1960s researchers working on *Hemoglobin Memphis* "assumed that the

molecule somehow mediated pain" (2001, 160). By looking at an Hb Memphis/S patient and his affected niece who had "little history of suffering from the typical pain crisis," Wailoo explains that certain physicians spent a considerable amount of effort researching whether or not *Hemoglobin Memphis* could indicate a possible approach to therapy (2001, 161).

9. For more on how African American and Black Britons negotiate identity, diaspora, and belonging through such quests, see Alondra Nelson (2008a, 2008b).

10. Mr. Washington spoke about his anticipated DNA passport at Harvard University as the invited guest of *The Harvard College Sierra Leone Initiative* for a panel celebrating the country's forty-seventh year of independence. Also see (Washington, 2008). In a quite different imagined use, medical anthropologist Karen-Sue Taussig discusses how people in the Netherlands circulated rumors of genetic identifiers becoming integrated into their passports in the early 1990s for surveillance and health reasons (See Taussig 2009, 2–3).

11. Since its early days, in 2003, the industry that many people now know as African "roots" genetic ancestry tracing has relied on two kinds of tests. One probe determines patterns in an individual's maternal line, through mitochondrial DNA markers, and constitutes about 0.5 percent of a person's genetic make-up. The other, which is only applicable in males, detects specific mutations present on the Y chromosome and may indicate as much—or as little—as 1 percent of a person's genetic background.

12. Wailoo points out, however, that black Americans did resource an evolutionary emphasis that the disease originated in Africa. He writes that in the early 1970s, "the disorder was increasingly understood as an African inheritance, a trace of authentic African identity among American blacks" (Wailoo 2001, 139, 144).

13. It was initially a team of Francophone West Africans, French (including Labie) and American researchers who postulated that these markers might serve as signposts that could reveal information about a given sample's geographic origins (Mears et al. 1981a, 606), yet it was the specific studies done by Labie's team (Pagnier et al. 1984) in the former French colonies in West Africa that remain the regional references for severity today in France and Senegal. With regard to genetically redressing the obscured origins of American Blacks disconnected from Africa by the slave trade, Dr. Elliot Vichinsky, a renowned sickle cell specialist in Oakland, California, told me in 1995, "This information only has to do with a few sites on one or two chromosomes, not the whole person." Similarly, in a 1997 conversation, Ronald Nagel, one of only two American co-authors on the 1984 seminal study, confided: "This idea is still sort of experimental. And this test is not regulated by any agency, like the FDA." It may be that since the African sickle cell haplotype discoverers were mostly French, and that African and Caribbean French seem to know their immediate historical roots, or exhibit less of a need to search them out, that the French team would not tout sickle cell haplotypes for African ancestry testing purposes beyond their medical labs. For their part, the American sickle cell geneticists saw the HbS haplotypes as too superficial to be informative for individual ancestry mapping.

14. Accordingly they wrote: "Of anthropological interest is that these haplotypes could provide an objective tool capable of defining the places of origin of Blacks dispersed through the Americas by the slave trade. This approach will allow the

calculation of the composition by African origin of many Caribbean and other New World Black communities, as long as they exhibit an appreciable HbS [sickle hemoglobin] gene frequency" (Pagnier et al. 1984, 1773).

15. To say that people in Senegal have different haplotypes from those in Benin and the Central African Republic means that they all possess the sickle cell mutation *not* because they necessarily inherited the gene from an ancestor they shared with people in the other two locales. Rather, these populations *co-possess* the disease-causing hemoglobin S allele because of evolutionary *coincidence*. Put otherwise, one sickle cell mutation arose in the ancestors of people who live in what is now Senegal, while two separate mutations appeared in the forebears of people in what are now the countries of Benin and the Central African Republic.

16. Anthropologist Margaret Lock's idea of local biologies (1993b, 2010) is important here, and will be discussed at length in chapter 1.

17. The most recent genetic studies concerned with fetal hemoglobin and sickle cell health are summarized by Higgs and Wood (2008) and will be more thoroughly discussed in chapter 1.

18. The biopolitical group diagnosis of mild Senegalese sickle cell, associated with molecular signature, falls in line with fraught colonial conceptions about Senegalese exceptionalism. As historians of Senegal have repeatedly pointed out, urban Senegalese, who lived in four specific communes including Dakar, were the only West Africans who could be considered for French citizenship starting with legislation that dated back to the 1848 French Revolution. Such a right and protection was not continuous, however, and had to be renewed by legislation in 1871. Even then, during the Third Republic (1870-1940), the special opportunity for Senegalese to become French citizens was usually reserved for cultural elites who would also renounce customary practices associated with "African culture." In other words, the exceptional status granted to urban Senegalese was more precisely only for "exceptional individuals" (Wilder 2005, 130). For most of the "*originaires*," as people living in the four communes were called, French citizenship was not at all a straightforward task. As historian anthropologist Gary Wilder points out: "Natives seeking citizenship would be required to formally renounce their customary personal status and place themselves and their families under the authority of French civil and political laws. . . . Among other criteria [including solvency], candidates for citizenship had to prove their devotion to France, read and write in French, and have adopted French cultural habits" (130). Eventually a 1932 citizenship decree also required local administrators to investigate a candidate's household before issuing an official "Certificate of Good Life and Morals," which meant evaluating "the differences between African and European domestic norms and practices" (Wilder, 133). As will be discussed in chapter 5 of this book, French colonial and postcolonial biological studies on sickle cell sought to differentiate Africans, as black peoples, through ideas of "race," compared within black populations.

19. Rose's point here is largely that molecular biology and the "technological reformation" that it presents allow one "to discover the biological basis of an illness, of infertility, of an adverse drug reaction in a cascade of coding sequences." . . . These bits of knowledge should not make one "resign oneself to fate but to open oneself to hope" (2007, 51). As I argue throughout, sickle cell patients' ability to embody

hope also allows them to rewrite otherwise debilitating diagnoses and in so doing upend any crude notion of genetic determinism. The enthusiasm Rose brings to this optimistic reading of biology, however, does not take into account how histories of inequality and global inequities might indeed limit the degree to which actors in places like Senegal live with constraints in their freedoms to make such "opportunities" about individual "choice" and "enterprise" (2007, 177).

20. One exception would be Nigeria where various sickle cell testing programs have been underway since the mid-1990s.

21. For examples of this hardening process, see Abby Lippman on "geneticization" (1991) and Troy Duster (2003) on the "prism of genetics." Also see Hedgecoe (2009) for a review. With regard to disease social movements in the United States, where "genes" were often used as catalysts for action, anthropologists Deborah Heath, Rayna Rapp and Karen-Sue Taussig did fieldwork among families who formed larger networks of patient advocacy to politicize and garner state attention for their lethal single gene Mendelian disorders. Heath, Rapp, and Taussig found that affected communities made the genetic nature of their under-researched afflictions central to defining their social networks in order to lobby for public funds from the U.S. congress. Patients largely emphasized their rights as citizens to health care resources through the hard category, and empirical reality, of the genetic nature of their disorders (see Rapp, Heath, and Tausig 2001 and Heath, Rapp, and Taussig 2007). Similarly in France, Michel Callon and Vololona Rabeharisoa show how French citizens with various forms of muscular dystrophy created an alliance in the form of a muscular dystrophy association wherein they emphasized "the gene" in their disease identity politics. Here the genetic nature of their diseases, and their rarity, became a simultaneous rallying point for public funding, research and eventual hopes for cures among the many affected. (See Rabeharisoa and Callon 1999)

Chapter One. Introduction: The Powers of Association

1. All names of patients and families used throughout are pseudonyms, with the exception of highly-visible patient advocates who are leaders of various sickle cell disease groups. Research physicians, geneticists, traditional healers, and other public health officials' real names are used since they are visible public figures whose published work and research I also engage throughout. I conducted all interviews in either French, Wolof, or both.

2. There are various genotypic forms of sickle cell disease. HbSS is the most common and the most severe. HbSC signifies that the person has inherited a hemoglobin C allele, found largely in West Africa, as well as an S allele from each parent. Because sickle cell can also merge with another hemoglobin disorder called beta thalassemia, a third form of the disease is HbS-thal, or sickle beta thalassemia. In this book, when speaking of sickle cell I am referring to HbSS, unless otherwise noted. Sickle cell disease is characterized by abnormal hemoglobin that causes red blood cells to become sickle shaped when deoxygenated. Due to various chemical reactions at the cellular level, these cells become rigid and are unable to move fluidly through the capillary system. Such "polymerized" cells also become viscous in addition to their rigidity. When enough sickled cells are present they prevent the flow of oxygen in the blood, clog the joints, and can

damage various tissues and organs of the body. The mere joint blockages cause excruciating pain, commonly called a "sickle cell crisis." Chronic anemia, tissue and organ damage, strokes, and infections can, in some cases, prove fatal.

3. The sickle cell allele is a misspelling in the genetic sequence that codes for the beta chain of hemoglobin.

4. Research for this book was largely conducted when sickle cell was still an "officially" invisible disease in Senegal during 1998–2001. Follow-up research trips were conducted in 2002, 2004, 2006, 2007, and complemented by *Skype*® video interviews in 2008 and 2009, with a final research trip in 2010. I witnessed events that marked a dramatic change in the public visibility of the disease during these latter years. Thus, the majority of the ethnography is set during this initial period, while I bring the reader up to date on more recent events throughout.

5. In her encyclopedic work, *Africa as Living Laboratory*, historian of science Helen Tilley argues that imperial scientific experiments carried out in Africa from 1870 to 1950, which raged from soil science to tropical medicine, cannot be seen as articulating knowledge that was inherently somehow "African," as opposed to more global, or "European." She writes: "[T]he continent of Africa and its peoples has been far more than an incidental backdrop: they provided the bricks and mortar of disciplines, theories, institutions and even laws. As we unpack this history it helps us to see how both European rule affected tropical Africa and how African experiences shaped key elements of the modern world" (2011, 314). Tilley makes no claim that this transnational relationship was somehow symmetrically and mutually beneficial for people in both settings. Her point is simply that we must rethink our notions of Africa as inherently marginal to the scientific enterprise.

6. One exception is anthropologist Peter Redfield (2008), who has begun research on human African trypanosomiasis, or sleeping sickness, which has recently been framed as a "neglected condition" in global health circles. Sleeping sickness is now officially getting attention through the label of "neglect. " Medical care for the disease in Uganda appears to be following a pattern of biopolitical intervention through humanitarianism that nonetheless produces a form of global citizenship based on acute local human needs that invoke pity in the west. Redfield argues that Western nations' biopolitical efforts to alleviate trypanosomiasis suffering, a reality that is far removed from those intervening on it, creates a form of global "citizenship at a distance" for African populations (*n.d.*).

7. For similar ethnographic chronicles of how everyday Africans are strategizing survival and economic viability in the face of economic crisis and uncertainty, See Makhulu, Buggenhagen, and Jackson (eds.) *Hard Work, Hard Times: Global Volatility and African Subjectivities* (2010).

8. The ways that sickle cell and other genetic disorders have emerged in human life, due to evolution and the larger forces (social, historical, disciplinary, ecological, and physiological) that allow biological traits their modern forms, do not have neat histories and, thus, do not have neat, consistent disease ontologies in the present. Regarding sickle cell anemia, part of the work of biomedicine is to render such irregularity regular, to come up with norms for, as one of my informants proclaimed, a "disease as individual as the person who has it!" Bodily experiences and cultural norms "descended" from multiple sources (from the past and from

afar) in Dakar have not yet been artificially streamlined by what Foucault (1984, 86) named "history [and physiology] in the traditional sense." Bodies, shaped by accidents of time, place, and culture, express biological traits in variable ways. Foucault offered a specific take on "genealogy" as a method to show "the heterogeneity of what was imagined [to be] consistent with itself" (82). In *Nietzsche, Genealogy, History,* he writes: "We believe . . . that the body obeys the exclusive laws of physiology and that it escapes the influence of history, but this . . . is false. The body is molded by a great many distinct regimens; it is broken down by the rhythms of work, rest, and holidays; it is poisoned by food or values, through eating habits or moral laws; it constructs resistances . . . Nothing in man not even his body is sufficiently stable to serve as the basis for self-recognition or for understanding other men" (87–88).

9. *Fagara xanthoxyloïdes* is sometimes spelled *zanthoxyloïdes,* while *dengidëk* is often confused with another plant called *genegidëk* (to be explained further in chapter 4).

10. We can also learn from the example of sickle cell anemia in Senegal by contrasting how one might follow its medical trajectory, social biography, and racialized legacy in other global contexts. A handful of historians and anthropologists have begun this work in the United States and France. Melbourne Tapper's *In the Blood* (1999) sifts through twentieth-century medical and physical anthropology texts regarding genetic proof of the "American Negro's" "*Anthropathology.*" Tapper convincingly demonstrates how science and medicine of this period were sites where American anxieties about white purity and black menace revived remnant polygenic ideas that American Negroes contained the biological blueprint for race degeneration. Tapper also highlights the flexibility of medical discourse to absorb empirical evidence of the disease appearing in "non-blacks" as mere proof of these groups' contamination, while mixing itself was interpreted by many as the reason why severe manifestations of the disease were thought to affect the "mixed" American Negro. Keith Wailoo's *Dying in the City of the Blues* (2001) takes up several of these themes with regard to sickle cell science conveying broader American anxieties about race, while it broadens the focus to span how the changing conceptions of the disease in American medicine in the mid to late twentieth century furthermore reflected macropolitics of health. On this point Wailoo demonstrates that black Americans and their ailments were often devalued at a human level, yet simultaneously valued as scientific objects and, later, political fodder in post–civil rights America. Wailoo begins a conversation about the tensions that torque politics of inclusion where people from across the political spectrum may advocate that racial injustices in health be addressed, even as such a push may risk reifying a notion of black—and potentially marred—biology. Most recently, medical anthropologist Carolyn Rouse (2009) has questioned the very possibility of true medical inclusion for a disease that still largely affects African-Americans. Rouse analyzes American sickle cell care in light of unequal treatment and health disparities broadly in the United States. Here, deep-seated ideas about black delinquency, drug addiction, criminality, violence, and low intelligence influence how nurses and doctors see and treat patients, despite these practitioners' commitments to equal care and, in some cases, specific efforts to upend racism in the clinic. In France two social scientists,

anthropologist Doris Bonnet and historian Agnès Lainé, have shown how the French medical establishment ideologically focuses on the "African" origins of patients with the disease, and continues to frame patient care in politically-laden ethnic terms. Both also demonstrate how sickle cell patients, like their disease, are seen to be from "elsewhere," rather than from Metropolitan France proper, which constantly "others" them within the health care system and within public perceptions of social sympathy for people with genetic disease more broadly (See Bonnet 2009; Lainé 2004).

11. As medical historian Keith Wailoo points out, in the U.S. context, it was not neglect but rather political attention given to sickle cell that provoked a public outcry in some sectors of society. It is too early to see how the larger Senegalese public will eventually judge a national focus on sickle cell, given the varied health priorities that could potentially compete with it. According to Wailoo, in the post–civil rights U.S. context, black Americans raised questions about prioritizing sickle cell given the myriad health problems plaguing the black population. He writes: " . . . black Americans wondered why sickle cell disease should be assigned a special status among pathologies when other health problems were even more important in black communities." In 1972, the Congressional Black Caucus embraced the Nixon administration's focus on sickle cell but also dubbed it part of the government's "twisted priorities" (Wailoo 2001, 192).

12. A damning book of investigative journalism by Abdou Latif Coulibaly (2009), coupled with radio programs by critical political commentators such as Souleymane Jules Diop, describe in stark terms the state's exorbitant spending. Luxury items, such as new cars for deputy ministers, and a new, unnecessary, tunnel and other embellishments along the Corniche West freeway for the 2008, eleventh summit of the Organization of the Islamic Conference (OIC), were incurred on public funds as roads in the hinterlands, where poor conditions lead to scores of preventable road deaths each year, went neglected. Also neglected were the city's 1959 drainage and sewer systems. Such irresponsibility in overseeing public works contributed to consecutive years of flooding, which displaced thousands of families, jeopardized water supplies, and of course led to an increase in infectious diseases such as malaria. The Senegalese paper *L'Observateur* reported that the NGO *AID Transparency, Senegal* also found that millions of dollars in aid money went unaccounted for in 2007, the years that much building on the Corniche took place (Diop 2007).

13. It is hard to ignore the fact that these target publics consist of women. Women are often unfairly blamed and made to carry the economic and emotional burden of their children's genetic diseases (See Fullwiley 2004, 177–79).

14. As political historian Linda Beck makes clear, Senegal is not a liberal democracy but is very much a clientelist democracy where long histories of patronage and informal special-interests provide actors with varying degrees of political access (2007, 33). Even as the National Sickle Cell Program launched, local specialists who were called on by the government to advise on education, health interventions, and spending felt as thought they were competing with officials who knew very little about the disease but who were already established in government health circles. According to Dr. Diagne, the fact that these insiders had no real experience with sickle cell often thwarted efforts to do realistic planning.

15. Besides spleen damage that compromises sicklers' immune response and makes them vulnerable to a range of infections, serious complications stem from the accumulation of deformed cells and the increased viscosity that slows blood flow, including cerebral strokes (often the cause of paralysis), chronic open leg ulcers, and femoral necrosis whereby bone mass in the hip begins to die. Each of these conditions produces varying degrees of handicap in adults with the disease, the world over.

16. Mme Wade's principal mission was to make sickle cell a public health priority of the United Nations so "that sicklers might benefit in terms of care and aid from the UN." Beginning in 2006, she publicly announced that the Senegalese state could not afford to subsidize sickle cell care, claiming that, "the cost is enormous, especially considering that 10 percent of the population is affected." See "Mme Viviane Wade: La Drépanocytose, un problème de santé publique" (Madame Vivian Wade: Sickle cell, A Public Health Problem) http://www.aes.sn/html/aes _page.php?xx_rubrique=La%20Presse&xx_texte_id=1061&xx_lang=FR&xx _mdr=&xx_trait= (accessed September 18, 2009).

17. Although there are many levels on which French and Senegalese researchers and patient advocates collaborate to further sickle cell knowledge, Senegal is not France, nor is it any longer an official French territory. I risk stating the obvious because independence in much of Africa is not a barefaced fact to be taken for granted, as economies everywhere are integrated and "interdependent" with varying benefits, or, too often, lack of benefits distributed beyond the rich and elite, especially for those in the global south (Ferguson 2006, 22–23). The colonial relationship between France and Senegal that formally ended in 1960 continues to exercise a certain power that scientists, even as cultural elites, on opposite sides of the North-South divide palpably face off over. Once the political capital of French West Africa, Dakar's geopolitical history and cultural memory centrally involve the French Hexagon. French remains the official language of the country and of its economy. French television and telecommunication companies control the airwaves and cell phone towers, while Paris often has a final word on Senegal's trade partners and market involvement. As recent neoliberal reforms have begun to shepherd in the privatization of previously state-run services, from the railways to water, the Senegalese stakeholders in these efforts are few. France also dominates banking, and its highly conservative lending patterns have consequences for the economic freedom of the larger finance sector. The former colonial power comes in as Senegal's largest bilateral foreign aid donor and largest imports trade partner.

18. The gene effect enjoys a quasi fact status in France, Senegal, and the United States.

19. Historically, what is now present-day Senegal has consisted of various peoples living in the general areas between and around the Senegal and Gambia Rivers. It has roughly spanned a geographical area from what is now Mauritania to southern Senegal. At the beginning of the second millennium, one of the most powerful of the region's precolonial states was called Tekrur, and it was largely comprised of people who are now known as the Toucouleur. In the eleventh century, the Tekrur monarchy was one of the first to embrace Islam in the region. Further south, legendary Wolof leader Ndiandiane Ndiaye integrated the Wolof states of Cayor, Baol, and Walo into the Djolof Kingdom in the thirteenth century. Some

of Senegal's various precolonial monarchies were attached to the multi-ethnic Mali Empire, which allowed the tributary societies under its hegemony to largely retain their cultural autonomy. From the mid-fifteenth century to the nineteenth century, first Islam and then French colonization influenced the formation of smaller aristocratic states, in some instances, with many monarchies prevailing that were based on caste systems of labor skill, and also on nobility. Thus, ethnic, religious, status, and geo-political identities overlapped. The point here is that the contemporary nation-state of Senegal is in no way to be taken as a naturalized entity, fixed in geographical space and time (for a review of Senegal's early history, see Gellar 2005, 15–26).

20. In a playful tone, many young Senegalese use the widespread slang adverb construction *Sénégalaisement* to qualify verbs of effort. In essence the speaker is attempting to calibrate his or her actions to an understanding of the slow pace of getting things done on the ground. Specifically, this usage is deployed for slow returns on economic and other political projects that have clear ends as aspirations, such as sickle cell patient advocates' goals of care subsidies and funding for their disease to be elaborated in later chapters. Of note is how this adverb construction renders survival strategies and ethics of "making do"—like the haplotype and health attitude discourses within biomedicine—as linked to specific notions of Senegalese *territorialization* (pace Deleuze) and subjectivity.

21. Senegalese university-trained botanists, who were also Muslim and practiced traditional healing, went so far as to say that we *cannot know* the deepest recesses of scientific knowledge, which would always remain out of our human reach. Moreover, they saw this level of knowledge as "hidden" [*laqatu*] from us, and reserved for God. Personal communication with El-Hadji Thalap Sarr, of IFAN (February 23, 2000), personal communication with Gaoussou Sambou (March 6, 2000).

22. Senegal under Abdoulaye Wade has deepened relations with the United States and has been heralded, especially during the Bush administration, as a model nation in terms of democratic governance. The USAID "Democracy and Governance" profile for the country opens with "Senegal is a democratic and predominantly Muslim nation, one of the most stable countries in an unstable region. A model of religious and ethnic tolerance, it plays a key role in conflict resolution in West Africa and beyond, and is committed to fighting terrorism. Senegal is an important partner of the United States because it has found a way to ensure social stability and religious tolerance without violence and repression." See http://www.usaid.gov/our_work/democracy_and_governance/regions/afr/senegal.html (accessed September 1, 2009).

23. Its theoretical import notwithstanding, the Senegalese sickle cell story highlights some of the shortcomings of co-production framings. Structurally and linguistically, co-production yields a neat, mutual arrangement, with very little attention to how political inequalities and history define the terms and products of the present "co-produced" entity in question. Embedded in the orderliness of the "co-production" concept lies a simultaneity of events which, when taken as parts of a co-produced result, often lose their political salience and historical genealogy.

24. Having done extensive fieldwork in the United States at multiple sickle cell centers, Carolyn Rouse concludes that, "healing and a sense of wellness for most sickle cell patients rely on more than access to allopathic medicine." Using Marxist framings, she goes onto say that, in the United States, "biomedicine has been fetishized, or is being worshipped well beyond its use-value" (2009, 255).

25. Dr. Souleymane Mboup of *Le Dantec* Hospital and the University of Dakar, in a collaboration with Max Essex of Harvard University, discovered HIV-2, a specifically milder form of HIV, in the blood of Senegalese patients in the mid-1980s. After years of following affected patients and doing longitudinal studies on them, it became clear to Mboup and his team that this form of the disease only eventually became virulent years after infection. In a strange resemblance to the economic, North-South research dynamics and biological findings that created "mild sickle cell anemia," poor Senegalese (mostly women forced into prostitution due to economic need) with HIV-2 were observed by the North-South research team to live healthier lives than others in Africa (those with HIV-1) and to display a particular local biology. Most had nearly normal T-cell counts for decades, compared with people elsewhere who had what was seen as the "Western" form of the virus, HIV-1. On a different register, Senegal has one of the lowest infection rates on the continent, with HIV-1 and HIV-2 combined, at less than 1 percent, although epidemiologists are now finding that "mild" HIV-2 is declining. (Gilbert 2009; Personal communication with Souleymane Mboup, March 23, 2011).

26. As discussed earlier in the text, RFLP stands for Restriction Fragment Length Polymorphism. Using enzymes that cut (actually digest) DNA at different restriction sites, the resulting restriction fragments are distinguished and separated according to their lengths. This technique was an early important tool in genetic sequence mapping and gene localization.

Chapter Two. Healthy Sicklers with "Mild" Disease: Local Illness Affects and Population-Level Effects

1. In *The Body Multiple*, Mol argues that patients' experiences of disease and professionals' medical conceptions of pathology "*exclude* one another" and "are *done* differently" (2002, 35–36). I argue that with mild sickle cell anemia, patient and professional practices may be done differently, but they surely do not exclude each other. To the contrary. French scientists' conceptions of genetic difference, patients' ethic of living well with their shared blood, and biomedical professional's needs to make do with economic health constraints all come together to enact this form of the disease. Mol would call this an incident where the scientific object, clinical object, and lived experience of the object "happen to coincide" (2002, 46).

2. For additional examples of how people in other global settings respond to health infrastructure scarcity and crisis, and in the process shape new subjectivities and intersubjective relations of care, see Brotherton 2008 and Han 2011.

3. Medical anthropologists working in countries with "developing economies" have shown that in some cases people with limited resources enter into illness for benefit (Das and Das 2006; Koch 2006; Petryna 2002) and, in others,

suffering is overlaid with technical glosses that free up state officials from obligations to correct root problems. In *Death Without Weeping*, Nancy Scheper-Hughes demonstrates the second dynamic in Northeastern Brazil, where a once socialized discourse on hunger became psychologized and is now articulated as the individualized disorder of "*nervoso.*" In this transformation, Scheper-Hughes argues, the "hungry body" once existed as a potent critique of the society in which it lived. Now the sick body "implicates no one, [while] . . . sickening social relations are gotten off the hook" (1992, 174). Hunger renamed as "nervousness" is treated by physicians with "tranquilizers, vitamins, sleeping pills, and elixirs" (1992, 169). For Scheper-Hughes, the specific configuration of "benefit" with regard to the illness category and its political contours for subjects' rights involved the state's exploitation of the subject-citizen for the sugar economy in which her starving informants toiled while triaging the lives of their children. Scheper-Hughes's informants emerge less as citizens with rights, than as denizens without them. Contrast this with Adriana Petryna's concept of "biological citizenship," whereby Chernobyl survivors in the Ukraine enacted and reconstructed radiation sickness and exposure as means to acquire the human health rights that they felt should have been accorded them as citizens. Similarly, in Georgia, Erin Koch found that healthy prison-inmates purchased infected TB sputum to pass off as their own since submitting this prized commodity to prison medical workers proved one of the only ways for them to gain the economic health benefits of more "upscale" prisons where many imagined that their basic human needs would finally be met. These works offer a powerful commentary on global affective orders and disorders and states' responsibilities to care for vulnerable citizens—as well as their failure to do so. In Senegal, for better or worse, people with sickle cell do not have recourse to even such compromised social securities.

4. In *The Republic of Therapy*, Vinh-Kim Nguyen writes of a very different dynamic concerning biology, economy, and kinship. He describes how the upsurge of HIV/AIDS activist groups in Ivory Coast and Burkina Faso went hand in hand with activists' hopes of securing donor funds for their specific organizations and philosophies of prevention. He writes, "On one hand, organizing communities of people living with HIV was about solidarity and self-help; on the other, well-meaning efforts to support 'empowerment' with much needed material support and confessional technologies of the self fostered competition and undermined trust" (2010, 84; chap. 3).

5. One area where the state influences care is through health insurance for state employees.

6. In Roitman's informants' lives, tax and price come to mean similar things when fungible goods yield margins of value for those who know how to manipulate them.

7. The CFA franc was created on December 26, 1945, when France ratified the Bretton Woods agreement and made its first declaration of parity to the IMF. At that time, it stood for *Franc des Colonies Françaises d'Afrique* (franc of the French Colonies of Africa). In 1958, it became *Franc de la Communauté Française d'Afrique* (franc of the French Community of Africa). Today, the denomination CFA franc

means *Franc de la Communauté Financière d'Afrique* (franc of the African Financial Community) and *Franc de la Coopération Financière en Afrique Centrale* (franc of Financial Cooperation in Central Africa) for countries belonging to the BEAC area (Bank of the Central African States).

8. Interview with Dr. Ibrahima Diagne, May 10, 2008.

9. Interview with Dr. Ibrahima Diagne, May 10, 2008.

10. Most recently, Wade even sold off parts of Senegal's territory to North Korea to finance a putatively "public" African Renaissance monument, which, at a cost $US27 million, proved to be an injurious affront to the many who live below the poverty line (Sy 2009). Insult was then added to injury when Wade filed a claim for intellectual property, "for thinking of the idea," through a U.S. patent in order to secure 35 percent of tourist-visit proceeds from the statue (Gilley 2010; Sy 2009).

11. Here he is referring to the protection against malaria that sickle cell confers.

12. This term refers to allowances often allocated by a head of household or a relative.

13. Priapism is a painful erection due to sickling and venous obstruction in the penis.

Chapter Three. The Biosocial Politics of Plants and People

1. Oxford English Dictionary, entry 7.

2. Girth is a sign of womanliness in Senegal. This bodily norm and aspiration will be discussed more in chapter 6.

3. Hydergine is costly by Senegalese standards, at about US$12 a box (the GDP per capita at this time was US$600). In real terms, this was more than two days' wages for many.

4. When I asked doctors at the CNTS about this possibility, they said that these two patients could be right, but that sometimes they get readouts where HbF is not present, or when the lab simply did not perform that analysis.

5. Their finding was that "After 48 hours of treatment, Fagaronine stimulated the Epo-R and y-globin (fetal hemoglobin) promoters by 2-to-3 fold and the promoter/ enhancer region of GATA-1 gene (necessary to all red blood cell genesis) by 3.2 fold" (Dupont et al. 2005, 489). Epo-R is a receptor for erythropoietin, a hormone that stimulates peripheral stem cells in the bone marrow to produce red blood cells.

6. A similar situation exists for "modern" pharmaceuticals, in this case their "illicit" sale in many Dakar market places. Didier Fassin takes up how such pills circulate in Senegal: they pass through the hands of street peddlers, the National Pharmacy (PNA) and a network of Mouride Muslims, while they are considered "marginal" and illegal yet are often sold in full view of the police. Fassin asks, how to qualify this black market? Is it "modern," since the pills clearly traverse circuits that are official and part of the legitimate economy, or "traditional," since they simultaneously constitute a profitable informal sector that benefits from Mouride commercial networks? (1992, 95–98)

7. Eric Courot's family name was previously Couillerot. In 2006, he told me that he shortened it "for simplicity."

8. One obvious example is the South African case of *Hoodia*, a plant used by the San of the Kalahari for centuries to quench thirst and possibly hunger. Going on writings from colonial botanical publications, the South African-based *Council for Scientific and Industrial Research* (CSIR) undertook research on Hoodia's

potential as an appetite suppressant for commercial application in the early 1990s. After a lengthy investigation, the CSIR patented the plant's constituent ingredients in 1997. Subsequently, in 1998, the CSIR and the British company *Phytopharm* entered into an agreement to commercialize Hoodia, while Phytopharm also entered into a licensing and royalty agreement with the pharmaceutical giant *Pfizer* in the hopes of developing an appetite suppressant for the dietary control of obesity, a market that was valued at US$3 billion per year in the United States alone (Wynberg and Chennells 2009, 97). It was not until 2001, however, that the San themselves learned of the commercial application of Hoodia. They were initially not only excluded from the potentially lucrative deals being struck, but moreover the CSIR told Phytopharm that the San, as a population, no longer existed (at the time they were 100,000 strong) (Wynberg and Chennells 2009, 101). Eventually, due to publicity and public outrage, a "benefits-sharing" agreement was worked out with San groups, but this has also proven incredibly lopsided (Wynberg and Laird 2009). With regards to fagara, sickle cell, unlike obesity, does not count as what I heard one French geneticist refer to as a "popular disorder."

9. One of the most successful sites for traditional healing and research into plants is an NGO called PROMETRA (*Promouvoir la médecine traditionelle*). They have a partnership with the METRAF (Medicines and Traditions of Africa) foundation of Senegal where they pursue intellectual property rights on specific forms of phytotherapy and hope to be able to commercialize certain products after sufficient studies have been conducted. See http://www.metraf.com/herbalmedprod.html. At present, they, like many healers who want state recognition, rehabilitation of their trade, and legitimacy, are still awaiting legislation that will regulate traditional healing.

10. Anthropologist Stacey Langwick makes a related point with regard to "cosmopolitan" nurses and nurse's aids in Tanzania. These professionals are forced by neoliberal economic cuts in the health sector to prescribe medications for the sick body that are seen to be commensurably effective to cure the problem at hand, irrespective of whether the therapies be "modern" or "traditional." She writes: "The modernist dualisms sedimented in the gates of the hospital and the prejudices of the nurses are being overwhelmed by the demands of everyday practice. Nurses are compelled to coordinate traditional medicine not only with but also within biomedicine. The implications of this change are both subjective and ontological" (2008, 437).

11. See World Health Organization, *Promoting the Role of Traditional Medicine in Health Systems: A Strategy for the African Region 2001–2010* (Harare, World Health Organization, 2000), document reference AFR/RC50/Doc.9/R.

12. The state paper, *Le Soleil* (May 8, 2010) recently published a piece called Médecine traditionnelle: « Il faut mettre de l'ordre », featuring an interview with the president of PROMETRA, Mme Boury Niang. It emphasizes that her work is "devoid of all charlatanism and she collaborates strictly with modern medicine." It goes on to stress the commercial potential of this state of "harmonization," since "thanks to the hospital structure in which she works, several research studies were undertaken that resulted in several patents." She ends the interview pleading with the state to institute the law regulating traditional medicine to protect

healers like herself as well as patients from "charlatanism." See http://www.leso leil.sn/article.php3?id_article=58859 (accessed June 23, 2010). Similarly in September of 2009, the *Soleil* ran a story citing the president of ENDA, Fatoumata Sy, who complained about Senegal's lack of a law to control traditional healing. For Sy, "without a regulatory framework, the traditional medicine sector will forever include all categories of practitioners such as the non-initiated, incompetent healers and charlatans coming from countries where they are forbid to practice due to laws [that they have in place]." See http://www.lesoleil.sn/article .php3?id_article=50454 (accessed June 23, 2010).

13. See *Base de données des tradi-praticiens*, Ministry of Health Publications, http:// www.sante.gouv.sn/spip.php?rubrique9 (accessed June 23, 2010).

14. The first publications on the effects of the Fagara plant on sickling were based on research in Nigeria; see Sofowora and Isaacs (1971) "Reversal of Sickling and Crenation in Erythrocytes by the Roots of *Fagara xanthoxyloïdes*," *Lloydia* 34(4): 383–85, and Sofowora et al. (1975) "Isolation and Characterization of an Anti-sickling Agent from *Fagara xanthoxyloïdes* root, *Lloydia* 38(3): 169–71. For research on the plant done in the Ivory Coast, see Londsdorfer et al. (1981) " Etude biologique préliminaire d'une plante africaine, *Fagara*," *Annaux de l'Université d'Abidjan* serie b, 15:281–87, and Londsdorfer et al. (1987) "De l'utilisation empirique de *Fagara xanthoxyloïdes* à ses propriétés pharmacologiques établies," *Afrique Pharmacie* 3:11–12. For studies done on the plant in the United States, see Honig et al. (1975) "Evaluation of Fagara Xanthoxyloïdes Root Extract in Sickle Cell Anemia Blood in Vitro," *Lloydia* 38(5): 387–90. In a direct response to the studies of Sofowora and Isaacs, this study reports that Fagara root extracts have no anti-sickling effect. However, the American researchers admit that their methods of preparing the root extract, as well as the scientific procedure itself, differ drastically from those of Sofowora and Isaacs. For a confirmatory study on Fagara's anti-sickling properties done in the United States see Abu et al. (1981) "Chromatographic Fractionation of Anti-sickling Agents in Fagara Xanthoxyloides," *Acta Haematologica*, 66:19–22.

15. The pharmaceuticals hydroxyurea, decitabine, and butyrate were all first used in the treatment of leukemia. Notable changes in HbF production in leukemia patients made them theoretically interesting as sickle cell therapies (for a review see Makis et al. 2006, 909–10).

16. It is still common practice in Senegal, as in the French system more broadly, for students to be assigned thesis topics by their advisors.

17. ENDA posts instructions for taking fagara, which is mixed with three other plants, for sickle cell on their website for "integrated development." They give patients specific directions for making an infusion, or tea, from the product. The following extract is from their website, http://madesahel.enda.sn/html/Presentation.html (accessed Nov. 28, 2006):

> Produit traditionnel contre les troubles de la dréponocytose [*sic*]
> Fagara (F) - Genegideck (W) - Barkèlé (P) - Noc (S) - Goro Mga (B)
>
> Chaque infusette contient 1.5 grammes de racine séchée et broyée.
>
> Mode d'emploi: faire bouillir l'infusette pendant deux minutes dans le contenu d'une tasse d'eau et boire à jeun. On peut sucrer.

> Posologie: en cas de crise, prendre une infusette matin, midi et soir, à jeun. En cas de crise aigüe, on peut prendre deux infusettes à la fois. Chez l'enfant de moins de 7 ans, boire la moitié d'une tasse.
>
> N.B.: Le produit a un effet préventif pendant 6 mois, si on le prend pendant 2 semaines à dose normale. Aucune contre-indication n'a été signalée jusqu'à ce jour.
>
> Ce produit, recommandé par les professeurs J. Kerharo et H. de Lauture, est utilisé par l'Association des Postes de Santé Privés Catholiques du Sénégal, APSPCS (B.P. 2407 - Tel. 821.79.54) avec l'appui d'ENDA-Medesahel (B.P. 6259 - Tel. 823.76.76).
>
> Un étui contient 9 infusettes.

See Keharo and De Lauture (2003). Note that their translation of fagara into Wolof is "genegideck," not dengidëk. The interchange of the two words is more common than not.

18. Emphasis added. See http://madesahel.enda.sn/ (accessed November 30, 2006).
19. Catholic nuns, who run health clinics in and around Dakar, rely on the French professor to supply them with fagara for sickle cell disease, since their patient population most often does not have access to health professionals who know enough about sickle cell to properly treat it. Patients from rural areas were usually prescribed expensive, outdated, and ineffective pharmaceuticals, such as hydergine, as I describe in the text. De Lauture's main contact among the nuns was a sister called Immaculata, who was originally from Ireland. She and others run a health clinic where sicklers frequently seek care in the small village of *Ker Moussa* renowned for its abbey, its goat cheese, and its monks' Gregorian chanting. The sisters view fagara and other medicinal plants as "God's medicines," as Immaculata told me in 2001. That they come to them from animist healers who later became Muslim, via a retired professor of medicine turned traditional healer, before ending up in their Catholic hands merely evinces God's will to "share his graces amongst all his children." The professor buys from Sambou and then repackages his herbs with the ENDA logo and telephone number. Small plastic bags of 1.5 grams are distributed throughout the region at Catholic Mission heath centers.
20. Sambou invited me to speak on sickle cell disease with him for Dakar radio station *DiamonoFM*. The host had planned a full hour with Sambou alone wherein he was to discuss sickle cell disease and his medications to treat it. He surprised her by bringing me along, so she permitted him to introduce me. He then told the listeners that I was an "American who was in Dakar studying under him," while I also possessed detailed knowledge on "the mechanics of the disease," which he might have to draw on.
21. In addition to the plant mixes that he had his sons prepare, Sambou's healing relied on prayer. At the beginning of every day he would pray and cite incantations in Wolof, Diola, and Arabic. When I first witnessed this, one of his sons worriedly asked me if I knew what he was saying; Sambou interrupted to tell me that it was a simple prayer of thanks and a request for guidance.
22. For the full editorial statement of the patient group that bills itself as the "Federation of People with Sickle Cell and the Thalassemias" (Federation des Malades

Drépanocytaires et Thalassemiques), also called SOS Globi, see http://www.sos globi.fr/cgi-bin/articles.php?lng=fr&pg=8542 (accessed August 31, 2009).

23. Letter, Dr. Andre Orsini to Dr. Cherif Rahimy. . . . This excerpt is also quoted on the Federations de Malades website in the VK500 "archive" in Gil Tchernia's "testimony." See http://www.sosglobi.fr/cgi-bin/articles.php?lng=fr&pg=8542 (accessed August 31, 2009).

24. For Tchernia's full posting detailing his exchanges and the various proposed phases of his collaborative study with Fagla Médégan, see http://www.sosglobi .fr/cgi-bin/articles.php?lng=fr&pg=8542. The passage cited in the text was translated from the French which reads:

> L'analyse des dossiers a montré que le caractère jugé favorable des effets du traitement ne reposait sur aucune méthodologie clinique sérieuse et sur aucun critère objectif. Les essais in vitro ont été entièrement négatifs. Monsieur Médégan venu pour en discuter s'est montré très abattu, a considéré que probablement nous n'avions pas reçu le bon lot du produit et a proposé de revenir lui-même assister à de nouvelles expérimentations avec les échantillons adaptés de son produit, ce que j'ai bien entendu accepté. Je ne l'ai jamais revu et l'expérimentation à l'aide du modèle murin n'a pas eu lieu.

25. A televised interview with Fagla Médégan aired in September of 2008, for the talk show *Vivement Dimanche*. He seemed to be there primarily because he knows the Italian Royal family, especially Princess Clotilde, now an award-winning French actress. Clotilde shared the stage with him and provided the not-so-obvious segue for host Michel Druker to ask about his research on VK500. During the interview Médégan talked about his research, and also purported to be an expert on the disease even though he made two false statements that outraged many in sickle cell circles; namely that "only Africans" get sickle cell, and more questionable, that sicklers cannot live past thirty or forty years old. See http://www .youtube.com/watch?v=C5TPdBWU10Q (accessed August 28, 2009).

26. The patent documents that are available to the public are mostly blank. The first page gives the crucial identifying information for Fagla Médégan, the publicity and registration numbers for the patent, as well as the principal use. It reads "a medicine primarily for the treatment of sickle cell or AIDS (médicament notamment pour le traitement de la drépanoctytose ou du SIDA)." A more detailed statement than the one sentence in the actual patent can be found in Médégan's database entry. It reads: "The present invention essentially concerns a useful composition that works as a medication. This composition consists primarily of an extract of the plant Fagara xanthoxyloïdes combined with [. . . other plants]. This composition is especially efficacious medicinally, notably in treatment regimens for sickle cell or AIDS. (La présente invention concerne essentiellement une composition utile comme médicament. Cette composition comprend notamment un extrait de la plante Fagara xanthoxyloïdes combiné en outre avec un extrait de la plante Securidaca longepedonculata, et/ou un extrait de la plante Uvaria chamae. Cette composition est notamment utile comme médicament notamment dans le cadre du traitement de la drépanocytose ou du SIDA). http:// fr.espacenet.com/publicationDetails/biblio?CC=FR&NR=2855056A1&KC=A1&

FT=D&date=20041126&DB=fr.espacenet.com&locale=fr_FR (accessed August 30, 2009).

27. See http://www.sosglobi.fr/cgi-bin/articles.php?lng=fr&pg=8542&prt=2 (accessed August 28, 2009).

28. Comparatively, one can buy a three-month supply of fagara, given that one makes, at a minimum, two 1.5 liter infusions, in local Dakar markets for *2.000 cfa* [US$4], while Sambou's mixture that contains other plants cost *5.000 cfa* [US$10] for a similar period.

29. The original letter in French reads:

> Niamey (Niger), le 02/09/99
>
> Bonjour Monsieur le Représentant.
>
> Comme prévu je vous envoie la documentation sur la drépanocytose.
>
> Nous sommes dans le même sitation [*sic*], mon ainé aussi est drépanocytaire SS. Avec ce nouveau produit, nous avons des raisons d'espérer. Ici à Niamey, j'ai deja une nièce aui [*sic*] a suivi le traitement et apparamment tout se passe bien. Elle n'a plus de crises. C'est d'ailleurs elle qui m'a envoyé cette documentation sur le produit. Je vous souhaite bonne réception et bon usage. Que dieu nous protege. Amen.
>
> Mme K. Mariama
>
> Projet sr/pf (orthographe d'original respectée)

Chapter Four. Attitudes of Care

1. Biomedical doctors in other African contexts recount similar approaches to diagnosis. Studying medical students in Malawi, Claire Wendland writes: "Several commented that their foreign colleagues, used to relying on radiologic and laboratory examinations, were not very good at physical diagnosis. Medical students from abroad did not know how to measure an enlarged liver with their hands, diagnose twins without an ultrasound, or confirm a ruptured tubal pregnancy without a pregnancy test" (2010, 174). As with doctors I encountered in Dakar, Wendland argues that medical students in Malawi thought that technology could be helpful for medical practice but that in its absence "resourcefulness" and human relations of care, empathy and "heart" were essential.

2. Modern equipment, for Rabinow, consists of potentially reconfigurable conceptual "tool kits" of logics and methods for social analysis of life's problems. He writes: "The challenge is three-fold: (1) to provide a toolkit of concepts for conducting inquiries into the contemporary world in its actuality; (2) to conduct those inquires in a manner that makes the relations, connections, and disjunctions between logos [reason] and ethos [life ethics] apparent and available to oneself and to others . . . to make those relations part of the inquiry itself as well as a part of life; (3) to take into account the pathos encountered and engendered by such an undertaking" (2003, 12). As concerns the modern cultural equipment and tools that Diagne and his colleagues felt could partially explain their contemporary world in its actuality, their "inquiries" on *semiologie,* fagara and the *attitude sénégalaise* remain mere mediations, which are nonetheless "part of life." These inquiries are somewhat stifled because these "tools" remain "available [mostly] to themselves," not others, while their research relations with their Northern col-

leagues as "connections" are also disjunctions that engender a certain pathos, and uneasiness.

3. The majority of practitioners I interviewed agreed that surveillance was key to Senegalese sickle cell care, but Diagne treated surveillance as primary. He always took the time to examine his small patients' bodies to make sure that infections and local parasites were not impairing their health. He examined their gait and visible level of energy or languor as they came into the office. He measured patients' bodies—head circumference, trunk, and full standing height—to ascertain growth values, which were dutifully listed in the charts. Patients were also weighed. This ritualized protocol of bodily contact and mutual familiarity of doctor and patient was specific to Diagne's practice and to those he eventually trained. The pediatrician found it important to ascertain the rate at which his patients were developing physically, since this disease can stunt growth. These measurements also served as a visible index that relayed to parents the fruits of their care as their children advanced in stature and in life. Diagne would inform parents of their children's numeric values and congratulate, or counsel, them and the child depending on his or her "progress." Although the CNTS formally serves as the adult sickle cell care site, many children figured among their patient population as well. Rarely were they "cared for" similarly, in part because CNTS practitioners did not have a pediatric focus.

4. In his study of Wolof family and kinship structures, carried out nearly fifty years ago and published in the mid 1980s, Senegalese sociologist Abdoulaye Bara Diop, writes: "relational ties (la parenté) are essentially transmitted through the blood. The expression bokk deret, which coveys blood ties, means "to have the same blood" (1985, 20). Yet, Diop also emphasized that blood-kinship references and certain hereditary diseases implicate the maternal more than the paternal side, a notion that many people in my research disagreed with. Diop writes, "The child is thus biologically a product of the two lineages. Physically, he depends on both his mother and father. However, if quantitatively what is inherited from the two sides balances out (on the one hand, the blood and flesh and, on the other, the bones and nerves) qualitatively the maternal line prevails" (ibid.). I made a point to meet with Diop to discuss how in my research it seemed that people were using kin expressions in ways that went beyond any clear notion of gendered heritage or closeness to one "line" over the other. His response was that Islam, with its patriarchal norms, has evened out people's thinking on heredity in the present. I did find, however, that unrelated people deployed a religious-like faith in their new kinships with others who also had HbS. I also found that women were often saddled with the burden of their children's everyday care, which provoked stress, existential anxiety, and fear in them about precipitously losing their child.

5. The Mouride Brotherhood is a prominent Sufi Islamic order in Senegal and the Senegalese diaspora. Adherents follow the teachings and life examples of Sërin Touba, or Cheikh Amadou Bamba, who was a Muslim mystic and ascetic spiritual leader who emphasized meditation and Qur'anic study, but, especially, hard work and industriousness as means to achieve salvation.

6. As medical anthropologist Carolyn Rouse has argued in Uncertain Suffering, specifics of organization also partially define the success of the four American Comprehensive Sickle Cell Centers where she conducted fieldwork (2009).

7. The question of the interrelation of persistent fetal hemoglobin and the sickle cell haplotypes seems to have been resolved for some in Paris who say that genetic studies have provided them enough evidence to show that the two are not *necessarily* related. However, these same geneticists, as well as sickle cell physicians, continue to connect the two conceptually.

8. See Thiam et al. (1990) "Les effets in vitro *de Fagara xanthoxyloïdes* Lam sur les érythrocytes drépanocytaires, *Dakar Médical* 35(1): 37–45.

9. Unfortunately the title was mistranslated into English, with a spelling error in the key word, "fagara": "In vitro effects of Fagaro xanthoxyloides Lam on drepanocytic erythrocytes."

10. Perhaps tellingly, psychiatry at *Fann* is now directed by Senegalese practitioners who not only advance ideas of the "individual" in Africa but also prescribe psychotropics and rely on the latest DSM as a diagnostic reference for their practice.

11. Shortly after the 2006 Dakar conference on sickle cell the *Soleil* state newspaper ran a story on the importance of traditional medicine for sickle cell. Thiam (whose first name is wrongly spelled Daouda) is quoted as saying that traditional plants work for sickle cell and that there needs to be "serious collaboration between doctors and traditional healers . . . we must accept our "colleagues" in the realm of traditional medicine." (Sané 2006)

12. Later our the interview I pushed him on this and he replied, "People say America is a melting pot [using the English term]; let us not forget that Africa is a melting pot too!"

Chapter Five. Localized Biologies: Mapping Race and Sickle Cell Difference in French West Africa

1. The federation of *l'Afrique Occidentale Française* consisted of the then territories of Côte d'Ivoire, Dahomey (now Benin), French Guinea (now Guinea), French Sudan (now Mali), Mauritania, Niger, Senegal, and Upper Volta (now Burkina Faso). For a contemporary proposal of African "dependency" rather than nominal "independence," in the face of market viability and responsible global connectedness, see Ferguson 2006, 22.

2. Senghor was Senegal's first president, who went on to rule for twenty years. He is perhaps better known as one of the founders (along with writers Aimé Césaire, Paulette and Jane Nardal, and Réné Maran from the French Antilles, and French Guyanese writer Léon-Gontran Damas, as well as Jamaican Claude McKay) of the *Négritude* movement. This political and literary movement was one that Senghor later described as "part of the struggle for liberation from the chains of [French] cultural colonization in favor of a new humanism" (See Senghor 1988, 136–37.) Senghor's mother, his father's third wife, was of the Peul nomadic ethnic group, while his father was from a successful feudalist Sereer family. His parents' ethnicities historically have some degree of culturally accepted tensions (*cal*), that often take the form of teasing, but that also trade in blunt stereotypes. His work often thematized cultural and racial sharing and complementarities, what he would later call "bi-cephalism." By his own account, Senghor's vision was informed by the fact that he "grew up in the heartland of Africa, at the crossroads of castes, races, and routes" (Irele 1977, 11). Senghor was awarded French citizenship and served in the military in the 1930s, as well as during WWII. He was elected

to represent Senegal in the National Assembly while living in Paris from 1945 through 1956, and was the first African accepted to the prestigious *Académie Française* for his literary works. For more on Senghor's life, writings and politics, see Janet G. Vaillant (1990) *Black, French, and African: A Life of Léopold Sédar Senghor*; Janet Spleth (1985) *Léopold Sédar Senghor*; Jacques-Louis Hymans (1971) *Léopold Sedar Senghor: An Intellectual Biography*; and Irving Leonard Markovitz (1969) *Léopold Sédar Senghor and the Politics of Negritude* (1969).

3. Teilhard de Chardin was a Jesuit and close friend of Senghor who likely influenced his thinking and writing regarding the physical differences and complementarities of different "types" of humans. He taught science in Egypt in 1905–1908, earned a doctorate in geology, botany, and zoology (as close as he could get to paleontology) from the Sorbonne in 1922, did archaeological work in China until the late 1940s (where he was present at the discovery of Peking Man), and, in 1928, spent two months traveling in East Africa, including Harrar and Somalia. For his biography and theory, see Ursula King 1996, and H. James Birx 1993.

4. The reasons for the federation's dissolution ranged from dissention on foreign policy toward France, including Mali's support of the FLN in Algeria (Mortimer 1972, 286), to disagreement on the distribution of offices and the Africanization of the civil service. Some feared that leaders in what is now Mali attempted to turn the religious leaders in Senegal against Senghor (Kurtz 1970, 406).

5. As of 1848, only Gorée and Saint-Louis were under French rule. Saint-Louis, on the Senegal River, was the first French colonial territory in Africa, settled in 1659. Gorée, a slave trading station just off the coast, was acquired from the Dutch in 1677 (although the French started trading there as early as 1624). In 1872 Gorée was named a commune, which included Dakar. Fifteen years later, in 1887, Dakar was made a commune independent from Gorée. The last site, Rufisque, a port and manufacturing center near Dakar, became a commune in 1880. Africans living within these areas were called "*originaires*" or " inhabitants" of these select areas, as distinct from people living in the interior lands of the territory of Senegal, and eventually throughout the rest of the AOF (Diouf 2001, 137–38). The idea behind the creation of the communes was that Africans living within the four cities would have all of the rights that French citizens possessed and would help to administer trade and facilitate the extension of French colonial power. The territory of Senegal had a special status, as Saint-Louis, then Dakar, was the capital of the AOF; those political privileges, in theory, set them apart from other Africans. This exceptionalism was not as straightforward in practice, however (See Gary Wilder 2005, chap. 5).

6. Anthropologist Doris Bonnet argues that in contemporary France, sickle cell, "a disease of origins," is linked to ethnologists' methods of classification, patients' political uses of their bodies to obtain medical visas, and geneticists' obsessions with group biological homogeneity, all of which articulate through sicklers' "identities" within and beyond France (2004, 49). She notes that despite the potential flexibility of identity constructions through the disease, a slippage occurs when origins and ethnicity are generalized and hardened, when "culture" is utilized as a "socio-biological paradigm (that takes the place of race and ethnicity), or serves as a 'toolkit' to explain everything" (Bonnet 2004, 61). In *Repenser l'hérédité*, Bonnet argues that a "patient's culture of origin" is often a euphemism

for race, and becomes a means for many French practitioners to generalize about rather than truly understand the populations they treat (2009, 86).

7. Archival records detailing the management, accounting, and financial anxieties of the CNTS between 1949 and 1957 make clear that obtaining enough equipment was a challenge, as were seemingly smaller tasks such as shuttling the personnel in from different areas and accounting for misused funds, such as unexplainable amounts of red wine being consumed and billed on the CNTS ledger. Allegedly, the wine was being imbibed by blood donors who were given a meal and beverage for their service, but as most were African and Muslim, it was likely not this population that ingested the massive quantities for which administrators were trying to account. Various correspondences and reports between actors at the CNTS and the Anthropological Mission in Senegal, as well as the *Musée de l'Homme* in Paris, on these issues can be found in *Les Archives Nationales du Sénégal*, "Centre de Transfusion Sanguine, 1949–57," Serie H, 1 H 62.

8. In his 1946 report for the Anthropological mission called *"Organisme d'enquête pour l'étude anthropologique des populations indigènes de l'AOF, alimentation et nutrition*, Pales wrote: For many years, doctors of the colonial troops, at the moment of recruitment, have taken the opportunity to measure thousands of Africans from all regions of the AOF... standing height, sitting stature, thoracic perimeter, weight. For the last five years they have added blood type to this picture..." (1946 Rapport no. 1, ORANA, p. 5, folder 163, Serie H, 1 H 92).

9. Historian Agnès Lainé argues that sickle cell testing in sub-Saharan Africa started with Hermann Lehmann, a British military doctor who worked in both India and East Africa. She cites him, without a bibliographic reference, as saying, "Sickleamia appears to be inversely proportional to the [amount of] contact the various tribes had with their most recent Hamitic invaders." She writes further on that "It is to Lehmann's works that we can date the conviction, among later authors, that the HbS gene was a black characteristic and that high frequencies of HbS [in some groups] should be interpreted as the marker that enracinates the black race to an African space" (2004, 29). The above quote attributed to Lehmann in Lainé is from a 1949 *Nature* paper that Lehmann published with A. B. Raper. Although they use the racial logics of "Hamitic" and "non-Hamitic" peoples, as well as language of "Caucasoid features" attributed to Hamitic "stocks," they claim, unlike Pales's, that their study in Uganda "was primarily medical" with a "bearing on anthropology" (1949, 494). Although they report on "a remarkable difference between certain African tribes" where "the incidence of the sickle-cell trait is uniformly low in the pastoral, Hamitic-tongued tribes," with the "Nilotic" tribes being "remarkably homogenous," while the "Bantu" tribes possess "a wide variation" (1949, 494), it seems an overstatement to claim that Lehmann's work was the causal impetus for sickle cell racial mapping in sub-Saharan Africa. The problem is that many studies on raciology, blood groups, and biological traits were already underway before Lehmann's various publications (which appeared as of 1949) (For a review of earlier raciology studies in the AOF see Bonnecase 2009). Historian-anthropologist Melbourne Tapper also argues that Lehman and Raper were informed by the Hamitic thesis, which they "legitimized by bringing hard serological evidence to its support" (Tapper 1999, 79). He does not, however, credit them with launching the colonial obsession with mapping race through

sickle cell. Tapper's history for sickle cell incidence mapping in tribal groups within Anglophone-colonized Africa begins in 1946 with E. A. Beet (1999, 64).

10. Most historians of French imperialism and colonial West Africa who have touched on questions of race end their studies with the interwar period. Ideas that were very much alive in the early 1940s, such as theorizing ways to concretize African identities, may have only just found a biogenetic basis on which to stand a few years later with the serological and trait studies done in the 1950s. With such questions in mind, I share Gary Wilder's view that strictly "periodizing transformation is always arbitrary and heuristic" (2005, 43).

11. The French researchers carrying out these studies in the AOF cite more than a dozen similar research efforts that had been conducted in the British colonies as early as 1943 in Nigeria (Smith 1943). Anthropologist Melbourne Tapper, concentrating on East African medical studies, argues that the British colonial medical corps pursued sickle cell "primarily as an ethnological matter, their main concern being what sickling (blood) could reveal about tribal histories, differences, and identities as well as about the very origin and true bioracial nature of the so-called African" (Tapper 2001, 335).

12. Not all subjects were used; for example sixty-seven subjects were excluded because of their extensive "heterogeneous" racial origins. The usable sample after the first year consisted of 2,302 people (Pales and Linhard 1952, 64).

13. In their 1966 work on world hemoglobin differences, hematologists H. Lehmann and R. Huntsman proposed that socioeconomic status, which they regarded as determining a population's ability to ward off malarial infections that could be lethal to sicklers, could also explain why certain populations had higher rates of sickle cell trait when compared to others. "In-breeding populations are particularly prone to accumulate a high frequency of unusual inherited character[istic]s. There is, however, yet another factor which may help to increase the sickling incidence in such primitive groups; though the malarial pressure may not be greater, the malarial death-rate will be increased under unfavorable and primitive conditions. Children, who might have overcome a mild infection of malignant malaria, may yet fall victim to it if there is in addition another cause of debility, such as malnutrition, or infection or infestation—all factors more associated with social status. Thus, a depressed social level will inflate the malarial death-rate, and the greater the number of children affected by this inflation of the malarial death-rate, the more significant will be the difference in the observed survival of sicklers over non-sicklers" (1966, 208).

14. See footnote 13.

15. These reports for Senegal are listed in the National Archives of Senegal, Serie G, 2G50/15, 2G51/15, 2G52/13, 2G53/25. For AOF reports, written by *the Haute Commission de l'Afrique Occidentale Française, Direction générale de la santé publique*, I read through the years spanning 1950 to 1953 and found no mention of sickle cell, or sickling (*sicklèmie*). See *Les Archives Nationales du Sénégal*, Serie G, 2G50/9, 2G51/8, 2G52/63.

16. The 1953 AOF report on public health in the colony lists over fifty diseases, most of which were potentially communicable. Some diseases were discussed in detail with notes on their prevention and treatment. Sickle cell, as a disease seen as inherent to but also confined to the natives, and that posed no threat to the

French, never figured in these reports even though various publications on the disease in the AOF had already appeared. Diseases listed during the years that Pales and Linhard were conducting their widespread sickle cell screening can be found in the AOF medical reports for the years 1951 and 1952, published in 1952 and 1953, documents Serie G, 2G 52/63 and 2G 53/7 at *Les Archives Nationales du Sénégal* in Dakar. Both are titled *Rapport Annuel, Haute Commission de l'Afrique Occidentale Française, Direction général de la santé publique.*

17. Historians of colonial health politics have pointed out that medicine in the AOF was long rife with racial hierarchies that were often rooted in European fears of contagion and fitness, both for their own health and power to rule, as well as for Africans' health and ability to provide labor (Keita 2007, 105–07). One instance of such racial ordering appeared in urban planning projects that separated French from African quarters through a philosophy of the *cordon sanitaire* (quarantine line). The actual construction of colonial communities was undertaken to contain disease, but it was also used to reinforce a political philosophy of French superior power concerning governance and health care (ibid, 100–101). Another instance of the institutionalization of hierarchy took place within medical education itself, and the eventual creation of African "auxiliary doctors," as they were called, who, it was understood, were always second rank. As Jean-Paul Bado points out, French colonial schools of medicine for native education were constructed to aid French doctors in Pondicherry, India (1863), Antananarivo, Madagascar (1896), and Hanoi, in what was then called Indochina (1902). Yet because of ideas within the French administration about "African intellectual insufficiencies and incapacity to follow scientific reasoning," the African medical school site was founded much later (1918) in Dakar and with some hesitation (Bado 1996, 217). It was only after massive shortages in medical personnel and trained French doctors available to serve in the colonies during World War I that the colonial administration realized they could no longer hold off training "indigenous doctors." This turn became an opportunity for the civilizing mission: their training emphasized scientific rationality and metaphysical empirical medicine. (Bado 1996, 218)

18. Medical historian Keith Wailoo has shown that cases of sickle cell anemia in "the white race" in the United States were thought to be a confirmation that sickling could be spread through "miscegenation," the term for interracial marriage in the early twentieth-century North American context. Among others, Wailoo cites M. A. Odgen's 1943 article, "Sickle Cell Anemia in the White Race," where one physician proclaimed sickle cell anemia a national health problem in the United States and argued that "Intermarriages between Negroes and White persons directly endanger the white race by transmission of the sickle cell trait." The physician concluded: "such intermarriages should therefore be prohibited by federal law." See Wailoo (1996, 306). Studies done in the 1940s and 1950s in the United States found that American blacks, who were also thought to have some Caucasian "admixture," had higher rates of sickle cell disease than "pure" blacks in Africa, who were thought to have higher rates of sickle cell trait. Some took such figures as proof that "race mixture could be disadvantageous." See R. Gates (letter) (1952) "Disadvantages of Race Mixture," *Nature*, 170: 896, and M. Tapper (1999) *In the Blood: Sickle Cell Anemia and the Politics of Race*, chapter 2.

19. For example, as Jean-Loup Amselle points out, Governor Faidherbe's affinity for the Peul, who, for him, more or less belonged to the intermittent race of "red" people, was in part due to the fact that he saw them as more fit to govern than their "black" neighbors, the Wolof and the Sérère. Nonetheless, they themselves were often mixed (Amselle 1996, 129).

20. Hirschfeld and Hirschfeld took advantage of the massive congregation of soldiers on the Macedonian front during the First World War, comprising sixteen nationalities, divided into the races of "European," "Intermediate," and "Afro-Asian," upon whom they performed the first "comprehensive" racial serological screenings. They concluded that races could be classified as discrete populations based on particular blood-group expressions. The Hirschfelds invented a schema called the "biochemical race index," the relation of the percentage of agglutinin b (Groups A and O) to the percentage of agglutinin a (Groups B and O) found in any and all populations. This sort of thinking enjoyed scientific status for only five years, but its underlying logic that "race" could be exposed by blood remained in place for much longer. Both E. Grove's work on geographically distinct Ainu populations with different blood types and L. Snyder's review of the biochemical racial indexes of the world's populations in 1926 found obvious anatomically similar "racial" groups sometimes inconsistently linked by blood-group percentages, the "biochemical race index." For a review of the literature and further explanation, the failings of early blood-race theories are compiled by Marks (1995) "Patterns of Variation in Human Populations," chapter 7 of *Human Biodiversity: Genes, Race and History*. For primary sources see Hirschfeld, H. and L. Hirschfeld (1919) "Serological Differences between the Blood of Different Races," *Lancet* (October 18): 675–79, E. L. Grove (1926) "On the Value of the Blood-Group Feature as a means of Determining Racial Relationship," *Journal of Immunology* 12(4): 251–62; L. Snyder (1926) "Human Blood Groups: Their Inheritance and Racial Significance," *American Journal of Physical Anthropology* 9:233–63, and J. Lewis and D. Henderson (1922) "The Racial Distribution of Isohemagglutinin Groups," *JAMA* 79: 14222–24.

21. Trait frequency here refers to *any* evidence of the trait, i.e., in those who actually possessed the disease, as well as those with just one HbS allele.

22. In a footnote they write: "We thank our comrades working in various hospital services for having facilitated our work" (1952, 64; fn 1).

23. For more on the fluidity of ethnic groups in what is now Senegal, see Makhtar Diouf (1998) *Sénégal les Ethnies et la Nation* (Dakar: Nouvelles Editions Africaines du Sénégal) p. 88.

24. For a history of the emergence of restriction endonuclease, an enzyme that digests fragments of DNA at specific points, and its use in spawning gene mapping possibilities, see Cook-Deegan (1994), chapter 2, "Mapping our Genes," and Kary Mullis et al. (1986) "Specific Enzymatic Amplification of DNA in Vitro: The Polymerase Chain Reaction," *Cold Spring Harbor Symposium in Quantitative Biology* 51:263–73.

25. Algeria is grouped with Benin because the Benin haplotype is found there.

26. Two other haplotypes were discovered a few years later in Cameroon and India by teams also led by D. Labie. See Lapoumeroulie et al. (1992) "A Novel Sickle Cell Gene of Yet Another Origin in Africa: The Cameroon Type," *Blood* 74: 225A (ab-

stract). Labie et al. (1989) "Haplotypes in Tribal Indians Bearing the Sickle Cell Gene: Evidence for the Unicentric Origin of the Bs Mutation and the Unicentric Origin of the Tribal Populations of India," *Human Biology* 61(4): 479–91.

27. Yet, in a triumphalist mode, Labie and her colleagues expressed doubt that the single-base pair polymorphisms found by Kan and Dozy would adequately prove sickle cell genetic diversity. Despite Kan and Dozy's 1978 finding and their own work, eleven other RFLP sites on the beta-globin gene had been found, Labie's team writes: "For this reason, attention is now centered on the use of multiple DNA polymorphisms in and around the *ß*-globin gene cluster for establishing the origin of the HbS gene. The conceptual basis for the use of the DNA polymorphisms located in the *ß*-globin gene cluster stems from the discovery of at least eleven sites accessible to detection by restriction endonucleases and several other sites detectable, at this point, only by sequence analysis. The 11 restriction endonuclease sites . . . should be expected to be closely linked to the *ß*-globin gene, and if the mutational event is reasonably recent a *ß*-globin gene mutation should be accompanied by a defined haplotype formed by the set of polymorphic DNA sequences found in the *ß*-globin-like gene cluster. Th[ese] sequences would be those preexisting in the chromosome before the mutational event" (Pagnier et al. 1984, 1771).

28. Sanofi is a major international pharmaceutical corporation.

29. These are the figures used in the 1984 paper, although in conversations both Labie and Diagne cited "85 percent" as the portion of people in Dakar who had the "Senegalese" genetic signature.

30. The title of this researcher's grant was "Pharmacogenetics and Therapeutic Approaches to Hereditary Illness," funded by INSERM unit 458.

31. In the seminal 1984 article that established the African haplotypes, collaborators in Dakar were thanked in the acknowledgements; however, the three names mentioned were all French. For many working on sickle cell today, the mentioning of French clinic heads allowed the Africans who gave blood and those who "carried out the real work" to be all but ignored. Corroborative studies were later conducted by joint French and African teams, but never with Senegalese researchers.

Chapter Six. Ordering Illness: Heterozygous "Trait" Suffering in the Land of the Mild Disease

1. The linguistic rendering of "sickle cell carrier" in French (*drépanocytaire AS*) is the same, despite the AS qualifier, as that which names one who has sickle cell disease (*drépanocytaire SS*) leading many to "sensibly" consider HbAS a mild form of HbSS disease.

2. The first widespread report of sudden death in young men with sickle cell trait in the United States happened during routine military activity at high altitudes (see Jones et al. 1970) and was published in the *New England Journal of Medicine*. Although several articles on the issue have appeared in this and other mainstream medical journals most are published in the specialized journal *Military Medicine*, or when they appear in other publications the studies have been carried out by medical researchers of the Armed Forces (such as Kark et al. 1987). Key articles by military personnel on the issue include: Q. Franklin and M. Compeggie (1999); K. Kerle (1996); M. Murray and P. Evans (1996); M. Sateriale and P. Hart (1985);

and P. Sherry (1990). For a lengthy review of sickle cell trait and exercise see J. Kark and T. Ward (1994). Lastly, celebrity black athletes figured prominently in the early 1970s public debates regarding the "normalcy" of sickle cell trait carriers. Their accounts varied and were ultimately used to differing ends, both to fund sickle cell testing legislation and then to call attention to its injustices. Regarding the first, in 1971, National League baseball pitcher Doc Ellis presented his own trait symptoms on national television for the congressional hearings that led to the passage of the *Sickle Cell Anemia Prevention Act* saying: "I have . . . aching in my joints. Plus I have fainting spells. I don't faint, but I get faint. And like today, during the first inning I felt that—faint, and the best thing that I did was just to stand still and shake it off." (*Congressional Record*, transcript, 1971, cited in Wailoo 2001, 169). Then in the 1980s when the U.S. Air Force made it a policy to dismiss all pilots with sickle cell trait, tri-star athlete Stephen Pullens, who was fired from piloting, filed a lawsuit and won. His case proved that carriers "affected with trait" were as physically robust as anyone, thus special handling (discrimination) of them was unwarranted. For more on the Pullens case, see Duster (2003, 27).

3. In previous interviews I carried out in Oakland, California, with African-Americans as a research assistant on a separate study called "Pathways to Genetic Screening" (DOE, DE-FG03-92ER61393), it was clear that certain American carriers did not understand their sickle trait as wholly distinct from the disease. This was evident in the language they used, calling their "trait" a "trace" of sickle cell in their bodies. However, I never encountered people with dramatic symptoms and suffering attributed to sickle cell trait in Oakland as I did in Dakar. In hindsight, it is clear to me that because this study was conducted in the United States, American researchers, like myself at the time, did not conceive that one could possibly suffer from symptoms and merely have one sickle hemoglobin allele, HbAS. Our categories of seeing sickle cell reflected those of the larger American medical field of the times, despite our position as social scientists professionally outside of it. As Arthur Kleinman notes in an early essay on somatization, "culture shapes disease first by shaping our explanations of disease" (1977, 4). It was not until years after my work on the Oakland project, when I went to do my own fieldwork in Dakar, that I would encounter sickle cell trait suffering as a disease option.

4. After medical reports of sudden death in black male army recruits during basic training at high altitudes were published in the New England Journal of Medicine (Jones et al. 1970), articles on sickle cell trait and, or, hemoglobin, then appeared in various publications which sparked much concern in the black community (see Hampton et al. 1974; Heller et al. 1979; Kark et al. 1987). Many studies discussed the trait and its risks, which had now become the basis for why blacks could only selectively perform in the military and in certain sectors of the Job Corps. Despite the fact that certain studies found no difference in mortality in "normals" and "sickle cell trait carriers" the Air Force grounded or fired their employees with sickle cell trait in the early and mid-1970s (Bowman 1977, 129). The effects of this were quickly understood through the framework and language of racism so familiar to American blacks at the tail end of civil rights (Bowman 1977, 128; Reilly 1976, 179).

5. As discussed in chapter 5, beginning in 1950 sickle cell disease and trait were *taken together* as similarities in kind.

6. Sickle hemoglobin (which accounts for as much as 50 percent of carriers' total hemoglobin) confers protection from falciparum plasmodia because the parasite *unwittingly provokes sickling* and, hence, the probability of being detected by the spleen and removed from circulation. In other words, as hematologist Lucio Luzzatto wrote years ago: by infecting a trait carrier, and thereby causing sickling of the red blood cells, "the parasite undertakes a suicidal infection" (Luzzatto, Nwachukup-Jarrett, and Reddy 1970, 321), as it would in a person with full-blown sickle cell disease (Luzzatto et al. 1970; Luzzatto and Pinching 1990, 342; Nagel and Flemming 1992, 355). Whether or not this interaction actually causes the pain and lassitude associated with the anemia and other complications of sickle cell disease, or trait, has never been posed as a biomedical research question and represents a strange void in the scientific literature.

7. During interviews with sickle cell specialists in Dakar, it quickly became clear that the association of sickle cell trait with symptoms was the norm. One younger physician at Albert Royer Children's Hospital called his unconventional refusal to diagnose the trait as a disease an effect of the "old" vs. the "new" school. He was referring to the fact that his older colleagues just next door at the National Blood Transfusion Center (CNTS) where adult sickle cell is treated were still carrying ideas from 1950s colonial medicine (which was not concerned with differentiating trait from disease).

8. Despite the normative practice of not treating the trait as debilitating in the United States and France, the issue constantly resurfaces in the American medical literature and most recently in 2009, in sports medicine, when the National Collegiate Athletic Association (NCAA) instituted a policy recommendation of testing trait carriers with the goal of avoiding sudden deaths on the court or field. During initial debate regarding the NCAA recommendations, Oakland-based sickle cell psychologist Marsha Treadwell underscored that testing could potentially mark certain players as risky investments, or "liabilities," for coaches and teams in the lucrative market of professional athletics. No doubt, NCAA sickle cell trait screening would also mean marking players of African descent in the U.S. context, which "could lead to inadvertent discrimination against minority players" (Allday 2009). Thus the question of trait suffering has been reopened the United States. For more, see "NCAA's Sickle Cell Test Plan Raises Fears," http://www.sfgate.com/cgi-bin/article.cgi?file=/c/a/2009/09/14/MN2P19LCJM .DTL (accessed September 14, 2009). Also see the NCAA's press release about their recommendations at: http://www.ncaa.org/wps/ncaa?key=/ncaa/ncaa/ media+and+events/press+room/news+release+archive/2009/announcements/ ncaa+news+release+--+ncaa+recommends+testing+to+confirm+sickle+cell+ trait+status+in+student-athletes (accessed September 14, 2009).

9. Moudou is the shortened from of Mamadou, a Wolofization of the name Mohamed. Many of these traders belong to the Senegalese Mouride Islamic brotherhood.

10. *Xés* (pronounced `hes) in Wolof means light-colored skin. The suffix "al" makes an imperative, thus *xésal* means "to make light-skinned" or "be light-skinned." *Xés* can perform the linguistic function of adjective, noun, or verb; indeed it is

simultaneously all three in many cases. The irony of this practice for the people of Léopold Sédar Senghor's and, by extension, *Negritude's*, homeland is great and warrants a separate analysis beyond the scope of this book.

11. Being Muslim rarely prevented people in Dakar from celebrating Christmas Eve.

12. For an explanation of Senegalese modes of feminine beauty and the ways women re-work religious interdictions to their favor see T. K. Biaya (2000).

13. Biaya details some of the ways *dirianke* women are explicitly engaged in seduction and wielding an "illicit carnal power." In his analysis, skin bleaching and the Muslim headscarf have come to go hand in hand. He says: "Depending on how it is worn, the headscarf may be understood to enhance the seductive power of the face, by which *suli* (the power of seduction) is not diminished but magnified. Consider what has happened in the city of Touba. Due to its erotic significance, the practice of *khessal* [sic] (depigmentation) was prohibited in this holy place by Mourid authorities; women visitors to the city now frequently evade the prohibition by wearing the headscarf!" (2000, 717).

14. The Victorian ideal of tuberculin beauty described by Susan Sontag, where "health becomes banal, even vulgar," provides another such example (1988, 26).

15. As stated in chapter 2, *drépano* is shorthand for the French term *drépanocytaire*, or sickler.

16. This case illustrates the subjective nature of health, as well as its individual norms: "the borderline between the normal and the pathological is imprecise for several individuals considered simultaneously but it is perfectly precise for one and the same individual considered successively" (Canguilhem 1991, 182).

Chapter Seven. The Work of Patient Advocacy

1. See http://webcast.un.org/ramgen/ondemand/pressconference/2009/pc090619 pm.rm (accessed October 10, 2009).

2. See http://usun.state.gov/briefing/statements/2009/125967.htm (accessed June 15, 2010).

3. RFLD, and later OILD, was made into a division of *Sud Développement*. The latter's website describes their mission as "an association d'aide et d'actions en développement agissant avec la participation active des bénéficaires. Il regroupe 18 associations partenaires de malades, des sections scientifiques dans plusieurs pays francophones, afin de développer un réseau international d'échange et d'entraide pour sensibiliser les communautés concernées et améliorer la prise en charge et le diagnostic, principalement dans les pays du Sud. Their website (http://www .drepanetworld.org/) provides an interactive space, chat room, and billboard for discussions between actors on both sides of the global divide.

4. The RFLD's logo was a globe, humanized and transformed into a human head sick with fever, presumably from sickle cell. It donned a red beret, which alluded to a red blood cell because of its shape. The globe's expression was visible tiredness. Its tongue hung out on one side of its mouth, while a thermometer poked out of the other. The caption below it read "*Tous unis contre la drépanocytose*" (All united against sickle cell disease).

5. OILD's homepage in 2005 emphasized the utility of the internet by encouraging users to take advantage of Drépanet saying, "La francophonie par l'usage de ces technologies donne enfin la possibilité aux acteurs, d'échanger et de s'entraider

au quotidien, au-delà des frontières, à l'échelle des individus" (*la francophonie*, or French language use, through these technologies [of the web] finally gives actors the possibility to have exchanges and to help each other, beyond their [national] frontiers, at the level of individuals.)

6. SOS Globi is not an acronym. It borrows "SOS" from the international code for a call for help in distress situations, while "globi" is a cartoon red blood cell that animates the group's brochures and videos. "Globi" is taken from hemo*globin*. As for APIPD, the acronym stands for the *Association pour l'information et la prévention de la drépanocytose* (The Association for Information on and the Prevention of Sickle Cell Disease).

7. Later when Petit-Phar stepped down, a genetic counselor from Henri Mondor, who was not of Caribbean origin, took his place. At this point, it was clear to outsiders that SOS Globi was being led by "medical staff," and not by affected communities. For more recent developments concerning identity and sickle cell advocacy groups in France, see Bonnet 2009, 28.

8. DOM-TOM is short hand for "Departments and Territories of France [Beyond the Mainland]."

9. When I visited Yves Beauzard's lab at St. Louis Hospital he in no way hid his exuberance, love even, for his transgenic mice. As I backed out of the lab upon entering because the urine smell of ammonia shocked my senses, he smiled and said with excitement: "They look like normal mice, but they aren't. They are transgenic mice to whom we owe a big Thank you. They have done a lot for the advancement of sickle cell, and they have helped a lot of patients." In the same conversation he said that it had been years since he actually worked with patients. The gap between the lab, the hospital, and patient groups could potentially narrow, if not close, with more communication and inclusion of patients in discussions on research agendas and the importance of current projects. The attitude of most doctors and scientists working on sickle cell is that the patient groups are agents to educate others on the disease, while serving as a support for families. The role patients and families of the AFM have in demanding, orchestrating, and finally funding research is unthinkable (to most practitioners) for sickle cell.

10. This was before the third international conference, which included a parallel awareness campaign that took place all over the city. In the postconference period they were inundated with additional new members.

11. Tambacounda is popularly understood to be one of the most remote and resource-poor areas of Senegal.

Conclusion: Economic and Health Futures amid Hope and Despair

1. In the introduction to *Hard Work, Hard Times* (2010) Beth Buggenhagen and co-authors Anne-Maria Makhulu and Stephen Jackson draw from some of these same events to drive home their larger point about global capital, economic crisis and Africans' strategies of desperation, in this case even courting death, as a way to ironically recover a sense of economic security.

2. When I interviewed Touty Niang of the ASD in 2010, she recounted how she hounded this official whenever she saw him at public events. In her words: "every time I see him, I tell him, 'eh, you know that sickle cell dossier is still on your desk.' And he responds, 'Madame, do you know how many diseases I have under

my charge? There's cancer, kidney disease, hypertension, heart disease . . . ' And I just stop him and say, sickle cell encompasses all of those disease risks and more. People with sickle cell get cancer, they have weak organs, enlarged hearts, risk of stroke and much more. You could be targeting all of the things you have under your charge if you just gave sickle cell the attention it deserves." She ended by telling me, "The problem is that people, even our government officials, are not properly educated on the disease. Chances are, he could not even grasp what I was talking about—that sickle cell disease affects all the systems of the body and addressing it could eliminate some of those other medical costs." This is both true and untrue as there are surely many cases of cancer, especially, as well as hypertension and heart disease that cannot be etiologically linked to morbidity with sickle cell. Touty was attempting to advance a clear politic to push sickle cell to the top of this politician's agenda, without success.

3. People with sickle cell in their families have varied responses to voluntary genetic testing as a tool for prevention. Women, in particular, imagined ways that partner testing might give them power to renegotiate arranged marriages. Both men and women drew upon Islam and more customary ideas of embryogenesis to think through the ethics of prenatal screening and therapeutic abortion (See Fullwiley 2004).

4. Touty's son died at the age of four from abscesses on his brain, likely due to a meningitis infection, not from sickle cell.

5. See Niang at, http://fr.allafrica.com/stories/201006180794.html (accessed June 30, 2010.)

6. This refers to a hematopoietic stem cell transplantation, which requires suppressing the immune system as well as running the risk of rejection that accompanies transplant technology in general.

7. Transcript of the Human Heredity and Health in Africa Press Conference in London, see http://www.genome.gov/highlightPassthru.cfm?link=/Pages/News room/Webcasts/Transcript-H3-AfricaPressConference.pdf (accessed July 14, 2010).

8. See NIGRHI 2010, http://www.genome.gov/27540081 (accessed June 30, 2010).

9. Transcript of the Human Heredity and Health in Africa Press Conference in London, see http://www.genome.gov/highlightPassthru.cfm?link=/Pages/News room/Webcasts/Transcript-H3-AfricaPressConference.pdf (accessed July 14, 2010).

REFERENCES

Abu, S., S. Anyaibe, and V. Headings. (1981) Chromatographic fractionation of anti-sickling agents in Fagara xanthoxyloides. *Acta Haematologia* 66 (1): 19–26.

Abu El-Haj, Nadia. (2007) The genetic reinscription of race. *Annual Review of Anthropology* 36: 283–300.

Alexander, N., D. Higgs, G. Dover, and G. R. Serjeant. (2004) Are there clinical phenotypes of homozygous sickle cell disease? *British Journal of Haematology* 126 (4): 606–11.

Allday, Erin. (2009) NCAA's sickle cell test plan raises fears. *San Francisco Chronicle*, September 14.

Allison, A. C. (1954) The distribution of the sickle-cell trait in East Africa and elsewhere, and its apparent relationship to the incidence of subtertian Malaria. *Transactions of the Royal Society of Tropical Medicine and Hygiene* 48 (4): 312–18.

Amselle, Jean-Loup. (1996) *Vers un multiculturalisme français: L'empire de la coutume.* Paris: Éditions Aubier.

———. (1998) *Mestizo Logics: Anthropology of Identity in Africa and Elsewhere.* Palo Alto, CA: Stanford University Press.

———. (2003) *Affirmative Exclusion: Cultural Pluralism and the Rule of Custom in France*, translated by J. M. Todd. Ithaca, NY: Cornell University Press.

Anseeuw, Ward. (2010) Agricultural policy in Africa—renewal or status quo?: A spotlight on Kenya and Sengal, in *The Political Economy of Africa*, edited by V. Padayachee. London: Routledge.

Antoine, Phillipe, Phillipe Bocquier, Abdou Salam Fall, Youssouf M. Guisse, and Jeanne Nanitelamio. (1995) *Les familles darkaroises face à la crise.* Montpellier: Éditions IRD.

Appadurai, Arjun. (1988) Putting hierarchy in its place. *Cultural Anthropology* 3 (10): 36–49.

Arab, Abdel. (2003) Researchers turn to schools to protect rare plants. Inter Press Service News Agency. May 28. http://www.ipsnews.net/news.asp?idnews=18447 (accessed June 19, 2009).

Ashforth, Adam. (2005) *Witchcraft, Violence, and Democracy in South Africa.* Chicago: University of Chicago Press.

Bachelard, Gaston. (2002 [1936]) *Études.* Paris: Librairie Philosophique.

Bado, Jean-Paul. (1996) *Médecine coloniale et grandes endémies en Afrique.* Paris: Karthala.

Balandier, Georges. (1966 [1957]) *Ambiguous Africa: Cultures in Collision*, translated by H. Weaver. New York: Pantheon.

Bangré, Habibou. (2003) Dans l'ombre de la drépanocytose. *Afrik.com*. July 25. http://www.afrik.com/article6399.html (accessed July 4, 2010).

Barataud, Bernard. (1992) *Au nom de nos enfants*. Paris: Editions J'ai Lu.

Bayart, Jean-François. (2005) *The Illusion of Cultural Identity*. Chicago: University of Chicago Press.

Beck, Linda J. (2008) *Brokering Democracy in Africa: The Rise of Clientelist Democracy in Senegal*. New York: Palgrave Macmillan.

Becker, Anne E. (1998) Postpartum illness in Fiji: A sociosomatic perspective. *Psychosomatic Medicine* 60: 431–38.

Benatar, Solomon R. (1998) Global disparities in health and human rights: A critical commentary. *American Journal of Public Health* 88 (2): 295–300.

Benkerrou, M., E. Denamur, and J. Elion. (2003) Information génétique et diagnostic prénatal dans la drépanocytose, in *La drépanocytose*, edited by R. Girot, P. Bégué, and F. Galactéros. Paris: John Libbey EuroText.

Bergson, Henri. (1998 [1911]) *Creative Evolution*, translated by A. Mitchell. Mineola, NY: Dover Publishers.

Betts, Raymond F. (2004 [1961]) *Assimilation and Association in French Colonial Theory, 1890–1914*. Lincoln: University of Nebraska Press.

Biaya, T. K. (2000) Crushing the pistachio: Eroticism in Senegal and the art of Ousmane Ndiaye Dago. *Public Culture* 12 (3): 707–20.

Birx, H. James. (1993) *Interpreting Evolution: Darwin and Teilhard de Chardin*. Amherst, NY: Prometheus Books.

Bonnecase, Vincent. (2009) Avoir faim en Afrique occidentale française: Investigations et représentations coloniales (1920–1960). *Revue d'Histoire des Sciences Humaines* 21: 151–74.

Bonnet, Doris. (2004) Drépanocytose et ethnicité, in *La drépanocytose: Regards croisés sur une maladie orpheline*, edited by A. Lainé. Paris: Karthala.

———. (2009) *Repenser l'hérédité*. Paris: Editions Archives Contemporaines.

Bowman, James E. (1977) Genetic screening and public policy. *Phylon* 38 (2): 117–42.

Bowman, James E., and Robert F. Murray. (1990) *Genetic Variation and Disorders in Peoples of African Origin*. Baltimore, MD: Johns Hopkins University Press.

Boye, Francois. (1993) Economic mechanisms in historical perspective, in *Senegal: Essays in Statecraft*, edited by M. C. Diop. Dakar: Codesria Book Series.

Brotherton, P. Sean. (2008) "We have to think like capitalists but continue being socialists": Medicalized subjectivities, emergent capital, and socialist entrepreneurs in post-Soviet Cuba. *American Ethnologist* 35 (2): 259–74.

Brydon L., S. Edwards, H. Jia, V. Mohamed-Ali, I. Zachary, J. F. Martin, and A. Steptoe. (2005) Psychological stress activates interleukin-1beta gene expression in human mononuclear cells. *Brain, Behavior, and Immunity* 19 (6): 540–46.

Bunn, H. F. (1997) Mechanisms of disease: pathogenesis and treatment of sickle cell disease. *New England Journal of Medicine* 337 (11): 762–69.

Callon, Michel, and John Law. (1982) On interests and their transformation: Enrollment and counter-enrollment. *Social Studies of Science* 12: 615–25.

Callon, Michel, Pierre Lascoumes, and Yannick Barthe. (2001) *Agir dans un monde incertain: Essaie sur la démocracie technique*. Paris: Seuil.

Canguilhem, Georges. (1988) *Ideology and Rationality in the History of the Life Sciences.* Cambridge, MA: MIT Press.

———. (1991 [1966]) *The Normal and the Pathological,* translated by C. R. Fawcett and R. S. Cohen. New York: Zone Books.

———. (1994) *A Vital Rationalist: Selected Writings from Georges Canguilhem,* translated by Francios Delaporte. New York: Zone Books.

———. (1998 [1965]) *La connaissance de la vie.* Paris: Librairie Philosophique.

Carsten, Janet. (2000) Introduction: Cultures of relatedness, in *Cultures of Relatedness: New Approaches to the Study of Kinship,* edited by Janet Carsten. Cambridge: Cambridge University Press.

———. (2001) Substantivism, antisubstantivism, and anti-antisubstantivism, in *Relative Values: Reconfiguring Kinship Studies,* edited by S. Franklin and S. McKinnon. Durham, NC: Duke University Press.

Carter, Donald M. (1997) *States of Grace: Senegalese in Italy and the New European Immigration.* Minneapolis: University of Minnesota Press.

Chang, Y. P., M. Maier-Redelsperger, K. D. Smith, L. Contu, R. Ducroco, et al. (1997) The relative importance of the x-linked FCP locus and beta-globin haplotypes in determining haemoglobin F levels: A study of SS patients homozygous for beta(S) haplotypes. *British Journal of Haematology* 96 (4): 806–14.

Clifford, James, and George E. Marcus. (1986) *Writing Culture: The Poetics and Politics of Ethnography.* Berkeley: University of California Press.

Collins, Francis S., Michael Morgan, and Aristides Patrinos. (2003) The human genome project: Lessons from large-scale biology. *Science* 300 (5617): 286–90.

Collomb, Henri. (1973) Rencontre de deux systèmes de soins: A propos de thérapeutiques des maladies mentales en Afrique. *Social Science & Medicine* 7:623–33.

Comaroff, John. (1980) *The Meaning of Marriage Payments.* New York: Academic Press.

Comaroff, John, and Jean Comaroff. (1992) *Ethnography and the Historical Imagination.* Chicago: Chicago University Press.

———. (2009) *Ethnicity, Inc.* Boulder: Westview Press.

Comoë, L., P. Jeannesson, C. Trentesaux, B. Desoize, and J-C. Jardillier. (1987) The antileukemic alkaloid fagaronine and the human K 562 leukemic cells: Effects on growth and induction of erythoid differentiation. *Leukemia Research* 11 (5): 445–51.

Comoë, L., Y. Carpentier, B. Desoize, and J. C. Jardillier. (1988) Effect of fagaronine on cell cycle progression of human erythroleukemia K562 cells. *Leukemia Research* 12 (8): 667–72.

Conklin, Alice. (1997) *A Mission to Civilize: The Republican Idea of Empire in France and West Africa, 1895–1930.* Palo Alto, CA: Stanford University Press.

Cook-Deegan, Robert. (1994) *The Gene Wars: Science, Politics, and the Human Genome.* New York: Norton and Company.

Coquery-Vidrovitch, Catherine. (2001) Nationalité et citoyenneté en Afrique Occidentale Français: Originaires et citoyens dans le Sénégal colonial. *Journal of African History* 42 (2): 285–305.

Coulibaly, Abdou Latif. (2009) *Contes et méscomptes de l'ANOCI (agence pour l'organisation de la conférence islamique).* Paris: L' Harmattan.

Das, Veena. (2007) *Life and Words: Violence and the Descent in to the Ordinary.* Berkeley: University of California Press.

Das, Veena, and Ranendra K. Das. (2006) Pharmaceuticals in urban ecologies: The register of the local, in *Global Pharmaceuticals: Ethics, Markets, Practices*, edited by Adriana Petryna, Andrew Lakoff, and Arthur Kleinman, 171–204. Durham, NC: Duke University Press.

Delgado, Christopher L., and Sidi Jammeh. (1991): Structural change in a hostile environment. Introduction in *The Political Economy of Senegal Under Structural Adjustment*, edited by Christopher L. Delgado and Sidi Jammeh. New York: Praeger.

Desrosières, Alain. (1998) *The Politics of Large Numbers: A History of Statistical Reasoning*. Translated by Camille Naish. Cambridge, MA: Harvard University Press.

Diagne, I., O. Ndiaye, C. Moreira, H. Signate-Sy, B. Camara, et al. (2000) Sickle cell disease in children in Dakar, Senegal. *Archives de Pédiatrie* 7 (1): 16–24.

Diaw, Fara. (1986) Drépanocytose: 50,000 élèves à sauver. *Le Soleil*, January 24.

Dieng, M. M. (2000) Le Khessal, une honte! *Le Soleil*. December 15.

Diggs, L. W., C. F. Ashmann, and Juanita Bibb. (1933) The incidence and significance of the sickle cell trait. *Annals of Internal Medicine* 7 (6): 769–78.

Diop, Abdoulaye Bara. (1985) *La famille wolof: tradition et changement*. Paris: Karthala.

Diop, Jules S. (2007). Révélations éffarantes de Aid Transparence Sénégal: Près de 2.477 milliards de francs détournés de mars 2000 à février 2007. http://www.seneweb.com/news/article/8587.php (accessed March 2, 2007).

Diop, S., S. O. Mokono, M. Ndiaye, A. O. Touré-Fall, D. Thiam, L. Diakhaté. (2003) *La drépanocytose homozygote après lâge de 20 ans: Suivi d'une cohorte de 108 patients au CHU de Dakar.* La Revue de Médecine Interne 24:711–15.

Diop, S., M. Cissé, A. O. Toure-Fall, D. Thiam, K. Fall, et al. (1999) La drépanocytose homozygote a Dakar: Influence du taux d'hemoglobine F, des facteurs socioculturels et économiques. *Dakar Médical* 44 (2): 171–74.

Diouf, Makhtar. (1998) *Sénégal: Les ethnies et la nation*. Dakar: Nouvelles Éditions Africaines du Sénégal.

Diouf, Mamadou. (2000) The Senegalese Murid trade diaspora and the making of a vernacular cosmopolitanism. *Public Culture* 12 (3): 679–702.

———. (2001) *Histoire du Sénégal: Le modele islamo-wolof et ses périphéries*. Paris: Maisonneuve & Larose.

Direction de la Prévision et de la Statistique, Programme des Nations Unies pour le Développement, et Département des Affaires Economiques et Sociales (DPS, PNUD, DAES) (2001) *La perception de la pauvreté au Sénégal: Volet statistique*. Dakar: DPS, PNUD, DAES.

———. (2003) *Situation économique et sociale du Sénégal, 2002–2003*. Dakar: DPS, PNUD, DAES

Dozon, Jean-Pierre. (1999) Les bété: Une création coloniale, in *Au coeur de l'ethnie: Ethnies, tribalisme et état en Afrique*, edited by J-L. Amselle and E. M'Bokolo. Paris: Le Découverte/Poche.

Dr Medegan Fagla Jérome - Vivement dimanche. (September 8, 2008). http://www.youtube.com/watch?v=C5TPdBWU10Q (accessed August 28, 2009).

Dunlop, David W. (1983) Health care financing: Recent experience in Africa. *Social Science & Medicine* 17 (24): 2017–25.

Dupont, Claude, Eric Couillerot, Reynald Gillet, Catherine Caron, Monique Zeches-Hanrot, et al. (2005) The benzophenanthridine alkaloid fagaronine induces erythroleukemic cell differentiation by gene activation. *Planta Medica* 71 (6): 489–94.

Duruflé, Gilles. (1994) *Le Sénégal peut-il sortir de la crise?* Paris: Editions Karthala.

Duster, Troy. (2003) *Back Door to Eugenics.* 2nd ed. New York: Routledge.

Duster, Troy, and Diane Beeson. (1996) *Pathways and Barriers to Genetic Testing and Screening: Molecular Genetics Meets the "High-Risk Family."* Final Report. Berkeley: Institute for the Study of Social Change, University of California, Berkeley.

Eaton, William A. (2002) Linus Pauling and sickle cell disease. *Biophysical Chemistry* 100 (2003): 109–16.

Ebin, Victoria. (1992) A la recherche de nouveaux poissons: Stratégies commerciales mouride en temps de crise. *Politique Africaine* 45: 86–99.

———. (1996) Making room versus creating space: The construction of spatial categories by itinerant Mouride traders, in *Making Muslim Space in America and Europe,* edited by Barbara Daly Metcalf. Berkeley: University of California Press.

Echenberg, Myron. (2002) *Black Death, White Medicine: Bubonic Plague and the Politics of Public Health in Colonial Senegal, 1914–1945.* Portsmouth, NH: Heinemann.

Elyachar, Julia. (2002) Empowerment money: The World Bank, non-governmental organizations, and the value of culture in Egypt. *Public Culture* 14 (3): 493–513.

———. (2005) *Markets of Dispossession.* Durham, NC: Duke University Press.

Embury, S. H., A. M. Dozy, J. Miller, J. R. Davis, K. M. Kleman, et al. (1982) Concurrent sickle-cell anemia and alpha-thalassemia: Effect on severity of anemia. *New England Journal of Medicine* 306 (5): 270–74.

Epstein, Steven. (2007) *Inclusion: The Politics of Difference in Medical Research.* Chicago: University of Chicago Press.

Evans, P., and M. J. Murray. (1997) Sudden exertional death and sickle cell trait. *American Family Physician* 55 (3): 784.

Farmer, Paul. (2003) *Pathologies of Power: Health, Human Rights, and the New War on the Poor.* Berkeley: University of California Press.

Fassin, Didier. (1992) *Pouvoir et maladie en Afrique.* Paris: Presses Universitaires de France.

———. (2003) The embodiment of inequality. *European Molecular Biology Organization Reports* 4:54.

———. (2007) *When Bodies Remember: Experiences and Politics of AIDS in South Africa.* Berkeley: University of California Press.

Fassin, Didier, and Eric Fassin. (1988) Traditional medicine and the stakes of legitimation in Senegal. *Social Science & Medicine* 27 (4): 353–57.

Faye, Abdou. (2004) Health-Senegal: Radio ads renew debate on traditional medicine. Inter Press Service News Agency. October 15.

Fédération des Malades. (2007) *Rappel sur le VK500.* June 5. http://www.sosglobi.fr/cgi-bin/articles.php?lng=fr&pg=8542 (accessed August 31, 2009).

Ferguson, James. (2006) *Global Shadows: Africa in the Neoliberal World Order.* Durham, NC: Duke University Press.

Feierman, Steven. (2000) Explanation and uncertainty in the medical world of Ghaambo. *Bulletin of the History of Medicine* 74 (2): 317–44.

Fleury, F., A. Sukhanova, A. Ianoul, J. Devy, I. Kudelina, et al. (2000) Molecular determinants of site-specific inhibition of human DNA topoisomerase I by fagaronine and ethoxidine: Relation to DNA binding. *Journal of Biological Chemistry* 275 (5): 3501–9.

Foley, Ellen E. (2008) Neoliberal reform and health dilemmas: Social hierarchy and therapeutic decision making in Senegal. *Medical Anthropology Quarterly* 22 (3): 257–73.

———. (2010) *Your Pocket is What Cures You: The Politics of Health in Senegal.* New Brunswick, NJ: Rutgers University Press.

Foucault, Michel. (1980) *The History of Sexuality.* New York: Vintage.

———. (1984) Nietzsche, genealogy, history, in *The Foucault Reader*, edited by Paul Rabinow. New York: Pantheon.

———. (1991) Introduction to *The Normal and the Pathological*, by Georges Canguilhem. New York: Zone Books.

———. (2005 [1982]) *The Hermeneutics of the Subject: Lectures at the Collège de France 1981–1982.* New York: Palgrave Macmillan.

Foucault, Michel, Luther H. Martin, Huck Gutman, and Patrick H. Hutton. (1988) *Technologies of the Self: A Seminar with Michel Foucault.* Amherst: University of Massachusetts Press.

Frame, M. (2000) What's wrong with her?: The stigmatizing effects of an invisible stigma. *Disability Studies Quarterly* 20:243–53.

Franklin, Sarah. (2000) Life itself: Global nature and the genetic imaginary, in *Global Nature, Global Culture*, edited by Celia Lury and Jackie Stacey. London: Sage Publications.

———. (2001) Biologization revisited, in *Relative Values: Reconfiguring Kinship Studies*, edited by Sarah Franklin and Susan McKinnon. Durham, NC: Duke University Press.

Franklin, Sarah, and Celia Roberts. (2006) *Born and Made: An Ethnography of Preimplantation Genetic Diagnosis.* Princeton, NJ: Princeton University Press.

Franklin, Q. J., and M. Compeggie. (1999) Splenic syndrome in sickle cell trait: Four case presentations and a review of the literature. *Military Medicine* 164 (3): 230–33.

Fullwiley, Duana. (2004) Discriminate biopower and everyday biopolitics: Views on sickle cell testing in Dakar. *Medical Anthropology* 23 (3): 157–94.

———. (2007) The molecularization of race: Institutionalizing racial difference in pharmacogenetics practice. *Science as Culture* 16 (1): 1–30.

———. (2008) The biologistical construction of race. *Social Studies of Science* 38 (5): 695–735.

Gandaho, Euloge R. (1998) VK500, l'exploit d'un pionnier béninois. *Le Matin.* November 6.

Gates, Ruggles. R. (1952) Disadvantages of race mixture. *Nature* 170: 896.

Geertz, Clifford. (2000) *Available Light: Anthropological Reflections on Philosophical Topics.* Princeton, NJ: Princeton University Press.

Gellar, Sheldon. (2005) *Democracy in Senegal: Tocquevillian Analytics in Africa.* New York: Palgrave Macmillan.

Gilbert, Hanna. (2009) Spinning Blood into Gold: Science, Sex Work and HIV-2 in Senegal. Ph.D. dissertation, Department of Anthropology, McGill University, Montreal, Canada.

Gilley, Bruce. (2010) The end of the African renaissance. *Washington Quarterly* 33 (4): 87–101.

Ginio, Ruth. (2006) *French Colonialism Unmasked: The Vichy Years in French West Africa*. Lincoln: University of Nebraska Press.

Girot, Robert, M. Maier-Redelsperger, D. Labie, and J. Elion. (1999) Traitement des hémoglobinopathies par "l'activation" de l'hémoglobine foetale. *Hématologie* 5 (6): 502–11.

Good, Byron J. (1994) *Medicine, Rationality and Experience: An Anthropological Perspective*. Cambridge: Cambridge University Press.

Gormley, Melinda. (2007) The first "molecular disease": A story of Linus Pauling, the intellectual patron. *Endeavor* 31 (2): 71–77.

Green, Linda. (1998) Lived lives and social suffering: Problems and concerns in medical anthropology. *Medical Anthropology Quarterly* 12 (1): 3–7.

Greenhalgh, Susan. (2001) *Under the Medical Gaze: Facts and Fictions of Chronic Pain*. Berkeley: University of California Press.

Grove, E. F. (1926) On the value of the blood-group feature as a means of determining racial relationship. *Journal of Immunology* 12:251–62.

Guisse, Cheikh Mbacké. (2006) Audit du fonds Taiwanais: Awa Guèye dans le viseur de l'IGE (Fonds Générales de L'Etat). *Seneweb.com.* May 18. http://www.seneweb.com/news/article/2530.php (accessed December 23, 2006).

Gusella, James F., Nancy S.Wexler, Michael P. Conneally, Susan L. Naylor, Mary Anne Anderson, et al. (1983) A polymorphic DNA marker genetically linked to Huntington's disease. *Nature* 306:234–48.

Guyer, Jane I. (2004) *Marginal Gains: Monetary Actions in Atlantic Africa*. Chicago: University of Chicago Press.

Hampton, M. L., J. Anderson, B. S. Lavizzo, and A. B. Bergman. (1974) Sickle cell "nondisease." *American Journal of Diseases of Children* 128 (1): 58–61.

Han, Clara. (2011) Symptoms of another life: Time, possibility, and domestic relations in Chile's credit economy. *Cultural Anthropology* 26:7–32.

Haraway, Donna. (1997) *Modest_Witness@Second_Millennium. FemaleMan©_Meets_OncoMouse™.* New York: Routledge.

———. (2003) *The Companion Species Manifesto: Dogs, People, and Significant Otherness.* Chicago: Prickly Paradigm Press.

Hayden, Cori. (2003) *When Nature Goes Public: The Making and Unmaking of Bioprospecting in Mexico*. Princeton, NJ: Princeton University Press.

Heath, Deborah, Rayna Rapp, and Karen-Sue Taussig. (2007) Genetic citizenship, in *A Companion to the Anthropology of Politics,* edited by David Nugent and Joan Vincent, 152–67. Malden, MA: Blackwell Publishers.

Hedgecoe, Adam. (2009) Geneticization: Debates and controversies. *Encyclopedia of Life Sciences (ELS)*. Chichester: John Wiley & Sons.

Heidegger, Martin. (1993 [1947]) Letter on humanism, in *Basic Writings,* edited by David Farrel Krell. New York: Harper Collins.

Heller, P., W. Best, R. Nelson, and J. Becktel. (1979). Clinical implications of sickle-cell trait and glucose-6-phosphate dehydrogenase deficiency in hospitalized black male patients. *New England Journal of Medicine* 300:1001–5.

Helmreich, Stephan. (2009) *Alien Ocean: Anthropological Voyages in Microbial Seas*. Berkeley: University of California Press.

Herzfeld, Michael. (2005) *Cultural Intimacy: Social Poetics in the Nation-State*. 2nd ed. New York: Routledge.

Higgs, D.R., and W. G.Wood. (2008) Genetic complexity in sickle cell disease. *Proceedings of the National Academy of Sciences* 105 (33): 11595–96.

Hirschfeld, L., and H. Hirshfeld. (1919) Serological differences between the blood of different races. *Lancet*: 675–79.

Hodges, J. H. (1950) The effects of racial mixtures upon erythrocytic sickling. *Blood* 5 (9): 804–10.

Honig, G. R., N. R. Farnsworth, C. Ferenc, and L. N. Vida. (1975) Evaluation of *Fagara zanthoxyloides* root extract in sickle cell anemia blood *in vitro. Journal of Natural Products* 38 (5): 387–90.

Hutchinson, Sharon Elaine. (1996) *Nuer Dilemmas: Coping with Money, War, and the State*. Berkeley: University of California Press.

———. (2000) Identity and substance: the broadening bases of relatedness among the Nuer of southern Sudan, in *Cultures of Relatedness: New Approaches to the Study of Kinship*, edited by Janet Carsten. Cambridge: Cambridge University Press.

Hymans, Jacques Louis. (1971) *Léopold Sédar Senghor: An Intellectual Bibliography*. Edinburgh: Edinburgh University Press.

Inhorn, Marica. (2003) *Local Babies, Global Science: Gender, Religion, and in Vitro Fertilization in Egypt*. New York: Routledge.

Irele, F. Abiola. (1977) *Selected Poems of Léopold Sédar Senghor*. Cambridge: University of Cambridge Press.

Isaacs-Sodeye, W. A., E. A. Sofowora, A. O. Williams, V. O. Marquis, A. A. Adekunle, et al. (1975) Extract of *Fagara zanthoxyloides* root in sickle cell anaemia: toxicology and preliminary clinical trials. *Acta Haematalogia* 53 (75): 158–64.

Jasanoff, Sheila. (2004) *Designs on Nature: Science and Democracy in Europe and the United States*. Princeton, NJ: Princeton University Press.

Johnson, G. Wesley. (1971) *The Emergence of Black Politics in Senegal: The Struggle for Power in the Four Communes, 1900–1920*. Palo Alto, CA: Stanford University Press.

Jones, Stephen R., Richard A. Binder, and Everett M. Donowho, Jr. (1970) Sudden death in sickle-cell trait. *New England Journal of Medicine* 282 (6): 323–25.

Kaly, Eugène. (2009) Médecine traditionnelle: Le projet de loi bientôt à l'Assemblée Nationale. *Le Soleil*. September 1. http://www.lesoleil.sn/article.php3?id_article =504454 (accessed July 2, 2010).

Kan, Y. W., and A. Dozy. (1978) Polymorphisms of DNA sequence adjacent to human beta-globin structural gene: Relationship to sickle cell mutation. *Proceedings of the National Academies of Sciences (USA)* 75 (11): 5631–35.

———. (1980) Evolution of the hemoglobin S and C genes in world populations. *Science* 209 (4454): 388–91.

Kark, J. A. (2000) Sickle cell trait. Online review article. http://sickle.bwh.harvard .edu/sickle_trait.html (accessed October 20, 2009).

Kark, J. A., D. M. Posey, H. R. Schumacher, and C. J. Ruehle. (1987) Sickle-cell trait as a risk factor for sudden death in physical training. *New England Journal of Medicine* 317 (13): 781–92.

Kark, J. A., and F. T. Ward. (1994) Exercise and hemoglobin S. *Seminars in Hematology* 31 (3): 181–225.

Keita, Maghan. (2007) *A Political Economy of Health Care in Senegal*. Leiden, Netherlands: Brill Publishers.

Kerharo, J., and H. de Lauture. (2003) Produit traditionnel contre les troubles de la dréponocytose.[sic] *ENDA madesahel, Application au Développement Inté-*

gré. http://madesahel.enda.sn/html/Presentation.html (accessed November 28, 2006).

Kerle, K. K. (1996) Exertional collapse and sudden death associated with sickle cell trait. *Military Medicine* 161 (12): 766–67.

Kete, C. V. (1998) Dépistage néonatale de la drépanocytose par la méthode d'iso-éléctrofocalisation de l'hémoglobine (cas de 518 nouveau-nés au centre hospitalier municipal Abass-Ndao de Dakar). Doctor of Pharmacy thesis. Faculty of Medicine and Pharmacy, University of Dakar, Cheikh Anta Diop.

King, Ursula. (1996) *Spirit of Fire: The Life and Vision of Teilhard de Chardin*. Maryknoll, NY: Orbis Books.

Kitamura, Makiko. (2007) To the Canary Islands and back: Going nowhere in Senegal. *The Immigration Here & There Project*. Northwestern University Medill School of Journalism. http://www.immigrationhereandthere.org/2007/02/post_11.php (accessed October 7, 2009).

Kleinman, Arthur. (1977) Depression, somatization and the new cross-cultural psychiatry. *Social Science & Medicine* 11 (1): 3–10.

——. (1997) "Everything that really matters": Social suffering, subjectivity, and the remaking of human experience in a disordering world. *Harvard Theological Review* 90: 315–35.

——. (2006) *What Really Matters: Living a Moral Life amidst Uncertainty and Danger*. New York: Oxford University Press.

Kleinman, Arthur, Veena Das, and Margaret Lock, eds. (1997) *Social Suffering*. Berkeley: University of California Press.

Koch, Erin. (2006) Beyond suspicion: Evidence, (un)certainty, and tuberculosis in Georgian prisons. *American Ethnologist* 33 (1): 50–62.

Konaté, Doulaye. (2008) Le paradigme de l'opposition tradition/modernité comme modèle d'analyse des réalités africaines, in *Petit précis de remise à niveau sur l'histoire africaine à l'usage du président Sarkozy*, edited by Adama Ba Konaré. Paris: Editions La Découverte.

Krieger, Nancy. (1992) The making of public health data: Paradigms, politics, and policy. *Journal of Public Health Policy* 13 (4): 412–27.

Kuhn, Thomas. (1993 [1962]) *The Structure of Scientific Revolutions*. 3rd ed. Chicago: University of Chicago Press.

Kundu, Joydeb Kumar, and Young-Joon Surh. (2008) Cancer chemopreventive and therapeutic potential of resveratrol: Mechanistic perspectives. *Cancer Letters* 269 (2): 243–61.

Kurtz, Donn M. (1970) Political integration in Africa: The Mali Federation. *Journal of Modern African Studies* 8 (3): 405–24.

Labie, Dominique, and Jacques Elion. (1996) Modulation polygénique des maladies monogéniques: L'exemple de la drépanocytose. *Médecine/Sciences* 12 (3): 341–49.

Labie D., J. Pagnier, C. Lapoumeroulie, F. Rouabhi, O. Dunda-Belkhodja, P. Chardin, C. Beldjord, H. Wajcman, M. E. Fabry, and R. L. Nagel. (1985) Common haplotype dependency of high Gy-globin gene expression and high Hb F levels in ß-thalassemia and sickle cell anemia patients. *Proceedings of the National Academies of Sciences* 82 (7): 2111–14.

Labie, D., R. Srinivas, O. Dunda, C. Dode, C. Lapoumeroulie, et al. (1989) Haplotypes in tribal Indians bearing the sickle cell gene: Evidence for the unicentric origin of the Bs mutation and the unicentric origin of the tribal populations of India. *Human Biology* 61 (4): 479–91.

Lagouge, M., C. Argmann, Z. Gerhard-Hines, H. Meziane, C. Lerin, et al. (2006) Resveratrol improves mitochondrial function and protects against metabolic disease by activating SIRT1 and PGC-1alpha. *Cell* 127 (6): 1109–22.

Lainé, Agnès. (2004) L'hémoglobine S, l'Afrique et l'Europe: Science et idéologies dans les représentations de la drépanocytose, in *La drépanocytose: Regards croisés sur une maladie orpheline*, edited by A. Lainé. Paris: Karthala.

Lakoff, Andrew. (2006) *Pharmaceutical Reason: Knowledge and Value in Global Psychiatry*. New York: Cambridge University Press.

Langwick, Stacey. (2008) Articulate(d) bodies: Traditional medicine in a Tanzanian hospital. *American Ethnologist* 35 (3): 428–39.

Lapoumeroulie, C., O. Dunda, R. Ducrocq, G. Trabuchet, M. Mony-Lobé, et al. (1992) A novel sickle cell mutation of yet another origin in Africa: The Cameroon type. *Human Genetics* 89 (3): 333–37.

Larsen, A. K., L. Grondard, J. Couprie, B. Desoize, L. Comoë, et al. (1993) The antileukemic alkaloid fagaronine is an inhibitor of DNA topoisomerases I and II. *Biochemical Pharmacology* 46 (8): 1403–12.

Latour, Bruno. (1993) *We Have Never Been Modern*. Cambridge, MA: Harvard University Press.

Lehmann, H. and A. B. Raper. (1949) Distribution of the sickle-cell trait in Uganda, and its ethnological significance. *Nature* 164 (4168): 494–95.

Lehmann, H., and M. Cutbush. (1952) Sickle-cell trait in southern India. *British Medical Journal* 1 (4755): 404.

Lettre, G., V. G. Sankaran, M. A. Bezzera, et al. (2008) DNA polymorphisms at the BCL11A, HBS1L-MYB, and beta-globin loci associate with fetal hemoglobin levels and pain crises in sickle cell disease. *Proceedings of the National Academy of Sciences* 105 (33): 11595–96.

Lewis, Julian H. (1942) *The Biology of the Negro*. Chicago: University of Chicago Press.

Lewis, J. H., and D. L. Henderson. (1922) The racial distribution of iso-hemagglutinin groups. *Journal of the American Medical Association* 79 (17): 1422–24.

Lipson, Juliene. (2004) Multiple chemical sensitivities: Stigma and social experiences. *Medical Anthropology Quarterly* 18 (2): 200–213.

Lippman, Abby. (1991) Prenatal genetic testing and screening: Constructing needs and reinforcing inequalities. *American Journal of Law and Medicine* 17 (1–2): 15–50.

Livingston, Julie. (2005) *Debility and the Moral Imagination in Botswana*. Bloomington: Indiana University Press.

Lô, Saliou Fatma. (2010) Médecine traditionnelle: "Il faut mettre de l'ordre," selon Boury Niang. *Le Solei*, May 8. http://www.lesoleil.sn/imprimer.php3?id_article=58859 (accessed July 2, 2010).

Lock, Margaret. (1993a) Cultivating the body: Anthropology and epistemologies of bodily practice and knowledge. *Annual Review of Anthropology* 22: 133–55.

———. (1993b) *Encounters with Aging: Mythologies of Menopause in Japan and North America*. Berkeley: University of California Press.

———. (1997) Decentering the natural body: Making difference matter. *Configurations* 5 (2): 267–92.

———. (2002) *Twice Dead: Organ Transplants and the Reinvention of Death*. Berkeley: University of California Press.

———. (2007) The final disruption, in *Reproductive Disruptions: Gender, Technology, and Biopolitics in the New Millennium*, edited by Marcia Inhorn. New York: Berghan Books.

Lock, Margaret, and Vinh-Kim Nguyen. (2010) *An Anthropology of Biomedicine*. Oxford: Wiley-Blackwell.

Londsdorfer, A., C. L. Hazaire, J. Lonsdorfer, F. Boutroustoni, R. Cabannes, et al. (1981) Étude biologique préliminaire d'une plante africaine, fagara. *Annaux de l'Université d'Abdijan* (serie b) 15:281–87.

———. (1987) De l'utilisation empirique de *Fagara xanthoxyloïdes* à ses propriétés pharmacologiques établies. *Afrique Pharmacie* 3:11–12.

Lu, Zhi-hong, and Martin H. Steinberg. (1996) Fetal hemoglobin in sickle cell anemia: Relation to regulatory sequences *cis* to the ß-globin gene. *Blood* 87 (4): 1604–11.

Luzzatto, L., and A. J. Pinching. (1990) Innate resistance to malaria: The intraerythrocytic cycle. *Blood Cells* 16 (2–3): 311–25.

Luzzatto, L., E. S. Nwachukup-Jarrett, and S. Reddy. (1970) Increased sickling of parasitised erythrocytes as mechanism of resistance against malaria in the sickle-cell trait. *Lancet* 1 (7642): 319–22.

Makhulu, Anne-Maria, Beth Buggenhagen, and Stephen Jackson. (2010) Introduction. Hard work, hard times: Global volatility and African subjectivities, in *Hard Work, Hard Times: Global Volatility and African Subjectivities*, edited by Anne-Maria Makhulu, Beth Buggenhagen, and Stephen Jackson. Berkeley: University of California Press.

Marcus, George E. (1998) *Ethnography through Thick and Thin*. Princeton, NJ: Princeton University Press.

Markovitz, Irving Leonard. (1969) *Léopold Sédar Senghor and the Politics of Negritude*. New York: Atheneum.

Marks, Jonathan. (1995) *Human Biodiversity: Genes, Race, and History*. New York: Aldine de Gruyter.

Mbembe, Achille. (2001) *On the Postcolony*. Berkeley: University of California Press.

Mbengue, Ousmane. (*n.d.*) Vers la création d'un conseil national des tradipraticiens. *Le Soleil online*. http://www.lesoleil.sn/article.php3?id_article=11732 (accessed July 2, 2010).

Mbodj, A. (*n.d.*) Alioune Aw, responsable du bureau de la médecine traditionnelle au ministère de la santé: "Organiser, réglementer et protéger le secteur contre le pillage." *Le Soleil online*. http://www.lesoleil.sn/article.php3?id_article_12005 (accessed July 2, 2010).

Mbodji, Mohamed. (1991) The Politics of Independence: 1960–1986, in *The Political Economy of Senegal under Structural Adjustment*, edited by Christopher L. Delgado and Sidi Jammeh. New York: Praeger.

Mbodj, M., O. Ndoye, M. Diarra, B. N. Mbaye, H. Sow Toure, et al. (2003) Sickle cell disease neonatal screening. First evaluation. *Dakar Medical* 48 (3): 202–5.

Mead, Margaret. (1973 [1928]) *Coming of Age in Samoa*. New York: William Morrow & Company, Inc.

Mears, J. G., H. M. Lachman, R. Cabannes, K. P. Amegnizin, D. Labie, et al. (1981a) Sickle gene: Its origin and diffusion from West Africa. *Journal of Clinical Investigation* 68 (3): 606–10.

Mears, J. G., C. Beldjord, M. Benabadji, Y. Belghiti, M. A. Baddou, et al. (1981b) The sickle gene polymorphism in North Africa. *Blood* 58 (3): 599–601.

Médégan Fagla, Jerôme. (2004) Medicament notamment pour le traitement de la drepanocytose ou du SIDA. *Institut National de la Propriété Industrielle*. http://fr.espacenet.com/publicationDetails/biblio?CC=FR&NR=2855056A1&KC=A1&FT=D&date=20041126&DB=fr.espacenet.com&locale=fr_FR.

Merleau-Ponty, Maurice. (2006 [1962]) *Phenomenology of Perception*. New York: Routledge.

Messmer, W. M., M. Tin-Wa, H.H.S. Fong, C. Bevelle, N. R. Farnsworth, et al. (1972) Fagaronine, a new tumor inhibitor isolated from *Fagara zanthoxyloides* Lam. (Rutaceae). *Journal of Pharmaceutical Sciences* 61 (11): 1858–59.

Ministère de L'Economie et des Finances, Direction de la Prévision et de la Statistique, and le Banque Mondiale. (2004) *Le pauvreté au Sénégal: De la devaluation de 1994 à 2001–2002. Report*. Dakar: Republic of Senegal and the World Bank.

Ministère de la Santé et de la Prévention (Sénégal). (2011) Programme National de Lutte contre la drépanocytose. http://www.sante.gouv.sn/spip.php?article73 (accessed March 31, 2011).

Mission conjointe OMS-CDE. (2002) Une mission conjointe OMS-CDE s'est déroulée au Bénin en vue d'évaluer la production à grande échelle du VK500, medicament mis au point par le Dr. Fagla Medegan pour le traitement des consequences de la drépanocytose.Partenariat. *Bulletin d'information du Centre pour le Développement de l'Entreprise* (January–February) 58:5.

Mol, Annemarie. (2002) *The Body Multiple: Ontology and Medical Practice*. Durham, NC: Duke University Press.

———. (2008) *The Logic of Care: Health and the Problem of Patient Choice*. New York: Routledge.

Montagu, Ashley. (1972 [1951]) *Statement on Race*. 3rd ed. New York: Oxford University Press.

Montoya, Michael J. (2007) Bioethnic conscription: Genes, race, and Mexicana/o ethnicity in diabetes research. *Cultural Anthropology* 22 (1): 94–128.

———. (2011) *Making the Mexican Diabetic: Race, Science, and the Genetics of Inequality*. Berkeley: University of California Press.

Moore, Donald S. (1998) Subaltern struggles and the politics of place: Remapping resistance in Zimbabwe's eastern highlands. *Cultural Anthropology* 13 (3): 344–81.

Morris, David B. (1997) About suffering: Voice, genre, and moral community, in *Social Suffering*, edited by Arthur Kleinman, Veena Das, and Margaret Lock. Berkeley: University of California Press.

Mortimer, Robert. (1972) From federalism to francophonia: Senghor's African policy. *African Studies Review* 5 (2): 283–306.

Mullis, K., F. Faloona, S. Scharf, R. Saiki, G. Horn, et al. (1986) Specific enzymatic amplification of DNA in vitro: The polymerase chain reaction. *Cold Spring Harbor Symposium in Quantitative Biology* 51:263–73.

Murray, M. J., and P. Evans. (1996) Sudden exertional death in a soldier with sickle cell trait. *Military Medicine* 161 (5): 303–5.

Mustapha, Hudita N. (1998) Sartorial ecumenes: African styles in a social and economic context, in *The Art of African Fashion*, edited by P. C. Fund. The Hague, Netherlands: Prince Claus Fund.

Nagel R. L., M. E. Fabry, J. Pagnier, I. Zohoun, H. Wajcman, V. Baudin, D. Labie. (1985) Hematologically and genetically distinct forms of sickle cell anemia in

Africa: The Senegal and the Benin Type. *New England Journal of Medicine* 312 (14): 880–84.

Nagel, R. L., S. Erlingsson, M. E. Fabry, H. Croizat, S. M. Susuka, et al. (1991) The Senegal DNA haplotype is associated with the amelioration of anemia in African-American sickle cell anemia patients. *Blood* 77 (6): 1371–75.

Nagel, R. L., and A. F. Fleming. (1992) Genetic epidemiology of the Bs gene. *Ballières Clinical Haematology* 5: 331–65.

National Genome Research Institute (NHGRI) (2010) NIH and Wellcome Trust announce partnership to support population-based genome studies in Africa. http://www.genome.gov/27540081 (accessed June 30, 2010).

National Institutes of Health, National Heart Lung and Blood Institute (NHLBI) (2002) *The Management of Sickle Cell Disease.* NIH publication No. 02–2117. Bethesda, Maryland. http://www.nhlbi.nih.gov/health/prof/blood/sickle/sc_mngt.pdf (accessed November 1, 2004).

Ndiaye, Mamadou Oumar. (2006) Comment 7.5 milliards de francs cfa détournés et planqués à Chypre: Micmacs autour de fonds Taiwanais alloues au Senegal. *Nettali.* December 14. http://nettali.net/Comment-7.5-milliards-de-francs.html (accessed July 10, 2010).

Ndiaye, S. (1994) Le mariage consanguin, in *La Population du Sénégal*, edited by Y. Charbit and S. Ndiaye. Paris: Direction de la Prévision et de la Statistique (Dakar) and Centre d'Etudes et de Recherches sur les Populations Africaines et Asiatiques (Paris).

Neel, James V. (1950) The population genetics of two inherited blood dyscrasias in man. *Cold Spring Harbor Symposiums in Quantitative Biology* 15:141–58.

Nelson, Alondra (2008a) The factness of diaspora, in *Revisiting Race in a Genomic Age*, edited by B. Koenig, S. S-J. Lee, and S. Richardson. New Brunswick, NJ: Rutgers University Press.

———. (2008b) Genetic genealogy testing and the pursuit of African ancestry. *Social Studies of Science* 38 (5): 759–83.

Nguyen, Vinh-Kim. (2004) Antiretroviral globalism, biopolitics, and therapeutic citizenship, in *Global Assemblages*, edited by Aihwa Ong and Stephen J. Collier. New York: Blackwell Publishing.

———. (2005) Uses and pleasures: Sexual modernity, HIV/AIDS, and confessional technologies in a West African metropolis, in *Sex in Development: Science, Sexuality, and Morality in Global Perspective*, edited by Vincanne Adams and Stacy Leigh Pigg. Durham, NC: Duke University Press.

———. (2010) *The Republic of Therapy: Triage and Sovereignty in West Africa's Time of AIDS.* Durham: Duke University Press.

Niang Issa. (2009) Adoption de la loi sur la médecine traditionnelle: Seul gage pour la sécurité des plants. *All Africa.com.* September 1. http://fr.allafrica.com/stories/200909010562.html (accessed July 2, 2010).

Niang Issa. (n.d.) Drépanocytose au Sénégal: 1700 enfants naissent chaque année avec la form grave de la maladie. *WalFadjri.* http://www.walf.sn/actualites/suite.php?rub=1&id_art=53362 (accessed October 20, 2009).

Nichter, Mark. (1981) Idioms of distress: Alternatives in the expression of psychosocial distress: A case study from South India. *Culture, Medicine and Psychiatry* 5(4): 379–408.

Odebivi, O. O., and E. A. Sofowora. (1979) Antimicrobial alkaloids from a Nigerian chewing stick (*Fagara zanthoxyloides*). *Planta Medica* 36 (3): 204–07.

Ogbu, Osita, and Mark Gallagher. (1992) Public expenditures and health care in Africa. *Social Science & Medicine* 34 (6): 615–24.

Orsini, André. (1999) Letter to Monsieur Le Professeur Girot, Hôpital Tenon, Paris, July 23.

Pagnier, J., J. G. Mears, O. Dunda-Belkhodja, K. E. Schaefer-Rego, C. Beldjord, et al. (1984) Evidence for the multicentric origin of the sickle cell hemoglobin gene in Africa. *Proceedings of the National Academy of Sciences of the United States of America* 18 (6): 1771–73.

Pagnier, J., O. Dunda-Belkhodja, I. Zohoun, J. Teyssier, H. Baya, et al. (1984) α- Thalassemia among sickle cell anemia patients in various African populations. *Human Genetics* 68 (4): 318–19.

Palca, J. (1991) On the track of an elusive disease. *Science* 254 (5039): 1726–28.

Pales, Léon, P. Gallais, J. Bert, and R. Fourquet. (1954) La sicklémie (sickle cell trait) chez certains populations Nigéro-Tchadiennnes de l'Afrique Occidentale Française. *L'Anthropologie* 58: 472–80.

Pales, Léon, and Jean Linhard. (1952) La sicklémie (sickle cell trait) en Afrique Occidentale Française: Vue de Dakar. *L'Anthropologie* 56: 53–86.

Pales, Léon, and André M. Serré. (1953) La sicklémie (sickle cell trait) en Afrique Occidentale Française (Haute Volta). *L'Anthropologie* 57: 61–67.

Pales, Léon, and M. Tassin-de-Saint Pereuse. (1954) *Raciologie Comparative des Populations de l'AOF. Cartes de Répartition de la Stature, de l'indice Cormique et de l'indice céphalique en Afrique Occidentale*. Dakar: Mission Anthropologique de L'AOF (and CNRS).

Palsamy, P., and S. Subramanian. (2008) Resveratrol, a natural phytoalexin, normalizes hyperglycemia in streptozotocin-nicotinamide induced experimental diabetic rats. *Biomedicine and Pharmacotherapy* 9 (62): 598–605.

Pálsson, Gisli. (2007) *Anthropology and the New Genetics*. Cambridge: Cambridge University Press.

Pathare, A., S. A. Kindi, S. Daar, and D. Dennison. (2003) Cytokines in Sickle Cell Disease. *Hematology* 8 (5): 329–37.

Pauling, Linus. (1970) Fifty years of progress in structural chemistry and molecular biology. *Daedalus* 99 (4): 988–1014.

Pauling, L., H. A. Itano, S. J. Singer, and I. C. Wells. (1949) Sickle-cell anemia, a molecular disease. *Science* 110:543–48.

Peterson, Kristin (Forthcoming) AIDS policies for markets and warriors: Dispossession, capital, and pharmaceuticals in Nigeria, in *Lively Capital: Biotechnologies, Ethics, and Governance in Global Markets*, edited by Kaushik Sunder Rajan. Durham: Duke University Press.

Petryna, Adriana. (2002) *Life Exposed: Biological Citizens after Chernobyl*. Princeton, NJ: Princeton University Press.

———. (2009) *When Experiments Travel: Clinical Trials and the Global Search for Human Subjects*. Princeton, NJ: Princeton University Press.

Plan National de Développement Sanitaire (PNDS)—Phase II: 2004–2008. (2004) *République du Sénégal, Ministère de la Santé*. April. http://www.beta.raes.sn/article233.html (accessed March 31, 2011).

Povinelli, Elizabeth A. (2006) *The Empire of Love*. Durham: Duke University Press.

Powars, D. R. (1990) Sickle cell anemia and major organ failure. *Hemoglobin* 14 (6): 573–98.

———. (1991a) Sickle cell anemia-beta-S-gene-cluster haplotypes as prognostic indicators of vital organ failure. *Seminars in Hematology* 28 (3): 202–8.

———. (1991b) Beta-S-gene-cluster haplotypes in sickle cell anemia: Clinical and hematologic features. *Hematology-Oncology Clinics of North America* 5 (3): 475–93.

Powars, D. R., L. S. Chan, and W. Shroeder. (1990) The variable expression of sickle cell disease is genetically determined. *Seminars in Hematology* 27 (4): 360–76.

Powars, D. R. and A. Hiti. (1993) Sickle cell anemia-beta(S)-gene cluster haplotypes as genetic markers for severe disease expression. *American Journal of Diseases of Children* 147 (11): 1197–1202.

Powars, D. R., L. S. Chan, A. Hiti, E. Ramicone, and C. Johnson. (2005) Outcome of sickle cell anemia: A 4-decade observational study of 1056 patients. *Medicine* 85 (6): 363–76.

Rabeharisoa, V., and M. Callon. (1998) L'implication des malades dans les activités de recherche soutenues par l'Association française contre les myopathies. *Sciences Sociales et Santé* 16 (3): 41–65.

———. (1999) *Les pouvoirs des malades: L'Association Française Contre les Myopathies et la Recherche*. Paris: Les Presses de L'Ecole des Mines de Paris.

Rabinow, Paul. (1996 [1992]) Artificiality and enlightenment: From sociobiology to biosociality, in *Essays on the Anthropology of Reason*. Princeton, NJ: Princeton University Press.

———. (2003) *Anthropos Today: Reflections on Modern Equipment*. Princeton, NJ: Princeton University Press.

———. (2008) *Marking Time: On the Anthropology of the Contemporary*. Princeton, NJ: Princeton University Press.

Raffles, Hugh. (2002) *In Amazonia: A Natural History*. Princeton, NJ: Princeton University Press.

———. (1999) "Local theory": Nature and the making of an Amazonian place. *Cultural Anthropology* 14 (3): 323–60.

Rahimy, Mohamed C., Doctor de République du Bénin. (1999) Letter to M. le Professeur Robert Girot, Hôpital Tenon, Paris, October 11.

———. (1999) Letter to André Orsini, Marseille, October 11.

Raper, Alan B. (1950) Sickle-cell disease in Africa and America: A comparison. *Journal of Tropical Medicine and Hygiene* 53: 49–53.

Rapp, Rayna. (1999) *Testing Women, Testing the Fetus: The Social Impact of Amniocentesis in America*. New York: Routledge.

Rapp, Rayna, Deborah Heath, and Karen Sue Taussig. (2001) Genealogical dis-ease: Where heredity abnormailty, biomedical explanation, and family responsibility meet, in *Relative Values: Reconfiguring Kinship Studies*, edited by Sarah Franklin and Susan McKinnon. Durham, NC: Duke University Press.

Reardon, Jenny. (2004) *Race to the Finish: Identity and Governance in an Age of Genomics*. Princeton, NJ: Princeton University Press.

Redfield, Peter. (2008) Doctors without borders and the moral economy of pharmaceuticals, in *Human Rights in Crisis*, edited by Alice Bullard. Hampshire, UK: Ashgate Press.

Reilly, P. (1976) State supported mass genetic screening program, in *Genetics and the Law*, edited by A. M. Annas and J. G. Annas. New York: Plenum Press.

Rice, Susan. E. (2009) Statement by Ambassador Susan E. Rice, U.S. Permanent Representative to the United Nations, on World Sickle Cell Disease Day. June 19. New York: U.S. Mission to the United Nations. http://usun.state.gov/briefing/statements/2009/125967.htm (accessed June 15, 2010).

Roberts, Elizabeth F. S. (2007) Extra embryos: Ethics, cryopreservation, and IVF in Ecuador and elsewhere. *American Ethnologist* 34 (1): 188–99.

Rodrigue, C. M., N. Arous, D. Bachir, J. Smith-Ravin, P. H. Romeo, et al. (2001) Resveratrol, a natural dietary phytoalexin, possesses similar properties to hydroxyurea towards erythroid differentiation. *British Journal of Haematology* 113 (2): 500–507.

Roitman, Janet. (2004) *Fiscal Disobedience: An Anthropology of Economic Regulation in Central Africa*. Princeton, NJ: Princeton University Press.

Rose, Nikolas. (2007) *The Politics of Life Itself: Biomedicine, Power, and Subjectivity in the Twenty-First Century*. Princeton, NJ: Princeton University Press.

Roth, E., D. Elbaum, E. Godoy, and R. L. Nagel. (1978) Hydergine and vincamine derivative LD 4298 exhibit no anti-sickling properties in vitro. *Nouvelle Revue Française d'Hématologie* 20 (4): 611–19

Rottenburg, Richard. (2009) Social and public experiments and new figurations of science and politics in postcolonial Africa. *Postcolonial Studies* 12 (4): 423–40.

Rouse, Carolyn. (2009) *Uncertain Suffering: Racial Health Care Disparities and Sickle Cell Disease*. Berkeley: University of California Press.

Sakho, Khadidiatou. (2008) Médecine traditionnelle au Sénégal: Les acteurs pour une loi décourageant la publicité mensongère et le charlatanisme. *Le Matin, Seneweb News*. August 27. http://www.seneweb.com/news/Societe/m-decine-traditionnelle-au-senegal-les-acteurs-pour-une-loi-d-courageant-la-publicit-mensong-re-et-le-charlatanisme_n_18210.html (accessed July 2, 2010).

Sané, Babacar Bachir. (2007) Alioune AW, Chef du Bureau de la Médecine traditionnelle: "La dernière décision concernant la loi sur la médecine traditionnelle revient à l'autorité." *Le Soleil*. February 2. http://lesoleil.sn/imprimer.php3?id_article=21198 (accessed July 2, 2010).

Sané, Idrissa. (2006) Traitement de la drépanocytose: Certains produits de la médecine traditionnelle seraient efficaces. *Le Soleil* November 25. http://www.lesoleil.sn/article.php3?id_article=18804 (accessed March 3, 2007).

———. (2010) Lutte contre la drépanocytose: L'Assemblée Nationale plaide pour le dépistage prénuptial. *Le Soleil*. May 5. http://lesoleil.sn/imprimer.php3?id_article=58725 (accessed July 2, 2010).

Sané, Idrissa, and Eugène Kaly. (2009) Sénégal: Prise en charge de la drépanocytose: Les tests de la greffe de moelle concluants. *Le Soleil*. January 23. http://fr.allafrica.com/stories/printable/200901230167.html (accessed June 16, 2009).

Sané, Idrissa, and Salimata Gassama. (2005) Abdou Fall devant les Députés: La loi sur la médecine traditionnelle sera bientôt déposée. *Le Soleil*. November 30. http://www.lesoleil.sn/article.php3?id_article=5213 (accessed July 2, 2010).

Sankaran, V. G., T. F. Menne, J. Xu, T. E. Akie, G. Lettre, et al. (2008) Human fetal hemoglobin expression is regulated by the developmental stage-specific repressor *BCL11A*. *Science* 322 (5909): 1839–42.

Sarr, D., A. M. Seck, and M. Ba. (1997) Quarante ans de psychiatrie au Sénégal (1938–1978), in *La folie au Sénégal*. Dakar: Association Des Chercheurs Sénégalais (ACS).

Sateriale, M. and P. Hart. (1985) Unexpected death in a black military recruit with sickle cell trait: Case report. *Military Medicine* 150 (11): 602–05.

Scheper-Hughes, Nancy. (1992) *Death without Weeping: The Violence of Everyday Life in Brazil*. Berkeley: University of California Press.

Scheper-Hughes, Nancy, and Margaret Lock. (1987) The mindful body: A prolegomenon to future work in medical anthropology. *Medical Anthropology Quarterly* 1 (1): 6–41.

———. (1991) The message in the bottle: Illness and the micropolitics of resistance. *Journal of Psychohistory* 18 (4): 409–32.

Sears, D. (1994) Sickle cell trait, in *Sickle Cell Disease: Basic Principles and Clinical Practice*, edited by S. Embury, R. Hebbel, N. Mohandas, and M. Steinberg. New York: Raven Press.

Seck, A. M., and D. Sarr. (1997) Approache thérapeutique de la folie au Sénégal, in *La Folie au Sénégal*. Dakar: Association Des Chercheurs Sénégalais (ACS).

Senghor, Leopold Sedar. (1959) *African Socialism*. A Report to the Constitutive Congress of the Party of African Federation. New York: American Society of African Culture.

———. (1988) *Ce que je Crois*. Paris: Grasset.

Sherry, P. (1990) Sickle cell trait and rhabdomyolysis: Case report and review of the literature. *Military Medicine* 155 (2): 59–61.

Shiva, Vandana. (1999) *Biopiracy: The Plunder of Nature and Knowledge*. Cambridge, MA: South End Press.

Shuster, S., W. Miller, A. Ratan, L. Tomsho, B. Giardine, et al. (2010) Complete Khoisan and Bantu genomes from Southern Africa. *Nature* 463 (7283): 943–47.

Snyder, L. H. (1926) Human blood groups: Their inheritance and racial significance. *American Journal of Physical Anthropology* 9:233–63.

Sofowora, E. A., and W. A. Issac-Sodeye. (1971) Reversal of sickling and crenation in erythrocytes by the root extract of *Fagara zanthoxyloides*. *Journal of Natural Products (Lloydia)* 34 (4): 383–85.

Sofowora, E. A., W. A. Isaac-Sodeye, and L. O. Ogunkoya. (1975) Isolation and characterization of an antisickling agent from *Fagara zanthoxyloides* root. *Journal of Natural Products (Lloydia)* 38 (2): 169–71.

Somerville, Carolyn M. (1991) The impact of the reforms on the urban population: How the Dakarois view the crisis, in *The Political Economy of Senegal Under Structural Adjustment*, edited by Christopher L. Delgado and Sidi Jammeh. New York: Praeger.

Sontag, Susan. (1988) *Illness as Metaphor*. New York: Farrar Straus and Giroux.

Sow, Ibrahima. (1997) Sur la notion de folie, in *La folie au Sénégal*. Dakar: Association Des Chercheurs Sénégalais (ACS).

Spleth, Janice S. (1985) *Léopold Sédar Senghor*. Boston: Twayne Publishers.

Statewatch. (2008) Spain: Annual statistics on the fight against illegal immigration published. *Statewatch News Online*. http://www.statewatch.org/news/2008/feb/03spain-imm-stats.htm (accessed October 7, 2009).

Steinberg, M. H. (2005) Predicting clinical severity in sickle cell anaemia. *British Journal of Haematology* 129 (4): 465–81.

Steinberg, M. H., and Adeboye H. Adewoye. (2006) Modifier genes and sickle cell anemia. *Current Opinion in Hematology* 13 (3): 131–36.

Steinberg, M. H., H. Hsu, R. L. Nagel, P. F. Milner, J. G. Adams, et al. (1995) Gender and haplotype effects upon hematological manifestations of adult sickle cell anemia. *American Journal of Hematology* 48 (3): 175.

Steinberg, M. H., and Ronald Nagel. (2001) Role of epistatic (modifier) genes in the modulation of the phenotypic diversity of sickle cell anemia. *Pediatric Pathology and Molecular Medicine* 20 (2): 123–36

Steptoe A., G.Willemsen, N. Owen, L. Flower, and V. Mohamed-Ali. (2001) Acute mental stress elicits delayed increases in circulating inflammatory cytokine levels. *Clinical Science* 101 (2): 193–94.

Stoler, Ann. (2008) *Against the Archival Grain: Epistemic Anxiety and Colonial Common Sense.* Princeton, NJ: Princeton University Press.

Stoller, Paul. (2002) *Money Has No Smell: The Africanization of New York City.* Chicago: University of Chicago Press.

Stoller, Paul, and J. T. McConatha. (2001) City life: West African communities in New York. *Journal of Contemporary Ethnography* 30 (6): 651–77.

Strasser, Bruno J. (2002) Linus Pauling's "molecular diseases": Between history and memory. *American Journal of Human Genetics* 115: 83–92.

Strathern, Andrew. (1996) *Body Thoughts.* Ann Arbor: University of Michigan Press.

Strathern, Marilyn. (1985) Kinship and economy: Constitutive orders of a provisional kind. *American Ethnologist* 12 (2): 191–209.

———. (1992) *Reproducing the Future: Essays on Anthropology, Kinship and the New Reproductive Technologies.* Manchester: Manchester University Press

———. (1999) What is intellectual property after?, in *Actor Network Theory and After*, edited by John Law and John Hassard. Oxford: Blackwell and The Sociological Review.

———. (2005) *Kinship, Law and the Unexpected: Relatives Are Always a Surprise.* New York: Cambridge University Press.

Stuart, Marie J., and Ronald Nagel. (2004) Sickle-cell disease. *Lancet* 264:1343–60.

Sullivan, Shannon, and Nancy Tuana. (2007) Introduction, in *Race and Epistemologies of Ignorance*, edited by Shannon Sullivan and Nancy Tuana. Albany: State University of New York Press.

Sy, Tidiane. (2009) Senegal colossus proves sore point. *BBC News.* November 16. http://news.bbc.co.uk/2/hi/africa/8353624.stm (accessed March 15, 2011).

Sylla, R., A. Diouf, B. Niane, B. Ndiaye, M. B. Guisse, et al. (1994) Pratique de la dépigmentation artificielle de la peau chez les femmes à Dakar et étude analytique des produits dits cosmétiques utilisés. *Dakar Médical* 39 (2): 223–26.

Taiwo, Oluronke, Hong-Xi Xu, and Song F. Lee. (1999) Antibacterial activities of extracts from Nigerian chewing sticks. *Phytotherapy Research* 13 (8): 675–79.

Tamouza, R., M. G. Neonato, M. Busson, F. Marzais, R. Girot, et al. (2002) Infectious complications in sickle cell disease are influenced by HLA class II alleles. *Human Immunology* 63 (3): 194–99.

Tamouza R., M. Busson, C. Fortier, I. Diagne, D. Diallo, et al. (2007) HLA-E*0101 allele in homozygous state favors severe bacterial infections in sickle cell anemia. *Human Immunology* 68 (10): 849–53.

Taussig, Karen-Sue. (2009) *Ordinary Genomes: Science, Citizenship, and Genetic Identities.* Durham, NC: Duke University Press.

Tapper, Melbourne. (1997) An "anthropathology" of the "American Negro": Anthropology, genetics, and the new racial science, 1940–1952. *Social History of Medicine* 10 (2): 263–89.

——. (2001) Blood/kinship, governmentality, and culture of order in colonial Africa, in *Relative Values: Reconfiguring Kinship Studies*, edited by Sarah Franklin and Susan McKinnon. Durham, NC: Duke University Press.

——. (1999) *In the Blood: Sickle Cell Anemia and the Politics of Race.* Philadelphia: University of Pennsylvania Press.

Thiam D., R. Bako, K. Seck Fall, and L. Diakhate. (1990) In vitro effects of Fagaro [*sic*] xanthoxyloides Lam on drepanocytic erythrocytes. *Dakar Médical* 35 (1): 37–45.

Tilley, Helen. (2011) *Africa as Living Laboratory: Empire, Development, and the Problem of Scientific Knowledge 1870–1950.* Chicago: Chicago University Press.

Tonda, Joseph. (2001) Le syndrome du prophète: Médecines africaines et précarités identitaires. *Cahiers d'Études Africaines* 1 (161): 139–62.

Tsing, Anna Lowenhaupt. (2005) *Friction: An Ethnography of Global Connection.* Princeton, NJ: Princeton University Press.

Turshen, Meredith. (1999) *Privatizing Health Services in Africa.* New Brunswick, NJ: Rutgers University Press.

Uda, M., R. Galanello, S. Sanna, G. Lettre, V. G. Sankaran, et al. (2008) Genome-wide association study shows BCL11A associated with persistent fetal hemoglobin and amelioration of the phenotype of beta-thalassemia. *Proceedings of the National Academy of Sciences USA* 105 (5): 1620–25.

United Nations. (2009) Resolution A/RES/63/237, Recognition of sickle-cell anaemia as a public health problem. From the *73rd plenary meeting 22 December 2008.* Sixty-third session, Agenda item 155. General Assembly, March 17, 2009. New York: United Nations.

United Nations Development Program. (2008) *United Nations Development Report, Senegal HDI Rank.* http://hdrstats.undp.org/en/countries/data_sheets/cty_ds_SEN.html (accessed August 22, 2009).

United Nations Educational, Scientific, and Cultural Organization (UNESCO). (2005) *Programme and Budget for 2006–2007.* 33 C/22. *Sickle-Cell Anaemia, a Public Health Priority.* Records of the General Conference, 33rd session. Paris: UNESCO.

United Nations Program (Joint) on HIV/AIDS (UNAIDS). (2009) *Country and Regional Information, Senegal.* http://www.unaids.org/en/regionscountries/countries/senegal/ (accessed March 20, 2011).

——. (2010) *The Global Report: UNAIDS report on the global AIDS epidemic 2010.* Geneva, Switzerland. http://www.unaids.org/globalreport/Global_report.htm (accessed March 9, 2011).

United Nations Webcast. (2009) Press Conference, UN Resolution on Sickle Cell as a Global Health Priority, and International Sickle Cell Anemia Day. http://webcast.un.org/ramgen/ondemand/pressconference/2009/pc090619pm.rm (accessed March 9, 2011).

United States Congress House Committee on Veterans' Affairs. Subcommittee on Hospitals. (1972) *Screening, Counseling, and Medical Treatment of Sickle Cell Anemia.* Hearings, Ninety-second Congress, first session, H.R. 11971. Washington, D.C.: U.S. Congress.

USAID (2005) *Senegal USAID.* http://www.usaid.gov/policy/budget/cbj2005/afr/sn.html (accessed May 3, 2006).

van de Walle, Nicolas. (2001) *African Economies and the Politics of Permanent Crisis, 1979–1999.* Cambridge: Cambridge University Press.

Vaillant, Janet G. (1990) *Black, French, and African: A Life of Léopold Sédar Senghor.* Cambridge, MA: Harvard University Press.

Vaughan, Meghan. (1991) *Curing Their Ills: Colonial Power and African Illness.* Palo Alto, CA: Stanford University Press.

Vora, Neha. (2008) Producing diasporas and globalization: Indian middle-class migrants in Dubai. *Anthropological Quarterly* 81 (2): 377–406.

Wade, Nicholas. (2008) New hints seen that red wine may slow aging. *New York Times.* June 4. http://www.nytimes.com/2008/06/04/health/research/04aging.html (accessed August 28, 2009).

Wade, Viviane. (2005) Allocution de Madame Viviane Wade. *Premiers Etats Généraux de la drépanocytose au monde.* http://www.drepabrazza.medicalistes.org/Mme Wade.htm (accessed February 27, 2007).

Wague, Tacko. (1987) *Contribution à L'Etude de Fagara Xanthoxyloïdes Lam (Rutacea) dans le Traitement de la Drépanocytose: Essais Pharmacologiques, Pharmacotechniques, Essais Cliniques.* Doctor of Pharmacy Thesis. Faculty of Medicine, University of Dakar, Cheikh Anta Diop.

Wailoo, Keith. (1996) Genetic marker of segregation: Sickle cell anemia, thalassemia, and racial ideology in American medical writing 1920–1950. *History and Philosophy of the Life Sciences* 18(3): 305–20.

———. (2001) *Dying in the City of the Blues: Sickle Cell Anemia and the Politics of Race and Health.* Chapel Hill: North Carolina Press.

———. (2003) Inventing the heterozygote: Molecular biology, racial identity and the narratives of sickle-cell disease, Tay-Sachs, and cystic fibrosis, in *Race, Nature, and the Politics of Difference*, edited by D. Moore, J. Kosek, and A. Pandian. Durham, NC: Duke University Press.

Ware, Nora. (1992) Suffering and the social construction of illness: The delegitimization of illness experience in chronic fatigue syndrome. *Medical Anthropology Quarterly* 64: 347–61.

Washington, Isaiah. (2008) DNA has memory: We are who we were. *Huffington Post.* February 19. http://www.huffingtonpost.com/isaiah-washington/dna-has-memory-we-are-wh_b_87450.html (accessed March 31, 2008).

Weatherall, David J. (2010) The inherited diseases of hemoglobin are an emerging global health burden. *Blood* 115 (22): 4331–36.

Wellcome Trust. (2010) Transcript of the Human Heredity and Health in Africa Press Conference in London. June 22. http://www.genome.gov/27540081 (accessed December 13, 2010).

Wendland, Claire L. (2010) *A Heart for the Work: Journeys through an African Medical School.* Chicago: University of Chicago Press.

Wexler, Alice. (1995) *Mapping Fate: A Memoir of Family, Risk, and Genetic Research.* Berkeley: University of California Press.

Wiesenfeld, S. L. (1967) Sickle-cell trait in human biological and cultural evolution: Development of agriculture causing increased malaria is bound to gene-pool changes causing malaria reduction. *Science* 157 (793): 1134–40.

Wilder, Gary. (2005) *The French Imperial Nation-State: Negritude and Colonial Humanism between the Two World Wars*. Chicago: University of Chicago Press.

Wilkinson, Doris. (1974) For whose benefit?: Politics and sickle cell. *Black Scholar* 5 (8): 26–31.

Williamson, Bob. (1995) Review: The end of an era. *Human Molecular Genetics* 4 (2): 149–51.

Wynberg, Rachel, and Roger Chennells. (2009) Green diamonds of the south: An overview of the *San-Hoodia* case. In Wynberg, Schroeder, and Chennells, *Indigenous Peoples, Consent and Benefit Sharing*.

Wynberg, Rachel, and Sarah Laird. (2009) Bioprospecting, access and benefit sharing: Revisiting the 'Grand Bargain.' In *Indigenous Peoples, Consent, and Benefit Sharing: Lessons from the San-Hoodia Case* ed. Rachel Wynberg, Doris Schroeder, and Roger Chennells. London: Springer.

Wittgenstein, Ludwig (1980 [1929]) *Culture and Value*. Chicago: University of Chicago Press.

Woolgar, Steve. (1981) Interests and explanation in the social study of science. *Social Studies of Science* 11 (3): 365–94.

World Health Organization. (1978) *The Promotion and Development of Traditional Medicine*. Report of a WHO meeting. November 28–December 2, 1977. Geneva, Switzerland.

———. (2002) *Traditional Medicine Strategy 2002–2005*. (WHO/EDM/TRM/2002.1). WHO Unofficial Documents. Geneva, Switzerland.

———. (2005) *Executive Board 117th Session. Sickle-cell Anaemia*. Report by the Secretariat. EB117/34. Geneva, Switzerland.

———. (2006a). *Fifty-ninth World Health Assembly. Sickle-Cell Anaemia*. Report by the Secretariat. A59/9. Geneva, Switzerland.

———. (2006b) *Provisional Agenda Item 11.4: Sickle Cell Anaemia, Report by the Secretariat*. A/59. Geneva, Switzerland.

———. (2006c) Sickle-cell disease and other haemoglobin disorders. Fact Sheet No. 308. August. http://www.who.int/mediacentre/factsheets/fs308/en/index.html (accessed October 1, 2009).

———. (2006d) *Sickle-Cell Disease in the African Region: Current Situation and the Way Forward*. Report of the Regional Director, AFR/RC56/17. Geneva, Switzerland: World Health Organization and the Regional Office for Africa.

World Health Organization. (2007a) *World Health Organization Global Health Observatory (WHOGHO), Senegal Country Statistics*. "General Government expenditure on health as % of total general government expenditure (4%)." http://apps .who.int/ghodata# (accessed June 30, 2010).

———. (2007b) *World Health Organization Global Health Observatory. Senegal Country Statistics*. "Per capita government expenditure on health at average exchange rate (US$) (30 USD, 2007)." http://apps.who.int/ghodata/# (accessed June 30, 2010).

———. (2007c) *World Health Organization Global Health Observatory. Senegal Country Statistics*. "Per capita total expenditure on health at average exchange rate (US$) (54USD, 2007)." http://apps.who.int/ghodata/# (accessed June 30, 2010).

———. (2008) *Management of haemoglobin disorders*. Report of a joint WHO-TIF meeting. Nicosia, Cyprus, 16–18 November 2007. (Appendix A: Sickle-cell anaemia. May 27, 2006 (WHA59.20). Geneva, Switzerland.

————. (2009a) *Stratégie de Coopération de l'OMS avec les pays, 2009–2013, Sénégal.* (WA 540 HS1). Bibliothèque de l'OMS/AFRO.

————. (2009b). *"Traditional medicine."* (WHA62.13). Agenda item 12.4. May 22. Sixty-second world health assembly. Geneva, Switzerland.

Yamakawa K., M. Matsunaga, T. Isowa, K. Kimura, K. Kasugai, M. Yoneda, H. Kaneko H. Ohira. (2009) Transient responses of inflammatory cytokines in acute stress. *Biological Psychology* 82 (1): 25–32.

York, E., and J. Brierre. (1971) How diligently should the diagnosis of sickle cell trait be pursued?: Clinical case report with military implications. *Military Medicine* 136 (1): 27–29.

Youm, Prosper. (1991) The economy since independence, in *The Political Economy of Senegal Under Structural Adjustment*, edited by Christopher L. Delgado and Sidi Jammeh. New York: Praeger.

INDEX

Italicized page numbers indicate figures, maps, or tables.

329